Becoming a Social Entrepreneur

What's it like to be a social entrepreneur – not a textbook social entrepreneur but one on the ground? This book offers an explanation. Michael Gordon, leading Social Entrepreneurship expert from the University of Michigan, spoke with more than one hundred social entrepreneurs – from six continents, young and old, just starting out to several decades in, addressing seemingly every societal problem of the day.

This book uses their words and experiences to provide a kaleidoscopic description of what it means to become a social entrepreneur. It ranges from the personal and emotional challenges they often face to the grand impact many hope to produce. It touches on the sublime but focuses on the everyday, highlighting the mistakes that have been made, the lessons learned and, especially, what advice they would give to those wanting to start a social venture.

This book presents the truth, not the varnish, and is ideal for use in the classroom with students studying social entrepreneurship, and for all new and experienced social entrepreneurs seeking real-life examples of how to overcome challenges. For anyone else, it offers a penetrating portrait of the lives of those committed to changing the world.

Michael Gordon is the Arthur F. Thurnau Professor of Social Entrepreneurship at the Ross School of Business, University of Michigan. He is the faculty director of the Center for Social Impact, the seat of social entrepreneurship at the Ross School with connections throughout the University of Michigan.

GW00771741

"Michael Gordon's research is informed by his many years of deep engagement with Ashoka's extended team of teams. This book provides broad, and nuanced, guidance to social entrepreneurs and deepens our knowledge of how they envision, enable and ensure new patterns of change. And more importantly, how their deepest impact is to help countless others to be changemakers."

Diana Wells, President Emerita,
Leadership Team Member, Ashoka.

"The title says it all: *Becoming a Social Entrepreneur: Starting Out, Scaling Up and Staying True* is the manual I wish I had at the start of my social venture journey. Over the years, I came to realize that the best advice came from my peers – fellow entrepreneurs who generously shared their wisdom, passion, frustration and success stories. Michael has done an amazing job of capturing the firsthand experience of a wide variety of changemakers, synthesizing lessons learned and translating their individual experiences into practical points of reference. This book is a must-read for every social entrepreneur, ecosystem partners who support their amazing work, and anyone who is curious about what makes a social entrepreneur 'tick.'"

Cynthia Koenig, Founder and CEO, Wello.

"An exhaustive, intimate survey of social entrepreneurs with varied, textured experience by one of the keenest observers of the field. A great read for anyone in the space and a must read for anyone aspiring to enter."

Fred de Sam Lazaro, Agents for Change correspondent,
PBS NewsHour, Director, Under-Told Stories Project.

"This book is a tour de force! It's an amazing resource for people who aspire to make the world a better place. Michael Gordon has succeeded in bringing together insights and wisdom from more than a hundred of the most inspiring individuals – social entrepreneurs who have overcome adversity and hardship to dedicate themselves to improving the common good."

Scott Sherman, Senior Director, Kravis Lab for Social Impact,
Claremont McKenna College, Founder,
Transformative Action Institute.

"A must-read book for aspiring and practicing social entrepreneurs. And an important read for everyone else. Prof. Michael Gordon deftly blends history, journalism, management and computer science, even rap music counseling to help readers better understand the past, present and future for social entrepreneurship. Demystifying first-hand accounts of really inconvenient truths to unparalleled positive social change accomplishments. Given our new change-defined era of increasing inequality, social fragmentation and global catastrophic risks, there's plenty of rich data and insights here to help us all see how everyone can and must be contributors to a better world through social entrepreneurship."

Bob Spoer, Chief Entrepreneur for People/Search, Ashoka.

"Michael's book stands out due to its breadth. Based on interviews from more than 100 practitioners, each of whom addresses unique societal problems across the globe, it may well be the most comprehensive study on social entrepreneurship to date. Though no two experiences are alike, together their perspectives let us know what it is actually like to be a social entrepreneur – both in the challenges they face, and, most importantly, how they rise above them."

Kyle Westaway, Managing Partner at Westaway Law,
Lecturer on Law at Harvard Law School,
author of Profit & Purpose.

"Michael, my friend and ally, and long-term OC Delegate, has penned this volume in the same way any successful social entrepreneur approaches their work: by practicing deep listening, by understanding the complexity and nuance of the issues at hand, and by providing true, concrete, incontrovertible value. As a result, *Becoming a Social Entrepreneur: Starting Out, Scaling Up and Staying True* stands alone in an ever-expanding milieu of books on the field of social entrepreneurship, beckoning forth future change-agents with clear, pragmatic and collective wisdom."

Topher Wilkins, CEO, Opportunity Collaboration,
Founder, Conveners.org.

"What do you need to know to be a social entrepreneur? Michael Gordon spent five years interviewing dozens of social entrepreneurs around the world to gain their insights and shape them into a broad and comprehensive how-to guide. It is both systematic and lively, full of rich examples that provides a roadmap for social entrepreneurs at any point in their journey."

Jerry Davis, Associate Dean for Business+Impact,
Michigan Ross School of Business.

"Carefully researched and packed with examples from over 100 social entrepreneurs, *Becoming a Social Entrepreneur: Starting Out, Scaling Up and Staying True* conveys what it takes to succeed as a social entrepreneur, creates a pathway for future research, and provides an engaging account for anyone curious about how to create a better world through enterprise."

Stuart L. Hart, University of Vermont,
author of Capitalism at the Crossroads.

"An essential handbook for aspiring social entrepreneurs and those who seek to partner with and support social enterprises. Filled with pragmatic advice and lessons learned from over 100 in-depth interviews with social change leaders. A must read!"

Ron Cordes and Marty Cordes, Co-Founders,
Cordes Foundation.

Becoming a Social Entrepreneur

Starting Out, Scaling Up and Staying True

Michael Gordon

Routledge
Taylor & Francis Group

LONDON AND NEW YORK

First published 2020
by Routledge
2 Park Square, Milton Park, Abingdon, Oxon OX14 4RN

and by Routledge
52 Vanderbilt Avenue, New York, NY 10017

Routledge is an imprint of the Taylor & Francis Group, an informa business

© 2020 Michael Gordon

British Library Cataloguing-in-Publication Data
A catalogue record for this book is available from the British Library

Library of Congress Cataloging-in-Publication Data
A catalog record has been requested for this book

ISBN: 978-0-367-19772-8 (hbk)
ISBN: 978-0-367-19773-5 (pbk)
ISBN: 978-0-429-24318-9 (ebk)

Typeset in Bembo
by Deanta Global Publishing Services, Chennai, India

MIX
Paper from
responsible sources
FSC
www.fsc.org
FSC® C013985

Printed in the United Kingdom
by Henry Ling Limited

Contents

Preface: Listening to social entrepreneurs

I BEGAN THIS BOOK WITH AN OBSESSION: TO KNOW WHAT SOCIAL ENTREPRENEURS WISHED THEY HAD KNOWN WHEN THEY WERE STARTING OUT. In what turned into an exhaustive investigation, I sought responses from still-early-stage entrepreneurs and from those with years, sometimes decades, of experience. I spent over five years digging in as much as I could.

This investigation has been more than exhilarating. I have met and spoken to over 100 people who have generously given me their time – allowing me to interview them and sharing their experiences and insights around my central question. They are a vibrant, committed bunch, living their lives for others as well as themselves, dedicated to making the world a better place. I am in their debt and grateful that people like them inhabit our planet.

Alas, there is no secret that social entrepreneurs suddenly alight upon. Their ideas often clash, they still struggle, there is always something else to learn or to try. Yet the threads of their unique experiences combine to form a fabric that is recognizable: a determination to make a difference; flexibility in seeking solutions that work; an inner sense of self; close friends or family that get them through the tough times. They embrace the tools of business, but they are not merely "in business." They are obsessed with results and driven by impact. They have a foot in a better future, and draw us toward it, too.

Although these social entrepreneurs do not all speak in one voice, what they have to say – individually and collectively – provides guidance, I hope, for others hoping to strike out on a similar path. I have listened with a critical ear so that I can present their ideas with nuance and in context. By presenting this chorus of viewpoints, I hope that you hear the diversity of insights that my interviewees – now my friends – shared with me. I hope as well that this chorus allows you to draw your own conclusions, to understand that there are many paths to the same destination, and to listen most intently to those voices that harmonize with your own.

Finally, I would direct all interested readers to profmichaelgordon.com where you will find more information about the topics covered in this book as well as related ideas.

Acknowledgments

I am grateful to so many people and already scared that I'll forget to mention someone who has been a major part of my getting this book from some inchoate state to the finish line (*please* accept my thanks; you know who you are – just between us).

Let me flip the script and begin by thanking my family. My grandfathers, father, and uncles were all entrepreneurs. I didn't know the term then, but in picking up scrap metal, collecting rags, recycling aluminium, among other things – and making viable businesses out of these activities – they influenced me subconsciously as I was growing up and instilled in me an admiration for entrepreneurs. I thank you for infusing me with an entrepreneurial spirit. And art: my dad loved to write. From his days as a war correspondent, writing for his hometown paper in Oak Park, Ill. about his experience in Germany during the Second World War; to his days writing plays, which he and his friends put on before I was old enough to watch them; to his poetry, which my sister Toby masterfully compiled – he was such an inspiration. His generosity and decency were just as artful. My Papa Walter did oil paintings of trains for me and could draw a great Abraham Lincoln. I like to think that my work has a bit of art in it.

No less influential were the women in my family. To my grandmothers – who immigrated to the United States as children and wanted their lives, and their children's and grandchildren's, to be full and meaningful – thank you. My mom was consumed by the events of the day, devouring the news, and being firmly on the side of the bending arc. I get much of my craving for social justice from her. Both of my sisters, Toby and Annie, fight the good fight every day – through education, art, and a generosity of spirit.

In my own (current) nuclear family, I was given free rein to do what this book required: travel, become engrossed in my work (and probably – make that *certainly* – overlook stuff right in front of my nose). My deepest thanks to Candy for never throwing up any obstacles to this work and your continual love, support, and understanding. Hannah and Molly: you are super young women who became smart, caring professionals – in some small part, I like to fool myself, because of my influence. I say "fool myself" because I think you were headed in that way on your own, but I'm proud that your work and mine can be spoken of in the same breath.

I've been blessed to have taught, and learned from, and worked with (current and former) students who want to do good in this world. I thank you all. But there are those with whom I have worked closely, who have supported this project through their research, coding, writing – and even their art. This is also where I'm especially fearful of omission. Let me first thank Cynthia Koenig (now a dear friend), who was instrumental in this project from beginning to end, from whom I've learned so much about being a social entrepreneur, and who supported this work in countless ways. There are two others I also want to single out for their tireless efforts: Suzanne Jacobs, who was extremely important during the coding phase of this project; and India Solomon, who carefully read and critiqued an earlier draft of this book. There are others who supported me, and all made this project better: David Foster, Savannah Onwochei, Britni Erez, Christina Arreaza Browne, Ovi Datta, Miranda Hency, Anna Prenzler, Jaclyn Borgiel, Sarvani Yellayi, Sarah Sisk, Hailey Hubbard, Emily Voytas, Cici Tan, and Estefania Nieto.

My academic home, the Ross School of Business, and the University of Michigan, more broadly, have provided a stimulating environment in which to consider issues of social justice and other topics in this book. I thank Jerry Davis, Jim Walsh, Paul Clyde, Stu Hart, and Ted London, among others, for the many conversations we've had on such issues. Ross, currently helmed by Scott DeRue, has been consistently supportive of my work.

I also acknowledge two other organizations that have shaped this work, directly and indirectly. First is Opportunity Collaboration (OC), run by Topher and Jorian Wilkins, and founded by Jonathan Lewis. OC is a gathering space for social entrepreneurs, impact investors, foundation directors, and other do-gooders, including a stray academic. I've made many friends there, some of whom have made it onto these pages and some of whom have worked with me on meaningful projects; there are many others with whom I've simply had a beer and who have been a great influence. Second is Ashoka, an organization I've personally had the privilege to work with in various ways over the years and which has done more to shape and harness social entrepreneurship and changemaking than any other. I thank both of these groups for involving me and, more importantly, for the work you do.

I've received excellent editorial support from Dean Bargh and wonderful transcription services from Robin Cohrs. Rebecca Marsh reached out when this book was still in progress and helped make it a reality. I thank them all.

Then there are others who have been important sources of support, whether they know it or not: Lora Vatalaro, George Abrahams, Perry Samson, Jeannie Ballew, Lad Tobin. And, of course, Leo and Dozer.

This book would not have been possible without the time generously granted to me by those I interviewed. You are inspirations. To say this book wouldn't be the same without you isn't hyperbole, but understatement. It wouldn't *be* without you. Thank you!

Introduction

THIS BOOK PROVIDES insiders' views on starting a social enterprise. You'll mostly hear the words of social entrepreneurs, which I've curated. They are an amazing lot, wrestling with the challenges of today, yet they are very real people. The messages they share in this book are hopeful, impassioned, poignant, determined, grounded in authentic experience – and, above all, useful for anyone really wanting to know what becoming a social entrepreneur is like. I can't wait for you to see for yourself.

But, first, a bit about how this came about. I wanted to understand the challenges confronting early-stage social entrepreneurs and how they were dealt with. I wanted to avoid "knowing in advance" what I was going to learn and, instead, actually learn. To do so, I interviewed 125 individuals,[1] digitally recording and transcribing their words. This was followed by a detailed process of coding and qualitative analysis (details of which are found in Appendix 1). What I hope I've produced is an organic account of social entrepreneurs' challenges, solutions, and advice. Rather than describing social entrepreneurship from a theoretical perspective, or providing an in-depth account of one or even a handful of social ventures, this book explores what it really takes to be, and become, a social entrepreneur.

BY CODING INTERVIEWS, I was able to determine the broad and the ever more refined themes describing the issues social entrepreneurs confront. Each of the broadest themes became a different "part" of the book, each with multiple chapters (the more refined themes), each chapter containing what might be considered illustrative vignettes. The parts and chapters are as follows.

Part 1: Before you

1. Lessons to learn. Social entrepreneurs before you have made mistakes and discovered what works. It is important to learn from them. Many people don't.
2. Are you a social entrepreneur? There are different definitions. Many social entrepreneurs initially don't realize the label applies to them.

Part 2: You

3. Before they were social entrepreneurs. Immersion is essential. It can be gained in different ways.
4. Ideas. What do good ideas look like? Where do they come from?
5. Necessity. Does your idea really need pursuing? Does it require a new venture to be started?
6. Join. If there is a way to join forces with an existing enterprise without starting your own, do it.
7. Personal challenges. Being a social entrepreneur takes a serious emotional toll.
8. The sanities of pro-social behavior. Despite their personal struggles and challenges, social entrepreneurs live with a sense of idealism, purpose, and congruence.
9. Committing. Starting a social enterprise is not a decision to take lightly. Be prepared for how it will change your life.
10. Gaining skills. Both experienced businesspeople and others explain that they still need additional skills to become social entrepreneurs, and they explain how they obtained them.

Part 3: Your team

11. Go team, go. It is exceedingly unlikely you can succeed without a strong team.
12. Co-founder. Your odds of success go up if you have a co-founder.
13. Team formation. What skills does your team need? What roles do you need your team members to play?
14. Hiring. How do you hire well? Why is hiring well so important? How do you hire overseas?
15. Compensation. How do you overcome a small budget and still attract quality employees?
16. Volunteers. Be aware that they can be a drain on your time and energy. Learn how to use them to great effect.
17. Training. Effective training overcomes skills deficits in your organization. Everyone can be trained for new, skilled jobs – professionals and those with aptitude but without formal education.
18. Culture. Effective social enterprises enlist employees' hearts and minds by placing a priority on trust and encouraging emotional and cognitive diversity.
19. Mentors. Social entrepreneurs need advisors and mentors, and these cover the range from brief acquaintances to decades-long relationships.
20. Networks. External organizations can dramatically extend what you do and can be essential to the success of your social enterprise.
21. Board. You must have a board of directors. Most social entrepreneurs choose them poorly and use them incorrectly.

Part 4: Your business model

22. Two businesses. Social entrepreneurs run an "impact business" and a "financial business." When they are in conflict, impact must take precedence.
23. Know your customers. You can place your customers in concentric circles: those furthest out represent every potential customer; those nearest the center are those exact customers you are targeting at the moment. In between are customers you may reach soon, but not now.
24. Value proposition. Others may be providing goods or services similar to yours. What makes yours best? And why should customers choose you?
25. The economics of your business. Understand the proper "unit of analysis" for your venture. Depending on your organization's activities, the proper unit of analysis could be: the single item, a pallet, or the number of retail outlets carrying your product. You calculate your "break even" in terms of your unit of analysis.
26. Value chain. There is a flow to what you do – from outside your organization (in the form of supplies and suppliers), to within it (where your organization makes a product), to outside again (the customers to whom you deliver it). You must understand this "value chain" and make sure that it is profitable for everyone, at every step of the way.
27. Revising your model. You likely will revise your model again and again.

Part 5: Running your business

28. Small ain't easy. Don't underestimate the challenge or complexity of starting and running a small business.
29. Selling your stuff. Are there customers ready to buy what you produce? You can test to find out. If the customers you need don't yet exist, one possibility is to create the market for your goods. Another is to change what you sell.
30. Operations. Take advantage of tried-and-true methods. When your operations are in less-developed parts of the world, you must flex to accommodate local customs and possibly conduct businesses with a combination of home-grown and seemingly out-of-date approaches.
31. Managing. You must manage your organization for results and your team to ensure harmonious relationships. You often need to defer to those with local knowledge when you operate overseas.
32. Legitimacy. Foreign social entrepreneurs are not always taken seriously, and can be taken advantage of.
33. Legal. Don't make choosing your legal structure take precedence over your business model. Use attorneys to guide you.
34. Expenses. You will have all sorts of expenses that you never considered. Still, sometimes you should spend more now to accommodate your greater needs later. And how do you and your organization stay afloat?

35. Fundraising. What are the basics of fundraising – for nonprofits and for-profits? Know the differences among funders, including the demands they will place on you.
36. Investors. Speak the language of investors and understand their logic. What do "impact investors" really care about?
37. Fundraising tips. Take tips from those who have successfully raised money. Don't chase every dollar and don't be tempted by large sums too soon.
38. Fundraising trajectories. Different organizations have followed different paths in their fundraising, including starting with personal funds, then obtaining grants, then generating revenues.
39. Funders' perspectives. Different funders follow different rules. Know your potential funder.
40. Seller, beware. Sometimes you should not sell to the buyer who is offering you the most money because it would be inconsistent with your mission.

Part 6: More than you: Impact

41. Scale. To maximize their impact, most, but not all, social enterprises aim to increase the number of beneficiaries they serve. Thinking about your scale, even at the outset, can set you up for success. Use the efforts others have already made to create success, and let others follow yours.
42. Measure. Measure your impact using the appropriate indicators, using the most appropriate techniques. When possible, explain why you were responsible for the change you've measured, not others. Use your gut when appropriate.
43. Poets versus Quants. Well-collected and -analyzed quantitative data are very useful, but there are also times when your gut can guide you effectively. There is a variety of approaches to consider in conducting evaluations, from doing it yourself to engaging outside experts.

Part 7: Beyond you

44. This moment. Sense this moment in history and link your efforts to those of others as part of a movement. Defy orthodoxy.
45. Beyond scale. See what you do as part of a larger whole extending across geographies and problems. Your work can affect systems, shift our views of human rights, and change history.
46. Our moment. Every one of us can be a changemaker. We must decide.

Notes

1 This number is a fair estimate, but an estimate nonetheless. This is because two of the interviews were conducted in large (5–10 person) group settings in which exact counts were not recorded.

Part 1

Before you

SOCIAL ENTREPRENEURS have come before you, as others will follow. None can equip you for all the challenges on your journey. But they've seen the terrain. Listen.

Listen when they tell you to learn from the past, but be critical of received wisdom.

Examine your efforts. Are you "mission-first?" Do you have an appropriate relationship to profit and markets? Are you aiming high enough?

ARE YOU A SOCIAL ENTREPRENEUR?

1 Lessons to learn

BECOMING AN EFFECTIVE SOCIAL ENTREPRENEUR, as with most worthwhile endeavors, requires learning: from history, from others, and from the results you produce. Learning also requires critically examining, experimenting; not leaping to accept others' beliefs; and recognizing that the circle of learning you draw from must include many people you may never have suspected could be your teachers.

Sanga's birthday

SANGA MOSES DOESN'T CELEBRATE HIS BIRTHDAY BECAUSE HE doesn't know exactly when he was born. "I have something in my passport, which is 30 January 1982, but that was a collaborative birth date. I didn't choose it alone. I chose it with my class. It's a long story."

Growing up in Uganda in extreme poverty, raised early on by a depressed, homeless father, and never knowing his mother until he was 15, Sanga is an unlikely social entrepreneur. Landmarks along his route out of poverty include owning his first pair of shoes at age 13; receiving a university degree in Kampala, the capital city; and working his way to a corner office as an accountant in the banking world. And now, he has ambitions to transform the lives of, and preserve the environment for, other Africans like himself.

Wise far beyond his years, Sanga tells me:

> What I've learned is that there are two most important friends you can have: friends who have succeeded and friends who people call failures. People who have, in the eyes of the world, failed have some lessons. They have maybe done some wrong things and they know what to avoid, and those can be very good lessons to help you know what to avoid. And friends who have succeeded can also tell you a few things about what really works, maybe. So having both friends is really important.

The friends you'll meet in this book are of both sorts, the truth being that most exhibit traits of each. As Sanga makes clear, it is not only those who are successful by traditional definitions that are worth listening to.

Lessons left on the ground

KICKSTART INTERNATIONAL HAS LIFTED WELL OVER ONE MILLION rural Africans out of poverty by creating and selling technology *appropriate* to its context. The company's former name, ApproTEC, made this explicit. Crucially, technology that is appropriate for poor farmers with small plots of land should be that which helps them make money; but this alone, as KickStart discovered, is not enough.

Martin Fisher, an engineer with a PhD from Stanford, and Nick Moon, a carpenter with interests in music, co-founded ApproTEC in 1991. A few years earlier, the appropriate technology movement had been declared dead. The idea behind the movement was sound: to help the poor in the developing world by deploying technologies that create jobs that require labor, not more efficient technologies that eliminate them. Because more than three-quarters of Africa's poor depend on farming, it was natural that many of these tools, too, should support farming. KickStart's best-known technology resembles a basic stair-stepper found in many health clubs, but it is used for drawing water out of the ground to irrigate small farms, not for a cardio workout or toning your abs.

While the appropriate technology movement was built on the idea of supporting economic development via productive, local labor, those who tried to put it into practice led it to its grave by overlooking many key issues. Martin and Nick took these issues to heart and resuscitated the movement via ApproTEC. For instance, they realized that technologies that support rural famers might be simple, but they must also consistently be of high-quality, durable, easily maintained, and easily repaired. Also, for all the apparent appeal of giving away technology to communities in need, their experience told them that the best way to get people to take full advantage of money-making technologies was to get them to buy them; they would then be valued as prized (and expensive) possessions.

Fisher laments the lack of understanding by the original practitioners of the appropriate technology movement.

> It's interesting to watch the 30-year cycles in development. When I first went to Kenya in 1985, I was at the very tail end of the appropriate technology movement, which started with E.F. Schumacher's book, *Small is Beautiful*.[1] Everybody got very excited. Hundreds of millions of dollars were spent on appropriate technology. By 1985, basically it was dead in the water. Everybody said, 'It didn't work; we're not interested in technology; it wasn't the solution.'

Although by his own reckoning he claims he's "just a dumb engineer," Martin thought there might be a place for it.

> So I spent the next five or six years making a lot of mistakes about [economic] development, working for ActionAid and learning a lot of lessons

about what doesn't work – but also looking back on the appropriate technology movement and sort of analyzing why that went wrong. And there was a huge number of reasons it went wrong, and, in retrospect, every mistake they could have made, they made.

Despite KickStart's success, others entered the technology arena and those mistakes are still being made.

Those lessons have not been learned. Negative lessons in development are never learned. So now I've been watching this new movement in appropriate technology. They call it 'technology,' they call it whatever. Very, very many of those same lessons we learned are about failures, and things people [always did] wrong are being repeated.

In its over two decades of operation KickStart has developed a keen understanding of the rural poor, how to develop markets for new products, and how to build lasting supply chains – among other insights. Such lessons – both on what works and what doesn't – will be shared as we delve into the customs and practices of social entrepreneurship.

Note

1 Schumacher, E.F., *Small is Beautiful: A Study of Economics as if People Mattered* (London: Blond & Briggs, 1973).

2 Are you a social entrepreneur?

SOCIAL ENTREPRENEURS FIND a way to harness the forces of business, but their focus is first on societal good and then on financial gain, profit, and money more generally – mainly as a means of achieving societal good. At least that is a sentiment most social entrepreneurs would subscribe to.

Social entrepreneurs' complicated relationship with markets is evidenced by a desire to allow supply and demand to spread social interventions widely and efficiently even while recognizing, as many do, that, too often, market mechanisms alone are not up to the task. This creates a spectrum of social entrepreneurship, with markets and profit being employed to different degrees, those societal problems that are the most intractable typically resisting pure market approaches. Along this spectrum lies a diverse array of social entrepreneurs, including some who do not even warrant the label and others with the requisite bona fides who have never stopped to look in the mirror.

A new wave

STRIPPED OF ALL EXCEPTIONS, a description of a social entrepreneur might read something like this: idealistic, passionate, focused, committed to a better world, skillful. And young – for social entrepreneurship carries with it an air of promise, vitality, and the new.

No one I interviewed exemplifies this more than Noor Siddiqui, just 18 years old when we spoke, but in possession of an accelerated wisdom bolstered by a Thiel Fellowship. Starting in 2011, Peter Thiel, co-founder of PayPal, has granted 20 teenagers a year a $100,000[1] stipend (each, over 2 years) *not* to go to college and instead to focus on entrepreneurship. In addition to the lavish funding, the chosen fellows move to Silicon Valley and are mentored by luminaries in the areas of entrepreneurship and supporting activities, including venture capital.

Fellows are selected based on their potential to make entrepreneurial breakthroughs rather than any ideas they might have before beginning their fellowship. Noor's first idea as a fellow was to advance the concept of microwork. Her project, WorkShare, offered employment opportunities for those not fulfilling their economic potential. As an example of a microwork opportunity, many firms need audio files transcribed to text for more convenient use: these audio files may be legal depositions, conference calls, webinars, or any of a large variety of other content. WorkShare's aim was to contract with these firms and also to establish partnerships in base-of-the-pyramid (very low-income, developing-world) locales so that under-employed college students could produce the transcriptions for an attractive wage. Noor recognizes that her efforts would fail to reach those at the very bottom of the economic pyramid, the so-called "bottom billion":[2]

> At the beginning of my fellowship, I was targeting the *bottom billion*, but ... realized that the people who I'm targeting had to be at the base-of-the-pyramid ... not the [very] bottom billion ... That is where [aid] needs to go. That's sort of like the sector of society that has been most neglected. ...
>
> Business for the most part can't reach the bottom billion, [but] a lot of businesses are doing interesting experiments with clean water distribution, trash pickup and things like that where they have reached the bottom billion. But, there are still 3 billion people at the base-of-the-pyramid. That's definitely a place where businesses should be making things more efficient and create more wealth.

Noor speaks to the tradeoffs between social entrepreneurship and ordinary entrepreneurship:

> If really talented people were getting the opportunity to make a lot of money saving the world, I think they'd prefer to do that. But now there's sort of a paradox, a false dichotomy put in place [based on] whether you want to do well for yourself personally or whether you want to do well for the world. I think that people need to understand that.
>
> Right now I'm seeing that the sweet spot between high impact and high profitability is a very small, very narrow type of business, and if the scope of that could become larger where high impact could mean high profitability in more areas, then I don't think we'd have to live with poverty anymore.

From the sweet spot toward profit

BEING IN THE SWEET SPOT where impact meets profit eliminates dueling incentives. Much more often, however, a social entrepreneur must move noticeably toward one of the extremes. Tacking toward profit makes a social enterprise more closely resemble an ordinary business. Some even argue that there is a false distinction between social enterprises and business in general, or certainly a blurry one. Cheryl Heller falls into this camp.

Cheryl has worked with small and large socially minded organizations in a variety of capacities. She founded the first Master's Program in Social Design at the School of Visual Arts (SVA) in New York City, has taught and coached high-potential social entrepreneurs at PopTech and the Unreasonable Institute, and founded and maintains a firm offering communication and innovation strategy consulting to firms around the world addressing social innovation and sustainability. She argues that the distinction between entrepreneurs and social entrepreneurs is counterproductive:

> I think that it is time that we ended the separation between entrepreneurs and social entrepreneurs and good [and bad] industries. We need to make this mainstream. We need to have successful entrepreneurs. We need to make this a sustainable economy, and addressing the needs of the planet and society ought to be a part of that. Don't think of [being a social entrepreneur] as some rarified, special, 'aren't you wonderful and cool and different?' Make it mainstream. The world does not need another nonprofit organization. It just doesn't. Figure out a way to make this a viable life that will thrill you, and thrill you because you are successful and you're creating good in the world.

Her consulting clients include companies such as Mars (the family business best known for its chocolates), whose founder's words nearly 70 years ago sound remarkably like those of a present-day progressive company: "The company's objective is the manufacture and distribution of food products in such manner as to promote a *mutuality of services and benefits among all stakeholders*" (emphasis mine).[3] For Mars, those stakeholders include all who are affected by its business: from those who grow and harvest cocoa, to communities where their plants are located, to employees, as well as those who hold shares of stock.

Cheryl finds common cause between the efforts of companies like Mars and the foundations she works with, such as those that are trying to revitalize Buffalo and to develop a model for other American cities:

> There is basically no aspect of industry that doesn't need to redefine itself right now. What they are struggling with gets expressed in very different ways, but it is all about how, without committing corporate suicide, to really begin to address some of the issues that social entrepreneurs are trying to address, and not be left behind. They are all connected.

Business can't do it alone

THE ROOT LOGIC OF MARKETS IS SIMPLE: if there is a way to make a buck, someone will find it, then do it. Even if it takes a sum of money to get started, it's worthwhile if you get it all back plus more. The logic is flawless for selling M&Ms, Snickers, and Mars bars. Or corn, carabiners, and cars. Yet markets can also fail.

Implicitly, selling any product or service depends on various support structures being in place. Noor Siddiqui relied on transcriptionists who had already learned English, grammar, and typing in universities and the better high schools. Those with more desperate needs for income were typically unqualified and too costly to train.

Martin Fisher (whom we will meet a number of times throughout the book) teases out the problems facing social entrepreneurs tackling deeply entrenched poverty:

> [We] should be trying to solve big problems. Not all of us are, but we should be. And a big problem is exactly a big problem because there's two things which have gone wrong. One is market failure and secondly there's government failure.

Government failures include not providing for basic needs (like sanitation, access to water, and protection from prevalent diseases), not providing hard and soft infrastructure (including education and roads), and not having suitable rules of law and stable, conflict-free environments.

Government failures can be closely linked to market failures. Poor or non-existent roads, an ill or ill-equipped workforce, and associated factors can critically impair a business's ability to make a profit. With these supports in place, markets bring together eager buyers and willing sellers; without them, a business may need to build roads itself, provide remedial education, or take other corrective actions that create favorable business conditions – none of which it is likely to do.

Market failures arise, too, when potential investors simply deem profits too small or the time to reap them too long compared to other options. In the developed world, this can be overcome, sometimes, by selling early versions (of Teslas, iPhones, genome sequencing) to those champing at the bit and willing to pay small fortunes to be early adopters. This is utterly unfeasible in the developing world for those far more essential products such as water irrigation pumps and solar lighting. Martin comments:

> The market is actually pretty good at solving its own problems. But, when you have a market failure, to think that the market is going to solve the problem – it's just ridiculous, right? If the market can solve the problem, it's *not* one of the world's big problems. ... You're not going to solve big problems and make money at the same time, because the market has failed.
>
> And this is a fundamental market failure: A private company will not [make the necessary investment of time and money to develop a market] when you're selling to the very poorest, very hardest-to-reach, most risk-averse people in the world – poor African farmers. How do we know that? Because African farmers are still using a machete and a hoe. If anybody could figure out [how to sell them better tools], they would have figured it out. The market is pretty good [at that].

Which market?

STATEMENTS ABOUT MARKETS CAN BE EASILY CONFUSED. Even as Martin Fisher explains about market failures, KickStart relies on markets extensively to get irrigation pumps to those smallholder farmers who will buy them. Farmers who buy these pumps will be able to grow cash crops to sell for a profit; shopkeepers who sell the pumps will also make money; those who deliver the pumps to the shopkeepers will, too; and so on, all the way back to the manufacturer. These interlocking market transactions are effective at what they do: finding a way to get products to people willing to pay.

But this does not mean that markets are infallible. In spite of KickStart's success in ensuring that all parties from manufacturers through distributors and salespeople make money – plus farmers themselves – the end-to-end endeavor is *not* profitable. (This seeming paradox will be explained in Chapter 26, "Chained value"; suffice to say here that it involves formidable expenses for research and development and, more critically, marketing.) Thus, market solutions can't be counted on to always go in and "fix" a problem.

Yet we believe the myth of markets as business oracle – accepting as an article of faith that they validate the wisdom of certain pursuits while tossing aside the rest, based solely on profit or loss. By the market's logic, KickStart should be jettisoned as unprofitable, despite creating financially secure lives for more than one million formerly impoverished people – an outcome that would be nothing to cheer about. However, the idea that profitability can and should be used to determine which societal problems to solve is gaining traction among social entrepreneurs, and most potential investors in social enterprises have long been sold on the idea.

Mission, not profit, lights the way

KATHERINE LUCEY WAS AN INVESTMENT BANKER FOR TWO DECADES helping finance large-scale power plants and energy infrastructure around the world. Now her life's work is in helping bring artificial light for the first time to rural African households through the company she founded, Solar Sister. As different as are high-tech finance and African poverty, they might as well belong to different centuries or different planets.

Solar Sister is a nonprofit organization that uses the power of the market "to eliminate energy poverty by empowering women with economic opportunity."[4] It equips village women with solar products, training, and marketing, transforming them into entrepreneurs. By organizing this distribution network, Solar Sister, like the entrepreneurs it supports, receives a commission on every sale. Villagers benefit from the goods being sold. Many, for the first time, have light after dark or can cook with solar stoves instead of burning noxious materials that are both harmful and expensive. Katherine explains the need not to let profits be Solar Sister's foremost concern:

> Solar Sister started from a mission of rural electrification, of giving people access to technology. And we're using the market as the most efficient and effective way to achieve that mission. Even if at some point in the future we get profits, as in [revenues] above our costs, those profits would be

plowed back into building out the market and extending it further. It's a big problem. So as far as I could see, we could always redeploy those profits back into mission rather than take those profits to bring them back to a shareholder. Because if you're a for-profit company, that's what you would be doing. You'd say, 'Those profits are mine because I invested in it.' Whereas we're mission–first, so we're saying those profits should still be applied to mission.

And yet she feels the tug to become a for-profit social enterprise:

I go back and forth on [for-profit] social enterprise. A lot of people are very focused on for-profit models as I think they are tired of the old aid and development mentality, and they think that the for-profit model is the antidote to that. I do think it's important to be able to make profits, and certainly to use markets and money. Actually, one of the best feedback loops you can have is: If people will buy it, then they value it; therefore, what you are doing is good work. Whereas, if they wouldn't buy it, then the fact that you're giving it away is probably not a good indication of the benefits that you're providing. I think profits are a great thing, but in our case we're a mission–first nonprofit. It makes sense for us.

Are you a social entrepreneur?

ARE YOU A SOCIAL ENTREPRENEUR? Or maybe a better question to begin with is: do you want to be?

The variations in social entrepreneurs' perspectives that we've touched on thus far revolve around profit. As David Bornstein, author and journalist, has pointed out, however, profitability is often regarded too coarsely.

I wrote a column in the *New York Times* about why there are so many places in the country where you can't get good food. That's because we have this model in our mind that something either has to be for-profit or nonprofit. Think of Whole Foods ... We think that it has to be returning, let's say, better than a 5% investment to be a for-profit company. When you think of something as a nonprofit, what is it if you think about it in investment terms? It's a minus-100% investment, right? You give money away and you never expect it to come back. So we have 105 percentage points between those two things, right?

There's no reason why we cannot have a minus-20% good food-selling business in the inner city that does a pretty good business, has a lower price point, sells all sorts of great stuff, and is subsidized by all the people who wanted it to happen. A minus-20% business is an incredible value for your buck, but we think about the world in binary terms and we don't actually recognize that there are so many opportunities that are between minus-100 and plus-5. And I would venture to say a lot of social businesses could actually figure out where they fall in those lines. ... This binary way of looking at the world – the market or the government [or pure nonprofits] – is really a false dichotomy.

David's comments suggest something more: a range of profitability is the flip side of a range of severity of problems that social entrepreneurs address. Of course, this correlation is not exact; but if the problem a social entrepreneur addresses has vast potential to make her rich, hers is probably just a traditional business.

Should Fitbit or Groupon be considered social enterprises? In their favor: counting steps creates an incentive to walk more, which is healthful. Groupon, the daily deal website, was actually conceived as a social enterprise to support discounted purchasing by groups. But only the blissfully ignorant or woefully naïve would believe that Fitbit, Inc. (worth $1.25 billion as I write) or Groupon (valued at more than $5 billion) are solving the world's most pressing problems.

In contrast, providing health care to those who have never seen a doctor, or education in locales where teachers don't show up or there are no books, belong to an entirely different conversation.

So, do you want to be a social entrepreneur? If you do, remember that the world's most severe problems can be addressed through social entrepreneurship – in fact, their severity calls out for tenacious, often innovative solutions and actors who seek a life of meaning – but this is rarely a path to riches.

Are you a social entrepreneur? (Take two)

Now, BACK TO THE FIRST QUESTION: *are* you a social entrepreneur? This is not as obvious as it seems. Among the interviews I conducted, when the concept of being a social entrepreneur came up, many people registered at least a note of surprise. Out of many such responses, here are three:

> We incorporated as a nonprofit organization, and the interesting thing was at that time I didn't know anything called 'social entrepreneurship.' All I knew was nonprofit and social value. But someone sent me a Facebook message and said, 'I've seen what you've been doing all these years. I think you're a social entrepreneur: you should apply for an Ashoka Fellowship.' And I [thought to myself], 'Whatever 'Ashoka' means.' So I went to the Ashoka website, and I [realized] that this was what I was trying to do. Because what I was doing was: I was using my skills to earn income and then to solve social problems. And so that was when the connection came.
>
> ('Gbenga Sesan, Founder/Executive Director,
> Paradigm Initiative)

I didn't set out to [be a social entrepreneur], but I am one, and I do consider myself one. What I've really grown to believe in the marrow of my bones, and understand, is that we're way off course in terms of the role that business plays in society. And we're measuring all the wrong things.

Business really should exist to serve the benefit of all, to serve the communities that they exist in, to improve the quality of life for everybody. That's the statement of the social entrepreneur. Plus, business is a wonderful thing. In my mind, it's the only domain in our world that has the ability, the bandwidth, and the power to move society to where it needs to be in enough time to keep us from going over the edge.

(Sandy Wiggins, Principal, Consilience LLC)

I don't think we ever as a company, or me ever as an entrepreneur, considered myself a *social* entrepreneur – what the heck is that? My husband, who joined the company eight years ago, likes to say, 'We like to sleep at night.' But even before he started saying that, I didn't even think what I was doing was anything that anyone wouldn't have done. I didn't have any expectation that what I was doing was any different than what anybody was doing.

I guess [my approach to business] was about just fulfilling my lifestyle. I knew I felt better when I ate this stuff [organic food], and so if I'm going to be involved in this ugly thing called business, I might as well do what I want for consumers. But the social part of the mission really – I say this a lot, and people I don't think believe me, but I really do believe it – there wasn't an ounce of philanthropy in this decision to go offshore [and make lives better for those I employed].

(Bena Burda, Founder, Clean Clothes Inc.
[formerly Maggie's Organics])

These statements conceal the accomplishments of these individuals. 'Gbenga Sesan was a Nigerian computer whiz-kid, and is now a computer specialist, who used his gifts to create meaningful employment in the area of information and computer technology for disadvantaged Nigerian youth. He did, indeed, become an Ashoka Fellow, among the strongest acknowledgments of a social entrepreneur's achievements and their potential. For more than a decade, Sandy Wiggins has been at the cutting edge of sustainability, local business, and social finance – each a tool for supporting people before profits. He served as chair of the U.S. Green Building Council, was founding chair of the Green Building Certification Institute, and played a significant role in LEED (Leadership in Energy and Environmental Design), an influential rating system for environmentally responsible buildings (more in Chapter 46, "Decide"). He is now a senior advisor to RSF Social Finance as well as principal of a consulting company directed at triple-bottom-line development. Bena Burda is the founder of Maggie's Organics (now Clean Clothes, Inc.), a maker of organic apparel for more than two decades. At a time when the idea of organics had little cachet, especially organic textiles, Maggie's pushed for organic fiber processing standards, and got them adopted by the Organic Trade Association. Maggie's also worked with a Nicaraguan development agency to develop a means of production where all workers shared in Maggie's success, leading to a worker-owned cooperative. In the years since its founding, Maggie's has consistently questioned conventional practices around supply, distribution, and manufacturing of organics – always leading to better products, a cleaner environment, and working conditions with more dignity, engagement, and money.

Like 'Gbenga, Sandy, and Bena, Sanga Moses didn't consider himself a social entrepreneur at the outset, either. He still doesn't, preferring to call himself "a social servant – someone who serves my community." True to this objective, he has offered franchise opportunities to poor Ugandan women to provide them a livelihood, even when interested investors advised him to consolidate operations in the name of efficiency and profitability.

Being a social entrepreneur

THESE EXAMPLES CAN BE CONSIDERED IN TWO WAYS: either they support the idea that labels don't matter and that successful social entrepreneurs succeed based on strong ideas, execution, and persistence (which I think is true). Or, they mean that social entrepreneurs can toil in unnecessary isolation from each other (which I think is "more true"). Andre Albuquerque, a lawyer, who was made an Ashoka Fellow for his work providing land-rights resolution and dignity for Brazil's urban poor without legal title to their property, tells me:

> I realized that I was a social entrepreneur only eight years after I was being a social entrepreneur. Had I had that clarity and talked to other social entrepreneurs ... and social venture capitalists – maybe at the time there wasn't something called social venture capital – or other people that maybe had walked the same or similar paths, I would probably have moved along more quickly than I did.

To that end, this book is for those who know they are social entrepreneurs, think they might be, or are deciding if they want to be. May you walk your path quickly, in solidarity, and with wisdom.

Notes

1 All dollar values quoted in this book are U.S. dollars.
2 Collier, Paul, *The Bottom Billion: Why the Poorest Countries are Failing and What Can Be Done About It* (Oxford: Oxford University Press, 2007).
3 Forrest E. Mars, Sr., 1947. Retrieved July 5, 2018 from: https://www.mars.com/global/doing-our-part/principles-in-action/business-segment-highlights
4 https://www.solarsister.org

Part 2

You

Taking on a serious societal problem means first understanding it. You may have been affected by that problem yourself, or you set out with the intention of understanding it. But you must, by necessity, become immersed in its essential nature so that your work forges an unmistakable connection between what is truly needed and what you provide.

Whether moved by the plight of a community or a threat to a majestic rainforest, the idea you put forward must be smart, effective, and connected to your problem's history.

Even then, you may not be required to launch a venture: it may be better to join others. And when starting your own venture *is* required, you should think twice, and then again, about the likely personal toll this will take. Are you truly ready to commit?

And then the work begins to make sure you're truly prepared.

3 Before they were social entrepreneurs

IT IS IMPOSSIBLE to be a successful social entrepreneur without genuine immersion. This might come from the circumstances you are born into, or it may be more intentional and planned, as when one becomes obsessed with confronting an injustice that is occurring halfway around the globe. As educated as you are, you cannot *know* your way into immersion: immersion is lived – and deeply. What separates the social entrepreneur is the meaning she ascribes to her experience: an interpretation mixing humility with a desire to learn, empathy and respect, and an abiding attitude to act and make a difference.

Immerse yourself

SANGA MOSES'S UPBRINGING IMMERSED HIM IN POVERTY; it was an inevitability of his birth. Jerry White's youth prepared him to work for social justice and organizing for action; this was part his nature, part upbringing. Zachary D. Kaufman, a white American, became immersed in post-genocide Rwanda as a young man. Through his scholarship but, more importantly, his direct contact with victims and perpetrators of atrocities, he was called to action as a social entrepreneur.

While their backgrounds and the social problems they address differ in so many ways, it is not at all a coincidence that meaningful experiences laid down a path that led them – as well as other social entrepreneurs we'll meet, and, truly, all successful social entrepreneurs – to become social entrepreneurs.

The importance of an immersive relationship is borne out, in fact, in many ways. Marina Kim is executive director of AshokaU and its co-founder along with Erin Krampetz. Ashoka, its parent organization, has been at the forefront of social entrepreneurship for more than 30 years, and no other organization has done as much to bring attention to, develop, and expand the field. Ashoka literally coined the phrase "social entrepreneur." As Ashoka has evolved, it has recognized the need to impart changemaking skills and attitudes (it also coined the term "changemaker") to those in all walks of life: parents, teachers, health care workers, and us all.

AshokaU is one of Ashoka's "everyone a changemaker" initiatives, focusing on colleges and universities. Marina has worked with students, professors, and administrators around the world to spark, support, and interconnect social innovation in higher education. She has met and worked with social entrepreneurs worldwide. She described two traits associated with successful social entrepreneurs. One is an exposure to injustice, coming from one's own experience or sometimes via a role model; the second is deep immersion in a situation requiring change, especially where one can say "I can contribute." Marina's remarks mirror my findings. Out of the 71 conceptual codes used in the 125 interviews I conducted (see Appendix 1), "Immersion" was the fifth most common.

Life comes at you hard

UNIVERSITY PROGRAMS NOW OFFER COURSES IN SOCIAL ENTREPRENEURSHIP, but many who take them do so out of curiosity rather than an intense desire to create social change. Sanga Moses' path was far different, even if he was the first in his rural Ugandan clan to attend college. Not knowing his mother and often living separated from his economically and emotionally struggling father, Sanga learned to take care of himself early. As he explains:

> I have been a business person all my life. It was out of necessity. I come from a broken family. ... My first business was actually selling milk in a plastic can. That was when I was maybe seven or eight, and then I started a barbershop when I was about 12 in school, to cut kids' hair. And then I started a computer training center in my village, which failed because no one came to study computers. Then I started a printing and publishing company, which still exists and my friend manages it. That one has been very successful.

These businesses varied in their sophistication. While some were informal, the printing business and another solar distribution business are formally registered, and both are still in operation. And this list only suggests the range of business ideas that Sanga's efforts have set in motion.

Sanga's intelligence and hard work landed him at Makerere University, in Kampala, Uganda, a highly prestigious university that has educated 12 former presidents from four African nations. His life there, in a city of 1.5 million, was dramatically different from the rural, pastoral existence of his youth, where the community kept cattle and moved with them through the seasons as they grazed, where children gathered wood for cooking, and where forests were abundant.

But, in less than two decades, his home in western Uganda has become a very different place. Whereas forests covered nearly half of Uganda a century ago, they now cover just one-fifth – having devastating economic effects for more than three-quarters of Uganda's population who rely on subsistence farming, and extensive forests, for their livelihoods.[1]

Equally notable has been the effect on girls' education. Sanga recalls collecting firewood as a child from nearby forests, but deforestation means the task now involves a journey of two to three hours. And this responsibility often falls to young girls, whose responsibilities at home for collecting wood prevent their regular attendance at school.[2]

This was the new Uganda that Sanga encountered as he traveled home one day, taking a break from his job – a position of prestige and professional accomplishment – at Financial Trust, a Tier I microfinance institution with full banking privileges conferred by the Ugandan government due to its size and financial performance. Seeing his sister carrying firewood when she should have been attending school was a turning point: his life was about to plunge into angst and uncertainty.

Survivor

JERRY WHITE, FOUNDER OF LANDMINE SURVIVORS NETWORK, WASN'T SURPRISED by the ease with which he interacted with global celebrities: as far as he was concerned, he had been practicing his whole life. Growing up in a small coastal town outside Boston, he received a good education, had supportive parents, and enjoyed the life he led. He was smart, athletic, and resourceful. His theatrical leanings, along with an enterprising nature, were evident early on:

> We used to put on plays every summer, from the time I was five years old, plays like *Mary Poppins* or *The Sound of Music* or *Willie Wonka*. Whatever it was, it didn't matter if they were produced great. They would be barefoot in a boathouse, with painted bed sheets, torn, hanging behind us showing the Alps for *The Sound of Music*.
>
> So, from an early age, I learned to produce plays and we would do them like a skit. [Or I'd be] taking an idea and re-scripting it, and then casting it and putting it on. Of course, the audience being mostly families and parents, on the beach in the summer, just loved it: they ate it up.

Jerry's mother instilled in him a strong sense of service and social justice:

> Even though we had privilege and wealth and an education, my mother always made sure that we were caring for the poor. Anyone underneath us was more important than those ahead of us or above us.

Through his upbringing, he embraced the ideal "of those to whom much is given, much is required."[3]

Over the years, his plays have been produced on the world stage, a stage that he has shared with heads of state, civil society leaders, politicians, celebrities, and others committed to social justice. Although in his youth this could not have been predicted, there is an unmistakable arc from the boathouse to his success as a social entrepreneur:

> I found myself in these Forrest Gump moments of working with Princess Diana and Queen Noor and King Hussein and many others [working in

support of landmine survivors]. I thought, 'Why does this feel so easy?' It's a lot of hard work, but I just feel like I was born to do this type of casting.

We're all on this rather fascinating stage and we need to maneuver and change things, or cast or rewrite certain scripts to bring a paradigm shift that would matter for social transformation and change in the world today. I happen to be in the category of loving to see increased justice and peace and equality and dignity and rights in the world. That must be part of my DNA – that I was raised to yearn for justice.

Off the track

IF AMI DAR HAD BEEN LOOKING FOR A WAY TO GET INVOLVED WITH SOCIAL CHANGE TODAY, he might have gone to the website Idealist.org. But when he was thinking about such things in 1985, Idealist wasn't around – because he hadn't invented it yet. Today, Idealist is a clearinghouse for people hoping to find meaningful opportunities to serve society by lending their talents through volunteer work, internships, or paid work in areas including: international development, global health, microfinance, and a host of concerns in the United States and the developed world. These opportunities are offered by nonprofit, governmental, and multinational organizations as well as progressive for-profits and social enterprises.

So how did a self-proclaimed "anti-student," who saw vast potential for connecting people with nonprofits (and now other socially minded organizations) around the world, get this idea? By backpacking around South America, where it came to him in a burst of inspiration. Of course, no one but a handful of scientists had ever heard of the internet then, so he had to wait nearly a decade for the Mosaic browser, and even then it offered only a faint glimmer of how powerful the connections he envisioned could be. Idealist today connects more than 100,000 site users every day to potential opportunities at 70,000 nonprofits around the world.[4]

Ami explains the importance of experiencing life with a sense of patience as you figure out your role in it:

> I think the most important thing for me to say to the 22-year-old, the 21- or 23-year-old, is that life doesn't work linearly. When you are 22, you think it does. You think that it's kindergarten, high school, job, death – that type of thing. It doesn't have to work that way.

A linear life would be one that follows a carefully developed plan. Ami's certainly didn't:

> I never went to college. I hated school as a kid, and so the moment I could get out, I got out of high school and never went back. I had to go into the [Israeli] army for three years. When I finished the army, I went backpacking. People sort of go backpacking for like a year. I went for two

and a half years. So I was 25, I'd done nothing with my life, but things worked out …

When you're 22, there's almost a deep psychological sense that any decision that you make now is going to completely affect your life forever. 'Oh my God, if I miss a year, if I waste a year now, what will happen?' Nothing! It will be fine. When you're 32, you won't look back at the year when you were 23 and bemoan that you missed a year. You actually enriched yourself somehow.

Ami would encourage you to explore without planning, see the world, and gain experiences that will shape you, directly or through serendipity:

My advice, basically, is that if there are things that you think you want to do – you want to learn a different language, you want to see a place in the world that you haven't seen – do it now if you possibly can. It gets tougher when you are 30, 40, 50, when you have kids and family and work and stuff.

Go to Costa Rica and work for the English-speaking newspaper there. They need your English. Speaking English in the United States is not a huge asset; there are lots of people who speak English. There are 300 million people who think they write well in English. [But] your English is a huge asset somewhere else.

So take a risk, jump off the track – it's okay. You can get back on later.

Invite the world in

Ashley Murray (now Muspratt) grew up in Andover, Massachusetts, attended a rigorous, private high school, enrolled at Bates College and "by October, I knew I was taking a year off. I was so restless and just kind of felt like, 'Get me out of here.'" *The Backdoor Guide to Short-Term Job Adventures*[5] got her out, leading her first to rural Ghana and then other destinations around the world.

The book was my bible. I found so many really cool [jobs]. All through college, I found all these really awesome internships. That book really changed my life, and that year off is what put me on this sanitation track.

Her first job-adventure was in a rural village called Anfoega, in the Volta Region in eastern Ghana. It was her first time in such undeveloped circumstances, the first step in her decade-long immersion in developing-world sanitation. Today, she laughs at her obsession with sanitation. "My friends are sick and tired of me talking about [poop]!" But when she arrived in Anfoega, she was unaccustomed to what she would experience:

It was my first time in a developing country and it was just this incredibly eye-opening experience in terms of the water and sanitation challenges.

We [the family she lived with] had a Kumasi ventilated improved pit latrine, a KVIP, that was actually in really good shape. It was the dual pit. But that was my first time ever using a pit latrine and we had to walk, I don't know, four minutes, five minutes to the well to get water.

During that first visit to Ghana, she taught biology and chemistry at a high school. That experience, while also new, had less impact on her than the problems she saw everywhere with sanitation – from open sewers, to toilet owners paying to have their toilets emptied (lest they become unusable), to round-the-clock dumping of human feces into the sea:

It was that exposure to sanitation [in Anfoega] and the times I was in Accra [the capital city], seeing how bad urban sanitation was. The confluence of science – the biology and chemistry – were intellectually stimulating. I consider bad sanitation the biggest environmental problem we face as a global society today, and I knew I wanted a career in environmental protection.

Ashley adds with a sense of guilty pleasure that the path that *The Backdoor Guide* has led her on through Africa, China, and elsewhere has been as adventuresome as promised: "[An added benefit of all this] is more selfish. Getting to live and work abroad – that is really appealing."

Knowing versus understanding

ZACHARY D. KAUFMAN WAS IN HIGH SCHOOL IN PITTSBURGH IN 1994 when the Rwandan genocide took place halfway around the world, where an estimated one-seventh of the country exterminated another seventh: one million people exterminating another million, entirely based on ethnicity. Even at that age, Zachary was attuned to atrocities:

My family is Jewish and several of our relatives were killed in the Holocaust. So, growing up, I learned a lot about the genocide against my own people and about the struggles of other victims of oppression and discrimination. I learned at an early age that it is vital to combat myths, misinformation, and misperceptions that lead to persecutions.

Zachary had a connection to the African continent as well. His mother was born and raised in South Africa, and, when Zachary was born, Nelson Mandela was in prison. Mandela was released in 1990 and three years later won the Nobel Peace prize, along with President F. W. de Klerk, just four months before the Rwandan extermination began:

The genocide in Rwanda raged for about 100 days, from April to July of 1994. At the time, I was in high school. Because of my mother's background, I was particularly interested in developments in Africa. Coupled with my family's experience in another genocide, I felt a visceral reaction to what was happening in Rwanda.

Zachary enrolled at Yale in 1996, taking courses related to human rights, the Holocaust, and the Rwandan genocide as he pursued a degree in political science. In his junior year, he studied human rights in the field, receiving a fellowship from a nonprofit organization, Humanity in Action, devoted to serving students' interests in human rights, which placed him in Denmark. As part of his application for his first job after college, he submitted a writing sample about a failed prosecution before the United Nations International Criminal Tribunal for Rwanda.

It doesn't take a great leap to conclude that this document must have been a convincing one, as he landed a job in the State Department's Bureau of Democracy, Human Rights and Labor, later moving to the U.S. Department of Justice's Office of Overseas Prosecutorial Development, Assistance, and Training. In these positions, he focused on issues of transitional justice in Rwanda, supporting efforts to bring criminal justice to the perpetrators of the country's genocide.

Despite his understanding of Rwanda from afar, nothing prepared him for what he would experience the first time he set foot in the country. When I ask him how important being on the ground was for him to get the inspiration for his social enterprise – a venture that would establish the country's first-ever public library – he responds:

> For me, it was crucial to take that first trip and to have traveled many times since to Rwanda. During the initial trip, the very first Rwandan I met, Ancilla, had survived the genocide. Her entire family was killed in front of her and Ancilla herself was hacked with a machete and left for dead. After she regained consciousness, she hid in the marshes for three months. After meeting Ancilla, I've sent spent a lot of time speaking with survivors and perpetrators of the genocide, combing through archives, and paying my respects at genocide sites around the country, where the smashed skulls, torn clothes, and blood stains of adult and child victims have been preserved.
>
> It's one thing to study something from afar. It's another thing to meet the people involved and see the carnage. Doing so has profoundly impacted me.

Zachary's social enterprise worked for more than a decade to help launch the Kigali Public Library, an undertaking to create a new culture of intellectual honesty and openness in a country where information has been used in the worst possible ways, as evidenced by the hate propaganda and the kill-lists that had fueled Rwanda's genocide.

Unflinching

ZACHARY D. KAUFMAN'S EXPERIENCES ON THE GROUND in Rwanda further extended his understanding of the country's genocide, and the challenges to its recovery:

> I started interviewing suspected perpetrators to learn why they had committed the horrors of which they were accused. The ones who admitted their crimes offered a variety of reasons. But genocide, of course, could never be justified.

Though the genocide occurred in mid-1994, its effects have been far-reaching:

> The direct victims – those who were killed and the ones who survived – were just the beginning of those who have suffered as a result of the genocide. Rape had been used as a deliberate tool of the genocide, and so I would argue that there was a second wave of the genocide a few years later, when women started dying from HIV and AIDS. Some of their children also contracted the disease *in utero*. Secondary effects of the genocide have thus included disease and orphans.

Rwanda has also had to deal with the enormous number of perpetrators of the genocide, a problem with ramifications touching almost every aspect of society:

> Some estimates hold that as many people killed as were killed during the genocide. If that's true, there were around a million perpetrators of genocide in Rwanda. The enormous number of both victims and perpetrators affected everything: economic development, political stability, social cohesion, the justice system, health care. The prisons weren't large enough to hold all of the perpetrators. Even if they were, if you kept such a massive amount of people in prison, they wouldn't be in the labor pool. How does a poor, tiny country, about the size of Maryland, address such gargantuan challenges? These are just some of the onerous and painful questions Rwanda faced.

THIS DEEP UNDERSTANDING prompted Zachary to respond emotionally in a personal, authentic way:

> I was overwhelmed with all sorts of feelings and just the enormity of the challenges that Rwanda faced in its post-genocide era. I looked around and it seemed like there was no limit on need ...
> [And] nobody was working on the library. People had prioritized other needs and other kinds of assistance work. It just seemed like a no-brainer [for me]. ... As someone with a very deep academic background

and academic focus, libraries have always been my sanctuaries and my playgrounds.

American Friends of the Kigali Public Library, the nonprofit he founded, helped build Rwanda's first public library, in its capital city. The decade-long project created a bridge from the past to the future, both for Rwanda and Zachary himself:

> Because my work for the U.S. government focused on Rwanda's perpetrators – on criminal justice, which also meant Rwanda's past – I really welcomed the opportunity to work on a project with – and focused on – Rwanda's survivors, Rwanda's youth, and Rwanda's future.

Real life

PATRICK DONOHUE WOKE UP ONE NIGHT TO A RAGING FIRE consuming nearby dwellings during his home stay in Kibera, the world's second largest slum, a section of Nairobi, Kenya, but with none of the capital city's modern trappings. He was a member of a team working at the base-of-the-pyramid to create a business jointly owned by a major U.S. corporation and Kiberan slum dwellers. The fire and its aftermath taught him how resilient Kiberan residents were:

> The experience was a positive for me just to see how the community came together and rebuilt. [Like the residents,] I wish it hadn't happened, but it was definitely a focusing experience.

Charlie Cavell would wake up every morning in an apartment with bars on the windows when he was a student at Wayne State University in Detroit. He explains that his neighbors were all on welfare or Supplemental Security Income. These circumstances impelled him to develop an innovative workforce development program for young, low-income Detroit residents, called Pay It Forward.

Fire or bars – what we wake up to is less important than being alerted to our circumstances and roused to action.

Experienced with meaning

IMMERSION DOESN'T NEED TO INVOLVE DRAMA, DESTITUTION, OR ATROCITY. But it must be meaningful. Lisa Ballantine, her husband, their children, and their closest friends went on a missionary trip for a year to the Dominican Republic. During this time away, they offered spiritual assistance and started a number of churches. But the experience had a secular impact, too:

> I just saw the need for practical assistance. It was great to give spiritual assistance also, but I just saw so many physical needs that the people had that

could be resolved with relatively simple solutions. And so few people were actually willing to do things like that. I was really amazed. It's simple things – education and health education – the simplest things really change lives.

She and her family returned to the United States so that her older children could go to high school. But an entrepreneurial process had been set in motion. While studying ceramics at Northern Illinois University, she learned about a simple ceramic water filter, a technology she knew could benefit the Dominican Republic community she had called home:

> They have a huge need for water and, like most [developing] countries, they have a tradition in ceramics. It's very well accepted by people, and it's highly effective. So I began studying it and decided, 'Okay, well, this is what I want to do.'

Six years after her first visit, she returned when her husband bought a mountain ("I'm not being facetious: he actually bought a mountain.") She returned to her former community,

> where the need was great: they had no running water and they were all drinking water from the river and they were all sick. We had all these high hopes, believing everything's going to go great. And, very quickly, everything fell apart.

The challenges Lisa faced were of a technical nature and not due to misdiagnosing the situation. Her experience living among those she would come to work with and support had led to a true understanding of their needs and how to address them. Together with her fixation on correcting the problem, it would eventually lead to better health and economic opportunities for her community.

Faux immersion

CERTAIN EXPERIENCES CAN MERELY MASQUERADE AS IMMERSION. Some service trips pack participants on airplanes and fly them to developing-world locations where they engage in community service. Participants might provide a fresh coat of paint to a school or church, a new look that lasts until another group arrives the next week with fresher paint.[6] From the perspective of the community, it's fair to ask if they would have been better served by doing the work themselves, and if the money associated with airfare, meals, and accommodation could have been put to better use. In any case, even from the point of view of immersion, such experiences can shield participants from the true rigors of a community more than they expose them.

DORY GANNES FOUNDED THE OLEVOLOS PROJECT, a boarding school in the Olevolos Village in Tanzania, which serves orphans and other disadvantaged students, ensuring they receive excellent education, personal and leadership development, and a variety of meaningful extracurricular activities. All educational and living expenses are covered. Importantly, the Olevelos Project works closely with the village council, the district commissioner, and local community members, who advise on every aspect of the school and volunteer their time to ensure students' experiences will benefit the community.

Dory explains what immersion does *not* look like:

> Never go somewhere for a month and then come back and decide you're going to start a venture. That's a bad decision. A month traveling internationally isn't going to enable us to have the knowledge of the communities with whom we're working to really have a good sense of what they need.
>
> I would add that we can't decide what people need. Everyone has their own needs, so you'd best stick very closely with the community and drive your organization according their needs, rather than your own.

She elaborates, with eloquent nuance, on how "your own" may often supersede what's best for a community:

> I don't think this idea of wanting to help and make a difference and change the world is enough to carry us on with our work … as we actually start doing it.
>
> We have to want to make a difference, [but] we have to be deeply indebted and respectful of the people who we're working with, humbled by their experiences and think less of ourselves and more of the others around us.
>
> Even the saying 'I want to make a difference': the structure and the framing of that — it's obviously centered around you. And then 'want' is a verb that is also very self-directed. It doesn't incorporate curiosity, it's based off of need. And 'make,' as in 'I want to *make* a difference': it's as though you're doing the work, when there are so many other hands that are a part of it.

By inviting the world in, we can gain broad and deep experience. It is our choice, then, how we interpret it. We can engage the problems we see or let them glance off us. Or, to paraphrase slightly John Anner, a wonderfully effective and witty social entrepreneur:

> You can either approach the Peace Corps as a two-year camping trip, or you can try to get serious.

Notes

1 Kanabahita, Charlotte, *Forestry Outlook Studies Africa (FOSA): Uganda* (Kampala: Forestry Department, Ministry of Water, Lands & Envirnoment, 2001).

2 Bizzarri, Mariangela, *Safe Access to Firewood and Alternative Energy in Uganda: An Appraisal Report* (2009). Retrieved July 6, 2018 from: http://www.genderconsult.org/res/doc/SAFE_Uganda.pdf

3 Something President John F. Kennedy famously said (http://www.americanrhetoric.com/speeches/jfkcommonwealthmass.htm) – paraphrasing Luke 12:48 (King James Version).

4 Kanani, Rahim, "Inside look: The story behind Idealist.org." *Forbes*, September 12, 2012. Retrieved July 6, 2018 from: https://www.forbes.com/sites/rahimkanani/2012/09/12/inside-look-the-story-behind-idealist-org/#51a5c5b9144a

5 Landes, Michael, *The Back Door Guide to Short-Term Job Adventures* (Ten Speed Press, 1997, 2000, 2005). It is out of print these days, but there is the backdoorjobs.com website and you can still find used copies.

6 Salmon, Jacqueline L., "Churches retool mission trips." *Washington Post*, July 5, 2008. Retrieved July 6, 2018 from: http://www.washingtonpost.com/wp-dyn/content/article/2008/07/04/AR2008070402233.html

4 Ideas

WHEN SOCIAL ENTREPRENEURS grab the headlines, it is often for an innovative, "cool" idea. Bad reason. Splashy and sexy are often the siren song of social entrepreneurship, crowding out what is most fundamental: will the idea really solve the problem it is addressing? Splashy and sexy may obscure other truths: good ideas emerge from worse ideas, and the best ideas may be assembled from a kit of pre-existing parts. Rarely is a good idea the first idea. There is one universal about every good idea, however: an unshakeable intention to produce societal impact, no matter what it takes.

Paths

THE WORK OF A SOCIAL ENTREPRENEUR consists of reaching out into the world to make it better – but also going deep inside. It is giving life to what others have noticed before; but also bringing forth something imaginative and new. It changes a life, a village, or a way of thinking. How can social entrepreneurs' ideas span so many different things? How can social entrepreneurs live lives of apparent contradiction?

Sludge

EVERY SOCIAL ENTREPRENEUR I INTERVIEWED AT SOME POINT DEVELOPED AN IDEA for a social venture, of course – some dazzling, others workmanlike, a few difficult to understand. But where do these ideas come from? And what are the pitfalls along the way?

Immersion provides a starting point from which to think about the lives of people who lack certain essentials. During Ashley Murray's mid-college year in Ghana, the problem she has since built her business around practically found her. "It was an incredibly eye-opening experience in terms of the water and sanitation challenges." Her business, Pivot Works (formerly Waste Enterprisers), takes human waste from pit latrines, septic systems, or sewer networks, converts the energy within it to "pivot fuel," and sells it to industry. Treating human waste as an input to manufacture fuel, not as something useless that needs treatment and disposal, can produce billions of dollars in economic value and create healthier, more sanitary cities – in a large part by relying on sunlight.[1]

But living abroad is not a passport to success as a social entrepreneur. Marina Kim, who views social entrepreneurship from a front-row seat at Ashoka.org, has seen many early-stage social entrepreneurs falter by rushing to develop a "cool idea" based on superficial exposure. Without meaningful field experience to provide a meaningful context, and lacking deeper analysis into the root causes of a problem, their prospects are far dimmer than Ashley's (who went on to get degrees in biology and engineering along with much additional experience with fecal sludge before starting her venture).

Impulse to act

WE HAVE ALREADY MET SANGA MOSES ON HIS JOURNEY HOME from his banking position in Kampala. When he encountered his 12-year-old sister on the road, walking ten kilometers with her firewood, she was crying. She was upset about missing school and Sanga knew that she was forfeiting her chance to create a satisfying life for herself. Sanga recounts:

> I told her I would talk to our mother, and bring her back to a school in the city where I worked so she wouldn't have to fetch wood. But when I spoke to my mother, she said, 'No, you can't do that. She's the only girl I have. I'm an old woman: I can't survive without her. If you take her, I'll be dead.'
>
> I went back to the city, but this conversation haunted me. I couldn't really live my life anymore. I was constantly thinking about my sister, at the verge of losing the only opportunity she had to a better life – that is, education. And as a child who grew up in a rural area, my own life was transformed by education.
>
> I wasn't sure what to do. All I knew was how to be an accountant and work in a financial institution. But one night, I asked myself, 'If I don't do something, who will? I am just complaining about what I can't do, and my sister can't go to school because she has to fetch wood.'

Sanga quit his job at the bank.

Developing an idea

IN THE MOVIE *ANNIE HALL*, a writer tries to impress his friend: "Right now it's only a notion. But I think I can get the money to make it into a concept, and later turn it into an idea" – a comedic line with a lot of truth to it.

Sanga was only at the notion stage. He wanted to help young girls like his sister get an education; he wanted to save Uganda's dwindling forests. But he had no idea how. As he thought about the problems he wanted to solve, he considered different possible solutions. One, a solar cooker, he had to reject when his mother, acting like a beta-tester, said she couldn't cook at night or use it when it was raining. Next, he approached a professor of sustainability at the university he had once attended, explaining the problem he was trying to solve.

> He said, 'Young man, I'm a professor. I have never done anything with my hands, but I have literature.' So he gave me books and papers and magazines.

Sanga spent the next week at home, reading during every waking hour:

> I read about all things – biogas for example, but it looked like it was hard to take to scale. I read about all sorts of things until I read about the possibility of converting agriculture waste into fuel and fertilizers, and that made a lot of sense to me because Uganda is an agricultural country.
>
> All sorts of studies had been made in Brazil; and you needed a kiln. I had never even seen what a kiln looks like, and I didn't know anything, but I read and I noted these things. And I went back to the professor and said, 'I think I know what I want to do.'

SANGA NOW HAD A CONCEPT. He was still looking to solidify his idea. He was on his way, but only later would Sanga understand that even a good idea is just another starting point. Creating a business around an idea is something entirely different from the idea itself. And something more difficult to achieve. But neither he nor we are there yet in our story.

The doctor and the priest

KEVIN STARR, WHOM I DESCRIBE ADMIRINGLY AS "THE SOCIAL ENTREPRENEUR WHISPERER," IS A PLAIN-SPOKEN DOCTOR and managing director of the Mulago Foundation, dedicated to "looking for the best solutions to the biggest problems in the poorest places." He insightfully distinguishes what works from what only seems to. He has written no-punches-pulled accounts of social enterprises. Among his articles are those that: decry impact investing for lack of impact;[2] demand that social enterprises describe what they do in an eight-word mission statement (a truncated form that would be considered sacrilege in business schools);[3] take down Greg Mortenson and his acclaimed Central Asia Institute for its slipshod management and fraudulent financial reporting;[4] and suggest redeploying for greater impact the money and talent that underwrite business plan competitions and innovation prizes.[5]

When Kevin talks (or writes), we should listen. He has an uncanny knack for synthesizing practical lessons from messy and varied experiences. He gets straight to the point about the questions that should be asked about any potential solution to a problem:

1. Is it really needed?
2. Does it work like it's supposed to?
3. Does it get to those who need it?
4. Will it be used right?[6]

Ideas fail for all these reasons. Even some lauded by the popular press. If the answer to any of these questions is "no," the Mulago Foundation will not consider you as a recipient of its charitable funds (and rightly so).

1. *Is it really needed?* One Laptop Per Child created laptops that didn't serve poor, overseas communities' educational needs at all (and sometimes dropped them by parachute into those communities).[7]
2. *Does it work like it's supposed to?* Better Place created an electrical vehicle system that allowed cars to quickly "swap out" an almost-drained battery and "swap in" one that was fully charged. Ultimately, a dearth of the necessary charging stations coupled with the batteries' limited range led to the company's bankruptcy in 2013.[8]
3. *Does it get to those who need it?* Roads, or the lack of them, make it close to impossible to distribute vitally needed goods in some of the world's poorest rural regions.
4. *Will it be used right?* A bednet provides a protective barrier against malarial mosquitos. But it is hot, so people sleep with their heads and arms exposed, eliminating its protection.

EARLIER IN HIS CAREER, ED CARDOZA was Vice President for Development at Partners in Health, the international NGO that works with local health providers in some of the world's poorest places to offer the best possible care. He jokingly downplays his role:

> I was immersed into hundreds of colleges throughout the United States that were reading *Mountains Beyond Mountains* [the popular account of Partners in Health] and was often the booby prize if Paul, Ophelia, or Jim couldn't go. I would show up and give a talk.

It should be noted that "Paul" is Dr. Paul Farmer, MacArthur Award recipient and Nobel Peace Prize nominee; "Ophelia" is Ophelia Dahl, Partners in Health board chair and executive director; and "Jim" is Jim Yong Kim MD, PhD, and current president at the World Bank. They, along with Tom White and Todd McCormack, co-founded Partners in Health.

After he left Partners in Health, Ed, now an ordained priest, founded Still Harbor, a Boston-based nonprofit that provides support for social entrepreneurs or others seeking change by helping them explore their interior worlds. It caters to those of any faith, as well as those who distrust institutions of faith. His spiritual (but nonetheless secular) perspective is the yang to Kevin Starr's yin. Ed, the theologian, explains the very challenge that comes with agreeing to take on a problem:

> First an individual comes to a profound sense that they've encountered a problem or a challenge. ... There are two things that then can happen. One is you can get the shit scared out of you and just want to run away and avert your eyes. The other is the invitation: 'Maybe I should do

something about this?' The invitation is really one of the most important parts of [becoming a social entrepreneur].

Most people shut down, he continues, but "we have to make sure that when folks start to get activated or catch fire that we feed that passion." That occurs by helping them observe a problem critically and determine how they can get involved:

> We help them do three things: You observe and you use the processes to really get a good idea about what is going on. Then you judge, not in a kind of moralistic, Victorian way, but in a way that looks at data, that looks at what's really going on. Then you say, 'I have observed. I have begun laying aside judgments. It's very clear to me that there are obstacles or impediments – how am I going to act?'
>
> Those three things are [essential]. You want to a) make sure they don't divert their gaze, and then b) once they begin to experience a problem, they don't get overwhelmed or think, 'Oh God, there's no hope here. This is just too complicated.'
>
> At that point, you have a really good understanding of: 'This is who I am. This is what I am seeing. This is what I'm hearing. And this is why I want to get involved.'

On whose shoulders?

IN 1965, DR. JACK GEIGER OPENED A CLINIC IN THE MISSISSIPPI DELTA, treating patients who were so poor that they were often suffering from severe malnutrition.[9] His treatment for these patients, as logical as it was straightforward, was to write prescriptions for food. Patients took their prescriptions to their local grocery store, which would fill them by giving families food, and Geiger's clinic used its funds to pay for it.

The Office of Economic Opportunity, created by President Lyndon Johnson to lead the "War on Poverty" and which was funding his clinic, was furious. They sent an official to set Geiger straight about the funds they were providing, which, as the official emphasized, were to be used for medical care. By his own account, Geiger responded, "The last time I checked my textbooks, the specific therapy for malnutrition was food."

IN THE MID-1990S, REBECCA ONIE BEGAN COLLEGE. She wanted to find a way to provide real, deep, and continuing engagement with social problems for college students, and, over a period of six months, spoke with physicians at what was then called Boston City Hospital.

> Essentially, I was asking them, 'If you had unlimited resources, what's the one thing you would give your patients?' And I heard the same story again and again, which is a story we've heard literally hundreds of times since then. 'Every day we have patients that come into the clinic and the kid has an ear

infection. I prescribe antibiotics but the real issue is that there's no food at home, or the family is living in a car. But I don't ask about those issues because there's nothing I could do.' And they would [add], 'I have 13 minutes with each patient. Patients are piling up in the clinic waiting room. I have no idea where the nearest food pantry is. I wasn't trained to do this, and I don't have any help.' ... Doctors also say, 'We know that access to these basic resources will have a more profound impact on the health of our patients than anything we're going to do in the four walls of the doctor's office.'

Rebecca's observations led to the formation of a nonprofit organization now called Health Leads. It uses a hybrid workforce (initially, college volunteers; now community health workers, social workers, and others as well) to help address patients' essential needs – such as food, housing, heat, etc. – by identifying and securing appropriate community resources. It now packages more than 20 years of experience into learning collaboratives, workshops, and tools and resources to support other health systems pursuing similar work.

Despite Geiger's landmark work and Health Leads' own, deeply similar, efforts, for a long time their lives never intersected.

[Then] just a few years ago, I got an email from somebody named Dr. Jack Geiger, who was one of the two physicians who founded the first community health center in the Mississippi Delta in the 1960s. ... What was fascinating about [this email] is, on the one hand, I feel this incredible sense of pride in actually being part of this longstanding sort of movement to try to have a health care system that is more squarely aligned with improving patient health. And at the same time am sobered by the idea that, if Dr. Geiger had this idea in 1968, why do I still walk into Boston Medical Center, decades later, and have doctors saying to me, 'On these issues we practice a "don't ask, don't tell" policy.'?

By her own admission, Health Leads is a "distinctly un-innovative model," except, in this author's view, in the rigorous, systematic way it recruits, trains, and deploys its workforce. Rebecca says:

The need we're trying to address and the model we're using to address it are profoundly simple, logical, intuitive, and uncontroversial. The challenge is: how do you change the system to align with that reality? I think that's the piece of work that is still undone.

AFTER HALF A CENTURY, Geiger's prescriptions for curing the medical establishment, along with poor patients, is finally gaining momentum. Kevin Starr, the Mulago Foundation managing director, talks about the biggest mistakes that social entrepreneurs make:

You need to familiarize yourself with the literature and understand what pitfalls await you and who has circumvented them successfully. You can't just reinvent. ... There really is a way of determining how others have asked the right thing in the right way.

Kevin's comments pertain to reinvention in all things, from marketing to distribution to measurement, and – in the present context – the generation and development of ideas.

Complexity from simpler parts

MICROENERGY CREDITS (MEC) WAS BUILT on the ideas and efforts of others. To appreciate the company, you must comprehend its jarring juxtapositions. In the developing world, it helps microfinance institutions in places such as Mongolia, Uganda, and India. In the developed world, it deals with giant financial firms, such as Citi, that are intent on buying carbon credits. Its support allows microfinance institutions to provide financing for energy products that replace kerosene, wood, or dung for cooking and heating, or that possibly provide a family with indoor lighting for the very first time. Its work with Wall Street and other firms lets them prepare for potential governmental regulation of carbon by participating in carbon markets.

While its microfinance partners sell products that might allow a poor, rural family to offset its carbon usage at a level of $5 per month, MEC will aggregate these small amounts to sell them for millions of dollars. Families living on a few dollars a day save money and live healthier lives, carbon's destructive effects on the planet are mitigated, and the natural environment is improved for the poor, for whom this is so badly needed. And all this is mediated by electrons, photons, and dollars that whiz through high-tech systems to monitor and monetize carbon.

April Allderdice (MEC's co-founder) has instructive words for social entrepreneurs that acknowledge her debt to others:

> When we started MicroEnergy Credits, we were building on so many other organizations and copying them as much as possible, emulating, taking pieces from a bunch of different ideas. I'm so grateful for the opportunities that I had to be in conferences or have jobs that allowed me to interview dozens of different people and really index all of these experiences, because they all came into play when we designed this model. This model could never have worked if people hadn't worked hard to create the carbon markets, hadn't done amazing work in microfinance and microfinance-plus [microfinance that offers additional products, such as maternal health care]. These were pieces that we pulled together.
>
> But now I'm seeing other people speaking to us, learning from our case studies, applying it to their model, seeing if we can work together. So there's a lot of that going on. It's very innovative, and I really support it.

Intention for impact

CONCERN IS THE SPARK THAT IGNITES A SOCIAL ENTERPRISE; what it truly becomes is derived from intention. Setting your intention to produce large-scale change, even as you embark, is a real possibility.

Dan Sutera had already started three tech businesses when he visited his friend, David Seidenfeld, in Zambia. Seidenfeld had first arrived there while in the Peace Corps and had developed deep connections. Dan quickly realized that his strong background and interests in technology could be translated to the Zambian context: "I was really inspired to start Impact Network, which is focused on bringing technology solutions to rural development." Very early, they made their focus improving education in Zambia – not building schools (which they also do) or making a single failing school function better, but improving education for all children in the country and, possibly, across the African continent. Dan explains:

> Half of the schools in Zambia are government schools and the other half were built by NGOs over the last 10–20 years and they've handed them off to the community. [But they've since] fallen apart because the communities weren't really equipped financially or otherwise to run them. So we're try-ing to come up with a system that's low-cost [$3 per month per student] – about a third of the cost of government schools – that can use the teachers that are currently there, the untrained teachers, and provide them with the tools and training to actually deliver really high-quality education.

He emphasizes the breadth of impact that Impact Network is hoping to achieve, and the perspective that is necessary:

> [What occupies me] a lot is thinking about the system. Are you trying to solve a problem or are you trying to change the system itself? Does the system need to be changed? Is it about building a school or is it about changing the way education is valued and distributed? I think that having that larger systems mind-set is very important as you think through what you want your model to achieve, and fit into the larger system.

With the intention to effect broad changes in education, they began:

> We started out with e-learning. We have ten e-learning schools in rural Zambia. We're trying to effect change inside the classroom. We run the schools from top to bottom, and the kids are using half-digital, half-offline curriculum, so it's a blended learning environment. It's all kind of a learning-by-doing philosophy; it was developed by Zambians and Zambian teachers.

Today, Impact Network serves over 6,000 students across 44 schools, partner-ing with the Ministry of Education and Mwabu, an organization that develops the curriculum and provides teacher support for Zambian students of all grade levels. Impact Network is conducting careful, randomized testing of the effectiveness of its schools.

Recover, integrate, act

JERRY WHITE, OF IRISH-CATHOLIC FAITH, attended Brown University, from which he graduated with honors, as the first non-Jew to major in Judaic studies. To enrich his studies, he chose to spend his junior year living abroad in Israel. During a camping trip in the Golan Heights, he stepped on a landmine, losing his left leg and badly injuring his right. He spent a year recovering. Yet he quickly rejects the notion that his path to social entrepreneurship was a succession of planned steps, and even more strenuously that it inevitably led to work to combat landmines and support survivors:

> Whenever I'm interviewed, people always go to a couple of things pretty fast, without foreplay. 'What happened to you?' As if my story, the dominant feature of my life, was stepping on a landmine. It is an interesting story, but I never even think of myself as an amputee. For me, it's not my fundamental story or preparation, and it has very little to do with me being a social entrepreneur.

A decade passed until his accident assumed a central role in his work life:

> I didn't speak about my accident publicly for ten years: 1995 was the first time I spoke publicly about my story, at the UN, when I was deciding to use it for the purposes of helping to negotiate and advocate for the ban on landmines.

Jerry describes his activities before he turned to the cause for which he is best known:

> I was doing entrepreneurial work. We had done maverick work at the Wisconsin Project for Nuclear Arms Control. That was before people were focused on nuclear non-proliferation. One of my first jobs was looking at countries where other people weren't looking. ... I was busy doing things, and personally I was just getting on with life after losing a leg: graduate from school, learn to walk on a prosthesis, get married, have four kids.

Then he met Ken Rutherford, another landmine survivor. He saw in Jerry an ally in the nascent cause of banning landmines:

> He said, 'Jerry, you are tracking the wrong weapon of mass destruction. Landmines can kill more people than nuclear, chemical, and biological

weapons combined. Why don't you get involved in this movement that's just starting up, calling for a ban on landmines?'

Together, Jerry and Ken founded Landmine Survivors Network in 1997, 13 years after Jerry's accident in Israel, and four years after Ken lost both his legs in Somalia. In the span between his accident and Landmine Survivor Network's founding, Jerry's ideas about survivors' true needs had crystalized:

> I was ripe enough to understand what my own trauma had meant, or not meant, to me. Most survivors, the entrepreneurial ones who go on to do interesting things, have perspective on what has happened to them. They have the perspective of the wisdom of survivorship, what it means to recover and move on.

For Jerry, the key idea was to fundamentally reframe the role that survivors should play in the anti-landmine movement:

> Where I saw the need was that there wasn't the platform for survivors to speak for themselves and advocate as the lifeblood of this movement. War victims and mine victims were treated like poster children – tokenized at a certain level. We would feel sorry for these victims and therefore try to ban the weapons to help those people in the posters. That wasn't sufficient.
>
> So the idea was fundamentally a belief system: that those affected by an issue such as landmines should be at the table negotiating the solution. And it's this principle of inclusion that follows all of my work: those most affected should be at the table. That's true for disability; it's true for minority rights; it's true for gender issues. In this case, it was true for survivor issues.

Jerry cautioned others overcoming personal hardship against acting too soon:

> I see too many people in this category of traumatic personal life experience, when survivorship turns to entrepreneurship. There's a danger, in fact, if you do it too soon, because then it doesn't take root.

Strong "number 2s"

LIKE MOTHS TO A FLAME, some people are drawn to the idea of becoming a social entrepreneur; but, for one reason or another, they never get an idea that truly captivates them. Of course, all ideas will change as an organization is formed: financial sustainability becomes important, for example, and all the things that will become key considerations crystallize as the "pure" idea changes into a "business model." But, even at the outset, some circle the flame but their idea is never illuminated.

Chris Mueller provides an illustration of flirting with social entrepreneurship but never committing to an idea. Mueller is smart, deeply interested in social causes, and has a strong business background. Before returning to business school to get an MBA, he reported to the CEO of a regional health service provider and "pretty much had full authority of running a 300-employee, mid-size company with 6 million dollars in revenue." But he sought something more:

> The next challenge that I wanted to take on, having run some businesses, was to start my own. I felt like I had developed the skills, the confidence, and the knowhow to do so. ... I know I am good at growing businesses that have already started and taking them to the next level, to scale. I have done that.

To this end, he studied entrepreneurship and was also part of a social-entrepreneurial team looking to deliver water to poor families in India. Ultimately, he never started his own social venture:

> What holds me back is the cause. I find that I have so many different interests and can get excited about so many different causes. I don't have this single running theme that I see that other people who have been successful as social entrepreneurs have. I was waiting for lightning to strike. Waiting for the big 'Aha!' world-changing, revolutionary idea. I wasted a lot of time. I was grasping at things, looking for this great idea ... I spun my wheels a lot ... bouncing back and forth.

CHRIS ALSO STEPPED BACK from starting a venture for personal reasons, believing that starting a marriage and starting a business at the same time wouldn't be fair to either. But perhaps his most valuable realization was about where his true talents lay – at least at that moment:

> I know that I am a good 'number 2,' and maybe my niche or my contribution in the social enterprise space will be being a 'number 2' to a social entrepreneur – being kind of the operations and business-development person. Because I naturally gravitate toward that.

Marina Kim, co-founder and executive director of AshokaU, the organization dedicated to preparing young adults to enter the world of social change, emphasizes the importance of these "number 2s." She speaks of the tremendous need for "next-generation social entrepreneurship marketing directors; next-generation finance people," and other skilled businesspeople of a new ilk. These people are not founders, but they are essential in social enterprises, and yet often lacking. "We need our education systems to make people competent to use those non-founder skills in social enterprises."

THE INGREDIENTS ARE ALL the same, no matter what the cake: a grab-hold-of-you problem that won't let go; relentless determination to make a difference,

no matter the obstacles; facing facts; and understanding past successes and failures. None of these ingredients guarantees your idea will succeed. But, absent
any of them, it is much more likely to fail.

Notes

1 Ashley Muspratt, *Pivot: Urban Sanitation Evolved* (April 5, 2016). Retrieved July 6, 2018
   from: http://cdn.cseindia.org/userfiles/ashley-mushpratt.pdf
2 Starr, Kevin, "The trouble with impact investing: Part 1." *Stanford Social Innovation Review,*
   January 24, 2012. Retrieved July 6, 2018 from: https://ssir.org/articles/entry/the_trou
   ble_with_impact_investing_part_1. Starr, Kevin, "The trouble with impact investing:
   Part 3." *Stanford Social Innovation Review,* July 11, 2012. Retrieved July 6, 2018 from: https
   ://ssir.org/articles/entry/the_trouble_with_impact_investing_p3
3 Starr, Kevin, "The eight-word mission statement." *Stanford Social Innovation Review,*
   September 18, 2012. Retrieved July 6, 2018 from: http://www.ssireview.org/blog/entry
   /the_eight_word_mission_statement
4 Starr, Kevin, "So what's it take to get fired around here?" *Stanford Social Innovation Review,*
   February 23, 2015. Retrieved July 6, 2018 from: http://www.ssireview.org/blog/entry/
   so_whats_it_take_to_get_fired_around_here
5 Starr, Kevin, "Dump the prizes." *Stanford Social Innovation Review,* August 22, 2013.
   Retrieved July 6, 2018 from: http://www.ssireview.org/blog/entry/dump_the_prizes
6 Starr, Kevin, "Getting beyond hype: Four questions to predict real impact." Mulago
   Foundation, September 2, 2014. Retrieved July 9, 2018 from: http://mulagofoundation.
   org/resources/getting-beyond-hype-four-questions-to-predict-real-impact
7 Robertson, Adi, "OLPC's $100 laptop was going to change the world – then it all went
   wrong." *The Verge,* April 16, 2018. Retrieved July 6, 2018 from: https://www.theverge
   .com/2018/4/16/17233946/olpcs-100-laptop-education-where-is-it-now
8 "Better Place: What went wrong for the electric car startup?" *The Guardian,* March 5,
   2013. Retrieved July 6, 2018 from: https://www.theguardian.com/environment/2013/
   mar/05/better-place-wrong-electric-car-startup
9 Geiger, H. Jack, "The first community health centers: A model of enduring value." *Journal
   of Ambulatory Care Management* 28(4) (2005): 313–20.

5 Necessity

BEFORE SOCIAL ENTREPRENEURS EVER GET STARTED, they should ask two questions: is it necessary to address my problem? And: is it necessary that I start an organization myself to address it? These questions may seem so basic that they don't need asking, but one in five people I interviewed suggested that social entrepreneurs don't ask them, or don't pay attention to their answers when they do.

This chapter offers some perspectives on these issues. Common pitfalls are those of mistaking having a market for what you do for the necessity of doing it, and rushing to start a new venture without considering your responsibility *not* to do so.

Is it necessary – *Really* necessary?

WHAT KIND OF ANSWER SHOULD YOU GIVE to the question "Is it necessary to address this problem?" Is this a yes–no question? Or is a relative answer better, such as, "It's more necessary than helping people find the nearest grocery store, but less necessary than ending world hunger"? As noted in Chapter 4, "The doctor and the priest," Kevin Starr uses binary questions to rule out potential ideas at the Mulago Foundation (Is it needed? Does it work like it's supposed to? Does it get to those who need it? Will it be used right?).[1]

Peter Singer, a moral philosopher concerned with doing good and ending poverty, explains that social benefits must be considered relative to each other.[2] For instance, you might believe, as he argues most people would, that preventing one case of preventable blindness is worth more than improving the experience of 1,000 people by upgrading a museum. (He is a bit tricky in how he elicits that preference by asking if you'd risk a one-in-a-thousand chance of going blind by attending the museum.) In any event, if the costs of those two outcomes are the same (or blindness prevention is less), that's where you should give your charitable dollars.

Another, quite interesting, way to look at necessity comes from Ross Baird, co-founder and CEO of Village Capital (VilCap), a nonprofit that provides financial and business support for social entrepreneurs around the world. Ross asks if people would still buy TOMS shoes if the company's "buy one, give one" policy (in which each customer purchase is matched by a similar donation to those in need) were replaced by "buy *ten*, give one." He speculates that, because of their looks, at least some people would continue to buy them even though many more would condemn the new policy. In this way, TOMS can be seen as an economically sustainable conventional business with a social component – to the extent that the private equity firm Bain Capital bought 50% of TOMS for $313 million.[3]

By way of contrast, he cites Simpa Networks, a company operating in India that provides affordable, modern energy to the poor. By sending text messages, poor households can "unlock" a solar energy system in their home for a limited time, buying and using energy for pennies at a time. Each of these installment payments leads to eventual ownership of an efficient solar energy system which they otherwise could never afford. This makes Simpa necessary in a way TOMS is not:

> Real, live on-grid power is better than Simpa, but Simpa is the best option for the poor. If Simpa were [to decide] they were going to stop selling to the poor, would it be a company killer? It probably would be, because non-poor people don't want to buy what Simpa is offering. It's solving a problem that is specific to low-income people in India.

TOMS's hypothetical "buy ten, give one" "may or may not be a company killer," he continues. Thus, impact is essential for Simpa, but not for TOMS. For this reason, VilCap asks the following question when assessing potential recipients of its seed capital investments:

> If you took the impact out of the business, would the company still be *surviving* – not thriving – but would the company still be surviving? If the answer is no, we really, really like that business.

Originality is not necessity

LACK OF ORIGINALITY must not be confused with lack of necessity. Parag Gupta started Waste Ventures to support those who pick through waste for a living to salvage materials for resale. The work is difficult, unhealthy, hazardous, and often a last resort; for their efforts, waste pickers receive only a tiny fraction of the economic value they create. Through a series of interrelated efforts, Waste Ventures transforms waste pickers' lives by identifying and helping finance efforts that get them off waste dumps and into dignified, "green" – and better-paying – waste collection jobs.

Parag was not the first person whose ambition was to support waste pickers. He had seen waste pickers throughout the world as a portfolio director for the Schwab Foundation for Social Entrepreneurship:

> Conducting due diligence, I'd always come across a waste picker organization. It's so ubiquitous and the need was just so great. I really saw an opportunity both to create social as well as environmental impact.

At Schwab, he also learned from some of the most successful social entre-preneurs in the field, some of whom began world-leading social enterprises. All were obsessed with scale, but Parag saw little of that among organizations working with waste pickers:

> There were a lot of common threads [among different waste picking organizations] and a lot of different interventions. I'd always be evaluating them from a lens [of]: 'Can we combine three or four of these different interventions around three or four different materials that one finds in household waste to create a commercially viable model that can scale?'

"Necessity," for Parag, wasn't being novel. It wasn't that there was a gaping hole to fill because no one was working on behalf of waste pickers. It was that no one was doing it in the large, systematic way that he envisioned – a way, he believed, that would eventually even attract sound, economic investment from the outside.

Markets don't define necessity

IN SOCIAL ENTREPRENEURSHIP, WHEN THE MARKET SPEAKS it can say the wrong things. When it howls that you have paying customers, you should not mistake that howl for your venture being absolutely necessary. When it reminds you that you don't, that may simply mean that you have more work to do.

Katherine Fulton, president of the Monitor Institute, has a sharp eye for fram-ing effective social solutions both through cutting-edge philanthropy and social enterprise. In language that evokes Einstein's supposed quote, "Everything should be made as simple as possible, but not simpler," Fulton remarks, "I think that everybody that can be in a business, should be." However, and here is the critical point, she also worries about the rush to define a problem as socially worthwhile only by its business prospects, suggesting instead that philanthropy remains necessary for social enterprise:

> Here's what I'm worried about. There's a whole bunch of problems in the world that can't be solved by a business, and that will never be funded by venture capitalists. So we have to look at a broader range [of solutions]. … We've got to be … using all the creativity in the world to solve the things that nobody who is trying to make money in the near term is going to go tackle.
> At the same time, anything that can make creative use of capital should be, because there really isn't going to be new government money [to solve many big problems]. I think that's pretty clear.

LET ME FINISH MY THOUGHT ABOUT MARKETS HOWLING in approval about your customers. Customers will be necessary, of course, to support a well-thought-out idea – even if those customers are your donors or charitable foundations.

But having customers does not mean that your idea is one that the world really needs.

One study examined the over-40,000 health care apps available on the iTunes app store.[4] While improving health is a noble social aim, these apps will not necessarily do this: most simply provide information, and there is little or no way to determine which information is accurate, let alone useful. Yet people will pay for them: only half of the apps are free, and even they are often only a "starter" version that you soon have to convert to a paid subscription. Furthermore, where medical need and health care spending is greatest in the general population (among those over 65 with chronic diseases), there are far fewer apps than there are for younger, healthier people. Even for those apps that do address chronic conditions, few are related to leading causes of death or patients' failing to adhere to their doctors' orders.

In the developing world as much as elsewhere, willingness to pay does not imply your idea is necessary. Kevin Starr (see Chapter 4, "The doctor and the priest" and this chapter, "Is it necessary – *really* necessary?") has excoriated a couple of ideas that received much favorable press and attracted lots of money. One is PlayPump, a merry-go-round that children push to pump water from a borehole to a tower 20 feet above ground. It is costly, tiring, typically neglected, and often only used by children when tourists pay them to snap their photo. The burden of pushing has mostly reverted to women (the children quickly tire of its novelty), and, in certain settings, it would need to be pushed 24 hours a day to meet a village's need for water. Yet PlayPump received pledges of more than $15 million from the Clinton Global Initiative – its paying "customer."

LifeStraw is another glitzy, now classic, "solution" that doesn't work, but it had its own particular set of customers. Kevin called it a "big ass straw with a filter" that you wear around your neck until you stumble upon an irrigation ditch. Though it's very good at removing almost all pathogens, you would have to drink through it (exhaustingly) for 20 minutes a day for the filter to work properly and for the straw to provide your daily requirements for water. It costs a poor person about one week's wages to buy (or the equivalent of $1,000 for someone in the U.S. making $50,000), and must be replaced every three years. Despite these unappealing features, it received $30 million in carbon credits for its contribution to reductions of the boiling of water – those buying the credits are its customers – even though it falls far short of producing that level of environmental benefit, by all informed estimates.[5] *Forbes* magazine hailed it as one of the "Ten things that will change the way we live."[6]

By all means, listen when the market speaks. Then ask more questions.

Notes

1 Starr, "Getting beyond hype."
2 Singer, Peter, *The Most Good You Can Do: How Effective Altruism Is Changing Ideas about Living Ethically* (New Haven, CT: Yale University Press, 2015).

3　Ronalds-Hannon, Eliza, and Bhasin, Kim, "Even Wall Street couldn't protect Toms Shoes from retail's storm." Bloomberg, May 3, 2018. Retrieved September 9, 2018 from: https ://www.bloomberg.com/news/articles/2018-05-03/even-wall-street-couldn-t-pro tect-toms-shoes-from-retail-s-storm

4　IMS Institute for Healthcare Informatics, *Patient Apps for Improved Healthcare: From Novelty to Mainstream* (October 2013). Retrieved July 9, 2018 from: http://moodle.univ-lille2 .fr/pluginfile.php/215345/mod_resource/content/0/IIHI_Patient_Apps_Report.pdf

5　Starr, Kevin, "Thirty million dollars, a little bit of carbon, and a lot of hot air." *Stanford Social Innovation Review*, June 16, 2011. Retrieved July 9, 2018 from: http://www.ssir eview.org/blog/entry/thirty_million_dollars_a_little_bit_of_carbon_and_a_lot_of_ hot_air

6　Ely, Breckinridge, "Ten things that will change the way we live." *Forbes*, February 17, 2006. Retrieved 27 September, 2018 from: https://www.forbes.com/2006/02/16/s ony-sun-cisco-cx_cd_0217feat_ls.html#1ba6f8d25955

6 Join

DON'T START A SOCIAL ENTERPRISE if you don't have to. It's one of the clearest messages I received. None of my interview subjects was ever prompted to talk about this, and yet I was offered the following unsolicited opinions:

> If someone is doing something similar to what you want to start, go work with that organization any day of the week.
>
> (Parag Gupta, Waste Ventures)

> Whenever possible, do not start something.
>
> (Rebecca Onie, Health Leads)

> You don't have to start an organization to make a difference. There are a lot of organizations that are doing a lot of good work.
>
> (Dan Sutera, Impact Network)

> There are dozens of cooking stoves or solar lighting devices [at the base-of-the-pyramid].
>
> (Jim Koch, Global Social Benefit Incubator)

And these quotes barely begin to express the breadth of this sentiment.

The siren call of social entrepreneurship

THERE IS ALLURE TO BEING A SOCIAL ENTREPRENEUR — to the detriment of the field. While I'm delighted that people are inspired to work in organizations that address real areas of concern, there are reasons why it's usually better to join a social enterprise than to start one.

Jessamyn Lau (now Shams-Lau) is the executive director of the Peery Foundation, a family foundation that invests in and supports social entrepreneurs. In her role, she is in contact with many young people who want to change the world with their ideas: "I talk to students who are desperate to go out and start something and be the one to come up with that silver-bullet

solution. I just want to say, 'Slow down!'" These are not bad people, of course
– quite the opposite. But in their callow enthusiasm they are chasing immature
dreams. Johan Cruyff, the former Dutch soccer player, once said, "Speed is
often confused with insight." *Act now!* is a foolhardy creed. Not only will you
get poor results, you will be showing deep disrespect for those you believe
you're serving.

Ashley Murray, co-founder of Pivot Works, the company that converts
sewage into energy, echoes this thought:

> There's this tendency in development work to treat developing countries
> as playgrounds and laboratories where it's so easy to just go and test some-
> thing. There are serious, serious consequences to that.
>
> A lot of really well-intentioned do-gooders go one semester to a coun-
> try, see something that has been a problem for hundreds of years. No one
> has solved it yet, and they think they have the solution to it and they're
> going to come back and start a business.
>
> I just caution against this kind of knee-jerk entrepreneurship. Really
> make sure you understand the sector, understand the problem, understand
> why it hasn't been solved before – before you think *you* are going to come
> in with the answer.

At Still Harbor, Ed Cardoza, as we saw in Chapter 4, "The doctor and the
priest," leads residents and guests through a three-stage observe–judge–act
sequence. It provides a framework for someone to integrate what she is seeing with a deeper sense of purpose for getting involved. It helps her "make
more profound decisions," Ed explains, which includes the choice of starting
or joining:

> We help people to understand that it's not always a good idea to create
> something. There are an awful lot of NGOs in the world. You go to a
> place like Haiti, there are 10,000 NGOs that are taking up lots of money
> and resources, that don't talk to each other necessarily, and that don't nec-
> essarily even do very good work.
>
> We talk in terms of leadership/followership capacity – of really being
> able to understand what is the responsible and right thing to do here. Only
> in some cases is the responsible and right thing to do to create an organiza-
> tion or an intervention that is going to significantly change the "how" and
> the "what" of [the way] things are done.

In the rest of the cases, you join.

Joining the chorus

THE MANDATE TO ACT RESPONSIBLY ALSO PERMEATES others' comments. At
an Ashoka event, Alan Webber, former managing editor of the *Harvard*

Business Review and co-founder of *Fast Company* – and himself an entrepreneur – quips:

> There are an enormously large number of startups that are replicating things that already exist. And so we kind of have the Department of Redundancy Department, where it's exciting because it's my idea, but I didn't really check the landscape and there are already *x* number of people already doing this, which you wouldn't do if you were really doing a business plan.

His co-panelist, Katherine Fulton of the Monitor Institute, adds to this, comparing the world today to that of a decade or two ago, noting how it should be so much easier now not to forge ahead with something redundant: "In 24 hours now or 48 hours, anybody with a computer and some curiosity and some smarts can figure out at least [the beginnings of who's doing what]. And that's huge."

The reasons not to start something when you can join are least of all to save yourself the difficulty or embarrassment of failing to get much done. The real reasons – the responsible reasons – are to better serve a cause.

Parag Gupta, whose Waste Ventures bolsters waste pickers' livelihood and dignity, claims that he never would have started this venture if he could have joined someone else. He warns of fragmenting the field: splitting it into many small pieces that are less effective than fewer organizations with better support and more muscle:

> The worst thing is to go off and you start something very similar to what someone else is doing. Ostensibly, you've hurt the field more than you've helped the field because you've now divided the philanthropic dollars, or social investment dollars, in a way that doesn't need to be divided.

Martin Fisher's work at KickStart, lifting subsistence African farmers out of poverty for decades, has won him all sorts of accolades. He confirms Parag's warning, despairing that, with so many new social entrepreneurs, he's still "… competing for the same limited money, which is getting spread very thin, and the truth is that donors and impact investors aren't particularly good at picking winners."

Kevin Starr, who views philanthropic funding from the investor's side of the table, points to the huge waste that results from every social enterprise going its own way: "There's a huge R&D [research and development] burden, which people don't quite understand. The burden of R&D and sometimes unwitting experimentation is tremendous."

Necessary and unwelcome

MARK HECKER OF REACH INCORPORATED has revolutionized tutoring in underprivileged schools and thought carefully about building an effective social enterprise. He, too, dissuades potential social entrepreneurs from starting ventures for the wrong reasons:

> What bothers me is the fact that it's become such a cool thing to be a social entrepreneur. My advice would be that it's not. Becoming a social entrepreneur should never drive what you're doing. Feeling an intense need to fix an injustice of some sort should be what drives you.

That intense need should push you to join someone else's efforts, though few try to:

> If you've really found that thing that you're passionate about and it needs to be fixed and you feel like you can fix it, the most important step in the process is to actually do a scan to see if anyone else is doing the work already. And I think it gets skipped by everyone.

Mark offers as an example someone who sought him out for help in starting a new organization to support teachers:

> I talked with a guy very recently who's interested in starting basically a teacher residency program. His reasoning to start it was because he did Teach for America and felt like his first year was wasted. And he was really taken aback by the fact that I said, 'All right, so what you want to do is go work for Teach for America and get them to pilot a program where, if someone's willing to make commitment of a third year, then you offer this support to them in year one. That's what you're trying to do: you're not trying to start a new organization.' I think on some levels he was kind of offended that he thought he had this [completely new] idea, and really he had this idea for tweaking what was being done.

Some social entrepreneur support organizations, however, know the importance of reviewing the ecosystem. Echoing Green has provided seed funding of $36 million over nearly 30 years to more than 600 social entrepreneurs. Some of them have gone on to make a very big mark, including the founders of Teach for America, City Year, and SKS Microfinance. As part of the application for funding from Echoing Green, applicants fill in an Innovation Matrix, a tool that Echoing Green fellows interviewed for this book found extremely useful despite its straightforward nature. Applicants fill in a template in which they describe three to five organizations most like their own. For each, they describe the similarities; and then they describe the differences, including ways that they think their organization is either better or fills an unmet need. The template is just two pages long.

MARK HEEDED HIS OWN ADVICE, looking to see if he could embed his idea in an existing organization. His idea was viewed favorably, but he couldn't find an organization that would invite him to join it.

I think actually intrapreneurship [acting entrepreneurially within an existing organization] is a much more valuable skill than entrepreneurship. See whether you think you'd have the ability to go work for [a suitable host organization] and influence the work that they're doing. I had some early discussions with some of the other organizations in D.C. telling them about my idea – organizations where I thought there were some similarities. And I had some senior level people say, 'I really like the idea and in our younger years we would have liked that. But you're not going to get the support you need here.'

MARK SUMS UP much of this chapter, citing the organizational and personal pitfalls of becoming a social entrepreneur:

It's a lot less sexy to say, 'I had this great idea, but it turned out with a little research that someone else was already doing it, so I'm interested in going to work for that organization.' That's a lot less sexy but it's also … really important. You might be the person that helps that organization get much better. That's really valuable. But it's not as hip these days to go about it that way.

If I didn't need to do this [venture on my own] I would be happy not to.

He adds further:

When the process … of becoming a social entrepreneur has nothing to do with passion for a cause – it has only to do with passion for being a social entrepreneur – that is misguided.

Misguided by disrespecting those you purport to serve. And misguided, as well, by potentially diverting resources from organizations that are far more deserving.

7 Personal challenges

SOCIAL ENTREPRENEURS' EMOTIONAL LIVES are far from settled – churning beneath the surface with uncertainty, risk, stress, rejection, and misunderstanding far more often than meets the eye. They are susceptible to burnout and find themselves leading one-dimensional lives. The organizations they lead, and then those whom they serve, suffer, too, when social entrepreneurs are not emotionally whole.

Not just action

SOCIAL ENTREPRENEUR. "Social": a view looking outward at society. "Entrepreneur": a person with a commitment to taking action. What the phrase *social entrepreneur* doesn't suggest is an inner world – of struggle and doubt, yet purpose and generosity – which must be cultivated for the social entrepreneur to leave a lasting mark, let alone make it through the day.

In tones that were confessional, those I interviewed spoke of the dark – at least, the darker – side of being a social entrepreneur. More than three-quarters described the emotional toll of being a social entrepreneur; more than half spoke of challenges to their commitment; and nearly everyone identified the character traits required to persevere. A statistical examination of interview transcripts underscored how tightly correlated these ideas were with each other.

Awards notwithstanding

THE DAYS ARE LONGER, THE RISKS ARE HIGHER, the resources are fewer, the results more stubborn. What keeps social entrepreneurs going?

When I began this project, asking the question, "What do you wish you knew when you began?", I fully expected certain types of responses: how do you raise money, who should be on your team, how do you find suitable partners – things that lie at the operational core of social entrepreneurship (and which we will get to). I was much less prepared to learn the dirty secrets of so many of the social entrepreneurs I spoke to (including many of the very successful ones): that stress can be overwhelming and burnout is rampant. But there is also a spirit among them of what I think is best called generosity, and that, along with other personal traits and outward supports, is what sustains social entrepreneurs.

JANE CHEN'S BACKGROUND MIGHT SUGGEST that she would coast to success as a social entrepreneur. She has a Master's degree from Harvard and an MBA from Stanford. She has experience in developing-country health care, has worked for the Clinton Foundation's HIV/AIDS organization, and was a consultant at the Monitor Group (now Monitor Deloitte) where she advised companies on their strategy. Along with three other students at Stanford, she developed an infant-warming technology that is far more affordable and much easier to use correctly than a standard incubator for keeping premature babies alive. Embrace, the organization she co-founded to bring the warmer to parts of the world where babies tragically die from hypothermia, garnered support from Echoing Green, Mulago's Rainer Arnhold Fellowship program, and TED. Jane was hailed as a Young Global Leader by the august World Economic Forum, and she was the Schwab Foundation's Social Entrepreneur of the Year. She and Embrace were featured in print and broadcast media including the *Wall Street Journal*, the *New York Times*, *Time* magazine, and ABC News. *The Economist* named her the winner of their Social and Economic Innovation Award. Jane was invited to the White House to meet with President Obama, and Beyoncé donated $125,000 to support her work.[1]

However, when she and I spoke, awards and accomplishments were not on the top of her mind. She offers more sobering advice to those looking to start a social enterprise:

> It's important to have a healthy amount of idealism, [because] if people knew how difficult it was, they may not do it. ... You should be ready to be in this for the long haul. We went into it thinking we would change the world in six months or a year, and that's just not how it works. If you're going to do this, be ready for a long-term commitment – if you truly want to make an impact.

Work intensity

NO SINGLE DOWNSIDE IS UNIQUE TO BEING A SOCIAL ENTREPRENEUR, but the fact that there are so many – the workload, the risks, personal rejection, misunderstanding, burnout, and even discrimination – should act as a red flare for those hesitating to take the plunge. I promise: I'm not trying to dissuade everyone from joining the noble and essential ranks of those already in the field – quite the opposite; but I am delivering a strong message to those who might become utterly dismayed because they hadn't been properly forewarned.

Social entrepreneurs face down difficult social issues with an intensity that may massively exceed their resources. Often, with little money and staff, they tap the one resource they imagine is inexhaustible: their time. Especially at the beginning, acting with abandon can seem the best way to attack a social problem. But not long thereafter, it is simply exhausting. Many interview subjects said the same thing in slightly different words, some of which are presented here:

> [My co-founder and I] were working 80–90 hours every single week. We did that for about four years straight with basically no vacations. It was incredibly intense. ... We were working crazy hours. And it was a whole lifestyle. It is the norm. Most startups do it. Most founders do it.
>
> (Derek Ellerman, Polaris)

> I spent the vast majority of my time in the beginning making every deci-sion. I micro-managed everything. ... It was pretty overwhelming. I was doing everything. ... I would come back at lunch and I would try to pass out for [a while] before going back into the field.
>
> (Derek Stafford, Unión MicroFinanza)

> At first, it was overwhelming. I found myself pulling [several] all-nighters in a row – one on Monday, one on Tuesday. It was awful. I quickly learned that I need sleep. So I began to become better at delegating. ...
>
> Every single second counts. I'm eating and I'm working at the same time. I have my laptop open. ... What I do now is that I work on my sta-tionary bike, so my workout has become a part of my work routine. If I'm typing out a report or making a presentation, I'm also getting my exercise on my stationary bike. ...
>
> [Among] the new people coming into social entrepreneurship who have sought me out there is not necessarily the understanding of how hard it can be and how you do have a lot of sleepless nights.
>
> (Grace Hsia, Warmilu)

Stress and risk

STARTUPS – NOT SOCIAL STARTUPS, BUT ALL STARTUPS – have a reputation for fail-ure that statistics, unfortunately, can't disprove. The Bureau of Labor Statistics and the Census Bureau present depressing survival rates,[2] and the same is true even at the Y Combinator, a three-month-long, Silicon Valley, in-residence support program for entrepreneurs that hand-picks fewer than one in twenty applicants, removes their financial worries with funding, and wraps them in advice and support from the best of the best. Ninety-three percent of the com-panies gaining this elite support still fail.[3]

Despite an absence of clear data about social entrepreneur startups specifi-cally,[4] it's nonetheless safe to assume the results are equally alarming – espe-cially when social entrepreneurs are scrapping to get donor funds or generate revenues from customers with little money, or are living on their own credit cards without a pit crew behind them. Although the vast majority of social entrepreneurs I interviewed were surviving, they were no strangers to stress or rejection. As one entrepreneur – who did in fact fold the tent on her venture when she couldn't tap its potential market – said to me:

> I got to a point where, when I think about my own talents and the challenges of the problem, I just didn't think they added up to the right match for me to pour my life's blood into. I've been broke for four years and don't have a safety net, and I really couldn't afford to keep doing it emotionally.

A recent graduate of an entrepreneurship program at the Open University in the UK explained that, although he had been in business before, "running your own produces stress and pressure that is horrendous. People make decisions they wouldn't without this pressure." He went on to explain that the antidote to this is taking the time to learn about yourself – a point we will land on soon – though, he added, the unrelenting pressure makes doing that unlikely.

Though seasoned social entrepreneurs may become inured to stress because they have experienced more of it, it doesn't go away. Martin Burt, co-founder of Fundación Paraguaya, an organization for which he has won many prestigious awards for his pioneering efforts in microfinance, education, and poverty alleviation, lists some of the problems that can bombard you:

> This thing will consume all your waking hours. If you do not have a supporting companion, you will feel too much tension. You suffer too much. … There are too many moments of financial difficulty in the organization. Staff crisis. Regulatory crisis. Hostile government. A difficult member. Having to fire a person you've hired who can't come to work on time.

Naturally, these aren't unique to social enterprises. But they are likely more acute when the problems being addressed are so compelling, and the resources necessary to address them adequately so short in supply.

You don't know your own venture

REJECTION IS NOT JUST NUMERICAL; it is personal. Even if only 5% of contestants in a business plan competition win and get funding, 100% of you is rejected when you don't. Still, that's mostly numbers. Worse is the feeling that something you care deeply about is mischaracterized or, even worse, casually brushed aside. Mark Hecker is a social worker turned teacher turned social entrepreneur whose out-of-school programs have stood traditional tutoring on its head. He takes inner-city high school students in the lowest quarter of their class – meaning that they can often be described as functionally illiterate – and trains them to tutor inner-city elementary-school kids who are much like they are, just a few years younger: poor, academically unsupported and struggling, and lacking anything resembling a positive experience with school. He also pays the tutors – a benefit that quickly becomes secondary to the positive regard in which the younger students hold them.

The program draws deeply on the worlds of social work and early literacy. It is practice-based and grounded in theory. And it works. In a year, younger students gain up to 1.5 grade levels of improvement in their reading level, and the tutors gain two grade levels. More than 90% of tutors graduate on time, with three-quarters reading at a higher grade level than average. And yet everyone thinks they know how he can do it better:

> [I wasn't] prepared for the loneliness. Also, because it's something that I created and it means so much to me, there's very little preparation for just the difficulty when everyone wants to pick it apart – whether it be business plan competitions, or fellowships, or just talking to a funder. Most meetings I have are people telling me how I could be better at what I do, and I've been doing it for three years: they've been talking about it for 30 minutes. Yet they feel like they can tell me all the faults of what I'm doing. … It's emotionally tough to just get beaten up a lot.

Mark is far from alone, with many others, such as Ross Baird of Village Capital, a self-described "relentless optimist," offering similar thoughts:

> When your passion is your work, the highs are higher and the lows are lower. Sometimes, if people so much as suggest, 'Oh, slow down. You shouldn't work so hard,' you take that incredibly personally because you're so passionate about what you do. If you've poured yourself and your passion into your venture and you hit a major bump in the road, that's not just a reflection on the idea, that can be a reflection on you. It's incredibly lonely to have your neck on the line as well as your venture's.

Misunderstood

BE PREPARED, as a social entrepreneur, for friends and family to take shots at you, ranging from: indifference …

> I'd say, 'I was reading an article in the *Harvard Business Review*,' and they'd say, 'Oh well, we just want talk about sports.'
> (Charlie Cavell, founder of Pay It Forward, a workforce
> development social enterprise)

… and trivialization …

> It's like going into the Peace Corps for two years and having a pivotal life-changing experience and when you come back your friends are like 'Awesome … Madagascar. How was it?' You know, as though you're going to answer 'good,' and then they'll say, 'We should all take a trip to the Bahamas.'
> (Adam Carver, founder of Impact Everyday, which links
> credit card "points" to financing for renewable energy projects)

... to snarky ...

> My friends would say, 'Grace, we don't see you. We know you're out
> there curing cancer or whatnot, but we don't know where you are or
> what you're doing.'
> (Grace Hsia, of Warmilu, makes infant warmers, and is not curing cancer)

... and even thinly disguised contempt:

> Some people in Paraguay said, 'You've got to be kidding. It's going to be
> a slave labor camp.' ... People thought that too much practice is going
> to take away from classroom time, assuming that what kids learn is [only]
> in the classroom. We have learned that students learn from practice if it
> is well done. Practice does not take away from learning, nor does it take
> away from classroom. It completely enhances it. But if you come from the
> old paradigm, any time the kid is outside the classroom, he is not learning.
> (Martin Burt, of Fundación Paraguaya, on combining a
> working farm with education)

Needless to say, your family may think you're throwing your life away:

> My own parents will say, 'This is really hard. You should just let this go
> and let them [the people in poverty who need her life-saving work] deal
> with it.'
>
> (Grace Hsia, co-founder of Warmilu)

Or:

> My family is not behind this at all. They don't understand it. They're
> rooting me on [when I] win a business plan competition. But that doesn't
> defray their anxiety that I'm going to graduate without a real job, or that
> I've got my head completely in the clouds and I'm going to turn out like
> their hippie friends from the '60s or '70s who are nowhere.
>
> (Adam Carver)

It is rough, but part of the territory, when those closest to you – whose experiences are far from your own – are not available in the way that you need them.

Burning your social enterprise

THE CULMINATION OF THE HARD WORK some social entrepreneurs put in – maybe
the unlucky ones, but probably just the unwitting – is burnout. I don't claim
that social entrepreneurs have a monopoly on burnout. When everywhere you
go becomes your office and everyone you've ever met – or who wants to meet
you – can email, text, tweet, or zing you – and expect you to instantly email,

text, tweet, or zing them back – stress certainly, and burnout maybe, will be rampant. And burnout among social entrepreneurs is common – *too* common, though not all succumb to it. (In my interviews, approximately one in five spoke of burning out.) Burnout exacts a cruel toll on social entrepreneurs, their organizations, those they serve, and grander movements toward social justice and a more equitable world.

The burnout that I'm speaking about is not figurative. This is the real, deeply affecting kind. Derek Stafford provides an example, describing the situation when he was starting up his enterprise to support Honduran coffee growers with financial, agricultural, and marketing support:

> [My life] was completely out of control. I literally lost 60 pounds in 102 days, and it was not a healthy process. It was just the stress. It was overwhelming. My back was killing me; I wasn't sleeping. My partner was very close to saying, 'You have to go home [to the United States] and like spend a week getting yourself back to health and then come back here,' because it was just awful.

He was, fortunately, "walked back" by his brother, a seasoned business consultant, who helped him deal with greater efficiency and emotional ease with all that was on his plate.

NOT ALL BURNOUT IS AS SEVERE as Derek Stafford's, at least by physical standards. But its effects can be devastating even – maybe even *especially* – when they evolve more subtly. Derek Ellerman started Polaris Project (now simply known as Polaris) with has partner, Katherine (Kat) Chon, because, once they learned how "horrific" bondage slavery is, it just "grabbed us and didn't let go." The tenacity with which they attacked the problem was no less than that with which the problem took over their psyches. Yet:

> The tragedy is you get trapped in [your work] over time. It's one of the myths that needs to be just shattered for people who are going into this work. They need to really understand that you can maintain that level of intensity [only] for a number of years. You may not even feel the effects that much because you are in the early stage and you are just fired up about it. But over time, if not even in those early years, the cost is already [enormous]. It's something to understand from the very earliest stage.

Polaris took perverse pride in its reputation for being a grueling place to work. In other nonprofits, "when one of their staff members complained, [the executive director] would say, 'If you don't like it, feel free to go work at Polaris Project.'" While employees at Polaris worked 60 hours a week, Derek and Kat were working 50% more. After several years, however, Derek explains, "Both of us burned out and took time to recover. We got so much done, but it was at significant cost. Our personal lives were basically non-existent during that entire four-year period because we just worked all the time."

Derek had begun another social enterprise before Polaris Project and, since growing Polaris into a national anti-trafficking organization, he has reflected deeply on the mistakes that social entrepreneurs make. He emphasizes the destructive irony that social entrepreneurs act with a caring attitude toward the cause they serve, even as they fail to treat themselves and their own staff similarly:

> Ultimately, the work that we're all doing is to enable people to live really full, meaningful lives. [But,] very often, not only the leadership, but organizations themselves, end up having either toxic environments or environments where the staff actually doing the work themselves can't have full and meaningful lives. Where they are actually burning out.
>
> There's a misalignment between the basic vision that we're all working towards and the means through which we're actually trying to get it done. [There's a flawed] logic behind that as well: we're sacrificing our lives to help others.

Myths and shells

THE SACRIFICES DEREK AND KAT DEMANDED hurt not only themselves and their staff but also their organization's work: "That level of intensity – it's unhealthy and it begins to affect judgment; it begins to affect all kinds of things that ultimately hurt the organization," Derek laments. Most critically, leadership suffers: "That martyr type of mentality doesn't work because, in the end, the organization is harmed. Leadership is much less effective and is more dysfunctional. It's a major area where there needs to be a lot of focus."

Derek – as well as others who have studied and advised social entrepreneurs – explain that when social entrepreneurs focus only on work, their personal development is thwarted, leaving them, and therefore their organizations, far from reaching their fullest potential:

> There's a misunderstanding about what it means to be an effective or transformative leader. I think a lot of what inspires social entrepreneurs are stories of other social entrepreneurs. We look to them and look at the Paul Farmer [MacArthur Award recipient and Nobel Peace Prize nominee; see Chapter 4, "The doctor and the priest"] and people like that who … their entire life is their work.
>
> What we don't see and hear in those stories is that the majority of people who operate like that ultimately hurt their organizations. Even if they're still at the helm, often there's both a tremendous amount of value they bring and a tremendous number of problems they bring. Because when you are simply 'all work' like this, you are not fully developing as a human being. You are not fully developing as a leader. That has its costs over time. It's really not the way to go.

Derek emphasizes how common this is, and how damaging the consequences:

> I have not yet encountered any leader who maintains that type of work intensity and unidimensional focus for any length of time who doesn't have some significant dysfunctionality. As a result, it's hurting the work in the organization and their leadership. I've never encountered a leader where, when they are doing that, that's not the case.
>
> In most cases, it's not like you need to look for it; it's actually glaringly obvious. You don't hear about it. People who read stories about social entrepreneurs don't see that. This is all behind-the-scenes stuff.
>
> In the worst-case scenarios, people who've been doing that for 40, 50 years — to be brutally honest, they're almost shells of human beings now because they really haven't given themselves the ability to have a full life. It's a tremendous sacrifice and not necessarily for the greater good.

LET THIS DISCUSSION serve as a caution. Social entrepreneurs' lives *are* emotionally daunting. Yet, as we will learn next, they are also animated by uncommon optimism, goodness, and often grace. This can sustain them, and for that, and all the good they do, we should be grateful.

Notes

1 From 2015, Embrace became part of Thrive Networks, also known as East Meets West.
2 Shane, Scott, "Start up failure rates: The definitive numbers." *Small Business Trends*, December 17, 2012. Retrieved March 29, 2015 from: http://smallbiztrends.com/2012/12/start-up-failure-rates-the-definitive-numbers.html
3 Blodget, Henry, "Dear entrepreneurs: Here's how bad your odds of success are." *Business Insider*, May 28, 2013. Retrieved March 29, 2015 from: http://www.businessinsider.com/startup-odds-of-success-2013-5
4 Comprehensive data is unavailable, but the Failure Institute published a report on the *Causes of Failure in Mexican Social Enterprises*, in which it states that of the 115 social enterprises studied only 5.2% lasted more than ten years. Retrieved July 9, 2018 from: https://thefailureinstitute.com/wp-content/uploads/2017/04/Causes-of-failure-in-social-enterprises-low-res.pdf

8 The sanities of pro-social behavior

I came away from so many of the interviews I conducted with feelings of inspiration, even awe, about what I had heard: not just about what these people had done as social entrepreneurs, but the kind of people they were as human beings. Yes, they felt a connection to a cause or a group that they cared about deeply that drove them to action until the job was done. But something more than that moved me. Certain patterns continually revealed themselves in what they said – patterns revolving around inner goodness, idealism, belief and purpose, and congruence between the world they wanted to see and the way they lived their lives.

In light of what you have read up to this point, I admit that this might seem confusing. Preceding chapters have covered the difficulty of being a social entrepreneur, the misunderstanding, the loneliness, even the frequent burnout. And yet now I'm writing that there is a set of extremely positive feelings and traits that social entrepreneurs repeatedly express.

Act for yourself; act for others

Maybe the confusion in some way reflects our conflicting ideas about people who act for the benefit of others. A century ago, Darwin wrote that humankind has evolved tendencies of goodness toward others that are even stronger than our desire for self-preservation.[1] In contrast, the preponderance of economic theory since that time has been rooted in the idea that, as rational beings, we act solely for our own personal advantage. Ironically, the man most commonly associated with that economic point of view, Adam Smith, wrote just the opposite:

> How selfish soever man may be supposed, there are evidently some principles in his nature, which interest him in the fortune of others, and render their happiness necessary to him, though he derives nothing from it except the pleasure of seeing it. Of this kind is pity or compassion, the emotion we feel for the misery of others.[2]

In still another twist, the Dalai Lama, the revered advocate of peace and promoter of spiritual development, advises that compassion should initially be cultivated through self-interest:

> if you simply admonish others to cultivate compassion, and if you do not give them the resources – particularly the rationale for its need – it is just wishful thinking. Whereas, if you explain [it] from the point of view of self-interest – it is for your own interest and well-being; it is essential – it makes a difference.[3]

Contemporary psychology is studying a set of salutary emotions which, in a literal sense, define well-being.[4] These fall into six categories, or "moral virtues" (and their associated, more specific, character "strengths"), namely: wisdom and knowledge (e.g. creativity, open-mindedness, and perspective); courage (e.g. persistence and integrity); humanity (e.g. love and generosity); justice (e.g. social responsibility and fairness); temperance (e.g. forgiveness and humility); and transcendence (e.g. gratitude, optimism, and purpose). These terms are closely associated with social entrepreneurship. Theoretical and empirical research suggests, at least in some cases, that people acting from empathy carry out altruistic acts, even when there is no external reward, recognition, diminishment of personal distress, or other "egoistic" explanation.[5] The tendency to be "good" may be hard-wired.[6]

Social entrepreneur is a broad term, encompassing everyone from health workers toiling in war-torn regions to office workers sipping coffee as they develop health-promoting apps. Among them there will be personality differences, even as their "moral virtues" predominate. Empathy may impel them to act for the benefit of others, but such actions might be at a personal cost when they are undertaken in stressful conditions and continually repeated. It may seem less of a paradox, then, that social entrepreneurs can soar to uncommon heights but also fall into despair, and they can burn out.

Without further attempting to untangle the two sides of social entrepreneurship – a life of extraordinary purpose, generosity, gratitude, and optimism on the one hand; of inner struggle on the other – it is important to acknowledge the role of those positive emotions. We can then begin to see how these "sanities" may be enhanced and developed.[7]

ACCORDING TO THE EMPATHY–ALTRUISM HYPOTHESIS, altruistic behavior is triggered when one feels empathy for another and then responds from a motivation to improve that person's welfare.[8] What does not count is simply feeling another's need but being unable or unwilling to respond, or responding with a primary goal of alleviating your own distress or making yourself feel better in some way, even if it helps the other person, too. Acting out of empathic concern to address great, continuing need (often involving entrenched problems affecting a great many people – exactly what social entrepreneurs face) requires a longer view. You must repeatedly act over time and likely change tactics – even if you are never sure what the best course of action is or even whether your efforts will ultimately succeed.

It is not surprising, therefore, that social entrepreneurs exhibit concern for others, altruism, and perseverance – as well as other traits appropriate to their calling such as resilience, flexibility, and patience. Each of these traits is associated with well-being,[9] and each was commonly brought up in interviews. In what follows, I will take a nuanced look at these traits.

EMPATHY LIES AT THE ROOT OF HELPING. Ashoka, the cultivator of social entrepreneurs and other changemakers, believes it is fundamental in creating a better world. Yet empathy has the potential to lead one astray, too. Martin Fisher, who has been in the field for decades, helping hundreds of thousands of people escape lives of poverty, cautions:

> Unbounded empathy won't solve problems. Empathy keeps me going. But to be effective, you must do analysis. Maybe *not* helping the poorest people is the best approach [if borne out by analysis suggesting you can thus help many more people].

In fact, the empathy–altruism hypothesis suggests that, before you act out of empathy, you take into consideration how your actions – or inaction – can do the most good. There is even some experimental evidence that *only* taking empathy into account can distort your judgment on such matters.[10] Yet relying on calculated cost–benefit analyses leaves many social entrepreneurs cold; if they are to be led astray, they would prefer that it be in the direction of too much empathy, not too little.

LIBERIA IS ONE OF THE POOREST COUNTRIES in the world, less prosperous than Afghanistan and Malawi and barely wealthier than Somalia.[11] The overall health of the country is close to the bottom, too, by several different measures.[12] None of this is helped by the fact that, for more than a quarter-century, Liberia has endured much civil unrest, including two civil wars (although from 2006–18 the country enjoyed something of a respite under Nobel Peace Prize winner President Ellen Johnson Sirleaf). It is in this context that Last Mile Health – formerly Tiyatien Health (meaning "justice in health" in Kwa, a Liberian dialect) – operates, its current name and former name both suggesting its challenges and its mission. In a country where health outcomes are already bad, and doctors are nearly non-existent, Last Mile Health serves Liberia's poorest, most remote, rural citizens. The backbone of its health delivery system is made up of local community members who act as primary care providers, diagnosing and treating common diseases, and making "referrals" to rural health clinics.

Last Mile Health has goals that go beyond serving south-east Liberia, where it began; it hopes to demonstrate that its model can be effective nationwide and beyond. Peter Luckow, who with Raj Panjabi co-founded Tiyatien Health, explains to me:

> We think that if we are able to really define this model at a county level of 125,000 people [comparable to a state in the United States], including

some more centralized cities as well as these very remote villages of 500 people, we will then be able to argue to the government and to other international actors that this is a model that has validity. It's a model that can produce better results at lesser costs.

Indeed, Last Mile Health is part of Results for Development's Center for Health Market Innovation program, which scours the globe for the best developing-world health care models. With this focus on providing and demonstrating its impact, you might expect that Last Mile Health would be unswayed by anything but proving the efficacy of its model. And, yet, that is not the case:

> One of the things we struggle with has been this idea of defining a focus and homing in on a single approach in a way that invests concentrated energy yielding really high-quality outcomes [to the exclusion of other ways of providing health care]. We've struggled, both as an organization and as individuals, with the idea of saying no in a place like south-east Liberia. There are so many challenges. There are so many barriers to accessing health care. We want to be doing whatever it takes to ensure that our patients have the type of care we want our own parents and our own family members to have.
>
> It's hard to then say no when [there are other] great ideas or important approaches to this work, whether it be in the hospital, whether it be in our front-line health worker model, whether it be in even things like getting a two-year-old with retinoblastoma, cancer of the eye, treatment that she needs in neighboring Mali. That's something we've been doing the past couple of weeks.

Empathy creates that freedom to think about all the needs of those they serve, even if their needs for care diverges from Last Mile's own mission:

> There's a balance that we need to strike that both provides the intensity of focus for paradigm-shifting quality, while also staying true to our empathetic roots, our compassionate personalities; that strikes a tone that, regardless of what comes to our table, we need to do something about it. We have an obligation to do something about it.
>
> That's something that we've struggled with over the past couple of years. It's something we still struggle with and, to be honest, it's something I hope we will always struggle with, because I think that's a very healthy tension to have.

Persistence

ANYONE WHO EVEN GETS A WHIFF OF BECOMING A SOCIAL ENTREPRENEUR recognizes the importance of persistence. It will keep you going in the face of critics and self-doubt – a virtue no one questions as being vital in addressing societal problems. Yet it may also obscure your options. And even blind you to the "why" that is essential to sustain you.

Mulago Foundation's Kevin Starr has funded Martin Fisher's work at KickStart for many years. Martin is arguably one of Mulago's strongest success stories, now even teaching would-be social entrepreneurs that Mulago supports through its Rainer Arnhold Fellows program. Mulago's abiding focus is creating impact so that the poorest of the poor are well-served by its grant dollars. Kevin has a deep understanding of what problems his foundation can meaningfully address, and which are better left alone. A serious red flag for him is the need for market creation:

> Typically, market failure means people really want something and the market's failing. They can't really get it at an affordable price, or it [can't be] distributed to them, or it's going to cost too much when it does. Or, basically, all the various reasons why the market doesn't work for poor people.
>
> But with market creation, there's this extra dimension of creating demand and awareness, and trying to persuade people that you do want this thing. That's where I rarely go anymore [as a funder]. Unless the social impact is so profound and the potential for impact goes so deep and broad into the population, it doesn't usually seem worth the expense and effort to try to create demand.

Creating demand and awareness, as Kevin has learned, is daunting because of all of the interlocking activities and behaviors that must come together. To be able to sell an irrigation pump successfully to very poor farmers:

> Farmers need a bunch of things to work. They need to know what to grow for the market, they need to know how to grow it, they need decent-quality inputs, and they need access to markets. And, when somebody has most of that lined up and *then* you throw in a KickStart pump, you get this exponential thing happening.
>
> But we found out the hard way [that that usually doesn't work]. We worked with another project some years ago where we just thought, 'We're going to get everybody in this program credit so they can get a pump. It will be perfect, and then they'll all have this magic tool.' It just completely failed because most of them didn't have all the other pieces in place to take advantage of the pump.

And yet these were the very same challenges KickStart faced when it started out several decades ago. I asked Kevin to speculate, with the experience he has now had as a funder, what his disposition would be if Martin approached him today as an early-stage social entrepreneur wanting to launch KickStart:

> With what we know about smallholder agriculture and about social start-ups, I would be looking at all the behaviors that need to change for your

rank-and-file smallholder farmers to use the KickStart pumps, and that list would be pretty long. And for all the other actors, it would be pretty long. [So] with the tools we have now, if Martin came to me today as an [early-stage] social entrepreneur instead of one of our most important teachers over the years, we might have some serious questions before funding him.

I would be a lot more leery of the idea given this notion of just figuring out all the behaviors that really had to change. It's a long list. I would be pointing a lot of this stuff out, and I'd be worried about it.

Kevin's concerns would not surprise Martin. They are not hypothetical, but real. KickStart has lived them and experienced plenty more. One of the problems was farmers hiding their financial success from friends and neighbors in case it encouraged them to ask to borrow money: this is in fact the worst possible outcome from the perspective of KickStart's endeavors to promote the success of its pump. So, how did Martin Fisher and KickStart endure years of challenge, working where markets have not only failed but needed to be created from the ground up; when the funders *du jour* are wary of giving grants year after year when they could be making investments with financial payback; when he not only had to redesign the pump several times but also the manufacturing system for making them and the supply chain for getting them to customers? How did he create an organization that has lifted more than a million people out of poverty? The answer, I believe, is persistence.

Flexibility

LESLEY SILVERTHORN (NOW MARINCOLA) HAD A PEDIGREE for ready success as a social entrepreneur. Or so it may have appeared. She had two degrees from Stanford, significant experience abroad, and had worked at Amazon developing solar-powered Kindles. Selling solar light to African villagers who get their light from candles or kerosene, or providing an effortless way of recharging their cell phones that might prevent hours of travel, would almost seem too easy. Especially when you *save* them money when they purchase your product.

Yet it was very far from easy. Even though villagers would pay $50 for a cell phone, $50 for solar lighting and power was out of the question. Like Martin Fisher, Lesley and her company, Angaza, ran into a problem of market creation: people were simply not ready to part with so much money for her product. This and other mistakes caught her off guard and took their toll:

I don't want to say this in terms of demotivating anyone. But I look back on what it's taken for me to get where we are, and it was incredibly difficult. ... There's so many things that a lot of just passionate entrepreneurs overlook in the beginning. All the hoops that they have to jump through to actually reach scale and get where they want to go ... I was naïve when I first started out. 'Oh yes, we'll be a startup. We'll do this. It'll be great.' ... It's so easy to just throw in the towel and give up because of the road-blocks out there for a social venture.

Lesley persevered. Angaza became less a company with a new solar prod-uct and more a company with a clever way of providing consumer financing for solar products. Its pay-as-you-go technology unlocks a village household's solar product for use, bit by bit, week by week, as customers send small pay-ments via their cell phones, until, finally, they own it outright.

Nonproductive persistence

IN CASES LIKE LESLEY'S, the appropriate response to mounting difficulties is to persist and look for ways to flex your approach. In other cases, though, per-sisting can be a fool's errand. The psychological literature has a term called *nonproductive persistence*.[13] As the name suggests, people will persist in a task even when it is fruitless; and people with high self-esteem may be most susceptible, even ignoring feedback that their efforts will be futile.

Ed Cardoza has seen this play out at Still Harbor, where he works with social entrepreneurs on integrating their inner and outer worlds. He counsels people whose inner worlds seem to be collapsing. Who experience a crisis of a personal nature when they begin to realize that things aren't going accord-ing to plan. Who are scared, who want to bail, who thought things would be much easier.

Ed works first to restore the integrity of the person. He then works with her to examine whether her idea and approach should be salvaged:

> There is a lot of self-doubt, the darkness descends ... Their 'why' is being challenged because, in their action, something is not working well. We go back and start to discern and reflect whether there's something signifi-cantly flawed in their idea or execution, or is it because the notion is so radical or so threatening or so challenging or so unconventional that it's just being dismissed out of hand for absolutely no real reason. Helping people through that process is a very difficult thing because it's very per-sonal at times.

Your goodness or mine?

OBSERVING HOW SOCIAL ENTREPRENEURS EXPRESS "GOODNESS" underlines their similarities even as it also reveals the incredible breadth of their personalities, circumstances, and approaches to improving the world. As just one example, recall Sanga Moses, whom we've already met: as a child abandoned in rural Uganda; as a college-educated banker; as a brother grieving the loss of oppor-tunity for his sister; as a would-be social entrepreneur who gave up his job to pursue an idea he knew next to nothing about through a business he had yet to begin. Sanga's idea was to manufacture what he now calls "green charcoal" from agricultural waste. This cleaner fuel would save villagers money as it created jobs for farmers and helped protect the environment.

Sanga's *business model* – a topic we will formally introduce and explore later – involved collecting agricultural waste that farmers had pre-processed before then processing it further in his facility. This all changed when he met Sarah, a distraught woman unable to support herself or her children, who sought Sanga's help. The encounter prompted Sanga to help Sarah gain employment through his company. He also fundamentally reorganized his business to be more inclusive. I asked Sanga if he had done that with a view to increasing the profitability of his business. His reply captures the generosity that is, I believe, within us all, but is set into motion more often, or with a wider orbit, among social entrepreneurs:

> I actually didn't do it for any business reasons. Now, I'll be frank with you. I don't think I'm a traditional businessman. I don't actually call myself a 'businessperson.' That's a term that other people use to describe me. I call myself a 'social servant' – someone who serves my community.

In truth, Sanga recognized the economic rewards he might be forgoing by acting as a social servant, not a profit-first businessperson. He also believes they are overshadowed by what he is gaining in return. He did a back-of-the-envelope calculation to show me the potential business opportunity: 3 million people in Uganda who could use green charcoal, 110 million in East Africa; a possible profit of $1 per kilo for an item that must be bought again and again:

> It is a very profitable business that could make me a billionaire. But I also know that it could make me very wealthy emotionally, in terms of what I believe in, and that's the piece that I care about most.
>
> I will tell you something that I believe in. I inherently believe that I can be a billionaire in many ways. … If I really wanted to be rich quickly, I'm sure I can do that.

With delicate politeness he points out the wide difference in our ages before nailing down his main point:

> But I sometimes wonder – maybe you can tell me, you've lived for a longer time than me? Currently, I can feed my family. I feel like I have more than what 80% of my countrymen have. I already feel that I have everything that I need. I don't know whether having an extra million dollars in my bank account will make me much happier. I doubt that.
>
> I inherently feel that if I see many people like Sarah happy, that could make me a happier man than having a million dollars in my account.

Reframe

REMEMBER MARK HECKER (Chapter 6, "Necessary and unwelcome"; Chapter 7, "You don't know your own venture"): a former social worker, then teacher, now an educational social entrepreneur whose tutoring program relies on inner-city high school students near the bottom of the class assisting struggling elementary school children nearby. He has made a habit of seeing virtue where others may not:

> A Master's degree in social work is very experience-based. The greatest gift my MSW [Master of Social Work] ever gave me was it gave me a really, really difficult first placement where I worked in a maximum-security juvenile facility for violent and sexual offenders. That, for me, has always taught me that there's no such thing as a hopeless kid.
>
> That's something that's part of every day for me. I've really taken it with me from that work.

A taste for equity

MEET PAUL SAGINAW, owner of the best delicatessen outside of New York City, Zingerman's Deli in my hometown of Ann Arbor, Michigan. Paul and his co-founder started Zingerman's in 1982, and it has since grown into a family of eight local businesses. But even when it was brand new, Zingerman's felt a deep responsibility to the community:

> We were giving back to the community from day one. For me, it's not something you do after you're successful. To me, it's the case that doing businesses is an obligation. And so it's a line item [in our budget]. It's rent, utilities, give back.

Paul is a straight-shooting, outgoing, big-thinking businessman/social-activist. He advocates for a "thriveable" wage for workers, not just a livable wage; and a "living return," not maximum return, for Zingerman's. From the beginning, Zingerman's would provide food to support local causes in the community. Then, when Zingerman's was still in its infancy, in 1988, Paul happened upon an article in a food magazine describing several photographers in New York City who rented a van to deliver food left over from fancy photo shoots to the Salvation Army. "I thought, 'that is just brilliant.' ... We were already giving at a high level as far as our percentage of sales or of our profit. But this got us to focus on it."

And so he put his own plan in motion, combining his love of food, knowledge of business, and hunger for a more just community. He approached a sandwich line supervisor who was thinking about going to law school, appealing to her to help him launch what has now become Food Gatherers: the first food rescue program in Michigan, just the third in the country, and the only one to grow out of a for-profit business, and now a four-star-rated nonprofit organization:

> I have this idea. We'll take you off your job, but I'll continue to pay you your salary. I am going to go around and talk to all the food establishments and see if they're willing to give us the food that they're not going to sell. And you go research what's the landscape out there. What organizations are feeding people? What are they lacking?
>
> I wanted to have this multiplier effect, so that we would just focus on food rescue. And I wanted to go to SOS [a county agency for the homeless] and say, 'If you have a dollar for food rescue, if we take that instead, I'm going to get you more food than you are because this is all we're going to do. And then you don't have to think about that. You just keep focusing on your mission.' And that's what we did.

Zingerman's launched Food Gatherers using its own resources, without at first seeking support from others (that would soon follow), and never seeking to derive business benefit by promoting its generosity:

> I said, 'Okay, we're going to get this going and Zingerman's is just going to fund it. We're going to pay the salaries. It's going to be housed in [our deli building]. And they will have our phone systems, our copiers, our mailing list; they will have everything. And then we'll ask for help from [other businesses] and volunteers.'

Paul established a 501(c)3 (a nonprofit business), created a board of directors, and hired his deli employee, then two others. Funding was unrestricted:

> I said, 'We're going to give you a big chunk of money every year. You don't have to come and ask for it. Go do the work of the mission. Don't think about [the financial side of] this, at least for a long time, okay? Here, take the money.'
>
> And then, later on, I realized that if we really wanted to, in a significant way, try to solve this seemingly intractable social issue, that I needed everybody's help. We needed everybody to have a role in hunger relief.

Paul's philosophy flows from a sense of abundance – believing you have everything you need, that it's your good fortune to share, and that giving away provides you with more, not less.

> What I like to think about is: I have some resource in abundance and I can willingly give that and in no measurable, perceptible way does it have any [negative] effect on my life. But, for the person or group that's receiving it, it could have an enormous impact. Then what's my obligation to do that?

He completes his thought:

> I have a lot of experience. We [Zingerman's] have great systems. I have knowledge in this area [food and community businesses]. I have energy. And so I can freely give of that, and what I get back is I get enormous joy.

WHEN FOCUS, PERSISTENCE, AND RESILIENCE are combined with empathy – likely the social entrepreneur's master emotion – we can expect not only reflexive good, but sustained good. But not every potential social entrepreneur is ready for the price of fully committing to a social enterprise, as we explore next.

Notes

1 Darwin, Charles, *The Descent of Man and Selection in Relation to Sex* (London: John Murray, 1871).
2 Smith, Adam, *The Theory of Moral Sentiments* (London/Edinburgh, 1759).
3 Ekman, Paul, "Global compassion: A conversation between the Dalai Lama and Paul Ekman." In *The Compassionate Instinct: The Science of Human Goodness*, ed. Keltner, Dacher, Marsh, David R., and Smith, Adam (New York: W.W. Norton, 2010).
4 Peterson, Christopher, and Seligman, Martin E.P., *Character Strengths and Virtues: A Handbook and Classification* (Cary, NC: Oxford University Press, 2004).
5 Batson, C. Daniel, and Shaw, Laura L., "Evidence for altruism: Toward a pluralism of prosocial motives." *Psychological Inquiry* 2(2) (1991): 107–22.
6 Keltner, Dacher, *Born to Be Good: The Science of a Meaningful Life* (New York: W.W. Norton, 2009).
7 Chapter 1 of Peterson and Seligman, *Character Strengths and Virtues* is titled "Introduction to a 'A manual of the sanities,'" a play on titles like the widely used *Diagnostic and Statistical Manual of Mental Disorders* ("DSM") by the American Psychiatric Association (APA) which denote negative mental and emotional conditions.
8 Batson, C. Daniel, *Altruism in Humans* (New York: Oxford University Press, 2011).
9 Peterson and Seligman, *Character Strengths and Virtues*.
10 Batson, C.D., and Ahmad, N., "Empathy-induced altruism in a prisoner's dilemma II: What if the target of empathy has defected?" *European Journal of Social Psychology* 31 (2001): 25–36.
11 "Country comparison: GDP per capita (PPP)." *CIA World Factbook*. Retrieved July 9, 2018 from: https://www.cia.gov/library/publications/the-world-factbook/rankorder/2004rank.html?countryname=Liberia&countrycode=li&regionCode=afr&rank=223#li
12 According to the *CIA Factbook*, maternal mortality is the eighth worst in the world; infant mortality ranks at number 15. Retrieved July 9, 2018 from: https://www.cia.gov/library/publications/the-world-factbook/geos/li.html
13 McFarlin, Dean B., Baumeister, Roy F., and Blascovich, Jim, "On knowing when to quit: Task failure, self-esteem, advice, and nonproductive persistence." *Journal of Personality* 52(2) (1984): 138–55.

9 Committing

WHEN YOU COMMIT TO YOUR SOCIAL ENTERPRISE, you are committing to something greater than yourself, setting up a never-ending potential challenge to care for yourself as you give yourself fully to your cause. Every social entrepreneur must negotiate this tension on her own terms. Those who are successful navigate by goodness and purpose, with wisdom their ultimate compass.

Ready? Really?

COMMITTING TO SOCIAL ENTREPRENEURSHIP is not something to undertake lightly, like trying more adventurous sushi. It's more like committing to marry, or to be in a long-term relationship. I mean this. Jason Caya, who worked to help poor women in India develop leadership and networking skills to support their microenterprises, tells me:

> To be smart about development work you need to get on the ground and get experience. That was some good advice I got when I was asking someone how to get into microfinance, and I wasn't ready to do it at that time. And this is how I knew: because he said, 'Cancel your lease, break up with your girlfriend, buy a plane ticket, go spend [significant time] on the ground.' And I was like, 'All right, thanks, that's good advice: I'm not ready to do that.' I wasn't actually ready for two more years until I finally did that.

Charlie Cavell, who founded the Detroit-based workforce development organization Pay It Forward, took the same test and "passed" it:

> I had a girlfriend at the time, and because of me working so hard [we] broke up because it was 'Do I hang out with her and spend lots of time with her, or do I do Pay It Forward and network?' … Now I don't have a girlfriend to distract me so that's a plus. That saves a lot of time.

SANGA MOSES HAD RACKED UP A NUMBER OF FIRSTS: first from his Ugandan village to go college; first to earn a corner office position at a bank; and first to quit a position of such prestige and security. To start a social enterprise. Which did not go over well with *his* girlfriend.

> She didn't approve that I left the bank job because it was kind of cool being a banker. In my country, white-collar jobs are everyone's dream. Everyone wants to be a banker, sit in a cool office, and put on a suit. I was rising through the ranks quickly.
>
> Actually, when I told my boss that I was quitting, he said, 'Why? Is it about money? I'll double your salary. Don't talk about that. Go back to your job.'
>
> Then I made a mistake. I went home and told my girlfriend, and she said, 'Where will you find a good job like that? You can't leave!'
>
> So, first of all, leaving the job was against her wish. Then, a few months down the road, I had no money. I had to sell everything, including my bed. That really didn't go down well with her, and she told me, 'If you want to waste your life, waste it alone. You are not going to waste my life as well.' So she slammed the door and left.

Leaving his job may have gone even worse with his mother: "She thought I had gone crazy, leaving a job at a bank and returning to this village. She called a witch doctor."

Sanga's mind was clear and focused, however, even if his heart was heavy. There had to be a better future for girls like his sister who had to carry wood on their heads instead of getting an education. Despite the incredulity of his girlfriend and mother, he would build the organization that eventually became Eco-Fuel Africa. Creating economic and educational opportunity for women and girls, as well as addressing his country's deforestation problem, was more than reason enough for him to commit wholeheartedly to his enterprise. Happily, he is now enjoying success both in business as well as his personal life:

> I was very unsure of myself [at the beginning], so I thought, 'I have really, really messed up my life. I don't want to mess someone else's life with mine, so I don't deserve [my girlfriend].' So I let her go. I didn't even try to contact her, but somehow she felt so guilty and they told me she was not eating and sleeping, and a few months later she called me and apologized and said, 'I lost an opportunity to stand with you when you needed me the most.' So I said, 'No, it should be me apologizing.' So she came back to my life and now we are married, and we have a daughter.

Always stepping on the gas

MARTIN FISHER HAS BEEN AT THE HELM of KickStart since 1991. The longevity of his organization, its operating income of nearly $7 million, and acclaim such as having received Charity Navigator's top rating might lead you to conclude that business is on cruise control and he is kicking back, enjoying fine Kenyan wine. Though he and I didn't discuss what he drinks – and I'm not sure if Kenya makes wine – we did talk about the priority that running a social enterprise places on your life:

> I can't say that I've sorted out the personal side too well. And I don't know that many people have. Occasionally, I meet a social entrepreneur who seems to have got a good balance, but it's certainly the exception rather than the rule. And even if you look at the top, you know – Muhammad Yunus or someone – he's on the road every day. Jane Goodall – on the road every day. I mean, they don't have a personal life to speak of. … I can't say that I've sorted out mine in a very good way, but I've certainly enjoyed my life.
>
> I still work way too hard. I still don't get enough sleep. I still travel way too much. But some people with stable lives … might look at us and say, 'Well, I wish I was doing something more meaningful' – right? So, we don't have anything to complain about, that's for sure.

When your venture gives you lemons

ED CARDOZA, WHOSE ORGANIZATION STILL HARBOR helps social entrepreneurs develop a fuller understanding of their sense of purpose, explains how commitment must be undertaken with a long view. Particularly when much is at stake, being a *social* entrepreneur requires much greater dedication than being "just" an entrepreneur:

> Most of these folks are not opening up lemonade stands or selling vintage PEZ candy dispensers. They're taking on problems that are profoundly important, and often lives are in the balance. They are taking on nutrition programs where, if they stop, people starve. They are taking on hospital structures where, if they stop, people die.

Ed makes sure that no one hides behind statistics and failure rates to cop out on a social venture. He encounters social entrepreneurs rationalizing that "some, maybe most, social ventures won't pan out: they'll just die off" as an excuse not to give theirs everything they've got:

> And I always tell people, 'If you want to do something that's a little bit more safe, do something like a lemonade stand. Because if you are going to go into a place like Liberia that's war-torn and start making promises to people who have had nothing but promises made and broken, it's probably best not to start that intervention.'

Breathe in

JEFF SKOLL INTRODUCED THE SKOLL WORLD FORUM, 2015, recalling the words of John Gardner, a true public servant in the governmental, private, and civic sectors: "Bet on good people doing good things." A moment later he added his personal advice: "Know your purpose and be dedicated to it." Despite all the challenges, social entrepreneurs who truly thrive are buoyed by a sense of goodness and purpose. As a counterpoint to the obstacles and challenges that I've felt have been important to document in these pages, I now want to offer a brief meditation on goodness and purpose – qualities that continually blossom on the most forbidding paths that social entrepreneurs tread, and about which it has been my pleasure to have social entrepreneurs talk to me.

Acting from values

WHEN LISA BALLANTINE (SEE CHAPTER 3, "EXPERIENCED WITH MEANING") RETURNED to the Dominican Republic after her first year-long stay as a missionary, it was to help the locals she had lived with, who had no running water and were getting sick from drinking water from the river. She had developed a water filter to remove contaminants, and it could be made locally. Her hopes for the community soared until she discovered the filter she had made and delivered was not as effective as she had believed. The filter is a ceramic pot with tiny holes coated with colloidal silver, a naturally occurring antibacterial. But, after a few months of use, the silver, which is much like a glaze, was wearing out and washing off, leaving filters without their antibacterial properties. Lisa was devastated:

> I couldn't sleep at night. I just thought of these mothers giving water to their babies that was contaminated. They didn't purify the water using other means [such as boiling or chlorination or another method of filtration] because they believed in the filter.

She had already spent $50,000: $30,000 from personal funds and $20,000 more from a grant, which she was talking with her husband about giving back. That would not be a business decision or one about how to protect the reputation of her young company, FilterPure.[1] It was about acting with "rightness," acting from goodness. I don't think the decision was religious, but it *was* consistent with the precepts of her – make that *any* – religion.

Lisa's flexibility ("Beyond any education, beyond anything that you could learn, just learn to be flexible"), coupled with her persistence, led to a solution, however. She used the internet to identify and contact David Webb, eventually a board member and technical advisor, but then a stranger with more than two decades' experience in water filtration. She recalls their first conversation:

> I said, 'Can you please help me? I'm here in the Dominican Republic, I'm doing this humanitarian project, and these filters are a mess. What can I do?' And he said, 'Oh, that's no problem at all. I can just tell you on the phone. The problem is the filter. The silver's washing out and it's oxidizing and so you need to fire the silver in.'

Lisa was shocked, but he was reassuring:

> I said, 'You're serious about this?' He's like, 'Yeah, it'll work fine, no problem.' So we figured out the right amount of silver: it's a much greater amount [than we were using] and there were some more technical things that we had to do. But, basically, once we fired that silver in, that thing worked like a charm.

The reworked process has enabled local communities in the Dominican Republic and Haiti to manufacture filters that are 99.9% effective in eliminating microbes and that last five years, while also creating badly needed jobs.

But the underlying recipe for FilterPure's success has never changed: Lisa's qualities as a person. When she discovered her filters were defective, she took them all back and broke them so that nobody would be tempted to use them again, despite the huge financial loss to the project.

> That is the most important thing. I feel that once we have given a family a filter they're going to trust that that filter's going to work. ... I feel so strongly about that – I could not give a filter to someone that I myself would not give my own children water from. I take it very personally. When I gave a filter to a family, if I didn't think that filter was working I couldn't sleep and I would go and I would take that filter back. ... We can give them a very good filter, and so why not? If we spend a little bit extra money we can make the filter 'excellent' as opposed to 'better.' Wouldn't you want that for your family?
>
> Sometimes, just because [our customers] are in the developing world or they're poor we think, 'Well, at least it's "better."' But is that okay if we can give them 'excellent?' That sort of thing just drives me.

Pushing forward

THE GENEROSITY OF SOCIAL ENTREPRENEURS leads them where most people won't go, providing rewards well beyond money but also moments of isolation, despair, and even questioning the path they've chosen. In the eddy of emotion, activity, and opportunity, a question that straightens out the mind and appeals to the heart is: "Why?"

Dan Sutera, the serial tech entrepreneur who set out to change the national educational system in Zambia (see Chapter 4, "Intention for impact"), has the experience and savvy to get things done. He knows what it's like to broker a deal with the Zambian Ministry of Education, as well how to create schools based on e-learning in a country with unreliable electricity. Yes, he knows about frustration. To deal with these situations, he also knows his "why."

> 'Why' is very important to be in touch with because the 'why' helps you to drive [on]. When you're starting something, it's very exciting and you want

to do it, but then at some point it gets hard. And so when it gets hard, then the 'why' helps you motivate yourself through [the difficulty]. ...

[Still,] it can't be all heart. You know, the 'why' is important, but you also have to be a professional when you're going about it, either as a volunteer or as a founder. You have to come at it from a professional angle and understand – really understand – what you're doing and be able to make those tough decisions that aren't just emotionally driven.

Charmed "whys"

YOUR "WHY" IS GOOD POST-IT MATERIAL. Even when not troubled by doubts or impatient for results – *more!, faster!* – social entrepreneurs' lives are far from meditative (a topic, incidentally, that I'll address soon), and staying on top of their business and personal priorities can get jammed aside by all kinds of "stuff."

Charlie Cavell overcame a trying childhood and then, barely 20, developed a model workforce development program, Pay It Forward, in partnership with the state of Michigan. He always had a purpose to his life. As a kid, he went to school to prepare for a profession: "When I was six, it was so I could become a cowboy, or when I was 12, to be an architect." A restless, relentlessly optimistic social entrepreneur, Charlie has a clear passion: starting a venture then finding a partner to run it. His temperament keeps him constantly on the lookout for new opportunities, and his boundless energy ensures he is plugged in to what is happening in social entrepreneurship in Detroit, and, for that matter, around the world. I ask him if he had a personal mission statement:

> I have it right here. It's 'I want to serve people, learn from people, teach people, and be mindful that I always leave a footprint, so I might as well try and make it a good footprint that I leave with people; and to help empower people to recognize their potential.'

As he speaks, he counts off each phrase by sliding another plastic bead on a bracelet he wears as a constant reminder of who he is:

> I get distracted easily, so it's helpful if it's right there. It's also on my bathroom mirror with my short-term and long-term goals. I wrote it out a little more than two years ago, right after starting Pay It Forward. But that has kind of been my MO for quite some time.

He adds a comment that suggests to me that he has carefully considered how these ideas work as an ensemble:

> I wake up with that purpose; but then that's good and bad because you close yourself off. You close doors and don't open windows to other opportunities to try and learn and do more things. So that's why the 'learning' part is there, because that's the balance. That's what it's about, right?

CHARLIE WAS NOT THE ONLY SOCIAL ENTREPRENEUR from whom I heard something like this. I heard this from another:

> The habit I've got is: I write something on paper and pin it on the wall – something that I believe is the big picture. Like maybe if I'm doubting that I can do something, I can write, 'I can do it,' and put it somewhere where I can see it every day.
>
> And every day I say, 'I can do it, I can do it!' Something like that. To me, it has been helpful to always remind myself that I can do it, maybe because I never had a lot of external support. It has been a very lonely journey. Somehow I feel that it doesn't matter where you come from. If you are trying to do something, at the beginning not many people will understand what you are trying to do, so you will have resistance. So remind yourself every day that you can do it ... When you fail, I don't think that's a crime. You've just tried and failed.

This social entrepreneur studies the work of self-help authors including Jim Rohn, Zig Ziglar, and Robert Kiyosaki. Yet, before you dismiss such study as self-deluding psychobabble (and I certainly don't), perhaps you'll reconsider when you learn a bit more about him:

> When I was a little boy, I picked a book out of the garbage pit. It didn't have a title. It didn't have a cover, so I don't even know what the title is. But it was about a man who wanted to go to Egypt to find a treasure or something. He didn't know the language, but somehow believed he could find it. And he embarked on this adventurous journey not knowing what to expect, with just the faith that he could find it.
>
> And somehow that truly changed my life, because he was a humble man but he believed that he could find the treasure. And I remember that he reached somewhere – I don't know what happened. I don't remember the entire story anymore, but he finally went to Egypt and found the treasure. I don't know if that's fiction or it's fact.

Yes, that man lives in Uganda; he is working to save the lives of women and girls, and to save his country's forests; he is absolutely authentic. Yes, he is Sanga Moses. And: Charlie Cavell traveled to Uganda to learn from him.

Critical "whys"

WHY ASK "WHY?" Sometimes, asking why may help you make decisions consistent with your mission; other times, to deal with disappointment or frustration. But the whys that are most crucial are those that help you have a meaningful career and fulfilling life. Social entrepreneurs, who typically thrive on taking action and getting results, may be reluctant to address these crucial whys, sometimes at great personal cost. Ed Cardoza has seen this play out time and time again at Still Harbor.

> Not everybody gets it. Most people are looking for the secret sauce. ... When you say to them, 'The secret sauce is community; it's creating space; it's building real processes for discernment and reflection,' they usually yawn and walk away.

Those who do get it are the ones whose walk, talk, and sense of purpose are fused:

> Not only do they understand how they do things, and what they do, they are able to tell you in a very clear, compelling voice why they do the things that they do.
>
> That, to me, is what we are trying to do when we are working with young people who are asking, 'How do I do something different in the world? How do I engage in meaning?'
>
> And what we say is, 'You need to start with that "why." You need to start with that purpose, that direction, that belief, that differentiating principle that says, "If I look at this problem, and as I look at this experience, this is what it raises in terms of my own values, my own beliefs, my own purpose."'
>
> That is how I direct [those looking for meaning] to be able to create a 'who' and 'what' that is fundamentally different than what other people are doing.

This deep reflection provides congruence between who you are and what you do. Such authentic alignment will sustain you, even in the toughest times, far more than any pep talk ever could.

Wisdom

SOCIAL ENTERPRISES PASS THROUGH DEVELOPMENTAL STAGES. Foundations and social venture capital firms create labels for these stages, using terms like "proof of concept stage," "early stage," "growth stage," and "mature stage." These labels provide useful distinctions for passing out cash, but financial needs are only one part of a social venture's development. As Jerry White points out, founders and their organizations can get stuck in various almost-psychological stages, impairing their abilities to truly have as large an effect as possible.

Unsurprisingly, young people starting social enterprises (and older people whose social enterprises are still young) get caught up in the excitement of creating, of doing, of "changing the world" – what Jerry and others consider the "ego" stage of being a social entrepreneur. As the terms connotes, operating from ego puts too much focus on the doer, too little on what needs to be done.

But, before we dismiss getting caught in the ego stage as the folly just of youth or inexperience, consider that Jerry himself was still snagged by ego when he began to lead the Campaign for a Mine-Free Israel in 2004. This would be a campaign to clean thousands of minefields in Israel, Palestine, and Jordan, and millions of buried mines, that were maiming children, innocent civilians, and tourists (like Jerry), without providing any military or security value at all. With 20 years' experience working with world leaders, Jerry knew he was ready to lead the campaign. Actually, he was mistaken, as he recounts in an article on leadership:

> I thought I was more than ready. I had already practiced my landmine leadership on a global scale. ... We had helped negotiate an innovative treaty to ban anti-personnel mines, now signed by 159 countries. ... I thought these credentials along with my personal experiences [as a land-mine survivor] would be enough to get Israel to take action.[2]

But the campaign failed – fortunately, this was just a setback, not ultimate defeat – because he had made the campaign about him, suggesting to military leaders that his views as a survivor as well as his previous successes in eliminating landmines should trump their views as defenders of Israel. As Jerry was to discover, he needed to act with generosity, to truly value others' views, to create space for all sides to win, not just tear down his opponents' arguments. To act from a place of wisdom, rather than ego.

Breathe out

THERE IS A STORY Derek Ellerman told me about saving babies drowning in the ocean. At first you rush in and save those closest to the shore, and then you go farther and farther into the waves until, at some point, you yourself start to drown. "When do you stop?" he asks. For Derek, the dilemma was not rhetorical but the harsh reality that confronted his staff and him with troublesome regularity. For the organizations he founded, one to combat police misconduct and abuse and then a second to combat human sex trafficking, there was always someone drowning:

> [Our staff] would say, 'I've already worked 12 hours today or 14 hours today, and if I don't stop and sleep, then I know what it's going to do to me. But if I do stop and sleep, then these survivors [of human trafficking] aren't going to get services [they need right away] or I'm not going to be able to be there for this police raid.' It's a brutal thing when you know what the consequences [of taking care of yourself] may be [for others].

He and his co-founder of Polaris, the social enterprise devoted to stopping human trafficking, were far from immune to this tension themselves, erring on the side of continual involvement, risking drowning, until they ultimately burned out. The experience taught him:

> Organizations need to help their founders and their staff from early on begin to understand how to deal with that quandary. To deal with that

dilemma in a way that's really healthy, [unlike] ... the two ways this it is normally dealt with: either you go all out and you have to drown yourself and you end up ultimately having diminished effectiveness as a leader. Or, you decide to become a 'super professional' and you work nine-to-five, and you set up these boundaries. But you deaden your heart in the process, and you desensitize yourself. Neither of those are good approaches. You need a much more skillful means to work with these really [difficult] and very real problems that you face in leadership.

He urges that early-stage social entrepreneurs – in such a rush to *do* – do not neglect their personal development as people, and as leaders.

So much of the focus, early on, is on the *doing* side. We want to know how to run programs, we want to know how to do finances, we want to get to all that stuff that's really urgent, in your face, and that [responds to] the explicit pressures that are upon you.

But, the area that is often neglected is the *being* side – the personal leadership development side. Being grounded in your personal development work and ideally also some significant spiritual practice of some kind. ...

It is important to really understand that personal and leadership development work is as important as your strategy, your management, and your actual program. That who you are as a person – being in a good space and constantly focusing on your own personal development – is both the foundation and the ceiling on your effectiveness a leader.

Working on personal development will serve your own organization and, as Derek notes, it is also vital "in order to do the bigger work ... necessary to take on huge challenges." Challenges (which we will examine later in detail) that demand building and working through networks, developing coalitions, and creating social movements. Challenges where potential leaders' attention to personal development can, sadly, be all too rare.

COMMITTING TO BECOME a social entrepreneur, then, goes beyond the decision to start a venture; it means an unwavering commitment to cause, and to yourself and your organization – for the duration. Being a social entrepreneur means being an attentive and skilled businessman (or woman). But, more, it is a calling.

Notes

1 FilterPure is now part of Wine to Water.
2 White, Jerry, "Explosive wisdom: What landmines teach us about liberation and leadership." *Kosmos*, Spring/Summer 2012.

10 Gaining skills

SOCIAL ENTREPRENEURS NEED THE SKILLS to translate good intentions into effective outcomes – whether through their efforts alone or combined with those of a co-founder, team members, volunteers, or others. Most of the people I interviewed acknowledged their own deficits, speaking almost wistfully of skill-sets other than their own. Those without a business degree envied those who had one. Those with business degrees found that their education didn't properly prepare them. And even those who had been front, center, and successful in the corporate world said that that experience guarantees nothing when you become a social entrepreneur.

And yet with pluck and resourcefulness, successful social entrepreneurs find a way to learn what they need to and rely on others when their own knowledge trails off. They become adept at understanding their markets, the unique value they create, and their business models; they learn about technology and technical issues to the degree necessary; and they recognize that soft skills, not just hard skills, are required to succeed.

Now, just a product

WHY IS RUNNING A SOCIAL ENTERPRISE SO HARD? The answer is simple. In comparison to a medium-to-large-sized business where you'll likely find: a chief executive officer, a chief operating officer, a chief financial officer, a chief information officer, a director of marketing, head of accounting, all their staff, plus a stable of product developers and testers, a legal department, and support personnel – and maybe a chef and a masseuse – in *your* social venture you'll find: you. That those you benefit may not have money to pay you, and you may have to constantly be on the lookout for money, only adds to your challenges. This is a daunting proposition for even the most seasoned businessperson. It can be paralyzing, terrifying – or, worse, seem inconsequential – for someone with no business experience whatsoever.

THREE OF THE FOUNDERS OF DIIME (Design Innovations for Infants and Mothers Everywhere; now part of Sisu Global Health) – Gillian Henker, Theresa Fisher, and Malvika Bhatia – confide their concerns about starting a business. Able engineers, they had developed a low-cost, easy-to-use medical device that could save many lives in the developing world:

> [We are] working on blood salvage for ruptured ectopic pregnancies. The situation in Ghana is: there's not an adequate supply of donated blood, so in cases of erupted ectopic pregnancies, a woman will lose almost half of her blood volume, like two liters of blood, and it's just sitting in her abdomen. And because there's no donor blood, the clinicians will actually reuse that blood. They scoop it out with a cup or a ladle, run it through a nurse's fingers to remove the largest clots, and then pour it into a funnel that's lined with gauze to filter out the smaller clots and put that back into a blood bag and transfuse it [with a lot of antibiotics].

The trio explain that Ghanaian clinicians brought them this problem adding, to no one's surprise, "There are a lot of problems with that situation." They set out to address them:

> What we've designed is a really simple streamlined system: a manual pump type of thing. You withdraw blood [from the abdomen] and then there's an internal filter that filters it; and when you compress it, it's connected directly to a blood bag so it immediately goes in and filters. So it's all in a contained system. It's a much more effective filtering process, so [it adheres to] much higher standards.

Undaunted by working in Ghana, working with a life-threatening medical condition, or working through the engineering details necessary to make their Hemafuse (as it is called) work, they were at sea in terms of how to make the transition from product to business. Each of these three women offers her perspective on the challenges they've faced. For ease of expression, I've run their words together:

> Our team is really lacking in any sort of business knowledge or experience, so that's been really challenging for us. Working on the business stuff takes longer to do because you have to study everything, including the basic learnings that we never got.
>
> We know we have a good technology and we know that the clinicians want it, but it's all the steps in between. We don't know how to get from 'we have this technology' to actually commercializing it.
>
> I think at this point it's an issue of we don't know what we don't know.

Language of enterprise

THE PERSPECTIVE A SOCIAL ENTREPRENEUR MUST ADOPT is that she has a product (or service) that someone finds valuable enough to pay for. That "someone" might be the same person who uses the product, or it may be a third party, such as an aid agency, which may pay for it then distribute it to others who cannot afford to pay. Several key issues arise from this simple framing. Jim Koch co-founded the Global Social Benefit Incubator (GSBI), which helps social entrepreneurs expand their ventures to create more societal good. As Jim explains, GSBI's focus in supporting social entrepreneurs begins with three fundamental concepts:

One: the value proposition. What we're really looking for is: is there something really unique here? And is the social entrepreneur really clear about who her market is, how her venture is differentiated, and what are the key activities in order to execute on that value proposition?

Two: target market analysis, and there is a venture capital bias here in Silicon Valley and probably reflected in our work as well. Is it a really big market? And is there potential for very, very large-scale impact? Is this value proposition likely to have real potential in terms of a major impact?

And, third: a business model. What are the expense drivers that evolve out of the value proposition, and what are the revenue drivers? And so can this value proposition [pay for itself] through some combination of earned income and grants, or some kind of hybrid organization?

Other, central, business ideas flow from these three concepts. For instance, articulating what is unique about how you create value underlies your mission statement, the very purpose of which is to boil down for the world (and yourself) what your organization is trying to accomplish. Another "for instance": defining your business model and all the costs associated with it means that you also understand a slew of financial topics, such as cost of goods sold, manufacturing overhead, and administrative overhead (which, collectively, determine how much it actually costs you to produce and deliver your product). Your business model will also give you a handle on your cash flow (the timing at which your money comes in and leaves your business can be more critical than the dollar amounts, per se).

Your business model is also dependent on your "value chain" and its associated incentives. The idea here is that your business operates within a chain of business activities, many of these likely performed by other businesses. Each of them must make enough money to stay in business if yours is to do so, too.

The skillful social entrepreneur develops, refines, and applies these ideas in practice, where their usefulness goes far beyond words on a page. These and other topics on designing and operating your venture are covered later in this book.

Prepare thyself!

YOU WOULD NOT WANT TO FIND YOURSELF on the other side of a chessboard from Bobby Smith, or at the opposite side of a fencing strip about to duel. You would be destroyed at both. Chess and fencing were Bobby's tickets out of poverty. Immigrants from Jamaica, his brothers, his mother, and he were not welcome in their new country, both harassed and attacked by others in the neighborhoods where they lived. They were also constantly on the move, being chased from location to location by eviction notices. His fourth-grade teacher in East Orange, New Jersey, Miss Rice, told him he would either become a drug dealer or a dropout. His own opinion was that he might end up on drugs or be dead. Not an auspicious beginning for someone who became a mentor to select social entrepreneurs.

Wanting more for her son, Bobby's mother steered him toward academic pursuits, including chess. He proved to be gifted, studying and playing his way to near Grand Master status. This level of attainment caught the notice of a prestigious Newark prep school, Saint Benedict's, where he was given a generous scholarship. He was also required to play a sport. Too short for basketball, he chose fencing, which he had never heard of but was attracted to when someone described it as "physical chess." In a short time, he was training with the Olympic team and might have participated in the Athens Olympics had he not received a fencing scholarship to Wayne State University, the school with the most fencing titles in the United States.

As committed to giving back as he is focused and dedicated, Bobby wanted to create opportunities for others like himself:

> I went from playing chess at a high level to getting a 90% reduced scholarship to a $30,000-a-year high school in Newark, New Jersey, to learning fencing, to getting a scholarship to New York [to train] with the Olympic team. [Starting a social venture] wasn't happenstance. I just woke up one day with this feeling that came over me, like I owed something to society even in just a small area.

He founded En Garde! Detroit, a hybrid social enterprise with both for-profit and nonprofit activities, aimed at teaching fencing to inner-city youth. With a magnetic personality and an offer that sells itself, he had no trouble attracting students who were as baffled by fencing as he once was: "I walk in and I show the kids that they'll learn how to use swords. It's not a hard question. Do you think kids are going to want to play with swords?"

His program embraced much more, however:

> The core function is fencing. [As] the kids are learning fencing, they're getting healthy, they're engaged with some really interesting exercises that help develop those muscle groups needed for the sport. They're learning about French culture and vocabulary, they have word banks, and we connect to a STEM [science, technology, engineering, and mathematics]-based education model.

By its third year of operations, En Garde! Detroit was training more youth to learn fencing than any other organization in the United States.

Before a fencing match begins, the referee calls "En garde," which Bobby explains is a call to "prepare thyself." En Garde! Detroit offers inner-city youth the opportunity to prepare themselves for a world very different from what they are used to. But how did Bobby prepare himself to start and run his social enterprise?

> I had to understand what a brand is, what a logo is, and I had to understand finance. I had to find my margins and figure out what my margins were. If I duplicate a free program in a school, what would I be left with and could I survive off that, and for how long? What was my cash flow? I mean, I had to learn it all, and all of that was difficult.

He learned all this through voracious self-study:

> It really was a struggle. First was finding the information, and because it didn't exist in an easy, academically rigorous format, I had to create the lessons myself.
>
> I downloaded case studies and I researched the greatest people who have ever put their hands to this field, and I just tried to see what I could learn or absorb. Bill Drayton, Muhammad Yunus. You start to read and you start to see what's going on, and I just kept learning.
>
> I would spend 15 hours a day [over a two-year period] – I called it my Bat Cave mode. No shaving, no haircuts. Tuna fish and macaroni, and that was it. I just kept learning until I learned how to develop En Garde! Detroit.

He wrote his business plan, which was vetted by Ascension Health, a billion-dollar nonprofit health care provider. "I guess my business plan was okay. We were funded for a significant amount." He garnered national attention, from among others the Hitachi Foundation's national program for young social entrepreneurs. He judiciously sought support from others:

> I definitely had people who would give me time. When I didn't understand what an ROI [return on investment] was, I found people who would sit down and answer some questions – definitely. But you can only ask for so much. A lot of it has to be on your own. But I definitely had some key mentors who would give me five minutes, ten minutes, to explain one or two things to me.

Bobby would be the first to agree this wasn't the easiest way to learn. Yet, without formally pursuing a business degree, he got a thorough business education: "If there was a program that I could have gone to, geared around developing social entrepreneurs, I would have benefited from it. But from what I know now, I already have an MBA. I definitely have an MBA already."

Learn

KATHERINE LUCEY, WHOM WE MET IN CHAPTER 2 ("MISSION, NOT PROFIT, LIGHTS THE WAY"), DOESN'T FENCE, but she does have an MBA degree and significant corporate experience. Like Bobby Smith, she had to teach herself how to start and run a social enterprise. Now an Ashoka Fellow, Katherine founded the innovative women's empowerment organization Solar Sister in 2009 after spending 20 years as an investment banker. As a banker, she had significant experience in the energy sector, with a focus on building power plants. She retired from banking because of her increasing disillusionment with the industry's dwindling respect for values, which had so long been the foundation for good banking, and its growing emphasis on greed and self-interest.

During her retirement, she took time to care for her five children and also spent time developing ways to combine her passions: empowering women and protecting the environment. She also worked with Solar Light for Africa, a small project focused on installing solar lights in Uganda, which inspired the concept of Solar Sister.

She then set out to start her own enterprise. Despite her MBA, 20 years in the corporate world, and being fluent in cutting deals and crunching numbers, she recognized that she did not have all the answers:

> I reverse-engineered every social enterprise out there and tried to figure out what's the business model, how they make money, how it works, what their impact is – is it for real or is it just a lot of fluff? What's their secret sauce? I looked at all of them and really tried to figure that out and tried to choose from the best and learn from that.

She analyzed and dissected all that she could, from cases about Africa, generally, to Uganda, specifically, and things about distributed solar especially:

> I examined everything. Look at my bookshelf; you'll see everything from Muhammad Yunus, to John Wood from Room to Read, to really everything that's available. I also looked at the businesses [themselves], the news, and whatever is out there – and there's a lot out there. I looked at both companies that are better known and also some of the smaller, lesser-known ones that are doing interesting things.

And she did not shy away from approaching others, online or in-person:

> It's been a really incredible learning experience. And, because you have the internet, because you have a lot of forums and opportunities – social enterprise is now kind of 'the thing' – there is opportunity to connect with people easily. I use social media a lot: Twitter especially has been a really great place for me to learn from people just by following along with them

and seeing what they're up to, and then connecting with them. I've built up a network of other people who are either going through the same way I'm going through with building social enterprises, or are further down the road than I am and I'm learning from them.

Becoming technical

SANGA MOSES WAS HAVING A SIMILAR EXPERIENCE with learning, mostly on his own, how to build a social venture from an idea. For him, the building comprised actual things, since there were machines at the heart of his desire to create clean, affordable energy in rural Uganda. But he had never seen them, didn't even know about them, and certainly was in no position to make them.

As you may recall, the professor of renewable energy at Makerere University, the largest in Uganda, whom Sanga approached for help, told him he had "never done anything with his hands," but he did give Sanga armfuls of books, journal articles, and magazines, which Sanga devoured. What he read was about things completely foreign to him: biogas, kilns, studies in Brazil where agricultural waste was converted into energy. But they led to ideas for the types of machines he would need to produce to have a go at a social venture putting local villagers to work producing cleaner energy. He returned to the professor, who, this time, made overtures to his students: "'This young man is crazy enough to think that he can solve the energy crisis in this country. Who wants to help him?' And every student was interested. They put their hands up."

Their interest was not matched by their knowledge, or the university's ability to provide any kind of financial support:

> The professor took me out and said, 'This university does not have a budget for that kind of research, so you have to finance it.' That wasn't going to stop me. But I also knew that these students didn't have the knowledge, but then I was willing to learn with them. So we experimented several times, failed several times, and tried again until we found something that almost worked. But 'almost' doesn't count.

Out of money, which he personally had fronted, and feeling defeated, Sanga and his team nonetheless persevered until it did.

Ask

CHARLIE CAVELL WAS BARELY OUT OF HIGH SCHOOL when he began a social venture to help poor, young Detroiters get job skills, then jobs. To say he was a seasoned businessperson would be entirely wrong, though he sometimes tried to convince others that he was. Charlie's own upbringing was challenging, including a series of stays in foster homes. By an early age, he was goal-directed. His outlook was always to help others. Well before he started

Pay It Forward, his innovative workforce preparation and placement effort, he began living by a personal mission focused outside himself: serving, teaching, and helping empower others; learning from them; and always considering the effects of his actions. With boundless energy, enthusiasm, a quick mind, and an itchy attitude to get things done – *now* (and, sometimes, details be damned) – he began college at 17, looking for a way to harness these traits for social good. This did not mean that Charlie knew anything about running a social business, and what he didn't know both baffled and frightened him when he began his venture:

> I didn't know how to incorporate as a 501(c)3 [a nonprofit charity]. I was extremely scared that somehow the IRS was going to take all $87 out of my bank account because I didn't fill out question 36(b) correctly. ... I didn't know about fundraising. ...

But he did have an entrepreneurial streak, remarking, "[Entrepreneurship] is a mind-set that you accumulate throughout life; it's either in you or it's not. It can lead you." It led him to act, sometimes too soon, often without enough preparation:

> When I was just starting off, for example, I would read something from a website or talk on the telephone with the person who ran the Earn and Learn program. But that didn't mean I understood it.
>
> Or I would say things about the problem that Pay It Forward tries to solve, but which [would discredit traditional] workforce development. I would say stuff being ignorant of how those other systems really work, or how the larger system – MEDC [Michigan Economic Development Corporation], or the Workforce Development Administration, or how the city of Detroit itself works, or does not work. ... I was basically just talking out my ass.

Despite his winning ways, "People began to call B.S. and I'd go, 'Oh, looks like I need to read that a little deeper'; or 'Maybe I completely misunderstood how that flow chart looked.'" He redoubled his efforts to understand the true nature of the problems he was addressing. "You have to do it, because you're doing it not for yourself but for something greater than that." He came to understand how much he needed others' advice, opinions, and perspective, and he began to ask for it:

> A big thing became just meeting with people to have coffee, or go to their office trying to sell the idea of what I was trying to do. A benefit I had was being open to being ignorant ... and that I was young and passionate. I would tell these stories about how it's tough out here, and I want to help address that, that I want to empower people so that they can choose their destiny. ... [And I'd ask,] 'So can you help?'

And people responded, providing grounded advice and introducing him to others. "So it was pretty much talking out my ass when I was beginning, and then learning."

New mistakes

KATHERINE FULTON of the Monitor Institute notes that, too often, social enterprises die "from a lethal combination of arrogance and ignorance." But, even before they die, they "waste time, energy, and resources – things take too long because people are not learning enough from other people's mistakes, and as fast as they can." She confesses to these sins early in her own career. She remarks that you don't have to do something yourself to learn from it: "Knowing isn't the same as doing." Great leaders, she points out, are humble and consistently curious. But then she notes a contradiction:

> The chutzpah just to be an entrepreneur actually requires a bit of arrogance. So then how could you combine that with the qualities of openness, of curiosity, that enable you to learn faster from other people's mistakes, so you make *new* mistakes?

Too cool for school?

AS THE CHINESE PROVERB "there are many paths to the top of the mountain" reminds us, attainment unfolds in various ways. The saying also observes that "the view at the top is always the same," but neatly sidesteps the obstacles that each path inevitably presents, too. There is not a perfect path. Nor a perfect way to acquire relevant business skills.

Adam Carver had already earned a Bachelor's in Business, worked several years on Wall Street, and served on two award-winning startups when he was enrolled in an MBA program emphasizing sustainable business and launched his own social startup. It failed.

Charlie Cavell knew as a teenager that he wanted to be a social entrepreneur – though he probably never used that term. He enrolled in college, took the courses he thought would best prepare him, and participated in on- and off-campus activities that got his hands much dirtier than by reading textbooks. His preparation, as you will recall, didn't prevent him from "talking out of [his] ass" in trying to operate his venture. But it succeeded.

April Allderdice, an MBA and Fulbright Scholar, was a strategy consultant at McKinsey and a project manager at Dahlberg Global Development Advisors before starting her own venture. The experience she gained could not always be applied directly to her venture, MicroEnergy Credits:

> Prioritization is one of the big challenges [in running your own venture] because you have to raise capital, operate at the same time, hire people, and [so much more]. ... As a strategy consultant, we had things called boat

charts, where each step is one leg of the boat. I used to make boat charts all the time for my clients, for myself, for my team. Step 1, Step 2, Step 3.

But what happens in a social enterprise or any entrepreneurial startup is they just get mushed together. Phase 1 never finishes on time: Phase 2 has to start. All of a sudden, you're having problems from Phase 3, but you didn't complete Phase 1 or 2. You're doing them all, so you must figure out how you're going to prioritize, because all three phases are important.

You have to constantly iterate, constantly raise the capital, constantly push the business forward, constantly be sourcing and finding new people and having a bench. There's a million things.

NONE OF THIS IS TO SUGGEST that a business education or corporate experience is counterproductive, a complete waste of your time, or places a curse on your venture. It's not – and I'm 100% certain about the curse part. Only that they don't insulate you from mistakes, either.

Two interviewees used almost identical language in saying, from their experience (one as a social entrepreneur, the other in leading an organization that supports them), that it is better to be an entrepreneur who comes to social problems than someone with an interest in social problems who becomes an entrepreneur. It is easier to pick up the "softer" (social) side than hardcore business skills, they believe.

Randall Kempner, executive director of the Aspen Network of Development Entrepreneurs (ANDE) is of this opinion. ANDE is an industry association comprised of more than 280 organizations in 150 countries that work to alleviate poverty by supporting small and growing businesses. These are businesses too big for microfinance but too small for international private equity investments. ANDE believes they are the most reliable ways to help eliminate poverty in emerging markets.

> First of all, people underestimate the importance of talent. They often start thinking about money first, and that that is often misguided. Before you start thinking about how much money you need, you need to recognize the importance of having a strong management team, or at least access to people who can serve in that role, whether they're mentors or peers or other people on whom you can call. ...
>
> You've got to get your business part right and then the social part needs to be integrated. But I fear that there are many that get caught up in the social impact. Many ANDE members believe that it only makes sense to support for-profit ventures. We think that's generally the appropriate model, because you immediately face the discipline of the market, helping you build something which is sustainable.
>
> Who do I think on the face of it is going to have more success: a business school graduate who is imbued with a social mission and those ideals, or a social work graduate who comes to social entrepreneurship without the business background? I'd take the business school student. That doesn't

mean he or she is going to be perfect. Business understanding is necessary, but not sufficient.

Others, including successful social entrepreneurs with business degrees, down-play this idea. They suggest that you can pick up business skills as you need them, even if this necessarily means you will occasionally stub your toe.

A British social entrepreneur who returned to get an MBA remarks that, in some ways, she knew more before she got her MBA, when she "wasn't as bogged down by too much knowledge." What she prized most from the degree was gaining emotional intelligence. Emotional intelligence encompasses skills and attitudes that help us go inward to identify and manage our own emotions. Equally important, it helps us engage others with empathy and deeper under-standing, so that we more easily find common ground. Emotional intelligence, this social entrepreneur felt, helped her become a convincing, effective leader.

Data

IAN FISK HAS RUN THE MENTOR CAPITAL NETWORK, formerly called the William James Foundation, for over a decade. It hosts a business plan competition, but you shouldn't enter it just for the cash. "I'd be perfectly happy to give out bags of money," he explains. "It just turns out that I don't have any." Winners do get modest prize money – not, apparently, in bags – but every entrant gets something much more valuable: extensive feedback from seasoned social entrepreneurs. Mentor Capital Network has helped launch or expand over 500 social enterprises. As one social entrepreneur explains, "The feedback was phenomenal. For two years, I carried it around in my backpack and always had it with me."

At Ian's disposal are 700 judges, 400 of whom participate in a given year, some of them being "super active." A number of them are luminaries in the field. A first round of judging reduces the pool of entrants; a second round determines who makes it to the presentation round, where winners are deter-mined. At each round, participants receive extensive written feedback on their business plans. All this generates lots of information:

> I get to read people's dreams, and I get to read what really smart people have to say about those dreams. ... Using our pool of mentors to provide feedback on the business plans, we average 20 pages of feedback per plan per round.

Equally important, he follows up with all participants, not just winners, to get status updates:

> We do standard follow-up interviews, which I assumed everybody [other competitions] did, but it turns out that most people don't, or they just follow up with their finalists. We call, or Skype, or email everybody we

can find every year. We ask everybody. 'How are you doing? How many people are you employing? What did you learn? What do you remember from our competition? What are the best practices?'

In addition, Mentor Capital Network uses "scorecards" that judges fill out when evaluating participants' business plans, asking, more or less the same questions year after year.

Ian recognizes the wealth, and value, of all the information he collects. One insight he gleaned is about which companies are likely to survive the longest. A company's "team score" strongly predicts its longevity, so he examined teams' composition to explore which were most likely to have a long life:

> I thought, 'What do they have in common?' And it wasn't founders' advanced degrees. We've had three Harvard PhDs. But PhDs are, on net, a negative. MBAs are, on net, neutral for a startup. Once a company reaches a certain size, they may be more valuable. ... Most MBA programs are designed for people to be vice-presidents at GE and they have value for that, but not for social startups.

Climb with others

PERMIT ME TO STRAIN THE METAPHOR: with different paths leading to the mountaintop, find yours and travel it with others. The best experience comes from sharing struggles and lessons with fellow travelers. A number of acclaimed organizations offer formal support to social entrepreneurs. Most have extremely competitive application processes; many cost a good deal of money. Among them, in no particular order other than alphabetical, are: Acumen Fund, Ashoka, Echoing Green, Global Social Business Incubator, Grassroots Business Fund, Starting Bloc, Unreasonable Institute, and Village Capital. Should you be in a position to participate – do. The mentoring (a topic we have yet to get to) will be from those who have "been to the top" to help you get there, too.

But the connections you'll make with other rising social entrepreneurs will likely be as valuable, as many attendees I spoke to would attest. As one of them expresses:

> Participating in the GSBI, the Santa Clara University Global Social Benefit Incubator, was great. You get connected in with people who are thinking the same thoughts and grappling with these same problems, both in a very academic and theoretical way and also in a very practical and hands-on way.

To the majority of early-stage social entrepreneurs who will never participate in these programs, do not despair: different paths lead to the same mountaintop, so find yours. It may be through a business incubator at a university or community college; a for-profit incubator that offers hands-on support; a group that gathers for regular business "pitch nights"; a co-working space where others are starting ventures – social or otherwise; or any other ecosystem where others, like you, see the top of the mountain and are figuring out how to get there.

WARMILU, A STUDENT-RUN BUSINESS, was in its first session at TechArb, a University of Michigan Venture Accelerator. DIIME, another student-originated business, was one session ahead of them. Grace Hsia, Warmilu's co-founder, explains the relationship that evolved:

> Gill and Theresa took me under their wing almost. They saw in us the same early struggles that they had: multiple co-founders, starting as a senior design project, producing a commodity-level medical device, going into an emerging market. Right away, they were able to offer advice, feedback, insight, and very deep critique, because the issues that were plaguing us were things that they had already resolved or were currently looking at resolving. And, because we were both in the medical device space, they talked about what we had to do for testing our medical device: 'This is the IRB [institutional review board] process here at the University of Michigan – make sure you talk to these people.' It helped so much.
>
> Because of our close relationship, while they were working on DIIME stuff or while I was working on Warmilu stuff, something [fortuitous] might happen: I might meet with a person and think, 'This is someone I need to introduce to DIIME,' or they might think, 'This is someone I need to introduce to Warmilu.' Having that kind of close and personal relationship helps your business grow. It sounds very simple, but building those relationships take time, and we were just very fortunate.

Despite Warmilu getting advice from faculty members, business practitioners, and others from many walks of life, their experience with DIIME was special:

> They were our peers. That made one of the biggest differences. Other individuals [at a civic-run business accelerator with which both companies were affiliated] were all 30 or older. But with Gill and Theresa, I was able to say, 'My team and I have final exams.' And they'd say, 'This is what we did.' When we both graduated, we were able to relate to each other as peers who were in the same boat. As they were progressing, we would progress too in a similar fashion, almost parallel to each other. And so they raised money just a year ahead of us, and then gave us advice on what we need to do to raise money.
>
> It's almost like a big brother/big sister type of relationship, and that made all the difference.

Soft skills

"HARD SKILLS" ARE THE GLAMOR SKILLS in social entrepreneurship – the "entrepreneurship" part of "social entrepreneurship," which strengthens your enterprise, and your ego for mastering them. Strategy, supply chains, marketing, fundraising, and the like. And yet …

… And yet people (like me, apparently) shouldn't say, write, or even think things like that. Because, most simply, they're not true. Even if failing at the basics of business means, as it certainly does, that you must find a better way, making it *all* about business misses the larger point for a social enterprise. "Hard skills" may be "hard" in the sense of being difficult to master – though anyone can gain enough fluency to have the right conversations – but "soft skills" are the true bedrock of social enterprise. Included among them are some qualities you will recall from earlier chapters (and not uniquely associated with *social* businesses): empathy, persistence, the establishment of work–personal boundaries (to prevent burnout), resilience, and effective communication. Incidentally, these soft skills may be every bit as difficult to master as any business skill.

EMPATHY DESERVES SINGLING OUT for its central role in keeping us attuned and staying committed to the needs of others. The Greater Good Science Center at the University of California, Berkeley, has collected into a single volume[1] scientific essays that offer insights into understanding and applying the principles of empathy. A key distinction, elucidated by Paul Ekman and reported by Daniel Goleman,[2] who has written extensively about emotional intelligence, is that empathy – sometimes called "perspective taking" – can be broken down into three distinct skills. Cognitive empathy entails knowing what someone else is thinking and feeling; yet you can know but still remain unmoved. Emotional empathy entails feeling what someone else is feeling; but you then risk becoming overwhelmed, and emotionally paralyzed, by these feelings yourself. Compassionate empathy strikes a balance between remaining unmoved and becoming overwhelmed. It is a skill one can develop to understand another's thoughts and feelings and spring into action.

Empathy can be taught by parents who model this trait and instruct their children in ways that heighten it. School curricula can explicitly include training on empathy. Ashoka has partnered with Mary Gordon's "Roots of Empathy" program[3] to advance this powerful idea so that schoolchildren grow up to be problem solvers. But even for the rest of us, well beyond the age of childhood, there are possibilities. Yoga, as one social entrepreneur I interviewed describes it, "is the sport of social entrepreneurs." Others use meditation as a way to gain perspective and mindful awareness. A sense of awe from listening to music or marveling at nature can move us away from self-interest to the interests of others. So can reading, especially literary fiction, which can allow us to create and experience in our minds worlds new to us, including worlds where we transcend our direct experience and, at least for a moment, deeply experience the world as someone else might.[4]

PETER LUCKOW, WHOM WE MET IN CHAPTER 8 ("ACT FOR YOURSELF; ACT FOR OTHERS"), co-founded Tiyatien Health (now called Last Mile Health), which works in the remotest parts of Liberia, bringing health care to that post-war country whose health needs have been so long neglected. To say that Tiyatien Health served those in need, but without resources, is an understatement. I ask Peter how a social entrepreneur might prepare herself to work in such an environment:

> We need to always be critical learners. I think that happens organically, given the type of people that this work draws in to the field. I also don't think we pay enough attention to literature, to poems, to art that helps us to understand the greater human dimension of this work. So, one of the things that we do is to ask 'What books are you reading now?' or bring things like poems to meetings, however silly that might sound to some people. What we've found at Tiyatien Health is that those types of art forms allow us to step back from the work and see the jungle amidst the trees. They have really allowed us to very directly create better programs, create stronger strategy, align our moral compasses and organization.
>
> I don't think [we do this enough] because there's this idea that we need to be running 24/7 – building programs, answering emails. So we don't spend enough time stepping away and reading literature or visiting museums, or whatever it may be. I do think that is an important dimension of this work, and an important dimension of creating strong leaders.

JUST BEFORE HE LEFT OFFICE, President Obama explained how important literature had been to his presidency. Shakespeare offered a window onto our essential character; Jhumpa Lahiri described the ambivalent experiences of immigrants; and authors like V. S. Naipaul helped him fight against the cynicism engendered by viewing the harshness of the world.[5]

Credibility

CAPABILITY AND AUTHENTICITY ARE THE INGREDIENTS necessary for earning the support of those you need to engage when you're a social entrepreneur. When either is absent, you'll struggle to gain traction.

When Charlie Cavell started Pay It Forward, he already was operating with a kind of street cred. His own living conditions could be mistaken for those of the misfortunate clients he wanted to serve. He didn't own a car, and once took the city bus to Biggby's Coffee to meet Kevin from MEDC (Michigan Economic Development Corporation), a state-run business assistance program he was hoping to attract as a partner. Charlie had actually never met Kevin, nor even been introduced to him. As Charlie explains:

> I had found his business card on someone's desk and cold-called him for two weeks straight, because it had his business line, his cell line, and his email. So I would call his business line, the next time send email, and then call on his cell and leave a voicemail. I kept doing that every other day, those three modes, until he got back with me two weeks later. I guess he thought, 'Well dang, I might as well get this kid to stop bugging me.'

When Kevin arrived, he was 45 minutes late, having been stuck in traffic on the highway. Charlie quickly forgave him, explaining that, because he rode the bus he could never be sure he'd be on time himself. The offhand remark captured Kevin's attention:

> Apparently, the week before Kevin and I had met, a bunch of people got robbed or a bus was sort of hijacked. Some people came on the bus and said, 'Everyone, empty out your wallets.' And so apparently that made my riding the bus seem more dangerous. So Kevin [felt], 'Wow, this guy is really trying to [build his venture].'

They spoke for two and a half hours. It was the beginning of the relationship that led to Pay It Forward becoming a model workforce development program for the entire state of Michigan. "It was my passion; it was my hustling."

Seizing opportunity

"STREET CRED" CAN BE EARNED IN LESS PERILOUS, but equally authentic, ways than riding city buses. Rebecca Onie (Chapter 4, "On whose shoulders?") provides a case in point. She recounts the beginning of a relationship with Dr. Barry Zuckerman that led to their founding of Health Leads, now a leader in the health care movement:

> I had just turned 18 when I called Barry – Dr. Zuckerman – for the first time, based on a *Boston Globe Magazine* article that I had read about his work. It talked about how his first hire as Chair of Pediatrics [at the Boston Medical Center] was a legal services attorney to represent patients. I had spent the prior nine months as an intern in the housing unit at Greater Boston Legal Services, seeing so many families come in presenting with housing issues but having an underlying health issue. So I cold-called him.
>
> By a total fortuity – Barry is obviously amazingly busy – his assistant put my call straight through to him. I remember sort of stumbling through the conversation with him and congratulating him on his good work, and telling him – it was obviously ludicrous in retrospect – that I thought there could be an important role for young people to play in his work.
>
> And one of [the reasons] Barry is such an eminent physician is that he has an unusual willingness to engage with unconventional pathways to improving primary care and pediatric care. And I think Barry was both struck by the audacity of the call and also by the fact that, really, at that point in time, there wasn't a core of young people in pediatrics in his clinic.

The challenge was laid down:

> He basically said, 'Why don't you go spend six months talking to some real doctors?' And so it was with his blessing, I had those conversations.

When you talk to Barry about that initial conversation, which we both remember, he says, 'I'll be honest, Rebecca. I just never thought I would hear from you again. I get these kinds of calls all the time and no one ever follows up.'

But I took his blessing literally and went straight to the clinic. And what's interesting is I next spoke to Barry about six months later when he called me and said, 'I'm hearing from all my docs that you're talking to them. So what are you learning?'

Yes, Rebecca was only an 18-year-old student. But she could be counted on:

And I think [gaining his trust and confidence] was just that, really. So much of building credibility as a very young social entrepreneur was simply about actually doing what I said I was going to do.

In-credible personalities

BEFORE CHARLIE CAVELL EVER MET Kevin for coffee, he had become, in his own mind at least, an expert on workforce development. He had studied the problem, figured out what was wrong with existing programs, and began telling everyone how to do things better. As you will recall, he eventually realized he was simply "talking out of [his] ass," glibly papering over gaping holes in his understanding.

This isn't so hard to understand: empathetic, energetic people who see societal problems feel an urgency to correct them. Even before they're ready. Even when they think they are. (To Charlie's great credit, he recognized his hubris, changed his attitude, and filled in those holes with genuine knowledge.)

In-credible winners

CREDIBILITY IS EARNED STEP BY STEP, though some steps are often confused with crossing the finish line rather than being – well – simply another step. The best example of this is winning a business plan competition along with prize money. Though winners' heads may swell even more than their pocketbooks, these social entrepreneurs sometimes suspect their accomplishments are, really, a bit hollow. Being recognized as a winner, they are encouraged to "go forward, build!", bidding farewell to the stage their ventures are really at, and acting as if they are something more advanced. Again: often before they're ready. Even if they think they are.

In-credulous: Talent doesn't have hues

YUSUF RANERA REES GREW UP IN SOUTH AFRICA, coming from an educated family of relative privilege, though he was strongly connected to Alexandria Township (the term used in that country for a "slum") through his parents' work as doctors. His father, in fact, became Nelson Mandela's doctor after his imprisonment, accompanying him on his first international trip. As for himself: "My best friend growing up was a son of a domestic worker."

Yusuf recognized that the opportunities that lay ahead of him were quite different from those of his best friend, or others of similar circumstances. He was able to leave Johannesburg to study at Harvard and Oxford, before working on Wall Street.

> Every time I went home during that period I would see people who were in poor communities here who had just as much talent as the people I was interacting with back in the States or back in England but who would never, ever get the chance that those people got.

Yet he realized something more:

> I felt that with entrepreneurship it's not too late. If you could identify the people with [demonstrated] talent and invest the kind of resources that I was getting at those institutions, those people could be as good as anybody in the world.

Thus emerged the idea for the Awethu Project, a hybrid (for-profit/nonprofit) company whose goal is identifying and developing high-potential entrepreneurs in under-resourced communities in South Africa, with the larger ambition of developing a model replicable across the African continent. Awethu's logic was appealing, as were Yusuf's academic pedigree, his background in economics and business, and his previous experience as a founder of a startup. He parlayed these credentials into a prestigious Echoing Green Fellowship, which awards recipients nearly six figures and provides mentorship and other support services for their social enterprises.

Despite the acclaim of winning a fellowship, he believed he needed to improve his model – make sure he was identifying the right potential entrepreneurs; and providing them the right training – before he sought more money to grow it larger:

> At the end of the Echoing Green conference I realized that social entrepreneurship is an industry right now. It's sexy and there's so much excitement around it. You can travel around the world for two years on the back of a good story – never having done anything.
>
> I didn't want to be like that. I felt like the one thing our business wasn't doing – everything else was nice: the partnerships were great, the funding, we're winning awards, the entrepreneurs are talented – was the entrepreneurs weren't making any money.

So he fixed that:

> So for four months, I cut off all external contacts with everyone. I just worked with the entrepreneurs, and we set aggressive, proper [business

and financial] targets. One dropped out, and the other three [exceeded] those targets. It proved to me that we could do it, it proved it to them, and it also created a small-scale proof-of-concept for us.

... I wanted to prove that this thing could work before asking other people to back it. I was more interested in working on it than I was in asking for money, even if that [created a financial] shortcoming initially.

Ultimately, by proving the success of the model, Awethu secured government funding aimed at supporting a thousand entrepreneurs by following a larger-scale, more systematic process.

RARELY DO YOU HAVE ALL THE SKILLS you need to succeed as a social entrepreneur – at the outset or, in fact, ever: translating good ideas into an effective business is daunting. But you always have the opportunity to learn. Whether you come from the arts and humanities or from business, there is always a need to learn to become a successful social entrepreneur, even as you may need to learn different things. How you learn may embrace self-study, coursework, identifying people who know what you don't and asking them to teach you, and developing relationships with peers where you pull each other along. You may need to learn how to make a kiln capable of converting agricultural waste into clean fuel. You must learn how to precisely specify your target market.

When you know, when you follow through, and when you truly can do, yours will be a credible, authentic voice for change – even as you fully acknowledge you may need additional skills, more knowledge, and help from others.

Notes

1 Keltner, Dacher, Marsh, Jason, and Smith, Jeremy Adam, eds., *The Compassionate Instinct: The Science of Goodness* (New York: W. W. Norton, 2010).
2 Goleman, Daniel, "How to help." In *The Compassionate Instinct: The Science of Human Goodness*, ed. Keltner, Dacher, Marsh, Jason, and Smith, Jeremy Adam (New York: W. W. Norton, 2010).
3 http://uk.rootsofempathy.org/mary-gordon
4 Oatley, Keith, "A feeling for fiction." In *The Compassionate Instinct: The Science of Human Goodness*, ed. Keltner, Dacher, Marsh, Jason, and Smith, Jeremy Adam (New York: W. W. Norton, 2010).
5 Kakutani, Michiko, "Obama's secret to surviving the White House years: Books." *New York Times*, January 16, 2017. Retrieved July 9, 2018 from: https://www.nytimes.com/2017/01/16/books/obamas-secret-to-surviving-the-white-house-years-books.html

Part 3

Your team

WHEN AN INDUSTRIALIST/PHILANTHROPIST, Nobel Prize winner/saint, and a techno-Buddhist agree on a fundamental point, perhaps there's something there:

> Teamwork is the ability to work together toward a common vision. The ability to direct individual accomplishments toward organizational objectives. It is the fuel that allows common people to attain uncommon results.
> (Andrew Carnegie)

> None of us, including me, ever do great things. But we can all do small things, with great love, and together we can do something wonderful.
> (Mother Teresa)

> Great things in business are never done by one person; they're done by a team of people.
> (Steve Jobs)

Accordingly, in this part of the book we move from "You" to "Your team." This begins with the acknowledgment that your venture is not about you – though many social entrepreneurs ignore this basic insight. Building effective teams begins with your earliest decisions, as ventures that are co-founded are more successful than those founded by a single individual. As your team grows beyond this nucleus, the roles you need filled and the skills necessary to fill them must outweigh whom you know and even your history of getting to where you are now.

The practicalities of forming and maintaining a team present peculiar challenges for social enterprises. Who should be your first hire? Indeed, what if you can't afford to hire at all – can volunteers succeed? And, when you can, how do you make your jobs as attractive as those paying more? Operating a social enterprise may often mean working overseas, in locales where you have limited background (and may be treated with suspicion, to put it kindly). How do you establish a foothold that respects local autonomy and develops local talent?

Even with the right people, do you have an appropriate culture? Are the best ideas being heard – from inside and outside your organization? Who should advise you? And who should hold you to account?

These issues about team might seem to impede your progress. But remember: it's not about you.

11 Go team, go

If the bus comes

ROSS BAIRD INVESTS IN SOCIAL ENTREPRENEURS, providing both training and money (see Chapter 5, "Is it necessary – Really necessary?" and Chapter 7, "You don't know your own venture"). Through Village Capital, the hybrid organization he runs, he identifies businesses he believes are capable of taking on, and taking out, some of society's most difficult social problems. Over time, Village Capital has seen its share of poor investment decisions, which it recasts as lessons to mitigate risk and examine opportunities more critically.

> Lesson one is entrepreneur and team. The big lesson learned is that there is this cult of the hero social entrepreneur, and it's really, really destructive for a lot of ventures. Entrepreneurs don't build ventures; teams build ventures. So you want someone who's going to hustle, you want someone who's been able to hack it together, and you also want someone who's built a team. Because what happens if the entrepreneur gets hit by a bus? What happens if the entrepreneur can sell but they can't manage a supply chain?

There's no "team" in "I"

A TEAM OF ONE IS LIKE A MARRIAGE OF ONE, maybe solitaire for two: a built-in contradiction, clearly not what it might claim to be. Lisa Ballantine (Chapter 3, "Experienced with meaning" and Chapter 9, "Acting from values") came to social enterprise after 20 years as a homemaker, home-school mom, and youth leader. "That was what I did," she explains. That was also before she and her husband moved to the Dominican Republic to help provide clean water to a local community by manufacturing and distributing ceramic filters. She knew nothing about ceramics, filters, manufacturing, or how to run a business. "I used to think that was a detriment, but now I think it was an asset," she explains, given her openness to finding solutions as she transitioned from "project" to "social enterprise":

I didn't ever get taught the way I was supposed to do things. And so I wasn't stuck in the way it had to be. ... What I learned about leadership – I'm actually pretty good at it – is that when you are limited in your capacity, you hire out. So what I did was I found people to do [various needed tasks] for me. ...

I depend heavily on and I listen to a lot of people. I ask a lot of questions. I say, 'How would you do this? What would you do?' So what I would be lacking I would go to others for. But then if it [turns out to be] a bad idea and is not working, I throw it away and start something new.

THERE IS A COROLLARY to hiring out what you can't do: Don't act "like" a lawyer, "like" an engineer, or even "like" someone who can stay organized – unless you really are.

We're in a huge transition right now because what I was doing mostly was administrative details, which was about to wreck the organization because I'm terrible at that stuff. I'm going to be turning all that over to [an administrator we just hired] so he'll be taking care of that because I'm a horrible administrator.

And then my job will be what I love to do. Setting the vision, speaking, drawing people in, empowering people on both sides. Empowering locals to make an amazing filter and change their lives. And empowering people in the developed world that they can make a difference in the lives of the people around the world.

It's not about you

AT A PANEL PUT ON BY ASHOKA.ORG, a conversation developed about why social ventures failed. Alan Webber, co-founder of *Fast Company*, poses this question:

The truth is that it's really hard to do a social entrepreneurial startup – they fail a lot. All startups fail a lot. If you were to look at the death certificates of social entrepreneurial startups and read the line where the post-mortem says 'cause of death,' what would we most likely see?

We have already heard from Katherine Fulton, noted strategist, author, entrepreneur, and past president of the Monitor Institute – itself a social enterprise seeking to understand and share best practices of social entrepreneurs. She responds without hesitation:

If there was an epitaph for somebody, one of the things would be, 'It was all about me.' If I think about my own experience, I think it took me about ten years – I thought I'd learned everything there was to learn by force of will. And the next ten years I learned all the things you couldn't [do that way].

Social entrepreneurship is an expression of values: it's a self-expression. And the hardest thing to learn is that you will succeed and fail entirely by how you can inspire others. Every great social [enterprise, including Ashoka] … is surrounded by a great community.

The core of a great community is, of course, your team, writ small and large: a potential co-founder, those you hire, those you engage as volunteers, your advisors and mentors, and others extending further out toward the periphery of your organization.

TEAMS BUILD VENTURES, not heroes. Though you can't, find a team member who can.

12 Co-founder

Start together

SELF-AWARE SOCIAL ENTREPRENEURS KNOW THEIR LIMITATIONS, while wise social entrepreneurs – according to data – find partners to help them overcome them. Katherine Fulton spells out the need to find others to complement you, even at the outset:

> It takes so many different skills and attributes to be successful. ... Know what you're good at and what you suck at. How is it that you get really smart from the get-go? By having a partner.
> ... [So] corresponding to 'it's not about me' is that it wouldn't have to be about you if you went with somebody. ... Be lucky enough to have somebody that has a mirror image set of skills to your own to start with, so that you can hold each other accountable and keep each other honest.

Marina Kim recognizes that this sentiment is borne out by the facts. As co-founder and executive director of AshokaU, she has seen many leading social enterprises and many others that flame out. A key reason: going it alone. According to data Ashoka has collected, organizations with co-founders are 60% more likely to succeed long-term than those with a single founder.

Invest together

COMPARED TO THOSE WHO CO-FOUND SOCIAL VENTURES, solo social entrepreneurs are emotionally isolated, under-skilled, and overworked; and they lack having someone equally invested in the venture who is always there to help work through problems and challenge their ideas.

When Dan Sutera speaks about entrepreneurship, he speaks from experience, having co-founded three tech businesses that provide essential digital services such as file sharing and confidential messaging. From this experience, he points out:

> When you look at the Y Combinators [an incubator for for-profit startups] and the for-profit side of things, it's very rare that you see a single CEO

that forges ahead. Two or more co-founders are the norm because it takes a great amount of energy and willpower to push forward every day. Look at Jobs and Wozniak, Gates and Allen, or Larry and Sergei. They all had co-founders.

Nor is this advice only for the tech crowd, or for-profit ventures. It is just as relevant for social entrepreneurs. Dan appreciates the crucial value of having a co-founder in subsequently launching his two Zambian social enterprises: Impact Network, a high-quality, low-cost educational system serving Zambian students; and Impact Enterprises, a for-profit company providing work-force development training and creating job opportunities for out-of-work Zambians (Zambia's unemployment problem is staggering: nearly two-thirds of all graduates are unemployed). Impact Enterprises arranges for outsourced work from large, foreign companies to create meaningful job opportunities for unemployed Zambian young adults. Dan reflects:

> When you have co-founders to lean on, you can help each other through difficult times and support each other emotionally, politically, financially – all of those things. I think it's really critical to have other key people on board that are equally as invested as you are. I think going it alone is very difficult.

When Dan first traveled to Zambia to visit a friend in the Peace Corps, he realized that the same tools and technologies that he used to provide services for businesses at home could also be provided to spur rural development in that African country. Yet his background had not prepared him for dealing with the decidedly poorer and lower-tech environment he found in Zambia, where power outages were common and coming in as an outsider required gaining the approval from both a tribal chief and the national Minister of Education. That is where his co-founder, David, made a great difference. Though not a Zambian, through his Peace Corps experience he had established meaningful relationships with a village, had learned the local language, and "learned about the culture – I mean, as much as is possible in two years." Most important was David's network:

> The network was through him and he really became good friends with a man on the ground, a Zambian guy named Daniel Mwanza who was the mayor of one of the towns – David likes to call him the Zambian Paul Farmer because he's just a really dynamic guy. Without that connection to really ground what we were doing and having that trustworthy – and trustworthy is really key – but also capable local contact to build our net-work from, it would have been really tough.

You or "yous"

The effort put into starting a venture can be so complete that it becomes difficult to remember that the focus of that work is the uneducated, the hungry, or those with little hope – not you. Sometimes, the surest way to work for "them" is by adding a co-founder – letting go of "you" *singular*, and becoming "you" *plural*. But only sometimes. The world of *for*-profit startups (where startups are almost two-thirds more likely to succeed long-term with a co-founder) resembles the social venture world in favoring co-founded ventures. CoFounderLab.com – a site devoted to helping people learn about and attract a co-founder, even online – explains that over 90% of high-growth companies have two or more founders.

Yet, even among straight-ahead for-profits, there remains a choice about whether to keep control of the venture you've created, or give it up in return for the likelihood of greater financial return.[1] In for-profit *social* enterprises, maintaining control may mean stronger social outcomes, even if profits suffer.

WHEN HIS COMPANY WAS QUITE YOUNG, Sanga Moses was approached by investors wanting to help him expand. He was concerned that they might insist on greater financial return by eliminating inefficient means of production, especially if they became part of his decision-making team. Yet Sanga's business, in ways that we will learn, came to rely on grassroots efforts of poor Ugandan women who used low-tech tools. That kind of "inefficiency" created economic and social value for their families and communities. Sanga resisted the temptation of taking the money so that he could retain control.

In other cases, giving up some control might be a valuable way to serve more people, right away. Jane Chen and Embrace (from Chapter 7, "Awards notwithstanding") eventually split off a for-profit company from the one that was founded as a nonprofit.[2] That led to investments by impact investment firms who provided money and advice in exchange for some ownership of the company. It also helped put Embrace on the paths both to providing more life-saving technologies for premature and low-birthweight infants whose extremely poor families had no ability to pay for the technology (the original market) *and* to other buyers who could afford to pay something.

Critical feedback

ADAM CARVER GOT THE MEMO about having a co-founder, but he couldn't find one: "A major mistake was not having a co-founder. I have asked people to come on board umpteen times. I haven't had any of them who's really bit."

The concepts underlying the credit card he envisioned touch on many ideas gaining popular currency. It's green – by raising money for clean energy. It embraces social finance – by allowing individuals to adopt a financial tool that contributes to societal well-being. It can be seen as a part of the "sharing economy" – where you share your unused credit card points with those investing in solar and wind projects (just like Uber-ites share their unused cars or Airbnbers share their unused homes). Yet, Adam describes how difficult it was for people to understand, let alone buy in to, what he was proposing:

> One problem I had is the way that I pitched the idea to different stake-holders. ... I pitched the idea as a concept that will change the world – a force for good that will inspire and ignite a movement. But I learned after a while that people don't want to be preached to, and that financers don't necessarily care about [non-monetary] green. ... I also learned that non-profits are skeptical and cynical about finance. That is just one mistake that I made.

He laments not having someone who might help him see his mistakes earlier, avoiding setbacks and aggravation: "[Because] I'm doing it alone and as a solo entrepreneur ... I make mistakes and I don't learn about them for months. I made small mistakes along the way and they compounded."

Building partnership

IF YOU RUSH INTO FINDING A CO-FOUNDER, you risk a partnership with cracks in its foundation. As important as what a co-founder provides – complementary skills, crucial moral support, a network that expands your own – is how co-founders relate. Building a social enterprise demands a shared vision, clear expectations, and, most of all, trust. Mary Lemmer, an experienced entrepreneur, describes her experience of starting a company with a co-founder she didn't know well.

> Even though we got along fine and everything, there's a level of trust and communication that you don't have with someone when you don't know them before starting a venture. Even if you want to solve a problem and you meet someone else that wants to solve that problem, before you go and solve that problem together, get to know each other.
>
> It's almost like a relationship. You don't just marry someone. You get to know them, you date, and you spend time together. Sometimes you get to know each other over a period of years before you take that dive.

Trust provides an opening for working through uncertainty, doubt, even fear – all of which will inevitably arise within any enterprise:

> It's really, really important to have a co-founder [and team] that you can trust with anything, because there are times when it's going to be hard. I mean, shit hits the fan, and you have to turn to your business partner and say, 'What are we going to do?'

Honest conversations also evolve from trust. Mary speaks candidly about the difficulty of having hard conversations with her co-founder: "There were topics that were always hard to talk about – like equity and ownership and roles. You bring it up and it wasn't this candid kind of conversation [but tentative and awkward]."

Expectations about culture were also left unstated, leaving that unsettled, too:

> I think if we had a good trusting business relationship, that would have helped in building the culture. We would have been able to talk about it more, and it would have been just one of those topics that came up easily.

If possible, every attempt should be made to lay expectations bare, perhaps especially when trust is less than complete. In the case of a for-profit venture, where there is the potential for financial return, many expectations can be spelled out in a formal business partnership agreement. The more clearly these are stated, and the more items they cover, the less the chance the venture will be hamstrung by unforeseen circumstances including: the opportunity to expand, one partner's desire to exit, the degree of effort put forth by each co-founder, and other potentially crippling issues.

A CO-FOUNDER CAN MAKE you smarter, prop you up emotionally, and do the jobs you can't. Add to that another network of contacts, and it's not hard to understand that co-founded social ventures are more likely to succeed. Yet, the choice of co-founder is vitally important. If there's not complete trust, remain solo. And never compromise your vision or values for additional expertise.

Notes

1 Wasserman, Noam, "The founder's dilemma." *Harvard Business Review* 86(2) (February 2008): 102–9. Retrieved July 9, 2018 from: https://hbr.org/2008/02/the-founders-dilemma

2 Chen, Jane, "Should your business be nonprofit or for-profit?" *Harvard Business Review*, February 1, 2013. Retrieved July 9, 2018 from: https://hbr.org/2013/02/should-your-business-be-nonpro

13 Team formation

Ross Baird, who funds and provides technical support to social entrepreneurs through Village Capital, knows that someone addressing an important problem with a good idea can still be successful even if he or she doesn't have any business experience; but they must be surrounded by a strong team.

> Figure out what your strengths are and build a team to fill in your weaknesses. There are some people who are terrific at sales, some people are terrific at design/user experience, and some people are great at engineering or coding – the nuts and bolts that make things work. It is very, very rare that someone will be good at all three of them. I would say if you were able to identify one or two that you're particularly good at and fill out the rest of the team, that's ideal.

School work to real work

The best classrooms provide a safe space to discuss history, analyze music, conduct scientific experiments, and create – anything from poems, to computer code, to ideas for social ventures. A classroom can become a safe refuge for many reasons: the guidance of the instructor, boundaries imposed by deadlines and the end of the semester, the provision of resources, and, at least at the college level, instructions so predictable that students can recite them in their sleep ("...now form teams that you'll be working with for the rest of the semester..."). Most social ventures that begin in a classroom end in a classroom.

But when students decide to make an actual "go" of their venture and the props of the classroom fall away, they don't glide effortlessly into the real world. The "*team* prop" that a classroom provides might seem the most likely to remain intact when a class is over. After all, a group of students who worked together well enough to want to continue their work for keeps should have something going for it.

It may not.

Embracing new roles

STUDENTS WHO BAND TOGETHER effectively as classmates to address real problems are, more or less, a haphazard collection of people working toward a common end. Despite their skills, if they transition into a real business there is no guarantee they will be effective as a team. A real-world team must have structure and defined roles.

Embrace began as school project out of Stanford. One of its early missteps was believing that its organizational structure might evolve more or less organically from team members' shared, sincere intentions to save the lives of low-birth-weight and premature infants. Jane Chen, one of Embrace's co-founders, explains one of the struggles her team had when it began working in earnest to address this problem:

> Putting in place a really clear organizational structure – that's really important. It doesn't matter if it's a for-profit or nonprofit. For any kind of organization, you just need a really clear structure in terms of roles and responsibilities and all of that. We didn't have that in place in the early days.
>
> We had four co-founders, and in the early days everyone kind of did everything. We didn't really have clear job descriptions, or a clear method for decision-making, or even reporting necessarily. And that eventually led to some frustration and lack of clarity. So I think it's important up front to have that very clear.

Jane offers advice that Embrace had received from one of its early organizational consultants: write job descriptions for each role your organization needs to fill – not descriptions to match co-founders' profiles, but to describe who would ultimately be the best person for the role.

> When you're building an organization, what should drive you the most is the mission that you're trying to reach, especially in a social enterprise. You really have to put your ego aside and think 'What are the qualities that are most important for this role?' rather than 'How can I force myself to fit into this function?'

Warm relationships

WARMILU ALSO PRODUCES AN AFFORDABLE TECHNOLOGY to save premature infants in the developing world. It, too, began as a school project, though a few years after Embrace and at a different university. "People problems" that lay comfortably beneath the surface during the class project rose less-than-comfortably to the surface when it became a business. Each team member's level of commitment was one of those "people problems." Grace Hsia, Warmilu's CEO, explains:

> Having five co-founders is very difficult, especially since we all began in a senior design group. Now, with a company, what happens is we're putting

in different time contributions and different amounts of effort because of the nature of the tasks, the time they involve, and other commitments.

This led to necessary, but difficult, conversations about money:

> When you're in a company, your work must be compensated. When you have two people, you can say 50/50. It's so much easier to have those conversations. … It became very clear that it's a lot harder with five compared to two, or one.

In the company's earliest stages, some co-founders worked outside jobs to support themselves while others didn't. This complicated questions about equity (stake of ownership of the company and thus benefiting personally from its success). After initially assigning equity based on the number of hours each co-founder worked, equity was awarded based on the perceived contribution of each member. Each co-founder divided the entire equity pie the way she thought was fairest. The average size of the slice a co-founder received determined her equity in the company. The openness of this approach led to important conversations about personal priorities, the value of everyone's efforts, and other issues that underlay current, and future, levels of commitment toward Warmilu.

HASHING OUT EQUITY was part of a larger process to create an effective, trusting culture. Money is almost always a tricky and touchy matter, since it puts a number on one's value and calls into question issues of fair treatment. These issues are not central to classroom conversations but become evident in a business, more so with multiple co-founders, and especially if they don't know each other particularly well. Grace comments on the need to manage personal tensions in a large team like hers: "You see more clashes in personalities and a lot faster" than when two people work out their differences. In a large team, people are always questioning: "'Why are you doing this?' and 'Why are you doing that?' Taking the time to build those personal relationships is crucial. It's something that we originally did not do."

When Warmilu began working on team relationships, it did so in a fashion that displayed unusual wisdom for such a young organization:

> Being conscious of growth – not just the company's growth but also personal growth – [is vital] because there is a huge team aspect to it. People can't be in a team without growing as a person, and that's something that we worried about. How are we going to achieve professional and team development when we're so young as a team?
>
> What keeps us together is this passion, this drive to be able to spread the warmth and save lives. Even if we want to tear our hair out, or we're really happy over a win that the team had, there's always the feeling that 'This is for the company, this is for saving infants' lives.' And that has helped bind together people who are very different.

Warmilu's mission to save infants' lives hastened both team members' and the organization's development:

> I think that we were fortunate in that, when you're working on something that has such an impact on people's lives, it matures you. It puts responsibility on you that you did not have before: to understand a conflict and to work the conflict in such a way that it's moving forward the cause. Then you're doing good, you're being responsible, and you're building – not just yourself, but the company – in a good way.

Organization structure: Benefit or crutch?

WELL-DEFINED ROLES AND RESPONSIBILITIES are imperative for any organization wanting to use its resources well, create a difference, and endure. But populating your organization chart too quickly can create problems. Parag Gupta, founder of Waste Ventures and another social venture before that, explains that creating your core team takes time – even luck. But getting this right expands the possibilities for your organization and creates greater certainty about its future:

> There's definitely some skill finding a core team. There's definitely team building, but I feel as if 50% of it's also luck in finding the right people to start something with you – who feel as passionately as you do and are willing to put in the time, the effort: the blood, sweat, and tears that's necessary.
>
> [A challenge in launching] is getting this team established as soon as possible and at the same time being really picky with who you bring on. ... At Waste Ventures I recruited for about six to nine months, and I'm still in that process. But we have a good core team now that can sustain [the venture] and accelerate it much further than I could do as an individual.

Parag's focus on finding an appropriate team is intended to insulate Waste Ventures from the fate of his previous venture, which dissolved when he left it: "One of my first learnings in creating a social enterprise was that, if it relies too much on [specific] people rather than procedure or operational structure, when key people leave, the whole organization cannot survive."

For this reason his preference has been for a carefully chosen core team plus relationships he establishes with local waste-collection groups that will outlast his own organization: "We're providing the scaffolding, ostensibly. But ideally they will run by themselves after a little time."

IN LIGHT OF THIS, IT MAY SEEM PARADOXICAL, but must also be stressed, that rote attention to team roles and responsibilities may thwart an organization's ambitions. Neglecting *how* you're doing things can cloud *why* you're doing them in the first place. Ed Cardoza of Still Harbor describes a growing Boston nonprofit he advised in which relationships were strained due to differences in longevity, blood spilt for the organization, race, class, and even being front-line or back-office. They tried to paper over these fraught divisions by perfecting the organizational structure.

> There was a lot of tension, and everybody was talking about roles and responsibilities. People always go for the least common denominator and then think there will be no conflict. 'If we just have a clean organizational structure, everybody will know the chain of command, and we'll have clear roles and responsibilities. Everything will be fine.'

Ed explained to them where the problem actually lay: in the false promise of structure, which led to them doing their work divorced from purpose:

> I turned and said, 'I don't think the question is about roles and responsibilities. ... I think you are losing sense of *why* this organization was created. I think you have absolutely no idea *how* [to act in alignment with the organization's overarching values and purpose]. You [only] understand what you are supposed to be doing because a plan was created that explains what needs to be done and how those things need to be measured.'

Resolving such difficulties with redefined roles and responsibilities is like creating music with a metronome – you get structure, measured and exact, but with no point, without heart. To create heart requires melody, harmony – "walking your why" (if you don't like that phrase, blame me, not Ed). Without that, there is no music.

Pluripotency

April Allderdice wants her employees to be pluripotent; she is delighted to have a pluripotent co-founder. This word is normally used in a scientific context and is possibly unfamiliar unless, like April, you're aware of the idea behind the 2012 Nobel Prize in medicine[1] describing how a mature, specialized cell (such as a nerve cell) can be genetically reprogrammed so that it can grow into a different kind of specialized cell – perhaps a muscle cell. April, as you now may have guessed, was trained as a scientist.

April's enterprise, MicroEnergy Credits, exhibits some of the complexity and specialization of a complex organism. It works simultaneously with microfinance institutions in locations as remote as Mongolia and with financiers at the center of the universe (at least in some of their minds); its product line includes simple, visible goods like solar systems for heating and lighting, and abstract, invisible credits tracked by sensors and traded over electronic markets. These all work together so that small microloans can be made to economically poor and energy-poor families in the developing world at affordable prices, because the carbon they avoid emitting from other fuel sources creates economic value people will pay for. MicroEnergy Credits benefited from having a pluripotent co-founder, particularly at its inception (and in fact most ventures would):

> The best part about my business partner is that he is a true entrepreneur, and so he's up for putting on any hat you give him. That is what you need. There was an NPR [National Public Radio] story about the Nobel Prize in medicine, about pluripotent cells. They're like stem cells. They're mature cells that become cells that can do any function in the body. You need pluripotent employees in a social enterprise. ... James [April's co-founder] and I joke about how much money we saved on his legal degree because he does so much legal work for us [he's not a lawyer]. ...
>
> I can't count the number of times that I've been grateful I have a partner in this, though it's not all roses having a partner. It's made the company a lot stronger and me a lot saner. Not to mention the fact that it was half his idea, too.

So, PLURIPOTENCY: where you simply reprogram someone great at sales to be great at engineering. Not so lucky? (Not everybody has a James.) Then think carefully about the roles you *need* for your organization, and not the roles that those already *in* your organization want to play: a big difference. Build a team for the long-term, as long-term as you can, and bring in people who want to grow with you. Create a meaningful division of labor, not chaos: develop an org chart. But never let its instructions on "how" to do your work obscure the real reason you're doing that work in the first place.

Note

1 "The 2012 Nobel Prize in Physiology or Medicine 2012: Press release." Retrieved July 10, 2018 from: http://www.nobelprize.org/nobel_prizes/medicine/laureates/2012/press.html

14 Hiring

HOWEVER OBVIOUS IT MAY SEEM, IT MUST BE SAID: invest the time to hire the best people for the jobs your venture needs. Your needs aren't anyone else's, so don't follow their hiring pattern or imitate their org chart. What do you need? Whether hiring in Kalamazoo or Kolkata, this will serve you. Hiring well means planning for the organization you want to become. You wouldn't short-change your planning, would you? Then don't short-change your hiring.

Talent is everywhere – look. Others share your values – talk. You may not know the hiring landscape – network.

Bad language, bad hires

LARGE CORPORATIONS CREATE JOBS our grandparents wouldn't recognize:[1] chief marketing officer, chief information officer, chief sustainability officer, chief people officer, chief listener, chief privacy officer, chief administrative officer, chief scientific and regulatory officer, chief quality and product integrity officer, chief strategy officer, chief digital officer, chief experience officer, and chief observance officer. And, of course, chief internet evangelist. How many of these jobs should be in your organization?

Kevin Starr, who has thought deeply about how to support and invest in social entrepreneurs, puts it succinctly:

> You don't need a CFO really early. You don't need a lot of people with a 'C' [for 'chief'] before their title. The main thing is actually understanding who you need and getting the right person. It may be one position. It may be a bunch.

He points to the example of Living Goods, an organization to which the Mulago Foundation, which Starr directs, has given more than $1.5 million in unrestricted grants in less than a decade. Living Goods uses a network of local women to provide public health education, diagnose diseases, and sell life-saving drugs, to combat malaria and diarrhea, as well as other disease-preventing products, including water filters and fortified food. By being trusted members of the communities that they are working with, these "health promoters" (whom Living Goods likens to door-to-door Avon Ladies) have provided critical "last mile" connections, bridging the chasm dividing effective health-promoting products and information from those who need them most but are too difficult to reach. As Kevin explains, the critical role that health promoters play was not understood when Living Goods began:

> Initially, none of us really understood the key hire for them – the char-acteristics of their key hire. The key hire for them turned out to be the village saleswomen, and who they needed to be and what characteristics they needed to have. They had pretty good generals in place already, but what they didn't know, and what none of us really realized, was you have to have dynamic saleswomen at the very foot-soldier level. And so that was their key hire. We had just never thought of it that way.

ACCORDING TO LIVING GOODS' WEBSITE,[2] randomized control studies have shown that child mortality has been reduced by 27% (at a cost of $2 per child) and the sale of fake medications (a trick too frequently played on poor commu-nities) has dropped by 50% thanks to its efforts. On top of this, Living Goods is creating good jobs for the health promoters they hire.

Mindful hiring

IAN FISK, EXECUTIVE DIRECTOR OF THE MENTOR CAPITAL NETWORK, KNOWS about business plans. He reads them for a living – hundreds and hundreds of them – along with the extensive feedback each is given as part of his organiza-tion's business plan competition. From this and following up with competitors over time, he knows that a strong team is extremely important if a for-profit social venture is to make it past its second birthday. He also has discerned how strong teams come about:

> It's not necessarily the way you think of it. I strongly suspect it has noth-ing to do with being a multiple-bottom-line business but is true across all entrepreneurs. It's also not 'Who are the individuals who are currently behind [the venture]?' It's 'Have they thought enough to know who they're going to need to be working with a year from now?'

Most don't, Ian continues; instead they prefer to determine the skills they will need on the fly:

> Many entrepreneurs believe, 'I'm just going to dive into this and then, when things change, I'll figure it out.' But, if you've actually thought it through, you might know who those people [whom you will need to hire] are, and you can keep an eye out for them as you grow.

He notes the statistical support for this observation: companies that anticipate their hiring needs are almost 0.75 points higher on a five-point scale, "which, on that scale, is a big deal. So, thinking about who they need to be working with in the future is the single most important piece, statistically [for obtaining a high team score]."

Basics of hiring

> We have learned to take our time on hiring because, if you make a mistake there, it's worth millions of dollars in time and energy.

THIS IS NOT A THROWAWAY COMMENT from someone who doesn't know business or how many zeroes are in "millions." It's a warning that comes from someone with years of business leadership who is as far from innumerate as could be: Steve Mariotti, founder of the Network for Teaching Entrepreneurship, before that an entrepreneur, and before that a treasury analyst at Ford Motor Company where he was lauded for his financial skills. He also has an MBA, a degree in business economics and, as a child, could do basic calculus. And multiply three-digit numbers in his head. Steve's four-part secret to hiring is as follows:

1. Hire the best:

> The difference between somebody who's an A+ in their work, whether it's a program director or a teacher or a writer, and somebody who's a C+, you can quantify it.

2. Spend the time to hire well:

> I used to view hiring as a waste of time. 'I've got to spend 12 hours of interviewing.' So I would just call people I knew and say, 'Do you want to come over and...' It was a big error. I didn't learn that [for almost a decade]. Every hour invested in interviewing, looking at resumes, talking and thinking about hiring reaps 100 hours in improved productivity, efficiency, and lowered cost. Half of what I do now is recruiting and thinking about who to put into different jobs and how to build a team so that you've got each person in the area that they're best at.

3. Forget about being the smartest person in the room:

> We try to hire up. When I go into a room, I like to know that 95% of the people there are smarter than I am. I have no ego in that. Ninety-five percent of what happens is determined by who is on the team.

4. Use your culture to your advantage:

> We've always tried to create a flexible work environment. I believe 72 people out of 85 on our executives are women. I believe we have nine

of our women executives who have children under five and work full-time. We have not lost an executive, I believe, after maternity leave in something like six years. We've tried to create a positive, family-oriented culture. It's how we compete to get top executives who want to raise families. And we're very careful to drive out discourtesy or anything that creates anxiety between people.

Away from home

WHEN CRAIG DEROY ENTERED A NEW TERRITORY, he depended on local knowledge. "We would go there and try to find the best people." I must add that he is talking about expanding his business as president of First American Title Insurance, and not Medeem, his African property protection business. In fuller context the quote reads:

> Rather than building our own title insurance shop in Poughkeepsie, we would go there and find the best people in town, usually acquire their business, take a stake in their business, keep them as owners and rely on them – because they knew their market better, to begin with, and they knew how to address their market.

And First American's approach in Poughkeepsie remained Medeem's approach in Ghana, and more recently Zambia:

> We started and stopped with their knowledge of that market, and I think that's something I came to Medeem with – relying on locals to help guide us as to the right approach for that market.
>
> It was all about the people. It was about who the principals were, whether they related well, whether we had the same philosophical approach in the market that's at First American. And the same is true when I went to Ghana.

Craig had no base of experience in Ghana when Medeem began. Finding the people he could count on depended on third parties:

> We had some really great contacts in Ghana, very senior-level, based on the relationships we had with CGI [Clinton Global Initiative] and with a couple of our early partners: Opportunity International [a microfinance institution] and ESRI [a provider of geographic information system tools].

Medeem leveraged these relationships to meet key local individuals to support its launch. "Advice like, 'You really have got to talk to Joe because Joe's the right guy. He knows this space and everybody respects him. He's well thought of. He's an honest broker' was indispensable."

Craig emphasizes that, in any business, and especially one on foreign soil, being humble and open is vital, and absolutely so in hiring:

> The only way you break through in these markets is to be a sponge and try to pick up as much as you can. ... Develop good contacts in the field you're looking to move into. Find people you can trust who will give you the benefit of their experience, and then find very good people in the geographic areas that you're looking to participate in. ... For us, this was particularly difficult because there was no predecessor [another company doing something similar].

The people the people you know know

MICROENERGY CREDITS, BASED IN SEATTLE, but operating continents away, knows the importance, and challenges, of finding the right people away from home: "In terms of fieldwork and finding people, we've had a lot of experiences – good and bad," explains MEC's CEO April Allderdice. To tip the scales in favor of "good," she relies on people she knows well to recommend those she doesn't know at all:

> We've primarily gone through networks of people that we know. When you're based in Seattle and you've got a team in Africa or a team in India, you have to trust them. That's the most important thing. I don't know if it's the right approach, but our approach has been to rely heavily on our personal networks: finding people that we really know, people that we know know them [those whom MEC hires].

MicroEnergy Credits also depends on successful relationships with small microfinance institutions in the same overseas locales. These are business partners, not employees, but they are integral to everything MEC does and are selected with the utmost care: "We definitely have vetting criteria that we understand will make them successful and to reach critical scale. They are really valuable field partners, and we treat them like clients. And that's so important."

MEC trains the microfinance partners on how to start lending for clean energy such as solar lighting systems, water purifiers, and efficient cook stoves, and connects them to funding from the carbon markets when they are ready. MEC helps them determine the best clean energy products to support as well:

> We provide customer service to them. At the same, we're bringing a lot of money to the table for them with the carbon funding, essentially, and [we're serving them by] providing our technical assistance.
>
> But it's a client relationship, and that's a relationship that I'm really comfortable working with. I have a lot of experience working with MFIs as a consultant, and I think it's a very dignified and respectful relationship. I think it can be very catalytic.

MEC bolsters its overseas work through its fellowship program. It hires young professionals, trains them, and gives them significant responsibility and experiences that help launch their social entrepreneurial careers. These hires create another layer of relationships between MEC and those it serves.

Talent is everywhere

WE HAVE MET DAN SUTERA in the contexts of intention (Chapter 4, "Intention for impact") and the benefits of co-founding (Chapter 12, "Invest together"), which helped him tap into local networks. He went to Zambia to travel, not to start a social enterprise, but, as we have seen, his friend David had served there in the Peace Corps, and that background, coupled with Dan's experience in technology startups, led to the creation of Impact Network and the subsequent launch of Impact Enterprises.

Dan and David launched Impact Network by leveraging David's relationship with Daniel Mwanza, a local mayor. Daniel was capable, trustworthy, and, equally importantly, local. The success of Impact Network depended significantly on Daniel's involvement. For about a year, Daniel worked for Impact Network on a part-time, volunteer basis. Then, to solidify their nascent organization, Impact Network hired Daniel and the team was built around him. He remains the regional director today.

Dan notes the realities of finding the people with the talent you need in a country like Zambia:

> One of the nice things about hiring local, depending on what level up the chain you're hiring, is that it tends to be cheaper. So, for instance, Daniel's salary is $300 a month and that's an amazing salary if you're living in a village. If you're living in the capital, it's a totally different story. ...
>
> [But] from an operations standpoint, we weren't able to find [enough] talent at the village level. We had to go to nearby towns and cities to find qualified employees to help manage the operations and run the schools: people that had graduated high school, not necessarily college, but were capable of communicating with us via email and Blackberry, and capable of filling out reports and that sort of thing.

Dan highlights the vast diversity in professional talent associated with different regions within the country:

> The human capacity issue there is a really interesting one, and I segment it into three levels. There are people in the rural villages, who tend to be farmers. In the towns you can find some of these professionals who are high school graduates, which is pretty good when you're in Zambia. And then if you go to Lusaka [Zambia's capital city], you can find the next level up, which is really professional – Master's degree professionals – who you can hire for $40,000 or $50,000 a year. They are just as good as people in

the U.S. that you would pay $100,000 or more. You can induce them to work in the villages if you pay them $50,000.

P.S.

EARLY-STAGE SOCIAL ENTREPRENEURS who don't have a ready-made network: take heart. It is possible to latch on to networks already in existence. ANDE (Aspen Network of Developmental Entrepreneurs) has members from more than 150 countries working to end poverty. Various social enterprise incubators and accelerators, such as the Global Social Benefit Institute, have well-established connections as well. Many universities and community colleges have scholars with regional ties who are ready and willing to provide advice. And there is no shortage of practitioner and academic conferences with reach into all corners of the world.

Vision attracts talent

AFTER SANGA MOSES LEARNED that his sister was skipping school because she had to fetch wood, but still before he quit his well-paying job, he wondered about his ability to pull off his vision of converting agricultural waste to fuel by creating the organization that was to become Eco-Fuel Africa. "I said to myself, 'I know nothing about this. I studied accounting. I've worked for a bank. How am I going to do this?'"

The answer lay in his ability to persuade – to persuade those with the right combination of skills and values to join him. The team Sanga assembled was diverse – ranging from poor, illiterate women who would use machinery to produce clean fuel, to university students and professors with advanced degrees who helped with technical challenges. The underlying approach Sanga took, however, was the same with everyone: building a foundation on an alignment of values.

> In my experience, the hardest [part of starting a social enterprise] is finding the right people. Once you find the right people, it's easy to find the right technology, the right model. The hardest part is finding people you can depend on, people who have the same motivation as you do, people who are honest.
>
> I've realized that many people: their biggest motivation is money, self-gratification. 'What's in it for me?' – And some of those people don't pass the test because it takes a lot of struggle to make an idea work, and sometimes the money doesn't come instantly. So such people quit easily once they realize that they are not going to make a quick buck instantly. They give up.
>
> So, finding the right people – who are willing to go an extra mile, who are willing to pay the price, who are willing to put what they believe in first and then care about the money later – is the hardest piece of the equation.

Despite at first having reservations about his own ability to identify and attract the appropriate people to his team, Sanga came to view this as "my biggest strength. Somehow I believed that I could find people who understand what I want to do, and then motivate them to join me to do this."

The people who Sanga succeeded in motivating to join him were given full measure of his trust. Not that this insulated Eco-Fuel Africa from all problems, but it created a climate conducive to solving problems and advancing the cause:

> Even now, I don't know how to build the entire machine because I have people that I have trusted and they believe in what I do, and I give them everything that they need and the trust. They make many mistakes, and sometimes they put me in so many problems because they spend more than what they budget ... But the most important thing is I trust them and I let them try and fail and try again. That's how we manage to [progress]. ... I trust people who have the skills and give them an opportunity to use them.

Notes

1 Goudreau, Jenna, "C is for silly: The new C-suite titles." *Forbes*, January 10, 2012. Retrieved July 10, 2018 from: https://www.forbes.com/sites/jennagoudreau/2012/01/10/c-is-for-silly-the-new-c-suite-titles/#21408cf22a01
2 https://livinggoods.org

15 Compensation

Looking to hire the best when you can't pay the best is a hard circle to square. But if your organization actively lives its values, you become a welcoming place for others to express and explore values like yours. And if working for you is a springboard to other opportunities, that also makes you attractive. Some social enterprises may explore non-monetary compensation, too.

Compensation: Values

Social enterprises invariably pay less than companies offering positions with equal responsibilities, whether in manufacturing, retailing, banking, or almost any other industry. For a job seeker holding a more lucrative offer, choosing to work for a social enterprise means placing meaning before money. Some do it, but as a professor who has counseled many talented students facing exactly that situation, I know that many more don't.

Startup social enterprises rely on a variety of strategies to compensate for not being able to offer hefty salaries. We will explore some of these strategies in the remainder of this chapter.

Sandy Wiggins, whom we first met in Chapter 2, "Are you a social entrepreneur? (Take two)", urges that your mission and your values be harnessed to create advantages in all aspects of business, even attracting talent. An accidental social entrepreneur, Sandy began his career in the construction industry, where he quickly advanced from crew member to foreman to running his own company. This was a prelude to the next several decades, during which he chaired the U.S. Green Building Council and was instrumental in helping develop its widely hailed LEED certification system. More recently, he has become involved in the construction of net zero buildings and even entire communities – projects that through intensive conservation and onsite, renewable generation are able to produce all the energy they require. He is also a leader in the "social finance" revolution, knowing that communities will never be whole until financial services truly serve everyday people and not simply those already with access to money. Sandy sees the guidelines he adheres to as the foundation for personal and business success:

> As we learn to act more responsibly and sustainably in our business and daily personal lives, not just environmentally but socially, we get happier. And that's what it's all about, right? Don't compromise. The most important thing you can do at an early stage is to clearly articulate your vision and your values – your guiding principles – and make those your touchstones for everything that you do. Keep coming back to them.
>
> And, if you do that, you'll be successful. It'll draw the people to you that you want to work with. It'll bring joy to your business, and as a result, you will be successful.

Compensation: Experience

Nigerian computer whiz-kid 'GBENGA SESAN recognizes that what he cannot offer his employees in salary he might make up for by the experience he is providing. Growing up poor in Akure, in the south-west of Nigeria about 500 km from Lagos, he was denied access to computers and mocked for even thinking he might be able to use them: "The computer teacher was much taller than I was, so he literally looked down at me and said, 'Sesan, a computer is not for people like you. You can't understand how to use computers.'"

From that point forward, 'Gbenga devoted himself to learning all he could about computers and, eventually, sharing what he knew with other poor Nigerian students. None of this was easy. "At my first computer school, we were given typewriters, not computers, to learn on because there were very few computers, and they didn't want us to break them." His training then escalated to writing programs in the BASIC programming language – on paper, still not on computers.

Yet he persisted, excelling to the point that he became Nigeria's first Information Technology Youth Ambassador, and later became a member of the United Nations Committee of eLeaders on Youth and ICT (information and communications technology), where he was especially involved in work on ICT and African youth. "I sort of became, in quotes, an expert on IT development and youth because I was young, so I had a fresh perspective." Over a six-year period, he traveled widely, speaking both to university students and less-well-heeled audiences, including one group in Lagos's best-known slum, Ajegunle:

> When I completed my usual training, the questions were different. The usual questions would be like 'How do I program in Java, or Cobra, or Python?' But these questions were 'So, my younger sister needs money to go to school. How do I make money to send her to school?'
>
> That influenced my training model. So my training model wasn't [any longer] just about tech-tech-tech: it was more about tech and

entrepreneurship, using tech to create value so you can earn an income. And that became the primary thing, because I felt that was where I was much more needed.

'Gbenga founded Paradigm Initiative (PI), a social enterprise that addresses the questions and concerns of students like those he met in Ajegunle by providing training in information technology, entrepreneurship, and life skills to help youth lift themselves out of poverty. PI works with youth in Ajegunle through a three-month intensive program and has also reached more than 50,000 young people across Nigeria with one-day or two-day training programs. 'Gbenga has opened the doors for those young people that have completed PI's training:

> People who have gone through the training tell stories; some of them got scholarships to go to an event in Zambia, and I can relate with them. One of them got a job with the UK High Commission in Abuja [Nigeria's capital city].

His employees flock to Paradigm Initiative because of the opportunities it generates for them. "Everyone who comes to work with the organization gets a lot of experience." Which also poses the perennial challenge for social enterprises:

> We have a human resource challenge because we do not have enough resources to pay them as much as, for example, banks or telecommunications would pay them. It's only natural for them to look at all the opportunities and all that. I want PI to pay as well as any organization anyone would want to work in. But, of course, it takes resources to make that happen.

'Gbenga knows personally the thrill of overcoming challenging circumstances:

> The first time I got on an airplane – I won't forget the date, November 11, 2001 – it was life-changing. I said to myself, 'Here I am, the young person who was told by a teacher I could never understand how to use technology, and I'm the same person who is invited by an international organization based on my knowledge of computers and what I thought could be useful in the future in terms of African development.'

His employees now see that same emotion lighting up the faces of the disadvantaged youth for whom they create opportunities through their efforts at PI. That is its own form of payoff.

Non-monetary economics

EVEN WHEN THEY ARE STRAPPED FOR CASH, social enterprises can arrange compensation using alternative economic approaches. One of these is timebanking.[1]

Timebanking involves doing an hour of work to earn an hour of timebanking credit, which can later be spent to receive an hour of work from another member in the timebanking system. It is a form of exchange that values labor that may not otherwise be compensated (say, driving a neighbor to a doctor's appointment) and which allows people to pay for services (tailoring, for instance) with their time instead of money. A software system lists what work is on offer and tracks credits that are banked for work performed, or spent for work received. It is not barter (and therefore not taxable) and does not depend on direct swaps between two individuals.

Derek Ellerman, serial social entrepreneur and adviser, describes how timebanking might be used to support a social enterprise:

> A system could be set up to leverage powerfully the work that [a social enterprise] is doing, doesn't involve money and, instead, taps into people's passion for the issue and for the community that you are creating for them. It's a really important option that early-stage social entrepreneurs should be aware of.

Timebanking may make enough difference to attract those who can't afford the time to work as a volunteer. "It allows you to set up an ecosystem that is potentially a lot more sustainable, even if you don't have the money [to pay providers] at all." Providers can be skilled professionals such as doctors or nurses, people who receive training and then provide a service such as helping people fill out their income tax forms, or people with a resource like a car that they can use to take the elderly on errands:

> You can create a pure volunteer system, but you could also set up a timebanking system where the people who are providing those services can essentially exchange services with the people who are receiving them [in the system]. That's a really basic example.
>
> It can get scaled out pretty significantly with very little funding. It's a really important option that a lot of people aren't aware of. And particularly in the populations where [social enterprise] work is happening, you often are dealing with other people who, like you, are in an early-stage organization and don't have a lot of money either [and who thus would be attracted to timebanking] and can extend the ecosystem further.

It's important to think about alternatives to standard currency transactions.

Hiring expresses values

AT THE TIME WE SPOKE, Mark Hecker had very recently moved his business out of his apartment into a separate office. More recently still, he had hired his second employee. To both of them, he offers health, life, dental, and vision insurance, and a retirement plan. I wonder about his striking concern for his employees' welfare. I ask him, "Was this a difficult decision for you, given that you could have easily justified not doing so, and could have decided to use this money for program activities instead?" His response reveals a philosophy of building a team that was expansive yet practical:

> For me it wasn't. I've always been a long-term thinker, and I think we need to build an organization that people are going to want to work at. On a separate level, I think the benefits [I offer] are really a values decision. I think a lot of organizations start off on a shoestring and say, 'When we get more established we'll start offering better benefits.' But you never feel like you have enough money. You'll never at some point say, 'Oh we have extra money. Let's increase those benefits now.'
>
> The conversation [I had with my board] was not 'How much money can we spend right now?' The question was 'What message do we think is important to deliver to employees that work here?'
>
> We wanted an organization where people want to work, people want to stay, and people want to support. The reality is that it's better to budget for what you actually need, and then perhaps you come up short, than to try to budget on a shoestring, and be cutting out the vision of what you actually want it to be.
>
> We want an organization that supports the individuals that work here, so that's how we're going to plan. And now it's my job to make sure we have the resources to support that vision.

Note

1 An idea whose early major proponent was Dr. Edgar S. Cahn, who created TimeBanking in 1980. See https://timebanks.org/about.

16 Volunteers

AT SOME POINT FOR EVERY SOCIAL ENTERPRISE, making use of volunteers is likely a necessity. But will that become a blessing or a curse? Well-designed volunteer programs are valuable for provider and recipient. Haphazard programs create chaos for organizations and leave volunteers disenchanted. Well-designed programs choose volunteers selectively, train them well, and use their talents well.

Local talent is not voluntary talent

LAST MILE HEALTH USES a series of "accompaniers" to bring needed health services and vital health information to those in the poorest and remotest parts of Liberia. This process is a cornerstone of Partners in Health's much acclaimed health delivery model,[1] where trained community health workers supplement the care provided by terribly scarce physicians and other health-service providers. They literally accompany individuals through the processes of learning about, preventing, diagnosing, or treating their illness. Indeed, Paul Famer, who co-founded Partners in Health, provided inputs from his experience with accompaniment in treating patients in Haiti to help Last Mile Health establish its own model in rural Liberia. Peter Luckow, co-founder of Last Mile Health, talks about his organization's reliance on accompaniers:

> The majority of our accompaniers are front-line health workers we hope will remain in the communities in which they are from. That does a couple of things, one of which is they're better-suited. They know the community better. They know the resources in the community so they're better able to provide care in the context with which they're familiar.

For reasons of both practicality and fairness, accompaniers are paid:

> One of the biggest challenges that the global health field faces in terms of community health workers is the issue of retention. Organizations will train health workers to do a vaccination campaign or give public health talks, and though they ask them to go off into the community, they often don't pay them; they don't value what they do for the organization. And

what we have seen in Liberia is that, when community health workers are not paid but instead asked to volunteer, retention rates are shockingly low – 0 or 5% a year.

We think it's crazy to expect these poorest of the poor in places like Liberia to volunteer their services and then to be shocked when they actually get a job and decide not to come back the next year to be a health worker.

For us it's about both selecting them from the community in which they're from and then paying them to do those services. We treat them just as we treat the rest of our staff in terms of monthly payments and access to the services and privileges that come with being an employee, just like our finance assistant is treated or our program director is.

Why would anyone volunteer?

WORKING AT A SOCIAL STARTUP: a warped board and two milk crates for an office, responsibilities that unfold like Venetian blinds, a work environment that alternates between too much to do and complete frenzy. Volunteering at a start-up: same description, but without pay. The best social enterprises determine how to build strength around their volunteers.

Volunteer structure

VOLUNTEERS CREATE GREAT VALUE – OR CHAOS – all depending on how they're organized and managed. An unfortunately large number of social entrepreneurs with whom I spoke described their experiences with volunteers as "break-even" at best: the effort they put into finding, training, directing, correcting, emailing, and even coddling volunteers was just about repaid by the good they did for the organization. And then there were the less fortunate ones.

For some social entrepreneurs, the situation could not have been more different. Their volunteers became essential contributors, the value they created far exceeding any disadvantage they caused. A major explanation for these different experiences lies in how volunteers' work was structured.

DEREK ELLERMAN AND KAT CHON, co-founders of Polaris, you may recall (Chapter 7, "Burning your social enterprise"), became increasingly appalled by human trafficking the more they learned about it. They committed themselves to doing all they could to create a world without slavery (mostly focusing on sex trafficking and labor trafficking), but as a startup lacked the staff and budget to match their ambitions. They addressed these deficits through the skillful use of volunteers. Some organizations accept as volunteers anyone with reasonable skills who sends a resume their way. Others wait until they need someone to do a job (perhaps website design) that they don't know how to do and then put out feelers for volunteers. Polaris's approach was 180 degrees different.

From its earliest days, Polaris relied on its fellowship program to develop and put to work a skilled workforce whose capabilities matched its particular needs. Fellows at Polaris are entirely unpaid volunteers, but it is worth pointing out that fellowships with other social enterprises may offer stipends, typically ranging from tiny to small. (To understand their size, they may provide enough money for volunteers to live abroad but not to save.) Derek explains the philosophy of Polaris's fellowship program:

> The world of getting resources to your organization early-phase is the world of getting volunteers and creating an incredible program – where people can really commit to being a part of your organization, and work there part-time or full-time. And having it not just be an internship program, but something far beyond that: a really powerful, valuable experience for people who make that kind of commitment. You don't need a lot of money, or any money oftentimes, to be able to create a program like that. The return that you get in terms of talent and passion and the people is huge for an early-stage startup.

The level of commitment among Polaris's fellows was in proportion to the value they received:

> [The program] is totally unpaid, but we gave them real work and real responsibility and actually allowed them to work on the front lines of the issue. ... The central thing to focus on is the value that you are providing the people who are putting their time in. The fellows we had run through the program were incredibly committed. They would work full-time and more than full-time. They would waitress in the evenings to pay for it. There's a level of really incredible commitment because we provided tremendous value both at the professional level in terms of [in-depth] training on the issue and a chance to do real-world work – not shuffling papers and getting coffee and things like that. Actually working in the program, and helping develop the programs. The culture was a very empowered culture, and there's a lot of freedom and responsibility that goes with that. We really believe in our people.

Polaris also admits fellows by classes, three classes a year, each lasting less than six months. The cohort structure contributes to the sense of belonging they feel:

> The other huge piece that is really critical is the community. We have such a close-knit community in the program, where it's not just you come into work and leave, but you really bond deeply with all the people you're working with. We always do a lot of social events and oftentimes, especially in the early days, people would work late at night together. There are tremendous community-based, belonging-based rewards [from] being part of a program like that. When you are doing social change work, it's not just about the issue. A lot of it is about the community in which you

are doing the work. To be very purposeful about creating that is a big part of making it work.

The fellowship program at Polaris created a workforce far beyond what Derek and Kat could do by themselves: "Early on, there were two paid staff: Kat and I. But, functionally, we had more capacity than any other trafficking organization in the D.C. area at that time, just because of [our fellowship program]."

The fellows program remains a backbone of Polaris:

> One of the reasons we were successful early on is that we developed a fellowship program that provided really in-depth training, mostly for college students and other folks who would otherwise be doing just an internship. … In the last ten years we've had about 400 fellows, three classes a year, and each class usually is from ten up to 20 fellows.

Select and train

A WELL-RUN VOLUNTEER PROGRAM enjoys its pick of applicants. At Polaris, 100–150 people might vie for just ten fellowship openings. To select the ten, Polaris uses a thorough interviewing process and then checks all references. As Derek Ellerman explains:

> It would almost be like hiring someone for a job. We put a lot of time in on the front end to make sure that we got people who not only were super-passionate and had the type of personality and character that we wanted, based on our own organizational culture, but who were really high-performers.

Polaris's selectivity is amply rewarded. Fellows can be given freedom and responsibility, truly extending Polaris's workforce rather than tagging along for the ride. In addition, less supervision is necessary than otherwise would be required:

> It's still a significant time commitment, of course, working with everyone. But, if you organize fellows into teams, natural leaders often arise, and fellows are all supporting each other and helping each other. In a sense it's almost easier [to have a team]. With a team of multiple people supporting each other and working together, it takes some of the burden off of [managing fellows].

As A COLLEGE SOPHOMORE, before she formed Health Leads, Rebecca Onie noticed over and over again a missing element of patient care: patients might be prescribed an antibiotic, but they also needed food, a place to live, heat, or a warm coat – none of which physicians could provide or even had the background, authority, or time to respond to. Even at hospitals with a better-than-average ratio of social workers to patients, there was such a bottleneck that patients' non-medical needs went unattended: "As recently as 2012, in the clinic at Boston Medical Center [where she first observed the problem], there were only two social workers for 24,000 pediatric patients, which is actually better than a lot of the clinics in which we work." Even at the very best hospitals in terms of numbers and quality of social workers,

> they pretty much don't do follow-up except in crisis – in domestic violence or child abuse. That's just not part of their protocol because if they were going to try to follow up with all the patients who need follow-up, they would be utterly swamped.

Health Leads' solution: create a program to fully address patients' social-health needs by filling doctors' prescriptions for the very things they ordinarily wouldn't prescribe, such as housing and food. And have ample staffing to remain in touch with patients until Health Leads finds the resources within the community to meet their needs.

For much of its history, Health Leads' on-the-ground workforce was all volunteer, and all college students, each of whom supported about a dozen patients a year. "It is quite time-intensive to see a family through from the initial intake and needs identification to securing the full set of resources that they need, and that requires a high-touch model." Though this extraordinarily high ratio of staff to patients presents a bottleneck to rapid expansion, it has done nothing to lead Health Leads to lower the standards for the volunteers it accepts into its program or the requirements once they join.

When she founded Health Leads as a student, Rebecca rejected the idea that volunteering should only require a few hours a week (and then only if you could squeeze them in), no training, and, in truth, was "something that never happened but will look really good on your resume." She prefers the metaphor of a college sports team:

> College sports teams are in some ways the ultimate in volunteerism. They say, 'This is going to be 20 or 30 hours a week, 6:00 am, six days a week, at some terrible field all the way across campus. And you're probably not even good enough to make the team. We're going to look at your performance and your team's performance and we're going to kick you out if you don't show up, or we're going to kick you out if you just don't perform.' There is a rigor to it, but also an investment made in the athletes.

At Health Leads, the rigor begins with the application, where up to nine in ten applicants are not selected as volunteers. "Recruitment is so critical, not because we're looking for college students who have years of experience doing this work, but college students who have a deep conviction around these issues and an appetite to learn." Once selected, volunteers undergo 16 hours of training before they ever set foot in a clinic. The training ensures a deep understanding of cultural competence and a thorough understanding of the resource landscape in the community. Health Leads develops some of its training content, but like other effective and efficient social enterprises, borrows from others whenever it can:

> We're certainly not the only organization that works to connect low-income individuals to community resources, so we have tapped their training to create our own Advocate Boot Camp ... My general approach on nearly every aspect of our model is there is enough that is hard about what we are trying to do, so that if there is any work, training or otherwise, that someone else has developed already or is better at [than what we are doing], we should be using their approach. It's incredibly opportunistic and also paired with real humility that it doesn't have to be proprietary and internally developed in order to be excellent.

Once in the clinic, volunteers receive day-to-day oversight and support from full-time staff with case management and social work experience, who themselves are supported by the Health Leads Reach™ platform, which monitors progress in delivering resources and allows them to better support volunteers. Every detail is important to volunteers' success: "We've spent a lot of time looking at what's the ratio between number of clients to a volunteer, and then number of volunteers per paid staff person."

Your team in the cloud

LISA BALLANTINE, you will recall, used the internet to identify and contact a ceramics expert when the antibacterial coating on the filters her company made was washing off. The internet also became a major tool for developing the volunteer workforce that undergirded the growth of her organization FilterPure. Lisa believes that FilterPure should grow organically, finding people with a passion for clean water, who would commit to the cause despite not being paid:

> As people begin to catch a heart for what you're doing, they begin to sign up and they will participate. They will give themselves to it, but they won't be motivated by the money. So, if the money runs out, you're still going to have them there. We have sort of a loose [hiring] plan. We have ideas of what we need, holes in the organization, but we wait for people to come on board because they love what we do.

Lisa uses the internet to reach out for those "with a heart for water," attracting volunteers who might fill some organizational holes, among them recent MBA graduates. As they put in their hours to prove themselves, they may be offered paid positions.

LISA RECOGNIZES HER OWN EFFORTS are linked to other clean water efforts around the globe. People in the developed world, she believes, must be empowered to advance the cause:

> To know that they can make a difference in the lives of the people around the world. That their input [is needed], not just money. That's the thing that we need to understand as nonprofits. The money will be there if people's hearts are in it. We need to show them how they can make a change.
>
> So many think, 'How could I do that? I don't live there. I don't [have the needed skills]. I don't know anything.' But you can make a phone call, you can put something on Facebook, you can tell people about [the challenges of clean water], you can learn about water, and you can affect the water in the United States. There are so many things that we can do here that we're not doing.

Note

1 Kidder, John Tracy, *Mountains beyond Mountains. From Harvard to Haiti: The Remarkable Story of One Man's Misison to Cure the World* (New York: Random House, 2003).

17 Training

BUILDING A TEAM CAN FEEL like fitting a multi-dimensional jigsaw puzzle together. You need skill on your team, sure. But must it walk in through the front door? Commitment to the cause may seem non-negotiable, but what about someone not as fully versed in your cause as you are? You want all-star talent, but have a minor-league budget. What can you do?

The organizations we see in this chapter show how training can be effective in addressing these challenges – among both well-educated professionals and semi-literate community members, in the world's every corner. Training can both build on one's existing experience or identify those with aptitude and talent and meld them into essential employees. Aptitude may lie undeveloped, until it blossoms through training.

Rooted in business

ROOT CAPITAL IS A FOUNDING MEMBER of the ANDE, a network of organizations that support entrepreneurship in low-income countries. Root Capital bridges the worlds of small farmers and major agricultural buyers, including Starbucks and Green Mountain Coffee, through its use of creative social finance. Most smallholder farmers are beset by problems that prevent their rise out of poverty: including inadequate knowledge, lack of money with which to invest in better farming methods, and, not least, access to global markets which pay far better than local communities. The importance of agriculture in the developing world has been widely noted, especially in terms of number of people employed and often in terms of overall national economic output.[1]

Root Capital believes that the key to lifting these farmers out of poverty is supporting small and growing local businesses that then support the farmers. Small and growing businesses – often supplier co-ops – have a degree of sophistication and market clout unlike the farmers themselves. Here is an example of how Root Capital might work with one of these co-ops:[2]

Root Capital makes a loan to the co-op, but only after the co-op has a signed agreement from Starbucks (or another larger purchaser) who promises to buy an agreed-to amount of coffee (or another agricultural product) from it at a specified future date. The co-op may then make small microloans to its farmer-members – loans they may use to buy higher-quality inputs or that provide some income to tide them over before they sell their coffee to the co-op. After harvest, the co-op receives farmers' coffee and sends it to Starbucks. Even before it is paid itself, the co-op uses funds from the loan to make partial payments to farmers when they turn over their coffee crop (lest they sell it to someone else). Starbucks eventually pays Root Capital (not the co-op) for the coffee the co-op provides. Root Capital takes the money it is owed, totaling the amount it lent the co-op plus interest, and sends the rest of the payment from Starbucks to the co-op. The co-op, in turn, pays farmers the balance they are owed for the coffee they have supplied (less what they may owe from any microloans). The timing and structure of these loans and their repayment lessen the risks and provide other benefits to all parties: Starbucks, the co-op, coffee farmers, and Root Capital.

But the training that Root Capital provides is just as vital. Via seminars, workshops, and other means, Root Capital advises the co-ops (and other small and growing businesses) it supports. This training includes financial management, in areas such as accounting, financial planning, cash management, and financial reporting. This support helps the co-op's day-to-day efforts and, just as importantly, it helps the co-op grow, reduce its risks, and be better positioned to receive a bank loan. Through partnerships, Root Capital may also arrange technical assistance in areas such as agriculture, marketing, and client relationships. These also strengthen co-ops' operational and financial strengths, enhancing their business opportunities.

Adaptive hiring

When Craig DeRoy built his small team in Ghana, he recruited for specific skills but also something more ineffable. Medeem, his new company, was embarking on an effort to provide property-rights protection to base-of-the-pyramid landholders:

> It's not at the level of formal government registration. That's not our job or our capability. We're not providing a title insurance product because we're not saying, 'This is yours.' We're just saying, 'Here's the evidence based on what you presented and that we've been able to collect based on neighbor interviews and other information [to make your claim to your land supportable].' Some interloper coming in arguably won't have that same documentation and will be at a disadvantage to simply displace you from the property.

Though the protection Medeem would offer would not be legally binding, Craig knew someone with a legal background in land rights would be essential:

> I knew we needed expertise in land rights, and so I started to ask and met some land lawyers. I found an individual who really was excited about the

notion of Medeem and who I thought would be a great leader, I guess is the best description, for starting an enterprise. Using his legal background was essential to understanding where we could bring our program and help serve the population we were looking to serve most effectively. He's now our country leader.

Because Medeem would be documenting land boundaries, that, too, was a skill Craig recruited for:

We also realized we needed technical expertise, so I looked for the best person I could find on a personal level – who had the strongest credentials but would work well with the team, saw the vision, embodied all that. So we got a technical surveyor to help us as well, and we built a team around [the two of] them.

SELLING WATER OR SELLING SOLAR COOKWARE: these are difficult sales, at first, when people are used to obtaining, for free, water from muddy rivers or dung for cooking fuel. More difficult is selling something like insurance, a service you always pay for but may never use, or use only on a distant future date. Medeem's land documentation services were like insurance in this regard, and maybe more mysterious to potential customers because of its use of high-tech gadgetry like GPS and its technology for digitally capturing and storing information. So it fell upon Medeem to sell not only its property certification services but the very need for them in the first place. Like those selling water, solar, or insurance, Medeem needed to create a market for its services where none existed.

What are the qualifications for a job you're making up for a product that doesn't exist? Craig continues, explaining how an individual with related experience could be given the necessary background and skills to play a key, new role:

The third member of the team was 'field.' We needed someone who really knew the field, so we went to the microfinance world and I found someone to lead that who is a remarkable young man. So we have three key core individuals.

I ask him to clarify the relationship between microfinance and Medeem: "You approached the microfinance world because they understand the landscape, not because you're offering microfinancial services, right?" Craig's response offers confirmation:

Right. It's because they understood the clients we were seeking to serve, and they already had sort of broken through, understood what their needs were, knew where they lived, knew their concerns, their opportunities. And we were also seeking a way to bridge the gap, see how we could fit into a more existing framework, because we're offering a brand-new product in a brand-new way. So the more we could assimilate with existing product lines and businesses, the better we'd be.

AT MEDEEM, where his core team was three people, no less than at First American, where Craig was president of one of the largest title companies in the United States, the rules for success were the same:

Anywhere you're operating in the world, it all comes down to people. You can talk about the metrics, you can talk about operations. It really comes down to the people, and the ability to choose the right people may be the hardest thing in business. You can be wrong in a lot of other ways and it will get resolved well if you've got the right people. If you have the wrong people, every problem becomes a big problem.

Learners and rockers

APRIL ALLDERDICE EARNED AN MBA and used to work for McKinsey, a premier management consulting firm. She knows the value of business skills and certainly does not shy away from hiring those with business degrees. But it is not a requirement.

Her organization MicroEnergy Credits looks for populations around the world who rely on high-carbon, low-tech, costly, and often unhealthy sources of fuel for heat and lighting and creates relationships with microfinance institutions to convert their clients to users of cleaner, more economical fuel sources. MEC has established relationships with microfinance institutions in various locales, including India, Mongolia, Uganda, and Kenya. For a young company, especially, operating in such far-flung geographies practically demands hiring individuals who can be counted on to work effectively and independently.

MEC's fellowship program is particularly important in providing this capability: "The fellows program is like McKinsey meets the Peace Corps," explains April. (Her co-founder's service in the Peace Corps, plus April's at McKinsey, suggest that this is not pure metaphor.) As soon as MEC signs a partnership agreement with a microfinance institution, it sends in a fellow to that locale. That person plays a key role, including managing MEC's profit and loss. Each fellow operates with autonomy, conducting what amounts to business "experiments" which, in turn, give MEC critical feedback about how to become a stronger company:

There were a lot of things that went into developing the fellows program. What we realized was that we needed a really smart problem-solver who was a really open-minded learner, and didn't have to know anything about microfinance or clean energy because we could teach them that. We needed a fast learner who is curious, can pick an idea up and then contextualize it, and find out how it really fits in with that microfinance institution.

Fellows are typically young professionals with some work experience who are eager to understand social enterprise. "They are standouts: they've really shown that they are problem-solvers or go-getters." They receive training to make them "really responsive to our structure, so we have structured learning materials, structured steps to follow, structured PowerPoints and spreadsheets and business models and market research formats."

Chosen few

WHEN SHE WAS AN INVESTMENT BANKER working on mergers and acquisitions, Katherine Lucey's colleagues arrived from select colleges with already-developed technical skills. In rural Uganda, Tanzania, and Nigeria, where she presides over Solar Sister (an organization we learned about in Chapter 2, "Mission, not profit, lights the way", and Chapter 10, "Learn"), the pipeline for talent could not be more different, yet the necessity for talent more similar.

Solar Sister empowers women to become entrepreneurs who sell solar products to African villagers. Katherine recognized that lighting could lift families out of poverty by increasing their productivity. To get lighting to them requires identifying, training, and supporting the right women to become entrepreneurs. "Our biggest challenges and most important accomplishments are recruiting, training, and retention – keeping them engaged."

Katherine quickly dispels the idea that all poor people in the developing world are cut out to be or want to be entrepreneurs:

> Finding the right women who really have this desire to be an entrepreneur, to be a businesswoman, and to run a business is challenging in environments where the ecosystem is very aid- and development-oriented. The kind of marketing and business and enterprise and entrepreneurship [that are central to being a Solar Sister entrepreneur] is not natural for everyone. So what we have to do is find those women who really get it, and really get that this is an opportunity for them, rather than [merely] a task.

Solar Sister does this in stages. First, it works with local women's groups to get referrals.

> Our first partner was called the Mothers' Union – that's like the church ladies of Uganda – out of the Anglican Church. In every little community, there's going to be a Mothers' Union committee, and it's a women's committee.

Even then, these referrals must be regarded with caution, since referrals may be for the most senior woman in the church, or someone who it is felt is owed a favor, and not necessarily the most promising entrepreneur. "So we try to help educate and train them, and help them help us select the right women."

Prospective entrepreneurs then submit an application. Solar Sister scrutinizes each one to try to get a sense of applicants' entrepreneurial potential: "They don't have to be extremely literate, but there does need to be an ability to maintain records and run a business. So there's some level of bookkeeping and business-keeping that's important there."

Next, Solar Sister meets with women and gives a presentation about the responsibilities and opportunities of working for the organization, followed by an interview. Those who make it through the interview process must give Solar Sister a small commitment fee to separate those who really want the opportunity from those who are less committed. "It's not a big commitment fee – not something that would prevent even someone who is in that level of income or non-income [from taking the next step]." All this gets you a trial with the organization:

> Then we have a trial period. We provide a training program, a training day, and after that training we have a one-month trial while they are a candidate. It's through that trial program that we really do sort out, because it turns out that people either are quite good at this and see the opportunity and are really eager and bring a lot of commitment to it, or don't. So that sorts things out pretty well.

Those women who survive the cut are registered as representatives of Solar Sister and given another full day of training, covering Solar Sister's products, salesmanship, record-keeping, and the like. A regional coordinator continues to follow up with each entrepreneur with ongoing mentorship, holding monthly meetings to provide more in-depth training on some aspect of the business – whether on better communications, or disassembling and cleaning or repairing a solar product.

Solar Sister's goal is to allow each woman to rise as far as possible, to fulfill her potential and increase her income (and, of course, help light Africa). For some entrepreneurs, this means understanding and selling more sophisticated products (such as plug-and-play solar home systems); for others, repair and service; and for others still, evaluating and creating custom designs. ("In your house you want four lights, you want to be able to run a radio, and you want a little solar refrigeration unit. You need 120 watts.") Katherine sums up how Solar Sister nurtures entrepreneurs:

> Our philosophy is to find the women who have that hunger to learn more and do more, and take this opportunity. And, if they demonstrate that, we will invest in them. We will provide them with more training and support, access to the supply chain, and access to capital. What we don't want is to have 50 women who are all sitting there passively at their desks, waiting for us to tell them how to get the motivation to do business. They've got to bring something.

Notes

1 International Development Association, *Agriculture: An Engine for Growth and Poverty Reduction* (IDA at Work series, 2009). Retrieved July 10, 2018 from: http://siteresources .worldbank.org/IDA/Resources/IDA-Agriculture.pdf
2 Based in part on Milder, Brian, "Closing the gap: Reaching the missing middle and rural poor through value chain finance." *Enterprise Development and Microfinance* 19(4) (October 2008): 301–16.

18 Culture

EFFECTIVE SOCIAL ENTERPRISES ENLIST employees' hearts and minds. Effective social enterprises engender trust and prize cognitive and emotional diversity. Effective social enterprises take a long view, helping sow their employees' future, while reaping the benefits of that support today.

Organizational software

ORG CHARTS = HARDWARE.
CULTURE = SOFTWARE.

While roles and responsibilities may be wired in, it is personal connections, relationships, and attitudes that determine whether an organization reaches its potential. Keeping people happy and engaged – creating a workforce held together by a sense of connection, contribution, and meaning – is even more important to a social enterprise than to a traditional enterprise, where greater perks and salaries can be strong bonds.

Zachary D. Kaufman (Chapter 3, "Immerse yourself") certainly understood this. At the organization he founded, American Friends of the Kigali Public Library (AFKPL), no one has ever been paid, and no one is full-time. What binds them into a workforce is largely Zachary himself. In a ten-year period during which he founded his enterprise, he was keeping busy: working full-time for the U.S. government; moving to Oxford for a doctorate; working part-time for three war crime tribunals; getting a law degree; and writing his first book (about Rwanda). "All of this about the library was on the side," he says. Yet Zachary still created a high-touch organization where he was the focal point:

> The organizations that I'd been involved in before starting AFKPL were quite hierarchal. ... What I learned from this experience was that people didn't want that.
>
> Everybody who was involved wanted to be in touch with me directly. They wanted to have conversations. If they wanted to have a briefing

about Rwanda, they usually wanted that to come from me. They wanted to get feedback from me on their work product.

Volunteers' preference to be connected to Zachary in their support of the library was not textbook-efficient, but it followed a strong logic:

> I thought that we would be able to structure [the organization] more [hierarchically] with committees, committee chairs, and so forth, but I quickly learned that there was a limit to that. Part of it was because, among the people who joined, many of them were my own friends and family. And if people join an organization for those personal relationships, they often want to do it so that they can spend time with those people. So that made sense to me. It wasn't very efficient, but it did make sense.

Even as the project progressed, Zachary saw the need to keep these relationships front and center:

> As we got larger and larger, I found that a higher and higher proportion of my time was spent on recruiting people, training people, reviewing their work, providing feedback, keeping them happy – all that stuff. Basically, if everybody is just in it as a volunteer, and as a part-time volunteer at that, morale is critical.

Zachary recognized that to keep morale high he also needed to spend a great deal of time sharing information:

> not just the challenges that we were facing, but also obviously good news. People mostly wanted to hear it directly from me, and so I found that actually a huge proportion of my time – and I didn't anticipate how much – was spent on these efforts.

Like them. Trust them. Be yourself.

WHAT'S ONE WAY TO CREATE an engaged culture in your social enterprise? Liking your team.

> Listen to your gut: it matters. It helps you, especially when you're working with other people. If you have a feeling about another person and that feeling is a negative one or [gives you] a tinge of discomfort, don't do it. Work with people who excite you.
>
> (Saul Garlick, ThinkImpact)

It's hard to have that excitement when there's a lack of trust (though hyper-vigilance and agitation may produce some excitement of the wrong kind).

Trust clearly underpins an effective team culture, and it cannot be taken for granted:

> The biggest learning for me is be a lot more careful about how I choose my team and who I surround myself with, because trust is fundamental, and it has to be authentic. Trust isn't built in a day.
>
> (Mary Lemmer, TerraPerks)

Valuing authenticity and vulnerability over pretense and posturing will create a more resilient culture. Recall Peter Luckow's explanation of why literature, poems, and art lend to the humanity of the organization he co-founded to address glaring health care needs in Liberia:

> They have really allowed us to very directly create better programs, create stronger strategy, align our moral compasses and organization.
>
> (Peter Luckow, Tiyatien Health)

Think different

A MIX OF TRUST, GENIALITY, AND AUTHENTICITY may bring a team closer together, but it leaves out a key ingredient of culture: diversity. Diversity can be separated into two types. One is cognitive diversity: the intellectual differences that characterize the perspectives, approaches, and available models we each possess to solve problems. The other is preference diversity, which corresponds to our values rather than to cognition. Scott Page has written about the superiority of cognitive diversity to individual brilliance in problem solving.[1] With the complexity and nuance of societal problems, cognitive diversity may be required to create headway, even if it means working with others with varying commitments to a cause.

MARY LEMMER CREATED A BUSINESS that would make money by getting people to use less energy. It relied on combining knowledge of behavioral economics, skillful use of social media and online rewards, and negotiations with utility companies. Alas, she was too early to the game for this business to succeed, but her attempt led her to realize that you might need to work with people with diverse skills and perspectives, but less passion than you have for the cause you are championing:

> Social entrepreneurs need to find that diversity on their team and in the ecosystem they create with mentors and advisors so that people ask those hard questions. The best way to do that is to not narrowly define what you're doing and what you're trying to accomplish. You have a mission. But there are a lot of elements to the problem you're trying to solve. [Suppose] there is a product element and you want to hire technical talent. You're not always going to sell them on, "We're saving people in India." You have to really think outside the box, and the best way to do that is to surround yourself with great people.

Emote different

JERRY WHITE EMPHASIZES the need for diversity in emotional tenor and disposition among members of a team. He explains that an organization dominated by a single personality type will necessarily be out of balance, and thus ineffective. The language Jerry uses is reminiscent of a playwright, actor, or theatrical producer (which he was during his childhood in New England) rather than being the hard-edged business-speak that often borrows from the military ("strategic advantage," "hostile takeover," "capturing market share"). Which might seem odd given his unavoidable connection to war – as a peace activist, landmine victim, and anti-landmine negotiator at the international level.

Jerry notes the stark contrast between Bill Drayton's personality and his own. Neither of these is "right" or "wrong" for social change work; you need them both, and others. Among other extraordinary achievements, Drayton founded Ashoka.org, the pre-eminent organization for supporting social entrepreneurs. Jerry, as you will recall, has been an activist and leader on the world stage:

> What's missing in this social entrepreneurship play is: where's the balance of your cast? It's the casting of the leaders, and then the balance has to show up in your strategies and in your teams. ...
>
> Drayton is a very strong 'air,' or analytic, and a thought leader. He is a lead professor, an analytic teacher, but that is not sufficient ... Where's the fire? Where's the earth? Where's the watery flow?

He explains how these other attitudinal elements must be there, too, to build an effective team – and ultimately even to create a movement (though that's a topic for later):

> You also need fiery leadership: those would-be advocates who like to lead campaigns and make change happen and break out of the box. Then you need watery sustaining conditions, those people who flow in and around. The type of people who sustain and nurture success. Then there are the earthy people who are always saying, 'Can we get practical right now and just do it? ... We can't talk about it to death.' ... Balance is essential. ...
>
> You cannot run your organization with ten Bill Draytons or 17 Jerry Whites. They will all fail. For every Bill Drayton, you need a Jerry White, and then you also need a this and a that and a lot of other things to make sure that the team happens.

Inward and outward

ED CARDOZA, THE SPIRITUAL–SECULAR ADVISOR to social entrepreneurs at Still Harbor, notes the frequent contradiction between the outward and inward behavior within social enterprises:

> There is high likelihood that, if people are vulnerable with one another and build systems of trust within their organization, they will

be unstoppable. But the weird thing that I've discovered is this: if you are an organization that takes care of the most vulnerable with love, compassion, and mercy, the likelihood that, at some point in the life of your organization, you will create a staffing environment that is not about mercy, compassion, and love – but actually the antithesis of those things – is pretty high.

What he is describing is an organization's culture: the values, norms, and practices that create what it feels like to be part of an organization and determine its effectiveness. Doing good is not enough to create a positive culture. Consider how the aspects of culture revealed in the following examples make a workplace safe or threatening, fair or unjust, susceptible or immune to influence, which Adam Grant states are defining traits of an organization's culture.[2]

As we saw, when they founded Polaris, Derek Ellerman and his co-founder worked with such intensity that they verged on emotional exhaustion (Chapter 7, "Burning your social enterprise"). Then they demanded the same when others joined the organization. You may recall Derek's rationale: if you see countless babies drowning in the ocean, you believe at first it's your job to save them all (as it is with victims of human trafficking, Polaris's mission). But, as you exhaust yourself with each rescue, you realize that you, yourself, will die if you act without regard for your own health and safety. Any organization built like this will be drowning from a sense of inundation. Happily, as the leaders at Polaris began to take better care of themselves, and looked out for the emotional well-being of their workforce, they became a more effective organization, rising to the level of a national leader in preventing human trafficking.

Ross Baird, now the president of Village Capital, describes his early career:

I had a mentor who asked me my very first day of the job what my dream job was, and what I wanted my next job to be after [the current] one. He said, 'I've managed 10,000 people in my life. I've found the biggest motivator of people in their current job is where it will get them next. It's my job to make sure that the next thing you want to do, if you're indispensable to our company, is something different or with greater responsibility within our company.'

That culture, one based on merit, meant working hard is both noticed and rewarded. A culture like this is fair in the way it promotes and lets people take control of their careers.

Health Leads, where Rebecca Onie uses an army of volunteers to staff the "social prescription" desks within medical clinics, provides a pathway to employment within that organization for interested, especially talented volunteers. But more important, as Rebecca explains, is how the experience at Health Leads prepares volunteers for related careers:

> A number of [former volunteers] are practicing primary care physicians and are very much still involved in Health Leads' work. They routinely come and participate in conversations that we're having about how to structure Health Leads' strategy. They also are really important evangelists. They explain, 'Even with all of the years of medical school and residency, this was the defining aspect of my medical career. My work now is an expression of that.'

Someone who volunteers at Health Leads is not "just a volunteer." Rather, she is someone volunteering in a safe (but rigorous) program, one that demands persistence and resourcefulness to fill prescriptions, and which actively nurtures the idea that what we do matters – because it does.

CULTURE ARISES IN MANY WAYS, but not, as is often thought, just by having a foosball table or "casual Fridays." Norms are key: Polaris's founders modeled working yourself to exhaustion, and that became the expectation at the organization. Values are just as important: Ross Baird's mentor's interest in his dream job let him know that personal development, and not just producing results, was of great importance.

We can also view culture as arising from organizational processes. Effective organizations establish processes that create positive motivations for work – a sense of engagement, working with purpose, and unleashing potential; and they stay clear of processes based on negative motives – emotional pressure, financial pressure, or simple inertia, as described in a *Harvard Business Review* article by McGregor and Doshi.[3] These authors assert that culture is the sum and interaction of processes that affect employees' motivation to perform.

From this vantage point, we can say: role design (a process) at Polaris was highly destructive. Until Polaris changed the way it (implicitly) defined the demands placed on those working there, emotional pressure was rampant, as maintaining a healthful personal existence lived in the shadow of acting from the unproductive (and unhealthful) emotional pressures of fear, despair, and guilt. Career advancement (another process) was exceptionally healthful where Ross Baird began his career. It coupled strong performance with unleashing potential. Ross is today living his dream. Creating organizational identity (yet another process) is vibrant at Health Leads. Staff and volunteers are coached to see the purpose behind their work and to recognize its connection to future opportunities for service. Thousands of former volunteers are themselves today socially conscious health practitioners or leaders in often related fields.

Notes

1 Page, Scott E., *The Difference: How the Power of Diversity Creates Better Groups, Firms, Schools, and Societies* (Princeton, NJ: Princeton University Press, 2007).

2 Grant, Adam, "The one question you should ask about every new job." *New York Times*, December 19, 2015. Retrieved July 10, 2018 from: http://www.nytimes.com/2015/12 /20/opinion/sunday/the-one-question-you-should-ask-about-every-new-job.html

3 McGregor, Lindsay, and Doshi, Neel, "How company culture shapes employee motivation." *Harvard Business Review*, November 25, 2015. Retrieved July 10, 2018 from: https ://hbr.org/2015/11/how-company-culture-shapes-employee-motivation

19 Mentors

MENTORS PROP YOU UP and tear you down, know more than you and learn from what you tell them, are long-time confidantes or one-time acquaintances. And you need them.

Others' shoes

IF THERE'S A SHORTCUT TO BECOMING A SOCIAL ENTREPRENEUR (and no one I spoke to claimed there was), it might be having a mentor. How you find one and use one are up for debate, as is even what a "mentor" means. But on the fact that they are vital there is strong agreement. This is a typical comment:

> One of the most concrete things [to prepare yourself] that really has huge value for people starting out is getting a mentor or someone who has actually done it. A social entrepreneur of some kind to individually mentor you and who you can call up with whatever your issues and problems are and have them walk you through it. There definitely are all these resources out there − books and different things − but there's something that's a huge value at a level of just real practicality you get from directly talking to someone who's walked this path before.
>
> (Derek Ellerman, Polaris)

Your mentor is good at what you are not:

> Management is a weakness I've been very aware of since starting the company and am actively trying to get better at. It was always something I brought up with mentors and asked for their advice if they were people that were in big management positions. I wanted really concrete kind of tips or advice on management and I got that.
>
> (Ashley Murray, Pivot Works)

Your mentor may make you uncomfortable:

> The first advice I'd offer is that it's critical to have at least two, but ideally more than two, folks who will tell you the things you do not want

to hear. I was really lucky to have mentors early on who evidenced their investment in my success by being really honest with me – both about my own leadership and about what would be necessary in order to achieve impact – and who would significantly challenge my thinking. And I think often those can be folks where you feel like, 'I actually don't really want to know what they have to say,' but if you bring them in, you are just radically more likely to be successful. So that's number one.

(Rebecca Onie, Health Leads)

You can't blame your mentor:

You need to be thinking independently and critically for yourself. It's not that they're going to tell you what to do and you're going to listen to them and just do what they say. Rather, a mentor is just a really good input to have amongst your many different inputs when you decide what you want to do. What you think is best. That's a game changer for a lot of people.

(Derek Ellerman, Polaris)

Don't be arrogant about what you think you know. But when you listen to somebody who is supposed to know more, simply because they say, 'Because that's the way it's done,' don't do it that way.

(Bena Burda, Clean Clothes Inc.)

One mentor or two?

WHAT CAN MENTORS AND ADVISORS do for you and your social venture? This is a partial list, based on what I heard. A mentor will:

- Listen.
- Provide emotional support.
- Tell you you're wrong.
- Confirm your hunches or more developed ideas.
- Offer technical support and expertise.
- Explain IRS filings.
- Provide constructive criticism and feedback.
- "Stress-test" your ideas.
- Be there when you need to reach out.
- Show you the ropes of running a business.
- Break you down, then build you up.
- Help you change your mind.
- Offer a different perspective, possibly from a related field.
- Tell you "No."
- Show you how things *really* work.
- Place you in their ecosystem.
- Help you enter a new geography or country.

- Help you know you're not crazy.
- Help you transition from "maybe if" to the real world of practice.

Does this sound useful?

AND THIS IS WHY social entrepreneurs typically have not one but many mentors and advisors. And why, with a co-founded organization, each co-founder may have several of her own.

Who's your mentor?

SINCE MENTORS ARE SO VALUABLE, it's somewhat surprising to find a lack of consensus about what a mentor really is. Jessamyn Lau of the Peery Foundation, shares a strong starting definition:

> I heard somebody describe the ideal mentor as somebody with grisly experience and empathetic listening skills. I think that's a pretty good summation: somebody who's going to be not only useful but somebody who you will want to work with as well.

Grisly experience would include "someone who has created an enterprise, who has struggled with it, who has been challenged by meeting payroll, who has walked the floor all night," as Jim Koch of the Global Social Benefit Incubator describes an effective mentor. It would exclude consultants, educators, foundation officers, and others who have worked closely with social enterprises without having started or run one. When empathetic listeners learn that *you* have been walking the floor all night, they react with genuine concern, even if they then launch into helping you correct your faulty business mechanics. Some venture capitalists who offer advice can fail the empathy test.

MENTORS' ADVICE COVERS the full gamut of what it means to be a social entrepreneur. Some may suggest fundamental changes to your business logic, as Ashley Murray, co-founder of Pivot, describes:

> I got some advice from one of my first mentors, who remains a mentor and is someone I'm in regular talks with. He said to me, 'You really might want to reconsider going from the pilot stage you've been working at to the stage of handling 1,200 tons of fecal sludge a day producing 70 tons of fuel [the stage Ashley was contemplating]. Isn't there a middle ground?'

He detailed the downside of going from pilot to full scale: since Pivot had never generated any revenue from converting fecal waste into fuel, the only possible way to raise the money necessary to fund the venture at full, commercial scale would be to hand over a huge stake in her company to investors:

> He really pushed me to come up with a middle stage requiring a much smaller amount of money [from investors] that would allow us to achieve

some really significant milestones that, assuming we achieved them, would make it much easier to raise a true Series A [venture capital funding]. And to do so without giving up as much of the company [in stock] because at that point we'd [be a more valuable company due to having a track record of sales].

OTHER TIMES, a mentor may just help you learn how to use a spreadsheet.

Wise moments

Sanga Moses rose from a homeless childhood where he raised himself to attending the nation's top university, living in the capital city, and working in a corner office at a bank. Yet he most values a "mentoring moment" from an unlikely source:

> The best advice that I've ever got came from a surprising source: a home-less man who asked me for a few bucks. And I didn't want to give him money before I knew who he was, because I didn't want to feed a drug problem. So I asked him for his story, to know how he got there and understand him as a person. And he told me, 'I have no story.'
>
> So I sat down with him and asked him, 'If you had an opportunity to change your life, to live your life again actually, what would you change?' And he told me something that totally changed my life. He looked at me, I saw tears in his eyes, and he said, 'Young man, if I had an opportunity to do it again, I would love more, give more, and care less about what other people think about me.'
>
> And that hit me, because those three things are dream stealers. Many people chase becoming rich and forget true love and people that are important in their lives. People who don't really love the community they work with and try to take everything from their community and never give back, they end up having a lot of money and nothing to do with it. ...
>
> Many people told me that [creating Eco-Fuel Africa] can't be done. Many people would ask me, 'Who do you think you are? Who is your father? Where do you come from? What does he do?' I would say, 'He's homeless; he doesn't have a job. So what?' You think people would stop attaching your value to who your father is and where you come from and what kind of background you come from. So if you don't really care about the perception of people towards you, I have discovered that you can go a long way.

Facets of support

MARINA KIM OFTEN BUMPS into social entrepreneurs. From her work at Ashoka, where she founded AshokaU, she knows that one trait of a successful social entrepreneur is having a role model or mentor. Role models and mentors are not the same, of course. The difference can be striking, yet both serve important roles. As Wanjiru Kamau-Rutenberg, director of African Women in Agricultural Research and Development and a social entrepreneur herself, explains:

> There's this really cool distinction that we're working with in Akili Dada [the social enterprise she co-founded to support young African women]: the difference between a role model and a mentor. A role model is someone you look up to who doesn't know you exist. Oprah is a role model for me. The way she has managed to acquire power and use it for good: that's a role model. A mentor is someone who cares about you and who's investing in you.
>
> It's important, then, for young people to have both. You're looking at the way they are living their lives and their authenticity. You're looking up to that and you're learning lessons from that.

She knowingly adds, "It's not going to be everything. Do not copy-paste somebody else's life.

Advisors play another overlapping role with mentors. Mentors, as I am using the term, lend their experience and offer advice, but with the overriding aim of supporting the social entrepreneur, even in times of difficulty. Advisors bring specialized skills or perspectives to a social enterprise. And, especially if they have a financial stake in a social enterprise, may connect failure with vulnerability. And possibly withdraw their support.

MARIA SPRINGER CO-FOUNDED LIVELYHOODS, a nonprofit sales network that arranges for poor Kenyan youth to sell clean energy technologies to lift themselves out of poverty. She knows well how advisors' expectations pressure you to paper over difficulties, and that one way for dealing with this tension is through peer mentoring:

> I have an advisory board and close mentors. But, in other cases, I rely on co-mentoring with other social entrepreneurs so that we can open up about things that sometimes you can't even open up to your close advisors about. When you're the CEO and the executive director of a company, sometimes you just have to hold it together – even if you aren't – because some of those great advisors you have want to be there for you; but at the same time people want to support successful people. I think it's very important to make a distinction between your advisors and mentors and co-mentors and friends. And make sure you have them all.

Maria's perspective – expressing vulnerability only to some of those who offer advice and support – was echoed by many, but not everyone. Nikki Henderson (now Nikki Silvestri), leader of a social enterprise working on issues of social justice, explains how she tired of making distinctions between those with whom she could be free to express herself and those she could not:

> Some people are able to maintain the different groups, but now if I don't have an advisor that I'm able to be completely transparent with, then I feel like at some point we're going to get to a very difficult conversation where I need advice on something that they can't give me because they can't go there. And, really, it's also because in this work in particular – justice-based work in a community of color and a low-income community – things that happen here are too urgent for folks that can't open their heart. I just don't have time for that.

Get your mentor – Now?

IN THE BLUSH OF EXCITEMENT at starting an organization, adrenaline (probably lack of sleep, too) may seduce you into overlooking your deficiencies. Next, you despair at the depth and breadth of what you don't know. Finally, you realize that it's time for a mentor. Though not a social entrepreneur, Jacob Harold describes his start as a program officer at the Hewlett Foundation in a way that applies to those who start enterprises:

> There was the honeymoon period of six months where I just was having a great time, traveling around, meeting with people; and then there was the six months of, 'Oh my God. I really don't know what I'm doing: I'm totally unqualified for this.' And then it kind of moved into a transitional part – here are the things I have to change about the way that I do my work in order to succeed. I just came to see my weaknesses ... I realized it gets back to humility. That you have to be humble and say, 'I need help on this. I need a coach. I need to build on my strengths and address my weaknesses.'

Who's your mentor?

THERE ARE MANY WAYS to find a mentor. One person's advice about how to find a mentor collides with another's. The opinions that follow suggest the broad spectrum of strategies to obtain support.

Ross Baird explains that mentoring can't be forced; it must evolve. Ross has been on both the receiving and giving ends of mentoring relationships, from his early work in education and social venture capital to leading an organization offering social venture capital and business support:

> Ask for advice all the time. Ask for advice from other entrepreneurs, ask for advice from funders, ask for advice from senior people at organizations you respect. You'll find if you get good advice you'll go back and keep asking. If you're a founder of a company, the only way that you can get

a good mentor is ask lots of people for advice. [But] you can't ever say, 'I want you to be my mentor.' That just happens.

CHARLIE CAVELL, FOUNDER OF THE WORKFORCE DEVELOPMENT organization Pay It Forward, once found a stray business card, as you may recall, and used its contact information to strike up a key relationship with a state of Michigan economic development organization. It may not surprise you, then, that he was equally adventuresome in seeking out mentors. I ask him if he had ever cold-called someone with the intention of obtaining a mentor:

> Yeah – John Van Camp, the CEO of Southwest Solutions. I emailed him and said, 'My name is Charlie and I do this thing called Pay It Forward, and I would love to listen and learn from you. I understand that you're probably busy, but if you have 30 minutes on one of these days coming up in the next two weeks, please let me know. I'd be more than happy to sit with you and get to know what you do better.'

Southwest Solutions is a mainstay in the south-west section of Detroit, serving the city for more than four decades. With a $50 million budget, it serves more than 25,000 citizens annually, offering more than 50 programs in areas such as mental health and wellness, education and youth services, housing support, economic development, and neighborhood revitalization. To say that John Van Camp is busy and in-demand is an understatement. So I ask Charlie what became of the email he sent: "We now get coffee every four to six weeks. In fact, what day is it? On Monday at 11:30, we're going to have coffee."

Charlie had reached out to John because Southwest Solutions was a leader in the same sphere of social services as Charlie's own organization. Although its budget was more than 100 times as large, it offered 50 programs to his one, and it counted its history in decades to his organization's months, they were concerned enough about Charlie to have him sign a non-compete agreement. For Charlie, John may have been "the one" (as another social entrepreneur described the ideal mentor she was hoping to find); at the very least, he was one of the ones.

Menteeship

WE DO A DISSERVICE BY DISASSOCIATING environmental problems from the problems of poverty. Yes, when we think "green" the tendency may be to conjure up mountains, forests, and rivers. And when we think of poverty, we may think first of urban decay, the need for jobs, and workforce development. And that apparent separation only widens when we believe we can address only one or the other at a time. In fact, the two are tightly linked. They are linked in that environmental problems plague the poor in urban areas in the forms of pollution and lack of green space; and in rural areas in forms of spoiled rivers and streams on which livelihoods and healthy lives depend. Not to mention that, rich or poor, we will suffer the same fate from unchecked climate change.

But poverty and the environment are also linked by the constructive potential to address them both at once. Van Jones co-founded the social justice organization Green For All to broaden the environmental movement to create inclusive, "green collar" jobs to help lift people out of poverty. These include jobs to weatherize housing, install solar panels, improve water infrastructure, and so much more. None of these can be outsourced, either, and thus they lock in livelihoods.

Nikki Henderson served as Van's executive aide at Green For All. "I had a front seat, and I saw more of him that year, I think, than even his family did. We were attached at the hip." She had a Master's degree, but he made her "staple things." She was an expert in public speaking, but Van didn't want her exercising those skills. He instead saw the raw potential he needed to mold. As Nikki explains:

> He told me, 'You're attractive, you're charismatic, and you're colored, which means that people are going to fall all over themselves and cater to your every need, and you have never put your time in. You have never had to do administrative work, you've never had to actually pay attention to detail. All of the things that hone an activist and sharpen your steel, you've never had to do, so you're soft. People like you that never have to put in their time end up becoming egotistical monsters, and that's completely unacceptable to me because you have real potential.'

If this sounds demanding, it was:

> I went home crying every other day not only because the job was hard, but because he really took the mentorship stuff seriously. Driving him to one event, we would get into a conversation about my ego and how it's actually the worst kind of ego to have because it does this and this and this and that. Or an opportunity that I missed when I wasn't taking notes was because of a particular leadership glitch that I have. He broke me down every day.

"Was Van's mentoring effective?" I ask, fairly certain how she'd answer: "It's the only thing that gave me the ability to do the job. I'm really clear about that." Nikki became the executive director of Green For All, executive director of Oakland's People's Grocery, and founded a venture aimed at food justice and then her own consultancy to help change systems and people's internal worlds. I ask her if Van remains her mentor:

> We don't actually communicate that often – maybe two or three times a year. But I feel like the way that he is still a mentor is that I still follow him very closely, just in media and with what his organization is doing.

[Van went on to serve as President Obama's green jobs advisor, is active in criminal justice reform among many other issues, and is a frequent political commentator on television.] And he connected me very closely to a lot of the people that are in the next ring outside of him.

A lot of the things that he taught me at Green For All I wasn't able to apply then, and so I find myself very often teaching things to my team that were things that he taught me that I just didn't have application for until now.

Moments, lifetimes

MENTORSHIP MAY BE A FLICKER:

I attend a lot of conferences. I engage in a lot of conversations and I find that 'mentorship moment' all the time. Mentors don't have to be aware of their mentoring, and I think this might be another lesson for the millennials: pay more attention to the substance of mentorship instead of the form of it. You hear something wonderful, you ask a question, you get the answer you want, and that's mentorship.

(Yuwei Shi, entrepreneur, social entrepreneur, and scholar)

But recognize that mentoring relationships can last many years:

All those people that circled back and said, 'Did you meet with this person I suggested?' or, 'Did they get back with you?' or, 'How are things?' I wanted to grab hold of them. Margaret Mead's quote about never underestimating what a group of small dedicated people can accomplish[1] – it's not, 'Never underestimate what one person working by themselves can accomplish,' right? It's that small group, it's that team, it's those champions. So, yeah, I want them with me.

(Charlie Cavell, Pay It Forward)

Note

1 "Never doubt that a small group of thoughtful, committed citizens can change the world; indeed, it's the only thing that ever has" (Margaret Mead).

20 Networks

THE "BIG BANG" THEORY OF NETWORKING might be: continually expand your universe of relationships to embrace more people, more organizations, more societies to receive sage advice, pertinent skills, and even hugs. You may not be looking to solve the cosmological constant problem, but just want to understand your taxes. Expand your network.

Network of support

CHARLIE CAVELL WAS BY NO MEANS the only founder who cold-called a prospective mentor (or advisor). But a more common way is by reaching out through a network of relationships. By attending trade shows, conferences, lectures, business plan competitions, and business incubators and accelerators, your Rolodex keeps growing (even if you've never spun a Rolodex in your life). Every entry is a prospective mentor. Perhaps of more importance are those they can connect you to, as Ashley Murray indicates:

> Relationships are so, so important, [as is] finding your champions. Because of a boss I had at IMI [a research institute], I got connected to the Gates Foundation and got to present my business model to them, got hired to do a consultancy, and then subsequently got this grant from them. I never would have had that connection [on my own]. Build relationships.

Ashley, who can be a cold-caller when her network's direct and indirect connections fail her, shares that most people you reach out to are willing to help:

> Most business execs, if you call them up, are going to be happy to talk to you – I've really found that. And I know I do. I get emails from people all the time: other people wanting to get into sanitation, or students at Berkeley that are [beginning a social enterprise]. And I'm totally happy to set up a Skype call with them. Yeah, we're all really busy and I think people appreciate that, but most people say, 'I want to help you.'

So I would encourage [cold-calling]. I send emails totally out of the blue to people I've never met before but are people I need to talk to. Usually you get a response, so I wouldn't be afraid. Ask – you just have to ask. Be willing to put yourself out there, and even if it seems a little awkward, just go for it. The worst you get is ignored or a 'no.'

Ashley's experience – that others are willing to make time for a conversation with someone they've never met, with that conversation possibly leading to a more enduring relationship – was echoed again and again among those I interviewed.

Relationships

WHERE YOUR TEAM ENDS is a matter of opinion. Is your team just those you pay? Your volunteers? Others? The most inclusive definition suggests an organization extending far beyond the walls of your office to include anyone with whom you have meaningful interactions. Here is an example of "team" viewed in this way. In the most remote reaches of Liberia, villagers are disconnected from the health care that they badly need. It takes extraordinary effort to reach them, let alone serve them adequately. As you recall, an organization that does so is Last Mile Health (formerly Tiyatien Health). Its co-founder Peter Luckow describes its diverse set of actors and the key roles each plays:

The idea is a really a novel partnership between clinical support staff in the U.S. and others like myself working with very community-oriented, community-rooted, humble, small organizations. We talk about it as almost working on the two margins of our global society. One of which is the poorest of the poor – the most marginalized, neglected population in Liberia; and, here in Boston, on the other end of the margin, with some of the best-trained, best-networked individuals who are providing health care in some of the finest hospitals in the world.

Despite their impeccable credentials, the Boston crew plays a supporting role, not the lead:

The bulk of our team are volunteers spending varying amounts of time in Liberia. We are as much as possible doing all of our program creation, and all of our curriculum creation actually, out of Liberia. And then it's checked by these teams in Boston.

This delegation is partly practical ("Many of the individuals who help do advisor work have fancy professorships or clinical appointments here in hospitals.

That only affords them the ability to spend a week or two a year in Liberia.")
It is also philosophical: the emphasis on listening to Zambian villagers is baked
into Last Mile Health's understanding of how to serve best, even as it has
access to some of the most progressive voices in rural health care, such as Paul
Farmer's Partners in Health (PIH):

> While PIH did advise us and help out in our model's creation and refine-
> ment, it really was, and continues to be, driven by the community, and is
> something that's very organic. When we were first creating this model, it
> was the community that said, 'We cannot wait for doctors to come to us
> in south-east Liberia. We need to be looking within our own community
> and figuring out another solution.' We've been able to create a culture
> in the organization that has allowed the patients' voices to be the main
> drivers.

Last Mile's governance structure relies on the wisdom of the people they serve:

> We formed an executive committee that's comprised of patients – women
> in addition to men, as well as some staff in the organization. That's become
> the main driver of our work in Liberia, similar to what a board of directors
> would be in the U.S. There have been meetings the executive committee
> has hosted with the community where patients have stood up and said,
> 'It's not enough only to be giving us HIV treatments; we also need to be
> given food if we're to grow healthier.' In those moments, those outspoken
> patients have been really the drivers of adding on new programs. Like, for
> example, supporting the agricultural cooperative that we now support or
> giving food stipends that we now give. It's been those moments that have
> really pushed our work forward.

Last Mile Health, of course, values the expertise it is blessed with through its
connections to the Boston medical community. But even as it seeks to take
advantage of this support, it resists the temptation to replace, rather than complement, Liberian wisdom with developed-world wisdom:

> We're still trying to home in on exactly what the balance looks like.
> This is one of the things which we talk proudly about – both here in
> Boston as well as the rainforest in Liberia. We think if we can channel
> those resources from a place like Boston to one of these most remote
> communities in Liberia that we'll really be able to do something special.
> If nothing else, really create a beacon of hope in Zwedru in south-east
> Liberia that starts to change people's minds – not only in terms of how
> health care is distributed, but also what's possible and what are the rights
> that can, and should, be afforded in places like Liberia, just as we aspire
> to here in Boston.

Help with your taxes, and maybe a hug

THEN THERE'S THE "STUFF" you have to deal with. Peter Luckow comments despairingly:

> An area that we've struggled with as an organization – and this is dry and unexciting, but it's a simple fact – is that there's a lot of leg work that needs to be done to build an organization. [Like] how the hell do you file annually with the IRS? How do you build strong financial systems? How do you build a board of directors? How do you build an organization with operational systems of communications, of finances, of legal processes that ensure that your work and programs will continue for the long haul? So much time is spent in the early startup stages of organizations wrestling with those questions, which is just reinventing the wheel over and over, because every organization struggles with these issues.
>
> We don't all need to be creating new financial systems when an organization down the street has already figured out how to deal with that. It's time that is taken away from programming. That's been one of the struggles in building up the foundation of our organization.

The best support Last Mile Health gets in addressing such practical matters comes from its peers:

> What's been most useful is that, here in south Boston, a number of organizations that are structured very similar to us – in being international nonprofits working in the health arena from a justice perspective – have come together to form a network that we're calling the 'Practice Network.' It's meant to figure out how we can be working with one another to strengthen our work around the world. There are organizations who are working in Mali and Nepal and Rwanda and elsewhere that now are coming together to share resources, develop some systems jointly, and hopefully one day even hire more backup staff who could be supporting all of our organizations in a way that would be more efficient than us all hiring our own.

MEMBERS IN THE PRACTICE NETWORK naturally relate to the much deeper "stuff" they have in common:

> The Practice Network also seeks to bring us together in community to support one another as leaders who are engaging in very stressful, very overwhelming work. I think that's something which very few organizations or even leaders in the social entrepreneurship realm seem to be dealing with: that interior formation side of this work, the more spiritual side that requires deep reflection, discernment, and community solidarity as we try and tackle the biggest challenges that our world faces.

Being in community with people who are both engaging in similar work and also willing to talk very openly and honestly about what it means to lose a patient in a place like Liberia, or what it means to feel like they are failing in developing good budgets that reflect their values – whatever the issue might be – [holds enormous value].

He expresses what so many others have said already about the stresses of social enterprise, adding how the Practice Network helps address them:

Not to say it's the same suffering by any means or the same severity, but I feel when we enter into solidarity with communities and families that are undergoing suffering, whether because of poverty, HIV, or sickness, that there is a certain level of suffering that we, as individuals, take on. And to neglect that or to not talk about that – the stress, the overwhelming nature of it – is to set ourselves up for burnout, for being less effective leaders, and being less effective in creating our own programs and envisioning the strategy of our organization.

I've seen a number of people who work in the arenas of global health or international development who go at it like hell for two or three or four years, but then just completely fizzle out because they can't take the stress, the emotion of it all, anymore.

What we've tried to do with the Practice Network – and what we struggled with and failed to do over the two or three years before it developed – is to give attention to ourselves, whether through communal critical reflection on some of these issues, or even saying, 'We know it's stepping away from the work to take a vacation for a week, or for three or four days, and that the patients we work with, and the staff in Liberia are working day in and day out at a such a higher level [of stress] than us. But still we need to be comfortable taking that time to tend to ourselves.' We've really started to place a much higher priority on that self-care side of the work.

Free lunch?

PRO BONO AND SHARED SUPPORT can be valuable when you find them – that is my main point – but they're not unalloyed windfalls. Mark Hecker, whose organization, Reach Incorporated, offers educational support to at-risk youth, explains the predicament of relying on others for support:

The most frustrating thing is when I have to spend a huge amount of time doing something I'm only going to do once. There's got to be a better way to do it. There are a lot of organizations out there that say, 'We can do all your backroom stuff; we can make this easier.' We went with this organization in D.C. called the Center for Nonprofit Advancement that brings nonprofits together so you can do group buying of insurance, and they try to make it really easy for you. As far as I could tell, it just added another layer to the bureaucracy, because now I had to fill out all their forms just so I could fill out all the benefits forms. ...

It would be less bothersome to me to have a fight in one of our classrooms than to deal with [employee] benefits. The program stuff I can handle. I understand what kids are like and that work. But it's the structural – the backroom – stuff that gets in my way.

The remedy Mark hopes for: finding and hiring someone with impeccable administrative and organization skills. The people who like doing those kinds of things, however, "are not the same people that start organizations. So we need to go find them."

21 Board

THE BEST RESOURCE THAT MOST SOCIAL ENTERPRISES fail to take advantage of is their board of directors. In the United States, states differ in their rules for corporations, but every corporation is required to have a board of directors, both for-profits and nonprofits. (Please don't take it from me, however; get legal advice.) The IRS makes this a requirement for 501(c)3s. What holds social ventures back from taking full advantage? Both a misunderstanding of how powerful boards can be as well as how they should operate.

Your board: Get interested

CAROL ERICKSON HAS SPENT HER ENTIRE CAREER working with the nonprofit and philanthropic community, including seven years as a senior program officer at the Bill and Melinda Gates Foundation working with a variety of NGOs. She now runs an independent consultancy for nonprofits, advising them on issues including organizational effectiveness, board development, and strategic planning. She provided her views on how social ventures can take advantage of their boards. Carol cautioned that her experience has entirely been with nonprofits. Nonetheless – and this view is mine – Carol's thoughts about effective board membership and governance apply to social ventures legally registered as for-profit corporations, particularly so when a venture and its board strongly prioritize social impact over financial return. According to Carol, the idea behind a board is quite simple:

> Having a group of people make decisions is better than one person making a decision. ... Having a board of smart people who are either elected or appointed to establish your policies, exercise fiscal responsibility, and oversee the management of an organization is really in the best public interest for a nonprofit in order to achieve its goals and its mission.

Fancy corporate boards may meet in lavish settings and provide compensation of tens of thousands of dollars a year per board member. While social ventures don't operate with this level of largesse, their boards often err in the opposite direction: being boards in name only, operating with complete informality, offering little, and potentially causing harm. Carol explains:

First and foremost you should try to find people whose primary reason for joining the board is a commitment to the mission of the organization, not a commitment to the founder as an individual, but somebody who really believes in the mission. That, to me, is absolutely critical to building a board of people who are going to want to roll up their sleeves and spend time on the organization.

Yet this, sadly, is often not the case. Too many boards resemble a family gathering or a reunion of college friends:

With many early-stage nonprofit leaders, the first thing they do when they establish a board is sign up their sister, or their mother, or their neighbor, or sometimes their husband. Your gut reaction is just to get people who you're close to to become your advisors. That creates this path that I see very often, where you have – instead of a governing board, which is what you want – a founder's board: people who are working in the best interest of their friend the founder, or their daughter the founder, as opposed to working in the best interest of the mission of the organization.

'GBENGA SESAN'S EXPERIENCE illustrates this. He stumbled when creating the initial board for his social venture, Paradigm Initiative:

A challenge that we're facing at the moment is with our board, the governance. I got it wrong at the beginning. I just wanted people who believed in my work, [more than] people who could provide governance oversight, who could say, 'You're wrong' and all that. That's been corrected. Fortunately, the first two years [his board's term] ends November, so we're getting a new board that will provide a lot more critical feedback, and some of them will also provide additional support in terms of fundraising and income generation.

In the extreme, legal conflicts of interest arise when, for instance, a founder appoints her spouse as board chair. This unseemly action may even cause the IRS to look more closely than you'd like at your annual tax documents, and funders not to look seriously at your venture at all. Carol remarks:

Relatives on a board – daughters, sons, spouses – and often best friends from college: that's fairly common. That, to me, really is a red flag in terms of knowing that this organization still is in the early development stages. They are probably not as sophisticated as you'd want them to be. Whether they're aware of that or not, it will be for the decision-maker in terms of whether they're more likely to get a grant or not.

AMONG THOSE I INTERVIEWED, there was a full range of board experiences: from those who didn't know a board was required ...

> I was selling this idea to friends and family who supported it because they trusted me, wanted to help me, and the kids were cute. I'm still working on getting a board together, so there are no people that are really pushing me, asking hard questions. I wish there were some people holding me back a little bit ... I wish I had some more guidance in the early stages to think more strategically.
>
> (Dory Gannes, Olevelos Project)

... to others who formed and used boards the way they are supposed to be.

Boards 101

Perched on high, looking down, you might see what successful boards do. From her work at the Gates Foundation and her own consultancy, Carol Erickson has had that vantage point, and she shares her perspective. Her comments apply to a governing board, though, mistakenly, many early-stage social enterprises operate with a founding board (friends, family) or none at all:

> Definitely, a governing board is responsible for selecting a chief executive officer.
>
> They're responsible for doing performance reviews of that chief executive officer.
>
> They're responsible for voting to approve an annual operating budget each year and voting if there are any major changes to it.
>
> A board would be expected to vote on any policy changes that might affect, for example, the mission or the purpose of the organization, or changes to constituents served.
>
> They're definitely supposed to be responsible for ensuring effective planning of the organization and monitoring the programs – making sure that they are effective.
>
> They should ensure that the organization has adequate financial resources and that they're behaving with legal and ethical integrity.

An effective governing board shapes and contours a social venture, without interfering with its daily activities:

> A true governing board really is not involved in the day-to-day operations of the programs, but they are involved in the overall oversight of the organization and making sure that the chief executive officer is doing his or her job.
>
> Big decisions like constituents served or locations you're working in: those are things that you definitely want your board involved in, in terms of the decision-making.

The boundary separating "big picture" and minutiae is not always obeyed, however:

> What I find is often really challenging are board members who are [too] involved and truly want to get down into the weeds of the programs – how those programs are being delivered on the ground – and make decisions about that. What you want your governing board to be focusing on is really the big-picture stuff and not so much the day-to-day. Hopefully, you have staff who are competent enough that they don't have to be micromanaged by your board at that level. It takes board members away from the bigger picture.

She punctuates the difference between "big picture" and "day-to-day" with a Christmas story:

> I remember a story from one of the first board members of Amazon who talked about one of the early board meetings when Amazon was just getting started. Here is this person – serving on the board with other prominent Seattle individuals – and one of the longest discussions that they had at the board meeting was on what kind of Christmas wrapping paper Amazon should be using.
>
> You don't want your board voting on what kind of wrapping paper you're using to send out your gifts: it's not a good use of their time. Their opinions may be important [on *other* matters!] and they may be able to contribute, but that day-to-day stuff is really best left to the staff.

As an early-stage founder, and likely also the CEO, what should you do when board members *do* act intrusively, to the detriment of your organization? Have a one-on-one conversation to steer them back in the direction of what their roles should be: "Just politely say, 'I've got this handled.' You don't want to alienate someone who otherwise is offering valuable service."

Formation

Effective boards expand the capability of a social venture, adding critical skills and perspectives. Carol Erickson shares her advice about forming a board:

> When I talk to people about forming a board, I try to get them to think about the big picture of the organization: what the organization needs in terms of expertise that might otherwise be lacking, whether it's legal expertise, financial or accounting expertise, communications and public relations. All of those things should come into play when someone is thinking about establishing a board.
>
> I think it's important for early-stage nonprofits to try to look at where their expertise gaps are, and how they can fill them with board members who can provide that free expertise.

Jane Chen and her co-founders did this when they began Embrace, their venture aimed at providing affordable alternatives to traditional incubators in the developing world:

> Right away we started recruiting [our board]. They were really critical because we lacked a lot of functional [meaning: business] and industry expertise. So we found people who could fill those gaps in. We couldn't be doing this without them.

THOUGH DIFFERENT STATES as well as the IRS may stipulate that an organization needs to have only a very small number of board members, Carol suggests that eight to a dozen people is often optimal. Even for a very early board, in its first year or two, five board members makes sense. Nonprofit boards should include a board chair, who oversees the entire board, runs meetings, and helps ensure the board's decisions are carried out; a vice chair, who will assume the role of the chair in two or three years; a secretary of the board who, among other tasks, helps ensure legal compliance; and a treasurer responsible for overseeing an organization's finances.

Much of the their work is done through subcommittees. Depending on an organization's finances, board members may either perform the work that the subcommittee recommends or simply offer advice. Typical committees include finance, fundraising, nominations and governance, evaluation, and, especially for small nonprofits otherwise lacking this capability, PR and communications. Each committee stays in regular communication with the organization's staff and the board's chair and vice chair, and updates the entire board at quarterly board meetings. Members of nonprofit boards who want to be paid for their expertise should be avoided; they raise the possibility of acting in their own best interest, rather than the mission of the organization.

Carol hastens to add that boards often don't resemble these specs at all:

> That's the way it works in the most highly functioning NGOs, but it doesn't always work like that when you've got a small NGO with just one or two staff and committees that are not meeting as often as you would want them to meet.

In fact, board meetings can be so infrequent as to neutralize a board:

> I was working with one group last year on board development, and the founder had come to me and said, 'I can't get my board to fundraise. They just won't do anything. Can you please help? Can you do a seminar or training for us to do this?' It turned out the issue wasn't so much that they weren't willing to fundraise. The issue was that they met only once a year, and none of the board members had been asked to fundraise when they agreed to serve. They really had no idea what the organization was doing. The founder wasn't keeping them informed, so they really didn't feel they

could advocate on behalf of the organization. It's interesting to see how a founder's perspective on the board can be completely askew from what is really happening and the source of the problem.

Don't shake on it

BOARDS SUFFER FROM THE RELATED DISEASE of operating without expectations. According to Carol Erickson:

> Everything is often kind of a handshake. There are suggested board contracts that are out there – the Foundation Center has a basic one that I often point people to. But I have yet to come across an NGO that I've worked with that had provided a list of written expectations of their board members before I encouraged it. You would just be amazed at how few board members fully understand what their expectations or responsibilities are, based on that handshake.

Fundamental misunderstandings are pervasive:

> Many people have no idea how often they're supposed to meet, how long their board service is supposed to be, whether or not they're expected to make a minimum financial contribution to the organization. These are just some basics that often just get completely thrown out the window because [asking someone to join your board] is just a conversation and things don't get conveyed, or things get mis-conveyed. So while I always encourage people to put those things in writing, it has only been recently, as of 2017, that I have organizations that are willing to do that.

Many founders also "make the serious mistake of not recognizing that board rotation is a serious issue … It is really, really critical in terms of maintaining enthusiasm and preventing board burnout [and ensuring fresh perspectives]."

Why these failures? Carol speculates that founders may be reluctant to put expectations in writing because they fear the legal repercussions if contracts are violated. "Regardless of whether you explain to them that there is really no one at the Treasury Department that oversees nonprofits who is out there enforcing all of this, they are just very, very reluctant to do so."

Things are beginning to change for the better, as Carol notes in a conversation two years after our first interview:

> In 2017, GuideStar [a nonprofit whose mission is to improve philanthropy by providing information that advances transparency, enables users to make better decisions, and encourages charitable giving] instituted new guidelines for evaluating all nonprofits whose 990 financial documents are publicly available on their site. Among the five questions GuideStar started asking about nonprofit board leadership practices is one about board

orientation and education: 'Does the board conduct a formal orientation for new board members and require all board members to sign a written agreement regarding their roles, responsibilities, and expectations?' Now, I just have to point to that GuideStar question, and every NGO says, 'Yes, we will do that.'

When people ask me about why GuideStar made those changes, I speculate that it was largely because of *60 Minutes'* exposure of the Central Asian Institute and Greg Mortenson's poor governance and financial oversight. Until the *60 Minutes* story and subsequent investigations broke, GuideStar had given the Central Asian Institute a five-star rating – largely based on how little they spent on fundraising and overhead/executive salaries. This was a huge turning point in the public's perception of non-profit oversight and how easily deception can occur when the right questions aren't asked.

ALL CORPORATIONS – nonprofits and for-profits – are required to have bylaws[1] and articles of incorporation, which should identify which issues the board will vote on, in contrast to others where voting is not needed. Carol points out that these vary widely in quality:

> Again, unfortunately there's no IRS police who are going through and saying, 'These are really good bylaws or you're missing X, Y, Z.' So for the most part, new NGO leaders are running their organization based on their own instincts.

Too often, organizations develop their bylaws the wrong way around. They find an attorney friend who can draw up the bylaws just to meet legal and IRS requirements and then they begin to recruit their board:

> The better way is informing people of your intentions to form a nonprofit and getting their advice throughout the process as you're developing those bylaws and documents of incorporation, and figuring out: How many people do we want to serve on this board? What should be their length of service? What should be the requirements? How many times should we meet? All of those things. Those decisions, which should be in bylaws, are better made by an informed group of people who are going to commit to the organization.

By abbreviating the process of creating bylaws and overlooking issues that make boards effective, organizations create documents barely worth the paper they're printed on.

> I've read some bylaws that are just not very rigorous. Again, you don't have the IRS going out there and reviewing your bylaws, unfortunately. Otherwise, I think a many of these smaller NGOs wouldn't pass the test.

You are not perfect

I MADE EXTRA, EXTRA, EXTRA darn sure that my board knew that I didn't know how to [do several mathematical tasks]. What I got from other executive directors was the fact that no executive director knows how to do the whole kit of what it takes, so you build a board that manages your weaknesses. So, really early on, the board had a sit-down with me to ask, 'Okay, what can you do and what can't you do?' So I don't need to have a board president that can go off and speak, because I can do that, but I do need to have a treasurer that is on his job or on her job, you know?

Sage advice from Nikki Henderson, who has served as executive director or founder of four social-justice-oriented organizations.

Yes, you raise money

MONEY AND SEX MAKE FOR UNCOMFORTABLE CONVERSATIONS. Fortunately, you only need to discuss one of them with prospective board members.

An expectation left out of most conversations with board members – before, and sometimes after, they join – is their responsibility for fundraising. Board members should understand when they sign up that this is part of the job. Still, there are better, and worse, ways to do it. To Carol Erickson, this is straightforward:

Often the expectation to fundraise is not articulated to board members. When I'm advising nonprofits, I basically tell them that I think every board member should make some sort of financial contribution, either personally or by soliciting others. Or, as is known in the nonprofit world, a *give* or a *get* contribution.

Even on boards of very early-stage ventures, that should be the expectation. Naturally, this can help bring in money when it may be in terribly short supply. But it also creates the advantage of creating awareness about your organization. Carol continues:

The more people you have out there tapping into their networks and their circle of friends and community members, the more people are going to be introduced to the organization's work, and the more potential supporters you can get.

As important as is the infusion of money and gaining greater notice, fundraising also serves as a double check on board members' commitment to the organization they are pledging to serve:

[Fundraising targets for different board members] is an important question and a very tricky one. I've seen some boards who set a minimum that is reachable by all of their board members, so if it's somebody who's just out of college, maybe the minimum is $100.

But what I see more effective NGOs doing is requiring a financial contribution of all of the board members that is meaningful to them. So not setting a minimum, or not saying it's $2,500 a year, give or get. But talking about contributions that are meaningful in members' philanthropic giving.

[In addition to them] serving on your board and making that commitment of time and expertise, you also want your board members to be committed financially to the organization. So each member's contribution should be one of his or her largest financial gifts to an NGO.

I've seen that discussion go on a far better path than those who say, 'You have to give at least $500 every year,' because people do have different philanthropic abilities.

THIS SHOW OF COMMITMENT can be attractive to potential funders, too:

Often foundations and other potential contributors will ask, 'Do you have 100% participation in terms of board member donations?' It's not an unreasonable question from a foundation or a potential donor to ask if the board members are all contributing, because if the board members don't believe in the organization, then why should another donor?

As WITH ANY WELL-INTENDED ACTIVITY, a board's fundraising can generate its own peculiar difficulties. Carol names two to steer clear of. The first is: avoid creating a board that only wants to give their money, not their time:

[I know of] a board of individuals who open up their networks, contact their friends, their college roommates, and everything in order to come up with a substantial amount of money each year. But many of them are just so busy they don't want to get involved in the governance of the organization. They just want to write their check and be left alone.

I think many NGOs would love to have a board of people who just want to write a check, but it can create a lot of problems in terms of financial oversight and [poor governance].

The second is: avoid fundraising targets that set your organization back: "I've got one client whose founder says, 'I want you to give until it hurts.'" That's practically an invitation for people to leave your board.

Smart and gray

DETERMINING THE ROLES YOUR BOARD members will play is one thing; determining who will occupy your board seats is another. So, what are the traits of those who should fill them? In a nutshell: smart, bold, strategic, independent-minded, result-oriented, experienced, committed. That was the advice of some of the most senior, most successful, and wisest social entrepreneurs I spoke to.

WHEN WE SPOKE, John Anner ran the nonprofit East Meets West (renamed Thrive Networks), an organization that makes smart investments in health, water, and education in the developing world to enhance local capability and capacity. John offers equally smart advice about the characteristics of his own board: "Our board members are used to taking risks. ... You should put on your board those who are smarter, more accomplished, and different from you." He emphasizes knowing what you're looking for and working your contacts to create your board. "Go one orbit beyond your personal network. Be prepared to be opportunistic."

IN 1984, MORE THAN TWO DECADES BEFORE the "International Year of Microfinance" and just a year after Muhammad Yunus founded the Grameen Bank, John Hatch and Rupert Scofield co-founded the microfinance institution FINCA. Taking an extremely entrepreneurial approach to providing funding, FINCA developed approaches to serve the poorest of the poor. Rupert, now the president of FINCA and author of *The Social Entrepreneur's Handbook*,[2] shares with me insights about who should sit on a board. First, find board members who will tap the brakes: "Young social entrepreneurs are so excited to change the world. They think they can do it all. Get gray hair on your board. They'll tell you to go slow. You'll hate it."

And, then, recognize how board members from the nonprofit and for-profit worlds may differ: "Venture capitalists will flee from your board if you don't listen to them. With nonprofits, it's different. They're more tolerant."

None of this suggests you should shun individuals from either sector. In fact, Carol Erickson insists nonprofits include both, since you don't want an all for-profit board who may have "no clue about how to even run a board meeting, or what their responsibilities are supposed to be, legally and ethically."

MARTIN BURT IS ONE OF THE MOST ACCOMPLISHED and celebrated change agents in Paraguay. Initially intent on reforming the country's government in the mid-1980s, he found his ideas unwelcome. Together with other visionary Paraguayan businessmen, he formed what now is recognized as the beginning of civil society there, Fundación Paraguaya. "Our background was a group of concerned citizens wanting to develop a professional unit to do what government is not doing and what business is not willing to do." They turned their efforts to eradicating poverty through microfinance, and later financial literacy and entrepreneurship education. The same group also created the country's largest environmental foundation. Martin remains executive director of the organization he and his cohorts began more than 30 years ago. It now also works in Tanzania and its lessons are disseminated worldwide through its learning network, "Teach a Man to Fish," operating out of the UK. Along the way, he has also served in local and national government, and has received numerous accolades from Ashoka, the Schwab Foundation/World Economic Forum, the Skoll Foundation, and other prestigious organizations supporting social entrepreneurship.

Martin takes a long view on social change and the role of a board. Although he suggests an early-stage social entrepreneur's board can be "light and loose," it is nonetheless essential for imposing financial and operational accountability, "or else he is going to crash." From the beginning, he advises, surround yourself with skilled, willing, and trusting supporters:

> First of all there has to be a personal trust. You can't bring in mercenaries. You can't bring in people that just want to be there to show off. There is a social entrepreneur; he or she needs to be surrounded by a support group who believe in him/her – but who are willing to accept the social entrepreneur, and also show and teach and educate. That is a role of a board.

Martin admits that his own board has sometimes impeded his organization's effectiveness. "We've made mistakes with certain board members who were not aligned. Everybody needs the same strategic alignment."

More often than not, though, trust and effective alignment with the board have led Fundación Paraguaya to strike out in new directions in pursuit of alleviating poverty – even in the face of uncertainty and disagreement. Martin explains the interplay he had with his board when his microfinance organization was presented with the opportunity to run a school:

> LaSalle Christian Brothers offered us a [failing] school. I had an emergency board meeting. I had to come up with a letter of intent over the weekend. I had a great board meeting at 7:00 on a Friday evening and I said, 'We have this opportunity: can I have a vote here? We're going to commit a lot of money until this thing breaks even. I will go and look for money.' Everybody said, 'Yes.' One board member said, 'Martin, I really doubt it that we're going to [succeed], but I vote for it. Let's go for it because it's a worthy cause.' And, of course, he is the happiest of them all because [it has succeeded spectacularly].

The board did not rubber-stamp its approval, but neither did it overrule Martin's wishes, as was its right:

> The board wanted to see financials. The board said, 'This is something that we can work with.' We did a very intelligent contract because we have very good lawyers on our board. We did an intelligent contract saying we'll take over the school but if something happens and we are incapable of [succeeding at] this thing, we will return it.

This episode underlines the conviction among Martin and his board that Fundación Paraguaya explore new avenues for alleviating poverty that might successfully extend what they already do:

> We take calculated risks. But the board insists that we take the risks. What kind of organization are we that we're going to lend [only] to small

businesses, 100% of which pay back? Are we hitting the right target population [if that happens]? Where's the risk? Who are we helping?

[The board embraces the] business community. It's concerned about poverty, convinced that market mechanisms are applicable to poverty reduction. But there's no greed. There is a sense of giving back. A sense of doing what is right. This is a very good board of directors. Without true governance, this would not have worked.

Being the founder and CEO does not mean that you do not surround yourself with serious board members. Or else it does not go. This is very, very important.

CAROL ERICKSON SUMS UP: "Surrounding yourself with a group of independent advisors is really the best way to get your organization focused on achieving its mission."

Notes

1 "A rule adopted by an organization chiefly for the government of its members and the regulation of its affairs" (Merriam-Webster).
2 Scofield, Rupert, *The Social Entrepreneur's Handbook: How to Start, Build, and Run a Business That Improves the World* (New York: McGraw-Hill, 2011).

Part 4

Your business model

Your business model is your blueprint for making money. But there are other types of funds. Mother Teresa spoke of "funds of love, of kindness, of understanding, of peace." For social entrepreneurs, there is a fund of impact, and it must be blueprinted, too, represented by your impact model.

Your business model enumerates and distinguishes all your potential customers to establish your focus. It differentiates your organization from others seeking to pursue the same business. It counts, analyzes, and calculates so you make prudent economic decisions. It acknowledges other firms with whom you will directly partner, and ensures that their incentives align with yours. And you will likely tweak it endlessly.

Your impact model begins with research and results in choices that guide your every decision toward societal impact. And it surpasses your business model.

22 Two businesses

SOCIAL ENTREPRENEURS MUST RUN TWO BUSINESSES: the one dealing with money, the other dealing with impact. Models help you understand their complexity – your business model guiding your finances and your impact model explaining the good you'll do. Though the idea of a business model may be better known, your impact model underpins everything you do.

Flying to Miami

NO ONE HAS EVER FLOWN INSIDE a model airplane from New York to Miami or lived in a set of architectural drawings. But replicas serve an important purpose when we come to design a plane, or build a house, or develop and run a business: they lay bare their essential nature, display relationships among their parts, expose flaws and unforeseen problems, and provide evidence of the "real thing" working because its model does.

At its most basic level, a *business model* explains the "money side" of a business: where will it come from? Where will it go? And in what amounts, and when? To stay in business, after all, you need enough to keep doing what you set out to do and still pay your bills, even if that means digging into your own pocket, taking out loans, or asking for contributions. But scratch the surface and you see that, to understand these issues, you need to understand others: from fundraising and marshaling your resources, to understanding your customers and serving them, to running your venture and, certainly not least in a social venture, creating genuine societal impact.

Each of these is part of the story you tell about your venture, both to yourself as well as investors and others outside your organization who, for your sake, need to understand it. Though business model "canvases" are becoming a form of popular communication shorthand, truly effective business models dive into far more detail than these can convey.

Your two businesses

YOU MAY NOT HAVE THOUGHT of it this way, but let Kevin Starr of the Mulago Foundation explain why every social entrepreneur has double the work of a standard startup:

> Everything flows from impact. You really are running two businesses. You're running a *business* business and you're running an *impact* business, and there are two models there. They may overlap completely, or they may not. One is the set of activities that you do to create impact, and the other is the set of activities you do to keep the lights on.

Together, your impact model and your business model describe the underlying logic of your venture. On the impact side, you explain why you're in business and how you keep score of the impact you create. On the business side, you explain how your business makes financial sense, for you and those you rely on. You might think of your impact model as part of your overall business model, or you may consider it separate from it. No matter: it always comes first.

Modeling impact

DREAMING OF SOCIAL IMPACT gets you moving. Modeling your social impact provides your essential compass. So, what goes into an impact model? First, a lot of thought and research. You'll never be fully informed about every aspect of the impact you hope to create, but you should be as fully informed as you can be. Do your homework, and use the results to stay on course. You may want a detailed narrative (pages long) for in-house use, and something shorter (a small slide deck) to share with others you want on your side. The elements described below belong in an impact model.

Description of the problem

Know the problem you are addressing. It is one thing to say that poverty is at an unacceptable level in the United States. But each of the following statements provides additional clarity and focus. For 2015, according to the Annie E. Casey Foundation:[1]

- The national poverty rate in the United States was 15%.
- Michigan's poverty rate was an almost identical 15.7%.
- Poverty rates were considerably higher for children – 21% nationally, 22% in Michigan.
- Detroit's poverty rate was a staggering 39.8%. Here, too, things were even worse for all children (58%) and especially for those five years or younger (60%).

- Poverty rates differed across races as well, with Michigan's poverty rates being: 47% for blacks, 30% for Hispanic/Latinos, and 15% for non-Hispanic whites.

Which "poverty problem" are you addressing?

Be clear about why you are solving it

Your reason for addressing a particular problem is more cogent when its consequences are fully understood. Addressing childhood poverty – which of course is important – becomes that much more compelling when you know that children growing up even in moderate poverty are up to eight times more likely to be poor in middle adulthood than children who never experienced poverty; and for very poor children, the difference is closer to fifty-fold.[2]

Necessity of your solution

What will you do? Explain your solution in terms of those you'll be serving – children in poverty, smallholder African farmers, victims of human trafficking – not according to the details of your technical approach. Describe the benefits you'll provide: how lives will be improved or how a wetland will be preserved. And why are those you serve better off with your intervention than with those of competitors? Are theirs too hard to use? Too hard to maintain? Why is yours necessary?

Metrics

Your analysis of the problem should hold water. The next question is: how much? That's where your impact metrics come in. Metrics are expressed in units such as calories, employment rates, or dropout statistics, not in adjectives like "healthier," "wealthier," or "wiser." Later, we'll look more closely at impact metrics. For the moment, I want to drive home the idea that this is something you think about at the start in developing an impact model, not after the fact.

Mission statement

KEVIN STARR EXPLAINS WITH BRUTAL clarity how a mission statement sums all this up:

> Mission statements in the social sector are often … word-salad, but there isn't a common *raison d'être* [as there is in for-profits, where everything revolves around making money]. We [as impact investors] want to know exactly [what] you're trying to accomplish. The tool that works for us is the eight-word mission statement. All we want is this: A verb, a target

population, and an outcome that implies something to measure – and we want it in eight words or less.[3]

As examples of how an eight-word mission statement is focused and specific, he cites: "Save kids' lives in Uganda"; "Rehabilitate coral reefs in the Western Pacific"; "Prevent maternal–child transmission of HIV in Africa"; "Get Zambian farmers out of poverty." Each explains *what* a social entrepreneur intends to achieve, not *how*. Each implies the metrics that will define successes: number of lives saved, number of reefs restored, etc.

Your product or service may provide many benefits. A rolling water wheel – an alternative to carrying water on your head – saves time, reduces the strain on necks and spines, and increases the odds of girls staying in school. But its chief benefit is better hydration from cleaner, distant water sources. Know your focus. Your impact model is your compass, and an eight-word mission statement is due north.

Notes

1 Data from Kids Count Data Center: A Project of the Annie E. Casey Foundation. Retrieved June 15, 2017 from: http://datacenter.kidscount.org
2 Wagmiller, Robert Lee, and Adelman, Robert M., "Childhood and intergenerational poverty: The long-term consequences of growing up poor." National Center for Children in Poverty, November 2009. Retrieved July 11, 2018 from: http://www.nccp.org/publications/pub_909.html
3 Starr, "The eight-word mission statement."

23 Know your customers

YOUR CUSTOMERS LIVE in concentric circles – the largest being those you ideally would serve but realistically can't. Within that are those you have the actual prospect of serving in the not-impossibly-distant future; and within that are those whom you are targeting now. Understanding these different potential markets will help you pay your bills and set your aspirations.

Your *business* business

LIKE YOUR IMPACT, your business needs to be modeled, too. Ultimately, your business model gets down to money and your venture staying afloat: how much comes in, how much flows out, and having enough to get started in the first place. But a discussion of money must involve some other things first, beginning with being clear – very clear – about your customers.

WHEN DIIME (which we heard about in Chapter 10, "Now, just a product"; "Climb with others") was a group of engineering students, the team was drawn to how technology could impact the lives of poor, developing-world mothers and infants. They also had the design chops to produce and test different medical devices, including one they settled on as their product: Hemafuse, which, as we have seen, is a device that allows blood to be safely captured and reused during a medical emergency. The team recognized that its skills, honed in college engineering labs, were well-suited for research, design, and preliminary testing. It also believed that lack of donated blood in Ghana created a need for the Hemafuse, and that it was something clinicians in Ghana wanted. Where the team was struggling was in how to translate this into a business that could make money:

> We're trying to find a partner to license our technology to manufacture it onwards. … We've been pivoting all summer because initially we were talking about building our own manufacturing facilities and doing that all ourselves. That was a crazy thought. And recently we've come to the realization that our expertise and our real value is in R&D [research and development]. And in collaborative design, where we know these are real problems that we're solving. But we don't know how to get from having

this technology to actually commercializing. The glaring problem is the business model, and it's something which we have little understanding of. We're trying to do more research to figure it out.

Knowing who your customers are might seem obvious, but think about DIIME's situation. Were their customers poor women with ectopic pregnancies, whose blood was often ladled from their own body and strained through gauze before being reused? Or were they the clinics that treated them? Or possibly nonprofit organizations that might buy Hemafuses in bulk to support many clinics operating on a shoestring?

Your business model must distinguish the individuals who are the ultimate beneficiaries of what you do from those who pay for it (your paying customers). They are often the same; but, when they're not, you need to understand and cater to them both.

FOR DIIME AND OTHERS, a place to start involves teasing apart the acronyms TAM, SAM, and SOM. Don't be surprised if investors or funders ask you about these — whether yours is a for-profit business or not. These terms indicate the size of the population you are serving, and thus the social impact you can create. For for-profit enterprises, they also give an indication of your potential profit, and so are of interest to investors. And be aware that these terms are sometimes used differently by different people.

TAM, or your Total Addressable Market, means everyone who might conceivably use your product or service some day, expressed in number of people (but knowing the associated number of sales and annual revenue as well is a good exercise). If you are starting a workforce development program for at-risk youth under the age of 18 in the United States, then every American fitting that profile is part of your TAM. (If you only ever hope to serve Detroiters, then they alone comprise your TAM.) Your TAM should be familiar: it is what you pointed to in your problem statement when you identified the magnitude of the problem.

SAM, or your Serviced Available Market, acknowledges there are limitations in reaching every one of your potential beneficiaries. It is a subset of TAM. Even if you eventually may want to serve all at-risk youth in the country, you would be held far short of that by, for example, only operating (at present) in New York City; by only having learning materials for English-language speakers; or by charging $150 for your training. Your SAM lets you know the best you could possibly do if your business model works to perfection under such limitations. Within your SAM, there may be different segments. Segmentation separates your SAM into different groups based on meaningful characteristics. You might segment by gender, by geography, by level of education, or permanence of one's housing (from temporary housing, to rental, to home ownership). Segmenting your SAM can allow you to group like members together and determine how best to appeal to them.

SOM is your Serviceable Obtainable Market, but it's much clearer just to call it your target market. It is a subset of SAM. Within your SAM, there may be certain segments you want to target now (in the next two to three years) and not just eventually. These make up your target market – *every*one in the segments you are choosing to serve now. This is not the same as your sales goals, about which you must be realistic that you will not reach everyone in your target market.

NONE OF THESE QUANTITIES is easy to come by, and, truth be told, you will almost always be guessing. But you can use a combination of research approaches to arrive at your estimates. If there are publicly available data, this can be a start. Statistical databases provide information about poverty, childhood mortality, and other issues of this sort, even though it may be less precise and focused than you need. Understanding your competitors' customers – and, yes, nonprofits as well as social enterprises compete – provides another perspective on your potential market. And, whenever you can, you should talk to those you think might use your product or service. This information will be invaluable both in identifying a more precise "segment" that you want to target with your offerings, and in helping you refine your ideas to serve them.

CHARLIE CAVELL'S WORKFORCE development program had just three qualifications for its target beneficiaries:

> You have to be 16–29, you have to be a Detroit resident, and you have to be low-income or lacking opportunity. That means: you come in the door with a tether on your ankle because you just got out of prison – okay, we take you. Because an issue that a lot of programs face is saying, 'We're only for single mothers between the ages of 18 and 21 who also live in this particular zip code.' Well dang, it's tough to have people fit into that qualification.

TAM SAM SOM ... mat ter

IF TAM, SAM, AND SOM WERE JUST ALPHABET SOUP, you could be excused for rolling your eyes and putting down your spoon. Instead, they can be essential to your finances and, so too, the impact you can have.

April Allderdice had worked with Grameen Bank in Bangladesh, acclaimed for its work in microfinance, but not its work in clean energy. As she explains: "At the beginning, Grameen was very similar to most other MFIs [microfinance institutions]. They had the MFI skill set. But they didn't know anything about energy."

But then Grameen began Grameen Shakti, a business that places solar energy systems in rural villages, finances them with microloans, and uses local village women, called "Solar Engineers," to install and maintain them. April helped them with this business, noticing its success: "It was a very successful business. I saw what they did and what worked, and I realized this is not rocket science. Any MFI can do this if they have the knowhow and some startup capital."

After leaving Grameen, she and her business partner became intent themselves on coupling energy-saving technology with microfinance. Their challenge was where to get the necessary startup funding for the enterprise they hoped to create. They considered the usual funders of nonprofits:

> We thought, 'Where are we going to get the seed capital? We're going to have to just get a big grant, so we'll get a grant from the Gates Foundation to do this.' But then we noticed that the carbon markets were $30 billion, and we said, 'Man, if we had 1% of that, we could [couple] every micro-finance institution with energy.'

Thirty billion dollars was the volume in tradable carbon credits in 2007, when they were devising their business model. When we spoke several years later, it had hit $120 billion. The World Bank notes[1] that there are currently more than 35 implemented mechanisms for trading (or taxing) carbon, covering regional (EU), national, and even subnational (California and city-level) plans. The price of carbon has, unfortunately (for the health of the planet), declined. Still, carbon is being traded in, among other places, Sweden, Shanghai, and Québec (with widely varying prices per ton of carbon in different locales). It is thought that international cooperation may lead to more uniform rates reflecting carbon's true value, totaling more than $400 billion by 2030, and $2 trillion by 2050.

These huge numbers – billions and trillions – were orders of magnitude beyond the TAM that April's organization, MicroEnergy Credits, or *any* organization for that matter, could ever reach. Even "1% of that [$30 billion]" – the basis of April's reverie – is an unimaginably high attainment, especially for a startup. But these numbers provided context for the overall size of the market, and opened up the possibility of her business model being based on financing from carbon credits.

CARBON CREDITS (OR OFFSETS) CAN BE "MANUFACTURED" in many different ways: planting trees, selling renewable energy projects, through activities such as insulating homes and buildings, and so on. Many parts of the developing world are home to carbon-reducing projects because their lax laws and regulations and their often primitive forms of energy production leave so much room for improvement. Brazil, India, Indonesia, Malaysia, Mexico, and Thailand are often attractive targets for projects. MicroEnergy Credits initially focused its own efforts on India, Mongolia, and Kenya. Replacing dirty energy (burning dung or kerosene, for instance) with cleaner energy (especially solar) was its method for lowering carbon and generating credits. Poor people using expensive, unclean energy sources in each of these countries (segments) became its target market.

Note

1 World Bank and Ecofys, *State and Trends of Carbon Pricing*. Washington, D.C., September 2015. Retrieved July 11, 2018 from: http://www.worldbank.org/content/dam/Worldbank/document/Climate/State-and-Trend-Report-2015.pdf

24 Value proposition

Why you?

QUITE THE OPPOSITE OF "WHY ME?" – a request to the heavens for an explanation when something unbearable occurs – "Why you?" forces you to articulate the reasons your offering is the best available solution for the market you're serving. Organizations often formalize their "Why yous?" in the form of a *value proposition*. You create your value proposition on the heels of understanding your customers' real problems, your competitors' solutions, and all the reasons that customers might elect not to buy from you. Like your pithy mission statement, your value proposition is short and to the point: a few sentences (at most) that explain why you provide your customers better solutions than all your competitors. Mostly, you keep this to yourself and not flaunt it before them.

Business 101 explains that you either compete by offering the lowest price or by having a better product (or service). But the market – not you – judges "better."

Sanga Moses' Eco-Fuel Africa's fuel pellets were made by local Ugandans, kept people's dwellings clean from the soot of charcoal or kerosene, and prevented deforestation (a contributor to climate change). None of this mattered to those who bought them: they were a good purchase to *them* because they saved customers time and money. Lisa Ballantine's ceramic water filters weren't the only way to obtain purer water in the Dominican Republic. But their convenience made them popular: you just pour water into a pot without mixing, boiling, or straining.

Many health initiatives, like Last Mile Health's efforts to provide health service to remote parts of Liberia, succeed because they rely on trusted local community members, even if their skills are quite limited, especially compared to better-trained personnel.

Reliability, availability of parts, service or support, and ease of obtaining a product or service are some of the other ways in which a social enterprise can compete. If you can't perfectly articulate why your customers should prefer you over their other options, why would they?

A FINAL NOTE: I mentioned earlier that any discussion of those you serve must distinguish the ultimate beneficiaries of what you do from those who pay you. And so you might need two distinct value propositions. For KickStart, for instance, the value proposition for farmers who buy a pump is that it's a proven way to quadruple their income or more; for foundations and donors who support KickStart, the emphasis would be on the cost-effectiveness of moving someone out of poverty ($65 per person) and the number of people thus far affected (1 million) and new jobs created (more than 200,000).

25 The economics of your business

BUSINESSES THAT MAKE ENDS meet must sell "enough." But how do you keep track: by the grape, the bunch, the pallet, or the truckload? Indeed, who you are – a small store rather than a distributor, say – determines the proper unit of analysis. From there, you can determine the volume necessary to generate a profit. In base-of-the-pyramid markets particularly, tiny profits per sale can result in significant profit in aggregate.

Accounting 101

THE FOLLOWING IS A RATHER SIMPLIFIED PRESENTATION OF THE MATH behind a business model, but it should give you the basic idea about numbers with which you must have a good working relationship. Let's suppose that you make and sell a single product, a rolling water drum similar to Wello's Water Wheel (such drums save time, prevent back and spine injuries, keep girls in school, and help provide cleaner water). Suppose you make each wheel for $12, sell wheels to various shops for $15 each, and they, in turn, sell the wheel for $20 to a person who will use it to transport water. So, for each water wheel that ends up being purchased by an end customer for $20, you make $3 and the shop makes $5.

Keeping things simple, suppose each shop receives (and sells) 20 water wheels. Then, from its perspective, it profits to the tune of $100 from these water wheels. Say you sell through 15 shops. Because your profit is $3 per wheel, your profit is $60 per shop. And because there are 15 shops, your total profit amounts to $900. (We can assume these are annual numbers. If they were monthly, then both shops' and your profit would be 12 times as large. And, if you happened to also sell a fancier water wheel through the same shops, you could make similar calculations to figure out what additional profits both you and the shops would make.)

For a small shop, each $5 it makes from a sale may be important. Its focus is rightly on each wheel sold – that is their unit of analysis. For you, selling through multiple shops, keeping an eye on every sale provides more detail than you need. Instead, your focus – your unit of analysis – is a shop, and the profit you make from working through it. Put a little differently, each shop needs to sell enough wheels to be profitable; you need to sell to enough shops to be profitable. In addition, focusing on the number of shops to which you sell creates the perspective you need for your venture to scale.

You may be thinking: Didn't I just read that each shop made $60 profit? And that I made $900? Yes, but such *gross profit* doesn't include expenses not directly associated with each wheel. For instance, a shopkeeper may need to pay rent ($10), have pay-as-you-go cell service ($5), and pay an assistant a modest salary ($12). These operating expenses must be deducted from a shopkeeper's gross profit to provide a *net profit* of $33 (or $27 less). (I'm assuming all these expenses apply just to selling water wheels.)

You have operating expenses, too, which reduce your gross profit. You may have rent ($45), you may draw a salary ($30), pay a salesperson ($25), stage plays to promote the wheel ($40), and have delivery expenses ($100). Your gross profit ($900) thereby drops by $240 to a net profit of $660. Your operating expenses aren't going away (let's not quibble about delivery expenses varying). So, if you had *no* shops that actually sold your wheels, you would lose $240. Fortunately, every shop you sell through – remember, a shop is your unit of analysis – provides you with $60 gross profit. So, you need to have four shops to "break even." This is your break-even point.

As I mentioned, this example is simplified. It's possible you have some one-time fixed costs (such as a machine you buy). You break even when your total revenues cover *all* your costs. Further, this may not happen during a single year, as we have been assuming. But once you cover your total cost, no matter when, you have broken even.

E pluribus business model

ONE SOCIAL ENTREPRENEUR TELLS ME, "I believe the number-one cause of death with all startups, including social ventures, is the inability to find a business model before you run out of money." To that let me add: even with an acceptable business model, it takes time to pick up steam to sustain the business.

The hallmark of many businesses focused on social outcomes is their tiny profits on each transaction. You may know the joke: "We lose money on every sale, but we make it up on volume." But if you *make* even a little bit on each sale, you can be sustainable.

You may recall Katherine Lucey saying that, to found Solar Sister, she "reverse-engineered every social enterprise out there and tried to figure out what's the business model – how they make money, how it works, what their impact is. Is it for real or is it just a lot of fluff?" Solar Sister is a nonprofit organization that distributes solar products designed and manufactured by others. It employs rural African women who receive payments based on commissions on what they sell. For every sale an entrepreneur makes, the profit is split, the entrepreneur and Solar Sister each receiving a portion. Solar Sister has a modest staff (five, when we spoke – quite small in relation to its 144-entrepreneur salesforce). Katherine explains how Solar Sister's business model depended on volume:

> At scale, we're a classic distribution company, which means that success is really volume and long-tail. ... The game is really that all of those little [profit] margins that we get off of every one of those sales will, at scale, cover all of the staff, all of the shipping, all of the marketing, all of the training, and all of that; but it doesn't yet, and it won't until we're quite large-scale.

In Katherine's break-even analysis, she would sum her unchanging, fixed costs (including staff salaries, marketing, and any rent); then, by knowing Solar Sister's (average) profit per entrepreneur (her unit of analysis), she could calculate the number of entrepreneurs she'd need to cover those costs. It would be a large number.

Poop and carbon

THERE IS NOTHING UNIQUE about Solar Sister's economics and its dependence on scale. I could have told you about MicroEnergy Credits. The ultimate purchasers of carbon credits are big financial firms like JPMorgan Chase and Citigroup. The only way MEC can sell carbon offsets to these firms is by accumulating tiny credits from many, many individuals who have replaced dung or kerosene with solar or biogas. I could have told you about Pivot Works, which converts human waste into industrial fuel. As founder Ashley Murray tells me:

> We define full-scale – it's somewhat arbitrary, but we're talking about building facilities at a scale that will serve about a million people per plant in terms of sanitation. We know that we have to be at a pretty critical scale to recover the costs of the equipment. We also know that we need to be able at a critical scale to make any dent in urban sanitation. ...
>
> And then, on the back end, we need to produce huge volumes of fuel if we're going to get a look from industries like cement and power plants, because they just burn so much fuel for hours. It's not worth their time if we can only provide them with several kilograms, or even hundreds of kilograms, of sludge a day. It just isn't enough. And I think that's awesome, because that enables us to serve more in sanitation, which is our mission.

26 Value chain

Chained value

HOW CAN A TREE BECOME A GUITAR? It is cut down, transported, sawn into boards, sold as lumber, purchased by a craftsperson, sliced, planed, sanded, shaped, and glued, fitted with tuning keys, strung with strings, and adorned with frets, a pick guard, and other functional and simply decorative niceties. Not because it takes music lessons. The business-speak for all this is that it passes through a value chain. A rudimentary value chain is drawn like a series of interlocking chevrons, something like this:

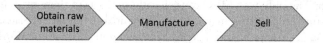

Only for a very rare product or service will one person or organization see something all the way from start to finish. For the rest, many parties play a role, linked together in a chain of activities, each of which creates additional value for an ultimate customer. Supporting these direct value-creating steps are ancillary activities, including marketing, technical support, legal services, and others, which provide important indirect supports.

IN THINKING ABOUT YOUR BUSINESS MODEL, one idea should stand out: everyone in your value chain must make money. Otherwise, why would they want to participate? (To be fair, some might do so based on a commitment to social impact. So we might more accurately say that everyone must see their incentives met.) To complicate the way your value chain operates, there is much we take for granted in the developed world that is not nearly as available in the developing world (and parts of the West), including roads, reliable vehicles, safe storage facilities, and much more. Your value chain must compensate for this.

KickStart's business model fundamentally acknowledges the incentives that bind it to its value chain partners. Though the organization makes irrigation pumps, it is anything but just a "pump company." Very intentionally, KickStart has established a set of linked activities where *everyone* makes money: farmers who use the pumps to grow crops, those who service them, those who sell them, those who stock and distribute them, and those who make them. KickStart's own revenues also exceed its costs, except for its marketing and R&D (research and development), which are supported through charitable donations. When possible, KickStart uses existing stores to sell through; when not, it creates other channels.

Every link matters

OR CONSIDER MICROENERGY CREDITS' MORE COMPLEX VALUE CHAIN, which is based on thousands or millions of people who currently cook or heat with products like wood, kerosene, or dung changing their energy-consumption behavior; microfinance institutions that are willing to learn about and make microloans for items like solar cookers; and large multinational corporations that want to buy these credits. As April Allderdice, MEC's CEO explains:

> MicroEnergy Credits is a financial intermediary that links microfinance institutions to the carbon markets. What that means is that we partner with microfinance institutions: we train them to start lending for clean energy such as solar lighting systems, water purifiers, and efficient cook stoves. And then, when they successfully do so, we connect them to funding from the carbon markets.
>
> What that means is that we've developed carbon projects [getting people to avoid using dirty energy by using low-carbon, clean energy technology purchased from microfinance institutions] and we've established off-take [offset] agreements with carbon purchasers. We buy the carbon credits, we sell them on the carbon markets, and we take a margin [i.e. percentage] on the sale, which is how we're sustainable. We pass on that carbon funding [to the microfinance institutions]. They can then use the funding to expand and sustain their programs. They can use it for marketing and client education, after-sales customer service, and maintenance. They can also use it to reduce the cost to the end user of the energy products.

MEC has sold carbon credits to EcoSecurities, Microsoft, and the countries of Sweden and Switzerland. These purchasers sign agreements, in advance, to buy carbon credits from MEC. These commitments in hand, MEC then commits to buy credits from the microfinance institutions with whom it partners. MEC's business model works only because all parties benefit. Those who buy a cook stove save money or time. Microfinance institutions now have a new source of profit by lending for products that their competitors won't. Big financial firms buy carbon credits in preparation for or compliance with carbon standards or to participate in a market from which they profit. For MEC, these linked incentives must be in place for it to facilitate the end-to-end flow of carbon financing by acting as a financial intermediary.

TRACING YOUR ORGANIZATION'S VALUE CHAIN is a necessary exercise in order to ensure its viability. Are all the "pieces" there for you, or do you need to create any of them? Does everyone stand to profit enough to be interested? Or might they be sufficiently motivated by social interests? Are there threats to your value chain, such as suppliers going out of business or finding more attractive customers than you? Until you feel confident you have the right answers to these questions, you need to re-examine these building blocks of your business model.

27 Revising your model

YOUR BUSINESS MODEL – how you will make money – eventually (and typically) will need to be put on a new path, whether nudged gently or yanked violently. Not because you've not given it enough thought, but because you're in business, and business provides feedback. Feedback can be illusory, too, especially when doled out in the form of adulation, awards, or recognition too soon. So: eyes open. Observe. Adjust.

Jazz

WRITERS READ, JOT DOWN, EDIT; composers listen, play with melodies, change notes; artists watch, apply brushstrokes, paint over. And so it is with business modelers: observe, craft, refine.

KEVIN STARR HAS SEEN MANY RISING social ENTREPRENEURS who study as Arnhold Fellows at the Mulago Foundation, which he directs. One is Jane Chen, the co-founder of Embrace. Her team had created a portable, easy-to-use incubator requiring no electricity while in use to give life-saving warmth to some of the 20 million premature and low-birth-weight babies born each year. She had seen; she had produced; it was time to refine, even if she didn't know it. Kevin comments on two adjustments necessary to get Embrace's business model right:

> Jane Chen [and Embrace] … launched a product without a clear customer. The real high-impact user that they bought into was the village midwife, and none of us had a clear idea how that village midwife was supposed to get this thing in her hands, and it wasn't designed yet to really be used by her. So we had two huge pieces that needed to be figured out before this product [even had a chance to create impact].

A FEW YEARS LATER, another firm, Warmilu, was forming to support the needs of low-birth-weight infants. Though its aims were similar to Embrace's, its technology was arguably more advanced by completely eliminating the need for electricity, even in readying a warmer for use. Despite this difference, Grace Hsia and the other co-founders studied Embrace to understand its business model: watching interviews, trying to dissect Embrace's experiences, including their challenge in reaching rural villages. From case studies and other documents, Grace and Warmilu were able to glean that Embrace faced difficulties

> not just with adoption, but also the price point at which they put their product, such that it was very difficult for those who are distributing to rural settings to even be able to distribute the product. They can't afford to buy it or carry it. ... I've heard that they've had challenges because of the pricing of their product, and it just has not been working out.

Of course, all this was second-hand information, as even those wanting to change the world are cagey about what information they are willing to share directly with each other. But it raised questions that Warmilu recognized it had to consider in determining how to make its own business a success.

CHANGING YOUR BUSINESS MODEL is not at all uncommon. Organizations may change their model in fundamental ways, such as changing their legal status (from nonprofit to for-profit or hybrid; and less often from for-profit to nonprofit). They may decide to license their product rather than being responsible for end-to-end manufacturing and distribution. They may target a new market segment and possibly vary their offering to better meet their requirements. The list goes on.

Embrace, as you will recall, eventually decided that it should adjust its tack to strengthen its financial position – creating a for-profit to sell a new line of warmers to private clinics, who could afford to pay a higher price than could poor villagers. These sales funneled money to the nonprofit through licensing fees, subsidizing Embrace's efforts to serve the truly poor living in villages.

Competition ain't a model

I WORRY ABOUT BUSINESS PLAN COMPETITIONS, though I have watched them, judged them, and even sponsored them. My concern is that they create an illusion of change, but change rarely results. After running five miles on a treadmill, you're still where you started, and I think many business plan competitions are like that. Especially when they're easy to enter (as most campus-based competitions are), it's educational and exciting to compete, but then the winners often pocket their prize winnings and then strike out to do something else. I will give props to both treadmills and competitions for creating good workouts, however.

Which is a rather roundabout way to introduce this next thought: it's dangerous to win a business plan competition and conclude that you're really in business. Some, certainly not all, business plan competitions pay winners a king's ransom. Each year, the prestigious Echoing Green competition, as an example, awards more than 50 fellowships of $80,000–$90,000 each (spread over 2 years), plus stipends for health insurance and for professional development. These financial awards are accompanied by technical support, pro bono partnerships, a dedicated portfolio manager, social support from chaplains and, as fellows to whom I've spoken claim is possibly the most important benefit of being a fellow: connections to other current and past fellows.

These accolades create a sense of ease that cuts against a grittier approach to growing a social venture that is based on pluck, resilience, and plain old hard work. As someone who was instrumental in shaping Echoing Green's competition tells me:

> The larger the cash prizes, the more likely the entrepreneur is to try and spend their way out of a problem. They don't leverage the power of scarcity. If they have $10,000 for a focus group or social media consultant, they will spend it. If they didn't have access to that capital they'd get out and do the hard work of face-to-face customer validation/rejection or spend two to three hours a day for a week learning leading social media strategies.

THE MOST INSIDIOUS ASPECTS of living off prize winnings are viewing them as validation that your business model is working, and, more troubling, parlaying your status as a winner to win other competitions. As you may recall (Chapter 10, "In-credulous: Talent doesn't have hues"), Yusuf Randera-Rees is the South African social entrepreneur whose organization Awethu identifies and supports those living in townships (slums) with the aptitude to become entrepreneurs but who lack the money, education, and other resources to fulfill their promise. And at this point let us recall his insight after becoming an Echoing Green Fellow: "You can travel around the world for two years on the back of a good story, never having done anything. I didn't want to be like that."

Take the money and …

ED CARDOZA OF STILL HARBOR, advisor to social entrepreneurs, explains the effects of unearned money interfering with effectively building your business:

> A number of pretty serious foundations and organizations take these incredible individuals with incredible ideas, and then just give money. That money comes pretty easily and the [venture] is actually able to get up [and running] in a year or two or three in significant ways. But really being able to continue the work takes a lot more than just simply giving people fellowships. It requires this depth of relationships and building relationships.
> We get a lot of those people at Still Harbor – and this is where I cringe: we see organizations that were created three years ago that got awards or fellowships or recognition that lead to money; they've built extraordinarily strong organizations. I'm talking about tending to 10,000, 25,000, 45,000 people, saving lots [of people]. They can show you the data. They're recognized by medical journals.

But they've been doing business in a highly unnatural way. In truth, they haven't been doing business at all:

> And, all of a sudden, the funding is pulled, and nobody has ever really thought about the fact that there's something about the intervention that is different than the business. They don't always produce revenue. If they don't produce revenue, has anyone talked to them about developing a fundraising plan and strategy in places where most of the funders don't necessarily fund ongoing direct service work, preferring fascinating or sexy [innovations]? That's where I always get nervous.

To sum this up: funding from competitions and other non-market sources of capital can provide money to help you launch (or grow). If you're lucky, you get feedback from experienced judges, too. But even when you win a business plan or receive a grant, all you've really received is the assent of a judge or grant officer who thought your plan and idea were good. Don't conclude that you've got a business model attractive enough to sustain you for the long run.

Yet Ed concedes the attractiveness of accepting such money, even at the sake of building longer-term solutions:

> Because money hangs in the balance, social entrepreneurs aren't going to say, 'If we do that, not only is it going to produce the wrong effect, it may actually create further damage.'

Fresh eyes

HAVE YOU EVER TRIED TO PROOFREAD something that you had written and rewritten so many times that you could no longer notice the errors no longer notice the errors? [*sic*]. This same problem can afflict business models, so one virtue of business plan competitions is the fresh perspective that they offer.

As I've described, April Allderdice of MicroEnergy Credits devised a business model based on using microfinance to reduce carbon emissions and selling the resulting carbon credits to large companies. She was well ahead of her time.

> Very early-stage, we did a business plan competition [UC Berkeley's Global Special Venture Business Plan Competition]. That really validated our business model, which really gave us the confidence that people will invest in this. It was such a new idea – a really different business model. Now, I'm finding that people say, 'Yeah, that works: no problem.' But, back then, people were saying, 'No way! You can't do that. How on earth are you going to do that?' So, I was actually surprised that we won but really excited, too.
>
> It was transformative for us. [Without the validation from the competition,] we might have been a nonprofit, we might have been an advisory

group. Based on feedback, we did a lot of revisions. The competition had several stages and we got feedback at every stage.

Among the judges were investors from Acumen Fund (the social venture capital fund) as well as more traditional San Francisco-based venture capitalists. While they were offering feedback and deciding winners, they were also viewing competitors from the lens of actual investment:

> Even after the competition, they connected us to other funds that would invest, and we got feedback when we pitched to them, too. I mean, there was a lot of advice on the business plan and it really helped us. We revised a lot, though the fundamental structure has remained surprisingly the same – the underlying concept. But there were a lot of tweaks where we needed to make it cleaner, tighter, easier to communicate. That happened at the business plan stage. And then, of course, in our early years after operating, we tested and tweaked some more.

Part 5

Running your business

THE ESSENTIAL ACTIVITIES of your small startup rival in scope those of a Fortune 500 firm, even with your skimpy staff and rounding-error budget. Size does not excuse you from product development, production, marketing, sales, or the other requisites of business. But, as a small player, often operating far from home and offering products or services the value of which convention is yet to recognize, the very market to which you want to sell must still be created, and even your legitimacy may be questioned.

Part 5 covers these issues along with others that social entrepreneurs face, such as choosing a legal status, fundraising, market testing, and managing your organization. While far from a textbook, this part offers hard-won advice from others whose paths seemed as daunting as yours.

28 Small ain't easy

Small businesses, still complex

TITLE INSURANCE IS THE BEDROCK of property ownership. It allows someone to buy a home or parcel of land without the fear that someone else will claim that it's theirs. A foundation of modern capitalism, insurance may appear to be as far from social entrepreneurship as imaginable. At least until you exercise your imagination, as did Craig DeRoy (see also Chapter 14, "Away from home" and Chapter 17, "Adaptive hiring").

A lawyer by training, Craig was president of First American Financial Corporation, a 125-year-old company worth $3 billion, whose largest subsidiary, First American Title Insurance Company, is the second largest title insurance company in the United States, with more than a quarter of the market. After taking early retirement, Craig founded Medeem, which provides evidence for Ghanaians (and now Zambians) to assert their ownership of property, although it falls short of the full legal protections actual title insurance offers in the United States. For a poor person, there may be no recourse when there is a dispute regarding property she owns, lives on, or where she has a business. And seizure of her property can be a devastating blow, even for a parcel that may appear meager to the outside world. Using a variety of digitized surveying and mapping technologies, Medeem works to help women, smallholder farmers, and other vulnerable citizens provide evidence that property is "in my name" – which is what the word *medeem* means in Twi, the native language of Ghana.

With 25 years of corporate experience, much of it relevant to Medeem's goals, it might seem that establishing this much smaller, simpler business would be a relatively easy affair for Craig. Yet when I ask him about the ease of starting Medeem compared to running a large international corporation he cautions:

> There are all kinds of challenges [in starting and running a small social enterprise]. It's no different than any of the businesses I was responsible for at First American … where I had responsibility for global title insurance operations as well as database businesses that would collect property information, property data, as well as credit reporting and credit information.

... You always have challenges with any business. Identifying what they are at the outset and then looking for ways to moderate them, mitigate them, overcome them is the natural consequence of being in business, by definition. So I wouldn't say it is different. The challenges are different, but no less or no greater than the challenges probably in starting any business I've been involved in.

He elaborates on the similarities among businesses, which are more significant than the differences:

[In a large corporate setting], you're facing common business concerns: what's your market, what's your product, how do you price it, how do you sell it, what's the margin on that product, how do you manufacture it effectively or sell it effectively to keep that margin, how can you grow your market? Those are common considerations, regardless of whether you are running a for-profit in the social impact space or a not-for-profit. You're really trying to figure out, 'How do I get my service or my product to have the most impact?' That translates to [the corporate equivalent of] 'How do I sell the most of it? How do I realize the most gain from that product?' It's a pretty equal translation. You could make that transition.

29 Selling your stuff

THOMAS J. WATSON, who headed IBM for more than 40 years, reportedly said during the Second World War that the world would never need more than five computers. Thomas Edison failed to understand the usefulness of his prototype movie camera, so never sought a European patent. These men of power misunderstood their markets. Similarly, consumers may fail, at least at first, to recognize the utility and importance of various products (bednets) or services (micro-insurance). This observation leads to two, slightly different, conclusions. One, you can do market testing to determine the readiness of customers to purchase (be empirical, then adjust your approach). Or, two, you might doggedly create the very market that is not yet ready to buy (be determined, and make it so).

That's a *what?*

IT MAY SEEM OBVIOUS, but products don't sell themselves. I've done in-class exercises where I've asked students to tell me where they've seen Coke being sold. The list is mind-boggling, including shacks in the poorest reaches of India and Africa, to way stations along routes to the top of the Himalayas. (As an interesting aside: the UK charity ColaLife distributes badly needed medicines such as oral rehydration salts in special, wedge-shaped packs placed between the necks of stacked Coke bottles that are already being delivered to remote locations.)

But social ventures aren't selling Coke. And prospective customers may have no idea why they'd ever want to spend their hard-earned money for the products or services social ventures offer. Your business model must acknowledge this. Martin Fisher, who has been creating wealth for smallholder African farmers for decades, explains the challenge, with all its ironies:

> What happens when you introduce a brand-new product [is] always that things take off very, very slowly. The investment to sell one product [after selling to relatively less-expensive-to-reach early adopters] goes up very quickly. You've got to build out a whole infrastructure.

In truth, he is talking about what happens in the developed West when you try to sell something new (as cell phones used to be), or sell things in new ways (as Amazon had to get people used to).

> Basically, it took 10–15 years for us [U.S. consumers] to adopt personal computers. For me, it was six or seven years before I bought one. It took me five or six years before I bought a cell phone. Overall, it took us 10 or 15 years to adopt cell phones, right? And we're the wealthiest people in the world. So it takes time. ... It took Amazon ten years and $3.5 billion to be profitable on a single book. And all they were doing is taking someone who buys a book and convincing them to buy it a different way.

MARTIN'S ORGANIZATION KickStart sells irrigation pumps to farmers with small plots of land. He compared selling them pumps to selling cell phones to people with similar incomes. Why do they buy cell phones? "Poor people aren't going to pay for time-saving devices: they're going to pay for money-making or money-saving devices. A small number for money-saving, a lot for money-making."

On this point, KickStart fares well compared to a cell phone. Its featured pump is even called the "MoneyMaker." But, on other points, the comparison falls apart. First, cell phones were a mature market before sales shifted to developing countries. They had been designed, were mass-produced, and sales prices were already dropping. KickStart's circumstances were 180 degrees the opposite. Cell phones also seduce you into thinking a better life lies right around the bend:

> I remember a friend telling me he was on one of the islands off of Sumatra [Indonesia] – an island with about 2 km of paved road, maybe three cars on it. Very, very rural. He was walking, came over a hill, miles away from anything, and there was huge billboard. What did it have? A picture of a guy in a skyscraper in Jakarta wearing a three-piece suit talking on a fucking cell phone. That is aspirational! Everybody will see it somewhere and that's what they want to be.

Yet, even in poor countries, farming carries a stigma. Martin continues:

> They didn't show some poor farmer talking on a cell phone. No, farming is not aspirational. In Kenya, if you're in school and you do badly, your teacher says, 'You're a loser: go dig in the field. You're going to be a farmer when you grow up.'

Oddly, even a MoneyMaker's money-making capabilities don't provide effective word-of-mouth advertising:

> It's a money-making device and it's much better than a cell phone. It's a fantastic money-making device. [But] if you make money, you don't tell

anybody about it. You don't even tell your family. If you do, they'll suck the money out of you.

No one even knows a farmer is making more money, or, if they suspect he's wealthier, they'll attribute it to anything but a pump:

> They don't realize [he's wealthier]. They see that you have done certain things. They have no idea how much money you've made or how you've made it. ...
>
> We literally have a case where the village was convinced that this particular entrepreneur who had one of our pumps was communing with the devil. How else could this loser have made money? He'd built a new house; he'd sent his kids to school. They set up a 24-hour watch for four or five weeks to figure out when he was communing with the devil.
>
> He's not going to say, 'No, it's this pump. I make a lot of money with it. I'm wealthy now.' In fact, he's going to hide his wealth and say, 'Yeah, this pump is okay.' And they're going to assume he's communing with the devil or, more likely, they're going to assume he got a nice remittance from some relative in the city who enabled him to put a new roof on his house.

For decades now, KickStart has been creating the market for irrigation pumps so that, eventually, it can sell them in volume. Its work to ready the market to purchase its goods remains a continuing challenge. KickStart's lessons must be taken to heart by anyone beginning to sell something appearing new, useless, unproven, or magical.

Aspiration versus illumination

IF POOR PEOPLE WANT cell phones, they surely want electricity, don't they? The logic seems sound, but it doesn't necessarily hold. Cell phones, as we've seen, have crossed the threshold from frill to necessity for many, even if they're the most expensive things that poor Indian fishermen, say, may ever buy. But electricity remains a frill, especially when there are other options like burning kerosene – even if they're more expensive, less convenient, and hazardous.

However, this wasn't obvious to Angaza when it thought about offering solar electricity systems to the poor. If customers paid $50 (or its equivalent in local currency) to purchase a cell phone, then, Angaza reasoned, they would see the value in purchasing home lighting for the same price. But they didn't. The firm hadn't considered that the financial outlay was simply too much – even though buying solar would soon pay for itself by eliminating the need to continually buy more kerosene. But *pure* logic and *consumers'* logic are different things.

ANYONE STRIVING TO UNDERSTAND customers must understand why they will adopt your product *and* why they won't. Customers failing to understand a product's benefit still bedevils KickStart. Too high an upfront cost tripped up Angaza. Products similar to yours that have under-delivered in the past are another common reason people won't buy. What may be most difficult, though, is underestimating how hard it is to get consumers to change their habits.

Kevin Starr outlines all the behavior changes that stand in the way of locally producing vitamin-enriched flour to combat malnutrition.[1] A local miller must get an appropriate mixing device, obtain the vitamin powder, understand how to use the mixer, actually use it, and be convinced to sell this new product; parents must buy this new (likely more expensive) product and then feed it to their kids; kids, even if their dwellings lack stocked pantries, have food preferences, and they must like a product enough to eat it.

The Mulago Foundation was one of Martin Fisher's early financial supporters and remains a fan of both Martin and the MoneyMaker, as you recall from Chapter 8, "Persistence." Yet, Kevin imagines how much more good KickStart could do if it were easier to change people's behavior:

> If you look at what a fantastic thing that pump is and what impact it has when people buy it, it's a really impressive thing. When you look at the sales figures, they're not and never have been [with approximately 7% penetration].

SMARTLY, ANGAZA'S EXPERIENCE in the field (see Chapter 8, "Flexibility") led to a diagnosis that its potential customers would pay for solar in small installments. Rather than making money by selling solar systems outright, they could provide pay-as-you-go (PAYG) systems that allowed users to pay for, and unlock, a limited amount of electricity, week by week, with each payment being applied toward ownership. After a year of payments, a user's payments would total the same $50 she would otherwise have paid at the outset, plus $2 more that was additional profit for Angaza. Instead of changing prospective customers' minds about paying upfront for solar lighting like they would for a cell phone, Angaza created a new business model. This did require developing new digital circuitry to put into their solar products, but it was less jarring than experiencing a head-on collision with users' behavior. Following my interviews with Lesley Silverthorn, Angaza's CEO, the firm has changed its business model yet again: it is now creating several variations of PAYG that are sold to manufacturers and distributors who embed the technology in the solar products they carry.

Who will buy?

SOMETHING HAPPENS BETWEEN having an idea and having a real business, and it isn't magic: it's testing.

Maybe you can relate to one of these experiences: you wrote a paper in college that you thought was brilliant (alas, your professor didn't agree).

You tell jokes that are really funny (but just to you). You've had a magical first date (but got rejected trying to get a second). If so, you will have an appreciation of the fact that a great business idea succeeds in your mind, but nowhere else, until you prove that it appeals to others: others who will use, and pay for, your product or service. There is some circularity here: to know if your idea is good enough for you to start a business, you first must determine if people will pay for it. To know if they'll pay, you must start a business.

This is where the concept of a *minimum viable product* (MVP) comes in. Popularized by Eric Ries[2] and Steve Blank,[3] it suggests that you test something that lacks features, is far from perfect, and will not be what you ultimately offer customers. But, in turn, it is inexpensive, can be put in front of people right away, and so lets you learn – *now,* rather than later – and respond by making adjustments instead of going forward on blind faith. Let's look at how this sentiment can play out.

As a scientist

YUWEI SHI, who combines the perspectives of a practitioner, academic researcher, entrepreneur, social entrepreneur, and funder, articulates the social entrepreneur's mandate:

> Don't be fixated on a particular theory, a particular perspective, a particular framework. Really do a deep dive to learn about context. [Use] fast experimentation, and don't be afraid of failure. Experiment – by it's very definition you will fail – as long as you learn something. Fast experimentation is the key.

Jane Chen, the co-founder of the baby-saving firm Embrace, was not part of my conversation with Yuwei, but she speaks as if she were right there, nodding in agreement:

> Prototyping, iterating – it's critical for anything you do, whether it's your business model, your distribution strategy, your marketing, your product development. It doesn't matter what. When you're trying something really innovative and novel that no one else has done before, you need to constantly experiment, iterate, and refine.
>
> [It's critical] to have an entrepreneurial attitude – a willingness to experiment, to constantly be running different experiments and trying to see what works and what doesn't ... Take a scientific process to your experimentation and have the humility to be okay with failing.
>
> Fail early, fail often. That is really important. Do that, and more than anything else, take your learnings, keep going, keep improving the model. ... I think it's really dangerous to be too wedded to one strategy.

She then pivots (a word entrepreneurs love) to specifically extol the minimum viable product:

> I really subscribe to a lot of the things Eric Ries talks about in *The Lean Startup* [including] the minimum viable product: instead of aiming for something perfect, just figure out what is the minimum you need to get something out there and quickly get customer feedback – because you can do as much market research as you want, but nothing will give you as rich data as just putting something out there. I would really encourage entrepreneurs to figure out what that minimum viable product is and get it to market as quickly as you can. Just start getting that feedback.

Minimum viable product

AN MVP is something that lets you learn real things about real customers. Creating MVPs is common practice in software development. It can mean presenting screenshots to potential users (even though the actual software doesn't yet exist) and seeing if they understand the interface you've produced. Even more minimal (and even further away from actual computer software) is simply showing hand drawings. Both are used to productive effect.

I've also seen various early-stage social entrepreneurs mock up systems that, when actually developed, would respond automatically to users' input. One that I'm thinking of would automatically alert users when certain items in their refrigerators are nearing expiration, so as to save them money and also put a dent in the 40% of food that goes to waste in the U.S. Yet, until the software was developed to track and report in this manner, the founders personally kept track of what was about to spoil for a group of trial customers and, by hand, sent them email alerts with the same information. This provided initial validation of their idea.

Probably what most MVPs are used for, though, is to see if there is any demand for your product and at what price. Ross Baird, whose Village Capital helps fund social entrepreneurs, explains the connection between MVPs and purchasing behavior:

> What's most impressive about the idea of a market-based solution to poverty is that what you come up with is so compelling to people who don't have a lot of money that they are willing to pay. They're willing to give you a little bit of the money that they have to solve the problem that your solution is solving.

Which is where evidence, not talk, means something: "The whole concept of a minimum viable product is that people saying they'll buy something isn't actually the same as people buying something." To illustrate the contrast, Ross explains that he'd be deeply skeptical if a potential investee found that, of 100 people asked, 60 said that they'd buy something.

We'd probably discount that to say, 'That means you've got probably six real customers out of that.' Nine in ten will not be telling you the truth. With us, in terms of evaluating a business, actual cash transactions are king and the rest of it is anecdotal evidence. If you got ten yeses in Kenya, I would heavily discount that.

To assist the potential investee, he recommends producing, and trying to sell, something resembling the final product:

Then I would say, 'What's the quickest you could actually give [potential customers] something that someone would pay something for?' We're relentlessly focused on that. What's the minimum amount of capital or minimum amount of effort you would need to actually have a cash exchange?

Analogs

WHAT AN MVP looks like depends on many things, not least on what has been done before. If others have developed something similar to what you envision, it may provide information to you about your potential customers. Kevin Starr explains how the Mulago Foundation has found that what is "really useful in working with [potential investees] is finding pre-existing analogs." He provides this illustration:

These guys had a device that could measure anemia [in the developing world]. It was like a $100 device, and they were going to have community health workers use it. The obvious question to me was: is there anything that expensive that community health workers have ever been issued and used? And, it turns out, there isn't.

This, in effect, put an end to the conversation.

As IN OTHER THINGS, exercising care in choosing an appropriate comparison is important. Lesley Silverthorn of Angaza knew the base-of-the-pyramid customers she was targeting were accustomed to small, hand-held solar devices, like flashlights or lanterns.

But they really weren't satisfied with, for example, another solar desk lamp that illuminated only the space for one child to read. They usually have four or five children; maybe even the neighbor children would come over and study with them … and you weren't really solving that problem with a very small-scale desk lamp, for example.

Angaza had a product combining solar and LED technologies that could fill the need for a more powerful, mounted lighting source. Angaza was aware that the price of its product was the same as a cell phone, which were commonplace.

But the similarity between its solar lighting system and cell phones was only that: their price; in other fundamental ways, they were not alike at all:

> We took a pretty hard look [and asked ourselves], 'What are they buying?' Cell phones were a big part of the analogy. A lot of these customers were spending $50 for a cell phone. Hands down, they just saw the value in a cell phone. A lot of it came down to status and freedom of having a cell phone. So we tried to basically optimize the SoLite for as much function-ality as we could provide but at the price point of a cell phone. Basically, even the average poor person in Kenya was buying a cell phone at that price.

But not their solar product, which was perceived as too expensive.

> The thing that we overlooked was there's a difference between buying a cell phone and buying a solar light. Buying a cell phone was so much [more accepted] – people trusted cell phones. They knew immediately what value a cell phone was adding in their life. Whereas a solar light ...
> We found we overlooked that hidden secret, I guess you could say. Essentially, even though we were priced at the price of the cell phone, we were selling a different product and that product had a much harder uptake in the market.

WHEN KEVIN STARR FINDS that kind of resistance, two questions come to his mind: why won't potential customers buy? And what might you do differ-ently so that they might? Lesley and her team had just answered the "why": lack of familiarity, and an absence of the "pull" from others' purchases to pave the way, conspired to erect too high a barrier for people to part with $50, even though they might want this powerful solar light. As to the second question – what might Angaza do differently? – there was an answer, and it laid the ground for an entirely new business: pay-as-you-go. For a $10 down payment, people could buy the light. They would then pay approximately $1 each week for one year for a precisely metered amount of energy (lamps can also be used to charge a cell phone). The entire exchange occurs automatically: the "release" of the energy to power the lamp as well as the metering rely on built-in hardware and software that connects to Angaza in the "cloud." The payment for each weekly transaction relies on nothing more than a cell phone and M-Pesa, the wildly popular mobile payment system in Kenya.

Importantly for Angaza, getting customers accustomed to such financing prepares them for larger, potentially more useful purchases in the future:

> We're using our current product as the entry-level product, but we defi-nitely expect when customers really gain full trust in our brand that they're going to upgrade to higher-power systems which can still be fully compat-ible with pay-as-you-go.

Easier than this?

YOU FACE STEEP DESIGN AND MANUFACTURING COSTS to develop a prototype, but without one you have no idea if your potential customers are really interested in what you want to produce. You're stymied. But somewhere there are analogs.

You envision selling rolling water drums in India. Another organization makes something similar, if inferior, to what you want to produce in Africa. Could you buy one and try to resell it in your geography? A third organization sells a water "backpack" – admittedly not a drum like yours, but still a conveyor for water. Might you buy one, see if your customers would purchase it? Will they *ever* pay for water?

What could be easier?

Pure

AN MVP GIVES YOU quick information, not final information, and its purpose should never be confused with a license to sell something simply because you've proven someone will buy it. Certain products need regulatory approval or one type of certification or another before they're allowed on the market. But continual testing – even when it is not specifically mandated – is your responsibility alone. And casual testing or quick testing can sometimes put lives at risk. Proof that someone will buy is not proof that you should sell.

Lisa Ballantine, as we've learned, embodies this belief. When she first got to the Dominican Republic, people were sick from the water they were drinking. So she launched an organization that made and distributed ceramic water filters, which removed impurities from the local water – but only for a few months, when the antibacterial properties washed off, leaving the filter useless, customers unsuspecting and still using them, and Lisa sick with worry that mothers were giving their babies contaminated water (see Chapter 9, "Acting from values"):

> We actually went back [to get] all the filters we had distributed – and we had distributed a couple hundred filters. I took them back and I broke all of them so that nobody would be tempted to use them again. It was a huge loss to our project financially but I feel really strongly [about giving these people something completely safe and effective].

Lisa and FilterPure were able to fix the problem through the generosity and knowledge of an expert whom Lisa identified over the internet who voluntarily gave of his knowledge. To ensure that such problems were behind them, FilterPure began testing every single batch it produces: "We do testing on the ground. We have a laboratory that we work with near the factory, and we do constant testing. Every month we send filters to be tested and approved. That is the most important thing."

Notes

1 Starr, Kevin, "Design for real impact: Design for the bottom billion." Forces for Good talk, June 2010. Retrieved July 11, 2018 from: https://www.slideshare.net/aynne/de sign-for-real-impact-0610
2 Ries, Eric, *The Lean Startup: How Constant Innovation Creates Radically Successful Businesses* (New York: Crown Business, 2011).
3 Blank, Steve, "Why the lean start-up changes everything." *Harvard Business Review*, May 2013. Retrieved July 11, 2018 from: https://hbr.org/2013/05/why-the-lean-start-up -changes-everything

30 Operations

YOUR PASSION FOR A CAUSE may not be met by your fervor for operations – but that's how you get things done, and you'd best do it well. Everyday dictums about achieving apply everywhere – forming an effective team, delegating effectively, and the like. Then there is the advice entrepreneurs are irresistibly tempted to ignore: imitate, don't innovate, when you can.

But special consideration is necessary when your operations are far from your home turf. Despite your wishes to the contrary, the technologies you want, the systems you need, the infrastructure you desire – none of these may be available. Thus your approaches to design, manufacturing, marketing, or distribution may become a combination of local habits, home-cooked systems, and even approaches imported to the present day from the dustbin of discarded systems of decades ago.

Running your *business* business

REMEMBER THE KEY LESSON from Part 4: you're running an impact business *and* a *business* business. If I could have asked for a show of hands to see how many of the 125 social entrepreneurs I interviewed started their venture for the joy of operating one, I'm sure not a single hand would have gone up. Maybe one or two would have said that they enjoy that part now, but far, far from most.

The aversion to running a business shows up in two different ways: (1) neglecting the "business" side entirely to focus solely on a burning social issue:

> I would have planned better. I would have had a strategic plan. I would have implemented a business plan much sooner. I would have sought consulting services. Even budgeting was something that I only did years and years later. I was getting to a point where, the more I was growing, the more disorganization I was creating.
>
> (Andre Albuquerque, founder of Terra Nova and an Ashoka Fellow [Terra Nova is devoted to empowering Brazilian squatter communities by helping them gain title to the land they occupy, while fairly compensating current land title-holders])

And (2) frustration (or dread) about all the "stuff" that must be dealt with even in a socially oriented business:

> When you read the books or the articles, they are always about the mountaintop points. They're always about the key connection that opened up all the doors, or the insight that somehow came. It's never about the 27 meetings you had that led to nothing.
>
> (Chris Mueller, in the earliest stages of contemplating a social venture)

> I can't tell you how many hours I wasted on [processing information]: hundreds and hundreds of hours every year.
>
> (Melissa Richer, Founder, Ayllu Initiative [an organization aimed at aggregating data about the base-of-the-pyramid to support scaling])

Rows and ducks

WHAT DO YOU DO WHEN YOUR DUCKS are on land, in the water, and flying through the air? What kind of row is that? You can try delegating, or letting lesser ducks fly off to someone else's pond. Whitney Smith, founder of Girls for a Change, suggests as much: "I still do boring stuff, but I've definitely tried my hardest to not do stuff that sucks the life out of me, because that leaves me kind of limp for the things that don't suck the life out of me."

BUT BORING STUFF WILL STILL NEED to be done. And part of the challenge may be in recognizing that the "boring stuff" is the "main stuff." Martin Fisher and KickStart's boring stuff might be marketing and market development. After all, the "exciting stuff" is addressing the needs of those living in poverty and creating robust economic systems that help farmers, distributors, shopkeepers, and many other African villagers. And designing durable, easy-to-use, locally appropriate, highly effective, affordable irrigation pumps. Exciting stuff that has lifted a million people out of poverty. Yet Martin explains why his marketing and market development efforts are so essential:

> In a way, they should [see the economic value in buying one of our pumps], but they don't. … There's a lot of things that we don't want, even though they could change our lives. So we went from being a technology design firm to being a marketing and sales firm. That's what we have to do and that's what we have to do well. And that's what we spend most of our money on. … We're a product company that does marketing and sales. We have to establish the supply chain as well, but then we have to figure out how to sell and market, and we spend all our time on innovative marketing and sales.

An online advertisement for KickStart's Head of Partnerships and Sales, Southern Africa Hub, lists some of the activities expected of the position:[1]

- Creating market development and sales plans.
- Selecting, developing, and managing distributor networks.

- Identifying new partners.
- Recruiting, managing, and coaching sales representatives.
- Conducting product demonstrations.
- Providing product training.
- Reporting on: impact, sales targets, new partnerships.
- Creating budgets.
- Managing budgets.
- Tracking data about pump users.
- Managing distributor accounts and collecting money owed.

Boring? Maybe. Essential? Absolutely.

By the book

TRAVELING UNPAVED ROADS and dealing with shopkeepers in small, anything-but-modern shops does not mean you can be unsystematic in your approach to business. KickStart knows this and adopts technology, adapts discarded approaches to business, and develops systems with the ability to reach deep into rural Africa.

> We're selling an aspirational lifestyle. We're experimenting all the time. We have a commissioned sales staff – highly selected, highly trained – out there in the field doing demonstrations. We're using hot prospecting systems – it's like Salesforce.com[2] for Africa that we've invented – out of cybercafés. Sales representatives enter their data, they get a work plan, and learn how to close the sales in the next week.

Outreach to remote smallholder farmers is equally well orchestrated:

> Live demonstrations absolutely have to happen, whether at retail shops, on market days, or street days. But, actually, they have to happen out at the farm, and there we partner with private companies, NGOs, governments – absolutely everybody. We get out on the farm because the farmer has to see it on the farm to believe it.

Marketing must be done very differently than how it is done in the present-day West. In important ways, systems that have outgrown their usefulness here remain essential where Twitter, Facebook, and even television and radio, have yet to catch on:

> The average person doesn't have a TV, doesn't watch a video. We use very hands-on marketing. It's marketing like we did in the '50s. I mean, the Fuller Brush guy, door to door. We're actually going farm to farm, demonstrating a pump. And, luckily, you can do it.
>
> It's expensive but it's not outrageous like it would be here nowadays. ... We are trying to prove, in a 'tipping point area' in western Kenya,

30 by 70 km, that we can get to this tipping point. We've been pouring extra money into that area – 1.2 million people live there – for the last two and a half, three years. We're at a point where now we have 90% awareness. Take a randomly selected GPS point – and we survey 550 of these – talk to the first farmer, and ask, 'What's the MoneyMaker pump?' Ninety percent know what it is.

Mimic

BY CREATING A KNOCK-OFF of Salesforce.com and bringing back its own version of Fuller Brush men, KickStart was playing the imitation game. It may be the most important game to play in running a business.

It is not a game only to play in the developing world. Before Rebecca Onie had ever heard of Dr. Jack Geiger, she unknowingly built on his ideas to get doctors to write, and Health Leads to fill, non-medical prescriptions. She is now more knowing and far more deliberate in adopting the best ideas from others. Health Leads' volunteers receive rigorous training in how to interact with and serve the needs of the patients they connect to resources including housing assistance, clothing, and food. The training is part borrowed, part custom:

> Our 13- to 18-hour training, as probably you'd expect, is a hybrid. It's both content that we've developed but … we're certainly not the only organization that works to connect low-income individuals to community resources, so we have tapped their training.

As we learned in Chapter 16, "Select and train," Health Leads plays the imitation game as often as it can, and "any piece of work … that someone else has developed already and/or is better, we should be using their approach."

KEVIN STARR would endorse Health Leads' opportunism:

> The most common mistake I see is the need to reinvent, which is a huge R&D burden people don't quite understand. One of the biggest mistakes I see is not understanding how much R&D you have to do, not understanding how many different things you're trying to innovate. I'll see people who think they're just innovating on one level, and in fact they're trying to do three things. And so, their burden of R&D and sometimes unwitting experimentation is tremendous.

Instead, imitate.

Design

CYNTHIA KOENIG IS A GIFTED PHOTOGRAPHER AND WRITER and an ardent conservationist. In the past, she gave as much thought to manufacturing and logistics as she did to how easy it is to get tap water from a faucet – that is, none. Now, she is obsessed by all three.

A staggering number of people throughout the world lack access to sufficient drinking water to meet their daily needs: somewhere between two-thirds and three-quarters of a billion people.[3] Cynthia founded Wello to help address this problem, creating a rolling water drum with handles to allow people to gather water from remote locations and move it with much less effort than transporting it on their heads (see also Chapter 25, "Accounting 101"). Wello's water containment drum is plastic, its handles metal, and, unless your garage is the size of an airplane hangar, you would consider it quite bulky.

AFTER ALL THE INTERVIEWS I'VE CONDUCTED, I've come to believe two things about operations. The obvious one is that they will differ widely from industry to industry and even business to business (when you've seen one supply chain, you've seen … well, one supply chain). But, and this second belief is my strong hunch, the operations surrounding a business that deals with a tangible product are trickier for an early-stage startup than for those who provide a service, especially when design, manufacturing, and distribution are all involved. Cynthia's experience with Wello is thereby instructive in understanding some of the challenges social entrepreneurs face in running their ventures and in recommending certain solutions.

A WELLO WATER WHEEL LOOKS LIKE A BARREL laid on its side with a lawnmower handle attached on both ends. Its action is similar to pushing a paint roller, though inside this particular roller there would be 50 liters of water drawn from a well or stream. To serve its purpose, the water wheel must: be easy to fill, be comfortable to push, roll smoothly, resist puncturing, slosh as little as possible, withstand heat and harsh conditions, last for several years (at least), be affordable, be transportable, be storable, and, yes, hold water without leaking. None of these features comes automatically and many were problematic.

The very idea of a wheel for transporting water required much thought, and this was chiefly gained by Cynthia and her team living with villagers. Water can also be carried: in a water backpack, for instance, or by a pack animal (although the villagers were surprisingly more concerned about the physical well-being of donkeys and oxen than that of schoolgirls who carried water on their heads in jerry cans). Wello engaged the firm Catapult Design to help determine the best solution for the types of villages Wello wanted to serve:

> One of their designers came over to India and spent time in the village with us with just some basic tools, where he was able to translate some of what we were hearing from consumers about their priorities, concerns, interests, likes, dislikes into something tangible. We experimented with lots of crazy things.

The early prototypes were looking at what was locally available: could we simply take something in the market and stick wheels on it, or repurpose it – present it in a new light? For example, there are a lot of toxic repurpose containers. Could we do something that would just line that container with something safe, so that the chemicals and fertilizers that had been sitting in the containers wouldn't leach into the water? People really didn't care about that, though. They would say, 'No, it's fine.' While we saw that as a need or a problem, consumers didn't.

Eliciting the most useful feedback meant sometimes ignoring what seemed central in favor of the periphery, as villagers discussed early versions of the Water Wheel:

We'd watch a lot and we would take videos. When we watched them, we noticed that while we were paying attention to one thing, something was happening in the rest of the room. We would use translators whose job was just to listen and then to tell us, 'When you were talking about X, Y, Z, actually there was a total side conversation about this or that, or people got really excited about this idea.'

More than anything else, though, design demanded patience:

Introducing something, getting feedback, but watching what happened more than anything else. Going back [to the village where prototypes had been distributed]. What were people still using? Who was using it? Who was the first one to try it? Who was the last one?

Does it hold water?

MOVING FROM DESIGN TO PRODUCTION surfaces new problems. On paper, architects create designs that always keep occupants dry. In practice, even new homes sometimes let in the rain. Cynthia's "architect," Catapult Design, "imagined a water wheel that didn't leak, and, at that point, it's really up to the manufacturer to fabricate a product that doesn't leak. When it did leak, that was on them."

On them – but, nevertheless, it leaked. Was this a problem with the company that made the mold to produce the wheel or with how that mold was used in manufacturing? Was it the way the cap was fabricated? Was the right kind of plastic being used ("there are probably hundreds when you get into the different blends available"), and even the right process for molding altogether? To an outsider, which Cynthia certainly was when she began, the process of reliably manufacturing a reliable water wheel was baffling:

I remember a time when I was asking myself what type of molding should I do? And some people would say, 'You're making a blow-molded product, so blow mold it.' And then someone else would say, 'You should rotomold it,' because they're thinking it's a small startup idea, it's basic: just do something basic. But no one would give me [the overall] context and say, 'Okay, here is what's going to happen: we will make the proto-type; it will be rotomolded. Then, once you have confidence, you'll go to a blow mold. Then maybe you will do an injection mold, but only when your volumes are at this level.' Finding the person who could come down to that level for me and explain it all: that just didn't happen.

Even had she understood these details in their entirety, she was unprepared for some of the tricks of the trade – or maybe they're better simply called "tricks." When plastic is molded it cures, and in the curing process the plastic shrinks. One batch of Water Wheels didn't shrink properly, for any of a number of possible reasons, which made the wheels stick in their handles: "It wasn't a great product experience, because it was hard to take the handle on and off." At first, the manufacturer argued that this was actually an improvement. With some effort, Cynthia convinced them that a wheel that wouldn't roll smoothly offered no particular advantage, and the manufacturer agreed to resolve the problem. "They'd say, 'Yeah, okay fine. We agree that's a problem – agree, agree, agree. Don't worry, we'll fix it.'" Cynthia reasoned that they should look at what had happened, then perhaps make a small modification to the injection-molded piece of the wheel. The manufacturer reasoned otherwise, giving workers utility knives to scrape off little pieces of plastic:

> That really didn't even achieve the purpose, and that was the part of the product that we wanted to have an especially thick wall because it's the weakest point. Why would you do anything to challenge the integrity of the weakest part when we've tried to strengthen it?

WELLO FACED OTHER CHALLENGES it was unprepared for, to say the least. One was that both its contract manufacturer and its mold maker did not always fol-low technical drawings:

> If you physically bring them something and say, 'Make this 20% bigger,' they're good at that. But to give them a drawing and say, 'Follow this exactly,' they did a lot backwards, because they weren't reading the draw-ings properly.

To navigate these plastic shoals, Cynthia engaged a design-manufacture con-sultancy, whom she learned about while commiserating with a fellow entre-preneur who ran clean water kiosks in Africa. The consultancy's expertise ranged from sealing plastic containers (from having worked with Keurig Green Mountain), to fabricating molds, to the capabilities of factories in emerging countries. They would advise Cynthia but also discuss issues directly with her manufacturers, often over Skype.

In due course, Cynthia also caught on to the peculiar logic of the envi-ronment in which she was working. Her contract manufacturer was already paying workers, even when they were just sitting around in the factory. So, why not have them scratch out imperfections in wheels with utility knives? Although making a small modification to a mold might only cost $500 – and truly fix the problem – Cynthia would need to pay it if she wanted to fundamentally address why her wheels were sticking in their handles – even though this should have been entirely unnecessary. Even to get into a factory in the first place to have a conversation, she would require an introduction – from someone local, and a man – otherwise she would never have been taken seriously. As for the leaking water wheel, the problem stemmed from its cap:

> It's about how to talk to someone who is really stubborn and is incentivized to do as little as possible. As far as they're concerned, they made a barrel, there's a cap on it, and it holds water – kind of – if you don't tip it over.

After first denying the problem ("it's fine, don't worry about it") and then overestimating their abilities their abilities to fix it ("we're great, we can do this"), the manufacturer hit upon its solution: take the strongest man in the factory to screw the cap on so tightly that it seals, even if no one can ever get it off.

> There was a lot of that. Technically, yes, they made a product with a cap, but how do you gently guide them in the right direction, suggesting that they don't want to admit that they don't know how to do it right?

Get moving

EVEN WHEN FLAWLESS WHEELS ROLL off a production line, they must keep rolling until they're in the hands of customers. When they stop moving is when the wheels fall off, in a manner of speaking:

> For our first and second production runs, we carried stock [to have on hand when someone wanted to buy from us], and then we learned how expensive it is to hold inventory, move inventory around, and to track it. We had to develop an inventory management system, and that's a less than perfect system.
>
> We rented [storage] space, and it's so expensive. We probably took a loss on about 50 or 100 units just because of the expense of warehousing for so long.

How did Wello improve on this situation, which was draining its resources, its income statement dripping in red ink? Some might say through luck; others might say "networking":

> Very early on, we were just trying to move one Water Wheel somewhere, like ship one from Mumbai to Rajasthan, and one of our interns – I don't

even know the story of how she connected with him – connected with a shipping agent whose business is in relocating people all around the world. He took an interest in Wello and said, 'I don't see why we couldn't ship your Water Wheels.'

Amit has since become an essential supporter and advisor. Cynthia explains that he often serves as a final check, especially when Cynthia is in the United States fundraising:

> I'll blind-carbon-copy him on emails to customers so he has a heads-up when they're asking for a quote. He makes it easy [to fill orders] … So, for example, right now I'm in the U.S., and we're in production this week. I've had a handful of calls with Amit, who's got a Google doc where he can see all of our purchase orders, the orders we're shipping. My team in India will be on the ground coordinating things and making sure invoices are filled out appropriately and that he's got all he needs to ship. But, between him and me, I'll just ask, 'Okay, is this all that needs to get done?' And he'll respond, 'Yep, got it done.'
>
> He's actually helped us out with warehousing and things like that, too. He's unpaid. I don't even know why he does this.

BY THIS POINT, Wello has been able to lower costs by holding less inventory, and for shorter periods of time, by pre-selling Water Wheels rather than stocking them:

> The last couple production runs, we've been pretty lucky in that we've been able to do make-to-order. We had a massive order come in, and we just said, 'All right, let's just do it, get it done.' Our most recent order, too, we're probably not going to hold too much stock.
>
> Our manufacturer doesn't give us floor space for very long, and our warehouse – it's just expensive.

Becoming sophisticated

THIS IS A GOOD TIME TO HAMMER HOME ONCE AGAIN the fact that all social ventures are really two businesses: one an impact business, the other a *business* business. An organization that was begun to improve the health needs of those with too little water and the lives of girls and women who transport it, Wello is continually morphing into a more sophisticated *business* business:

> If we had more bandwidth, we could have someone on ops and logistics to optimize [what we do]. When does the cost of holding inventory outweigh the cost of keeping it in Mumbai versus storing it out in Rajasthan somewhere? Where *is* the best place to store it? All those kinds of things?

As we grow, we're increasingly becoming – I wouldn't say a manufacturing company, because we outsource that – but we're a logistics company. And no one on our team, myself included, has that kind of skillset or that kind of inclination. It's a lot like writing with your left hand, and that's been a big challenge.

As a startup you're moving so quickly through different growth phases – it's like dog years. Three months go by, and I could swear it's been five years. Having a team that grows with you through that is really challenging.

Notes

1 Retrieved April 4, 2016 from: http://www.kickstart.org/about-us/job-openings.php
2 Salesforce is the world's number one customer relationship management system, supporting sales, marketing, and business analysis.
3 UNICEF, "World Water Day: Nearly 750 million people still without adequate drinking water – UNICEF." Press release, March 20, 2015. Retrieved July 11, 2018 from: https://www.unicef.org/media/media_81329.html

31 Managing

A QUICK GLOSS on social entrepreneurs as managers:

- Most aren't eager or experienced.
- The tools that might support them aren't readily available.
- They can join networks where members provide mutual support through advice and shared services.
- Effective managers pay attention to more than results, insisting also on fair pay and focusing on the well-being of staff and teams.
- Running a business where you are a foreigner and a part-time resident is possible, but it takes skill to understand when to step back and when to assert your authority.

What you didn't sign up for

THERE ARE MORE THAN 1.8 MILLION BOOKS on "management" on Amazon according to a keyword search. This is not one of them. But I will share some oft-repeated observations about management, and then offer a few of the suggestions that I found most thought-provoking. The observations begin with Martin Fisher getting straight to the point:

> This is a generalization, but I think pretty good, for most entrepreneurs. They're good at two things: having a vision and getting the [initial] detail right. If you don't have a vision, you don't start. If you don't get the initial details right, you don't get off the ground. But growing an organization, management, systems, employment, management meetings – entrepreneurs are usually bored by that stuff and they're not very good at it.

Martin's thoughts are echoed again and again, as if shouted in a tunnel:

> I used to hate being a manager; I don't hate it as much anymore, but I like to just do my work. I love to surround myself with people who don't need to be managed.

> (Ashley Murray, Pivot Works)

I think I'm good at starting something, and whether I'm actually good at this or not I'm sure is up to the Pay It Forward staff to decide. I don't like being the day-to-day manager.

(Charlie Cavell, Pay It Forward)

Neither of us [the two co-founders] had a lot of management experience, just like a lot of early-stage entrepreneurs. This is often a pretty steep learning curve for folks starting out, and a lot of it, honestly, we just often learned the hard way through doing it wrong and having to course-correct based on feedback. A lot of it was pretty organic, in terms of the learning process. More than probably needed to be.

(Derek Ellerman, Polaris)

Right now I'm dealing with a lot of lawyers because we're trying to get our legal registration finalized. When I heard about red tape, I just never really believed how red it would be. I have three interns on staff right now and then we have two staff members and then we have sales agents. So a lot of my time is managing various projects that are going on and following up with people.

(Maria Springer, LivelyHoods)

Managing: Pro tips

DEREK ELLERMAN EXPLAINS the inefficiencies inherent in being a small startup:

One of the really important areas that we need to transform in helping early-stage social entrepreneurs prepare for their work is to have the tools that are going to help them be more efficient in management so they don't have to work as much as we did, for example. A lot of [our efforts] were based on inefficiency.

AS YOU MAY RECALL, Last Mile Health worked through this very issue. Headquartered in Boston, it finds support from other Boston-area nonprofits through an affiliation it helped create that calls itself the "Practice Network." The Practice Network provides various ingredients Derek suggested the field needs, including: jointly developed systems, shared resources, and practical advice about how to get everyday tasks done.

Less organic, ready-made support systems are available, as well, including Taproot, which designs and offers pro bono programs in which skilled volunteers offer their services to mission-driven organizations online, and face-to-face in major U.S. cities. These services cover business needs such as human resource management, accounting, marketing, as well as strategic planning, and IT. You might find volunteers for an administrative task on Idealist.org. And, often for a relatively small price, you can contract with someone who has a special skill – say accounting, tax preparation, grant writing, and many others – through "freelance" outsourcing sites such as Upwork.

Tips from the front lines

IF YOU CAN'T TURN yourself inside out to begin to love management, try these workable suggestions from our interviewees.

- Get a "business partner with amazing management skills."
- "Sustain yourself, support those working for you, and don't sell yourself out."
- "Keep an 'open action' list, which shows each person's assigned tasks."
- "Think about who is on your team and what's going to motivate them. It takes a lot of communication and a lot of understanding of incentives."
- "Have a mentor or peers on whom you can call."

Ninja management

WAYNE GRETZKY, THE HOCKEY GREAT, famously said, "I skate to where the puck is going to be, not where it has been." Most managers skate to the puck, but then there are the ninjas. John Anner, CEO of the Dream Corps, speaks of the three focal areas that define where the puck is heading:

> [Staff on every level] have really got to manage three things simultaneously. One is the results of whatever it is they're working on; the second is the process by which those results are obtained, … because you can't just run roughshod over everybody else in the office; and third is relationships. Maintaining relationships allows you to be much more effective. So, if you're really shy and retiring and won't ask people for help, you just can't get out of your own little circle. Or if you're an 'emergency creator' – somebody who's always dumping things in people's laps at the last minute – you're not paying attention to that relationship piece and people don't like working with you.

NIKKI HENDERSON, currently a consultant on personal and community wellness, speaks to the three distinct levels of management that must each be acknowledged:

> The management of the team as a team [as opposed to managing individuals] is completely indispensable. The day and the minute that that falls through the cracks – quote unquote 'because of the work' – is the day that the team starts to crack apart and the work stops happening. Recognizing competing interests and establishing accountability to the larger vision can only happen collectively.
>
> And managing a team is a very different skillset than running an organization. So if you don't know how to manage a team but you know how

to run an organization, then you need someone there who can manage the team. That was definitely something that came up ... When the [executive director was away, spending time on organizational issues] you needed [someone] who is there in the office, so people can go into their office when they were having trouble with their supervisor, or who knew when we needed that staff meeting where we didn't talk about the work and just talked about how we were doing because one of our staff people just got hit by a car. If you don't get to see that kind of stuff, then you won't know [about issues affecting your team]. And then it's going to show up in all these crazy ways and you won't even know how it happened.

Stranger in a strange land

RUNNING A BUSINESS OVERSEAS would be easier if the laws of physics didn't prevent you from being two places at once. (Let's overlook the physics of quantum entanglement, which suggests this possibility.) For business, at least, you must be close to the action – if that's overseas, it's overseas – *and* close to the money, which you often must raise back home.

Americans may take for granted what they know about their home country, at least until they begin to operate outside it. Cynthia Koenig, who founded Wello, the organization that manufactures and sells rolling water drums in India, found this out:

> Even though I've never run a business in the U.S., there are things I know about business in the U.S., or banking, or how to ask good questions, or who to ask for something. In India, I'm like five rungs below the ladder [compared to the] knowledge that an average Indian would have of the same things. What any business strives for is efficiency, and I'm much less efficient. It's not a great place for me to add value to the company.

In India, Cynthia can be the proverbial stranger in a strange land. She cited, as an example, a sales tax that arose overnight, without any notification beforehand, which caught her, but not Indians, completely off guard.

> I had to have ten – maybe not ten, but definitely five – conversations with people where I'd say, 'So that happened overnight? And there was no evidence it was coming down the pipeline? Nobody had a clue, everyone was taken by surprise?' I had to ask questions like 'Won't our customers think that we're just total hacks if we didn't know it was increased? What kind of a business are we?' That doesn't inspire confidence.
>
> That's an example of why [I must leave certain details to native-born teammates]. I'm slower; it's more frustrating for me to be in that role for everyone. I don't have that context and that intuition. If you're going to do business in a foreign country, then you should have people in that

country who are primarily responsible for the day-to-day. Or you've got to be fully committed to move up that super-steep learning curve.

Cynthia is careful, however, to differentiate foreign customs, which baffle her, and probing deeply for business knowledge, which she regards as her American legacy:

> You've got to be very close to the work at hand. So, through our design process, I was actually a better person to do that than one of my colleagues who was born and raised in India, because all of my assumptions had to be validated. I didn't know anything, so I had to understand everything. That helped us get to [important decisions]. And that's useful at certain stages.

WHEN CYNTHIA IS IN THE UNITED STATES, where it has become increasingly necessary for her to be for fundraising purposes, her presence is still felt in India. Skype means voice and video is but a screen away – though countless interviewees warned about relying too heavily on a digital presence, while often being completely addicted at the same time. But it is vitally important to *appear* present, even when you're across an ocean. Cynthia explains that, before a quality control inspection, she checked in with both the factory and her team:

> I said to the factory, 'Take good care of them. They're nervous about this, so make sure you don't give them anything to be nervous about. Help me coach these guys.' Even though to my team, the reality I expressed was 'Don't let them get away with anything, right?'

CYNTHIA ALSO EXPLAINS how she learned to lean on others to help her negotiate India's business terrain:

> Much of what I [experience] is not unique to my being a foreigner in India. It's just the reality of a really cumbersome bureaucracy – a system that is still rife with corruption, with a lot of fear. So relying on external advisors: it's important.

And connections to others who know local customs and mores, and who command a level of respect or influence, carry weight apart from any advice they give:

> I think I'm aware of and thoughtful about understanding my place in this society. How do people perceive me? It's important for me to be perceived as someone who is connected. I might not always be here [in India], but I'm deeply connected. My place in relation to other people, in the fabric of Indian society at large, is really helpful.

32 Legitimacy

Taken seriously

RUNNING A BUSINESS OUTSIDE your country of citizenship means you might look different than most, be ignorant of local customs, not like the food, or even know the language. It can also shroud your business in suspicion, making your affairs seem neither local nor foreign but making your life miserable.

Although Cynthia Koenig, an American woman and the founder of Wello, had challenges with designing, manufacturing, and distributing water wheels, quotidian things like application forms and bank accounts were more frustrating:

> The biggest challenge is just legitimizing the business – all the bureaucracy, the red tape, the paperwork, the stupid amount of forms, and just things I need to stamp and sign. Easily, when in India, half my day can go to mind-numbing paperwork that takes you in circles.

A typical example was establishing a bank account:

> Banks – all of them are terrible. There will often be, or I will think that there will be, a very clear process: 'My company is registered, and the company would like to open a bank account. What's involved?' But on any given day, there might be five documents or 15 documents. Which one is it – is it five or 15?

Cynthia actually needed to open two Indian accounts, the first time acting on her own behalf, the next time with the support from an Indian attorney:

> With my first bank account, the bank refused to allow us to transfer funds in. It was a huge mess. [When I needed to open] a second bank account, my lawyer just called and he said, 'I'm going to send someone over; open a bank account for her.' And he submitted a few things, but none of the insane amount of paperwork that was required the first time around.
>
> The biggest thing is: how risky are you? And when the senior partner at one of the biggest law firms in India says, 'I'm sending you someone,'

that person is probably not a risk, right? When he says, 'You can use my home address on this, it's fine' – not a risk; this guy's not going anywhere.

Though Wello is legally registered as an Indian company, it is continually viewed with wariness by bureaucratic institutions that appear intent on sending Cynthia on transatlantic scavenger hunts. Cynthia describes a recent experience requiring proof of address for a renewal: "It was basically just like renewing your driver's license: it should be that simple." She had one of the particular forms of identification requested, but not another; she also had a backpack full of other things with her address on them: "all these things that I'd used the first time around, but now they weren't sufficient." The agency's remedy?

> They send me on this total wild goose chase and start claiming that I'm going to need to 'Apostille' documents in America. [That means] you have to take a document back to the Secretary of State of the state where the document was issued. But my passport was issued by the Department of State. I don't even know how you'd Apostille that. Finally I just said, 'Forget it, this is ridiculous: I'm not doing it,' and they said, 'Okay.'
>
> This happens over and over. I have a lot of frustration when it comes to there being different rules for different people. Depending on who is signing off, who you are, and what the purpose is, any number of different rules might apply to you.

This would appear to be something more than just a matter of Cynthia being female or American. Whatever the "rules" are, they are inconsistent, often unfathomable:

> One minute [being an American woman] works in my favor, another it's a bigger risk, depending on who it is. For example, with selling our product, my team doesn't really let me talk to customers because the perception is then that Wello is some internationally funded organization and doesn't need money, and why should they pay for a product? But it also can be really useful in terms of opening doors. I can get us meetings with any corporate, but my team are the ones who need to walk through that door and actually have the conversation.

I ask Cynthia how she could possibly know on which occasions her presence was expected and valued, rather than her team's. "My team is better at that than I am. They'll be able to tell who are the people who will [expect to see me]. They're better at it."

33 Legal

This chapter contains advice and tips from lawyers and social entrepreneurs who have sought legal advice (as all should). Your legal registration has a strong bearing on how you take money in – although nonprofits can generate revenue and for-profits can fundraise. It also determines how easy it is for you to be acquired by another business, if that becomes your desire.

The legal form of registration that best suits your needs may not be obvious, particularly with new legal forms having emerged and with non-legal certifications enhancing – or confusing – the choices you can make. Further, the form of registration you choose is not permanent, should you need to change it.

Legal turn

I've spoken with many social entrepreneurs who make the same mistake: prioritizing their legal status before their business model. (Before I get too far, I remind you – again – to seek legal advice, not mine.) Three representative quotes illustrate the confusion. Each is from someone yet to launch their venture:

> The major decision and the fork in the road was whether to go for-profit or not nonprofit. And, although I have a tremendous amount of respect for nonprofits, I do believe that the force of financial markets are far too powerful to ignore in trying to craft an enterprise.
>
> The biggest question is what kind of legal structure will we take? In my mind, the mission is a social mission. It's to give nonprofits a tool for fundraising and connecting with volunteers. But, if we run a sweepstakes, how will that play into it legally, depending on what sort of legal structure we take? Sustainability is a big factor, and a web tool, I think, doesn't necessarily fit the nonprofit model as much as it might a for-profit model or an L3C or B corp.
>
> I've decided on a hybrid model of a foundation with drop-down SBIC [small business investment company] Impact/Early Stage Funds.

YOUR LEGAL REGISTRATION DETERMINES THE WAYS that you can obtain funding and the ways that you can exit your business when it's time. It does not stipulate that you are, or are not, able to generate revenue to support your venture. It places restrictions on enriching shareholders (only for-profits have this option) and can remove the burden (in the case of nonprofits) of having shareholders or investors who expect financial returns.

The illustrative quotes I began with reveal that these founders have reflected on their legal options, possibly before they should have. Starting a business – for-profit, nonprofit, hybrid, or otherwise – entails the kinds of considerations that have been presented pertaining to your business model. Those are for you to determine; but leave the lawyering to lawyers.

Deborah Burand, a clinical professor at University of Michigan Law School at the time we spoke (and now at NYU Law), has represented both large and small organizations working at the frontiers of societal impact. She explains:

> I think the biggest issue [in the legal form you adopt] is whether or not it limits your fundraising capacity, and that really depends on who do you think the capital is going to come in from? … At the risk of self-promotion for lawyers, I would always talk to a lawyer at the business *planning* stage. Because there are lots of options and there are lots of tax consequences to those choices that you're making.

THERE IS A GROWING NUMBER of ways to legally organize your venture: for-profit (with its various forms including C-corporations, LLCs, and others), nonprofit, and various newer forms (such as L3Cs, Benefit Corporations, and Social Purpose Corporations). On top of this are dual registrations (in other words, to have twinned nonprofit/for-profit organizations, or to be registered in two countries), certification (B Corp certification), and state-to-state variations in what is permissible.

From the attorneys I heard from on the matter (five altogether), three ideas stood out. First, an exotic legal form may not be necessary. You want your venture to create societal good; and you may be able to do so by adopting a traditional corporate form. Deborah's legal clinic helped DIIME – the firm devoted to promoting the health of infants and mothers in the developing world by creating medical devices such as the Hemafuse – reorganize as a Michigan-based social enterprise by adding provisions to its articles of incorporation that made DIIME similar to a benefit corporation, even though the state of Michigan did not recognize that designation.[1] DIIME's charter made explicit its social mission to improve health, and permitted it to take into consideration interests that could compromise its profit-maximizing ability, including the interests of the customers for their products, their communities, and employees. The legal language protected the directors if they took actions investors might construe as not acting in the best financial interest of the firm.

Second, the right legal form may be neither obvious nor what you think it should be. Derek Stafford helped form Unión MicroFinanza (now Aldea Development) to provide small microfinance loans to small coffee growers in the La Unión region of Honduras. As is often the case with microfinance, these loans were made with interest rates that were extraordinarily high by U.S. standards, but below those charged by other lenders in the region. The IRS had problems with Unión MicroFinanza calling itself a nonprofit. They said, "So you're going to be giving out hundreds of thousands of loans, charging very large interest? Who might even consider you serious?"

Yet the organization worked very closely with several pro bono lawyers to make it all make sense to the IRS. "One of the ways it makes sense is that none of us take any money out of it [as profit or income]."

Third, only a handful of lawyers are familiar with the ins and outs of the laws and customs surrounding social ventures. You can find them by asking your counterparts at ventures similar to yours. But, as DIIME learned, talented, diligent lawyers can master the relevant law and, as theirs did, even devise new legal approaches to support you. As Deborah comments, however, obtaining qualified advice from someone learning on your dime can be costly:

> [Using an attorney unfamiliar with social business] is less what I'm con-
> cerned about. I think the issues are really on the advising side, not in the
> 'what do you incorporate as?' side, which goes to really helping the client
> to think through not only what do they want to be today, but what do
> they want to be tomorrow, where are they headed, and what are different
> ways to get there.
>
> The other issue goes to the pricing of that kind of advice and services.
> I think that, actually, is almost the bigger issue – finding affordable advice.
> Because lawyers will learn alongside their client, but the challenge is does
> a client want to pay for that learning? We don't have a private bar where
> this is sort of off-the-shelf: 'I've done it a hundred times. Come on in,
> I can give you advice and you don't have to pay for my coming up the
> learning curve.' I think [the concern is] more that issue than it is the qual-
> ity of the advice.

U-turn

DEBORAH BURAND HAS BEEN AN ATTORNEY in the private sector, the governmental sector, the quasi-governmental sector (OPIC), the nonprofit sector,
and in academia. Her words to social entrepreneurs contemplating their legal
options: "The sooner you get a lawyer involved, the less likely it will be expensive later to undo things." And you may undo things when there is good
reason.

EMBRACE, THE ORGANIZATION FORMED TO SAVE premature infants living
in the developing world suffering from hypothermia but without access to

incubators, realized that, as a nonprofit, it was too difficult to raise the amount of money it needed to meet its goals for growth. It formed a for-profit organization, Embrace Innovations, to expand its reach and serve slightly wealthier customers who would be treated in private clinics. Embrace, the original nonprofit, retained the intellectual property rights to the underlying technology, licensed it to its new-born sister, and used licensing fees to continue to serve those in the most desperate financial circumstances.

SAUL GARLICK FOUNDED AN ORGANIZATION, ThinkImpact, designed to offer college-aged students immersive experiences at base-of-the-pyramid locales. His organization taught participating students the importance of using market mechanisms to serve these communities. Eventually, Saul decided that his organization, too, should be market-based and converted from a nonprofit to a for-profit company.

JONATHAN LEWIS FOUNDED MicroCredit Enterprises (renamed MCE Social Capital) to mobilize funds for microfinance institutions (MFIs). Surprisingly, loaning money to well-run microfinance institutions is a safe transaction in that they are extremely likely to repay the loan, with interest. Yet banks are reluctant to do so, largely because of the perception of risk and the due diligence necessary to identify those MFIs worthy of an investment. MCE Social Capital removes both of these risks for lenders. MCE has assembled a group of high-net-worth individuals along with foundations, nonprofits, and others which, in effect, pool together money that is only spent (in fact, only collected) to cover bad loans made by microfinance institutions (or financial institutions making slightly larger loans). The process works as follows. Financial institutions loan money to MCE, which identifies MFIs it believes are well run and which serve the very poor; the money MCE receives is on-lent to microfinance institutions overseas which, in turn, lend it to poor, mostly female, mostly rural, entrepreneurs (sometimes providing accompanying support services including health education or training in business). When all goes as expected, entrepreneurs repay their loans to the MFI, which initiates repayment from the MFI to MCE, and from MCE to its own lenders.

However, all does not always go well, with 0.8% of the MFIs to whom MCE lends being unable to repay MCE due to failure of their own clients to repay them or from other business difficulties. That is when the virtual pool of money MCE has amassed comes into play. Those who have pledged money whenever there is a need to cover bad debts now give MCE the money it requires to repay the loan it took out to support the MFI. In the vast majority of cases (the other 99.2%), all does go well, having allowed MCE to make $100 million in loans in more than 30 countries over the last decade.

When it was founded, MCE was a for-profit. Legal registration was necessary, of course, to form a corporation that could take out loans from other financial institutions. But the decision to be a for-profit organization was not given enough attention. When MCE first had to call on its guarantors to pony up because one of the MFIs it had lent to couldn't repay, MCE realized that a legal adjustment would be wise. Operating as a for-profit, guarantors were simply forking over money to MCE. If MCE were a nonprofit, however, these payments could be considered tax-deductible contributions. And, thus, MCE is now a nonprofit.

Legalitie$

MY HAND ON A BIBLE (or the Quran or the Torah): I'm not a lawyer. But I did talk to one (actually several) who were familiar with social enterprises, as well as, of course, social entrepreneurs dealing with the legalities of money.

LAWYERS FAMILIAR WITH SOCIAL ENTERPRISES shared these thoughts:

- Be careful with the legal form you choose. It impacts your source of funds.
- There are differences between how you legally register your company – as a C-corporation, an LLC, a 501(c)3, etc. – and things that only sound legal (like B-corp certification).
- Some legal forms are viewed as being less liquid. LLCs, for instance, have a reputation for making it hard for investors to recoup their money.
- The state of affairs is emerging (through IRS rulings and court rulings). Be advised.
- Fancier mechanisms, including L3Cs and Benefit Corporations, may provide no actual advantage that can't be built into more traditional legal structures. For instance, traditional corporations (C-corps) have successfully included provisions that previously were only found in Benefit Corporation documents. And program-related investments (PRIs) have been made in charities and corporations that advance a foundation's mission; L3Cs provide no unique opportunity for foundations that make PRIs.

SOCIAL ENTREPRENEURS ADDED:

- Our lawyers suggest that acting as a company (LLC) and not a corporation is simple and provides flexibility (note any contradiction?).
- And their investors didn't mind.
- We can (and have): added a for-profit business on top of our nonprofit.
- We can (and have): added a nonprofit business on top of our for-profit.
- We can (and have): reversed our legal status from a nonprofit to a for-profit.
- We can (and have): reversed our legal status from a for-profit to a nonprofit.
- We can (and have): shifted the nationality of our business registration.
- This stuff seems like it *should* be so easy:

I said this to the lawyer and the accountant: 'I thought this would be so black and white.' It is just shocking to me, given how many companies are registered and how many companies are multinational. I'm not doing anything new, structurally. I thought it would be the most straightforward answer: Go in, just tell me what kind of company I should register as, and I'll register it. And instead it was weeks of back and forth. I still don't get why this is so complicated.

And don't ask me. (Have I mentioned I'm not a lawyer?)

Note

1 Masson, John, "Michigan business breakthrough benefits U-M startup." Michigan Law, University of Michigan, June 3, 2013. Retrieved July 11, 2018 from: https://www.law .umich.edu/newsandinfo/features/Pages/Business-First-Benefits-Michigan-Benefit-C orporation.aspx

34 Expenses

WHICH ONE OF THESE is not like the others?

- Starting a social enterprise.
- Working endless hours.
- Putting others' needs before your own.
- *Making a lot of money.*

(Hint: look for the italics.)

How do you keep your social enterprise afloat?
How do you pay your own bills?
And, by the way, you should buy more than you can afford now, because one
  day you'll need it.

Ramen

WILL BE YOUR STAPLE (is there something less expensive?).

Tuna fish will seem upscale (tempeh for the vegetarians?).

And x will be the number of years you'll go without receiving a cent from your startup (most said "at least 2"; many said a few more; one said "10"). One social entrepreneur puts it starkly: "The first couple of years you have to assume that you really won't be taking a salary almost. Maybe paying for expenses, if you're lucky."

Afloat

WHEN THE MONEY STOPS COMING IN (through grants, gifts, investments, or revenues), it will not be courteous enough to also stop sluicing out of your coffers. How can you cope?

There is no official strategy called "the Robin Hood," but, if there were, Bobby Smith should have patented it. After all, his social enterprise En Garde! Detroit gave swords to children (see Chapter 10, "Prepare thyself!"). But, more to the point, he created two activities: first, fencing lessons that his commercial clients could provide to their employees; second, lessons for poor, Detroit children who had seen much barbed wire but never a sabre. The instruction to both groups led to better fitness, better health, and better discipline. But only the first group paid, and their payments subsidized the classes offered to young students. His highly paid instructors, including one Olympics fencing coach, all had built into their contracts that they would provide free instruction for the kids. Bobby did this all without ever needing to form a nonprofit. Touché!

THERESA FISHER WAS AN ENGINEER who was designing and developing a medical device to ensure safer pregnancies in Kenya (see Chapter 10, "Now, just a product"), but it would be a long time until the money started to flow in. Yet there were bills to pay, including hefty sums to support manufacturing and testing early-stage medical devices. Her strategy for staying afloat financially might be dubbed "Home Depot," for she helped pay her company's bills by working a second eight-hour day stocking lumber and other distinctly non-medical items.

MARTIN FISHER, FROM WHOM WE'VE HEARD throughout this book, held a PhD in mechanical engineering and had ambitions to create tools to lift African farmers and their communities out of poverty. But the money he required was nowhere to be had. To support his work, he was able to put his engineering skills to use, but in ways not even remotely connected to his goals: building latrines for Somali refugees:

> We went off to the refugee camps and spent two years building toilets because that was the only way we could get money to run the rest of our program. It was a multi-million-dollar project, and you get whatever it was – 8.5% overhead. Without that, we would have been dead. We installed 45,000 pit latrines and developed a new technology.

He even saw the benefit in being unencumbered by investors at that early stage, who, not unreasonably, want their investees to hew to a predictable path:

> All that had nothing to do with our mission. But you have to be willing to try things when you don't have any money. If we'd had a donor or an investor, they would have said, 'Oh, what are you doing over there?'

TO STAY AFLOAT, stay resourceful.

Waves roll in, waves roll out

LET'S BE FRANK. You'll find many more ways for money to flow out than in. Unmanaged, this can be a problem; terribly unmanaged, it can sound your death knell. John Anner, who has run impressive nonprofits with the sagacity of a seasoned for-profit executive, sums up the mistakes that too many early-stage social entrepreneurs make: "When you launch, you need enough money to do your work. You're dead if you lack cash flow at critical junctures. You need much more money than you think. You need healthy cash reserves."

This does not mean economizing at all costs. He also advises spending money early to prepare for growth later: "Small business systems don't work well when you get big. So buy more than you need at the beginning [to be ready for growth and to avoid the double expense of buying small now, then large later]."

These systems might be for IT, accounting, HR, or other supports necessary for you to function without quills, reams of paper, and a green eyeshade.

Rolling out

IN NO PARTICULAR ORDER, and absolutely far from exhaustive, is the following list of expenses. May they spark the right balance between terror and prudence about the outlays that your organization has failed to consider. I heard them all:

- A "fancier" whatever-you-do to meet investors' demands.
- Paying for your employees' benefits.
- Conducting clinical trials or pre-clinical testing.
- Ethical committee fees.
- Customs and import/export duties.
- Retainer fees for independent evaluators.
- Patent fees.
- Hiring musicians and performance artists to advertise your product.
- Paying for focus-group participation.
- Providing working capital loans to those who sell your goods.
- Conducting surveys.
- Creating your own distribution network.

35 Fundraising

THIS IS THE FIRST of five chapters on fundraising (and investors), a reflection of how fully ensnared by fundraising social entrepreneurs can be. Here, I describe some basic concepts and emphasize its challenging nature. You will also hear a note of caution sounded: although you gain through fundraising, there is always something that you give up in return.

Financing: Appetizer

FOR THOSE WHO HAVE NEVER STARTED A BUSINESS, figuring out how to get money to launch, and then maintain, a social venture is daunting. A few preliminaries will set the stage and demonstrate that a social venture can use a combination of different forms of financing, some more relevant for early-stage ventures and some better suited to later-stage ventures. Every social venture must chart its own financial course.

You can receive funding that you will never have to pay back: this can be in the form of a gift or donation (from an individual or organization) or a grant (typically from a foundation or possibly a corporation). As a rule, this kind of funding goes to nonprofits. You can also receive money from those who expect repayment. This will ordinarily take the form of a loan (from someone you know or an investor interested in your work), or it can arise because someone became a part-owner of your organization (by receiving shares of your company). Loans are more typical for for-profit organizations than nonprofits, while equity (giving investors shares in your organization) applies only to for-profits.

Among more exotic forms of financing, you can receive a loan that, after a while, makes your lenders partial owners of your organization (convertible debt). Or you can issue shares in your company (even if a nonprofit) that generate payments to shareholders based on how much revenue your organization produces (quasi-equity).

Confused? Read on.

Strings attached

A DEVELOPMENT OFFICER AT A LARGE NONPROFIT emphasized that all money comes with strings attached. Investors will want financial returns, foundations will want impact, philanthropists will want to leave their mark, and family and friends who spot you money will want to feel proud and a part of what you're doing. Make sure you understand the strings and can live with them.

There is also the matter of capital intensity, which is business-speak for "Do you need a lot of money or only a little?" The capital intensity of offering entrepreneurial training and other services, for instance, can be very low, from several hundred dollars to less than $10,000 to get started. In contrast, when Angaza was just a small team of four, as Lesley Silverthorn explains, its expenses were much higher:

> To pay our bills we need $300,000 every year. As a hardware, or physical products company, there are a lot of costs just going into R&D as well as power sources [plus] the amount we have to spend on physical prototyping and manufacturing.

Funding from different sources (from people you know to large institutions) and of different types (donations, loans, grants, partial ownership) often vary dramatically in the amount of money they provide.

The challenge of fundraising

JOHN ANNER LIKES FUNDRAISING, probably because he likes people and likes challenges – although others with the same bent take dance lessons, bowl, or play cards but, for the life of them, wouldn't become fundraisers. Does he "think different?"

> Fundraising is really all about being able to tell your story persuasively to the right people. It's a really interesting, multi-dimensional chess game because, number one, you have to know who the right people are. You really only have two kinds of people on your donor list: people who give you money, and useless people. I just find that whole process of trying to figure out who those folks are and how to get to them to be endlessly fascinating.

And it must really take hard work to find yourself filed in John's "useless people" category:

> Persistence over time matters a lot. One of my biggest fundraising tips is: unless somebody just absolutely, vehemently, to your face, is screaming and yelling and tells you, 'No,' they're really just saying, 'Not yet.' It's just amazing how, over time, people will eventually find a way to fund you as

long as you don't come across like you're resenting it and you're not laying this guilt trip on them. Just be yourself.

Hot truth

THERE IS AN ADAGE, which many swear by: "If you want advice, ask for money; if you want money, ask for advice." But, first, you have to identify the person you want to ask.

Adam Carver flew cross-country to hear a speech given by Sandy Wiggins on responsible banking, just to get a few minutes with him. Others may act more locally, like Raquel Donoso, formerly CEO at the Latino Community Foundation, who explains, "If there are particular funders I've researched who I'm interested in, I make sure if they are speaking somewhere, I am at that somewhere."

WHEN YOU HAVE YOUR MOMENT, be prepared to take advantage. This may, as strange as it seems, require more sweat – actual perspiration – than idle listening. John Anner explains:

> I don't listen to funders! Foundation people are more rigidly trained than almost any other group of people. I know never to tell a potential [funder] what's really going on, so I don't listen to anything they say. What I pay attention to is what they do: who else they are funding, what grants they've made, what they are publishing, what conferences they attend. And a lot of your job is to figure out exactly what their framework for understanding the world is and then how to describe what you do in that framework. ... It turns out there's endless numbers of ways that you can explain the same thing in a different way to a different audience, and so your job is to know who that audience is and what they want to hear.

Even when it's a sweaty men's group:

> A few years ago, I was trying to track down this one donor, and he was attending this conference and so I went and attended. It was, unfortunately, one of these conferences where there was a men's group – it was like 50 of us, there was chanting and noise. But it gets hot, so everybody takes off their shirt and everybody's sweating, and I find myself right next to the guy.
>
> He's a large, hairy individual. And then the group leader says, 'Now turn to the person next to you and give them the "hug of the universe" or whatever,' and I thought, 'Oh no!' Sure enough, I wound up spending most of the night with this guy, talking about his failed romances and all the things he had done wrong in his life, and I wound up getting a $100,000 donation out of it. *That's* being a good listener, I think, and being willing to go that final mile.

John Anner is not like you

Not in what he does to raise money, but in that he likes doing it. Most social entrepreneurs find it endlessly tiresome, continually irksome. No single person whom I interviewed said, in its entirety, exactly what I'm about to quote in this section. But every constituent part of this quote *was* uttered, verbatim, by someone expressing frustration with fundraising. I've created this "mashup" – as if one social entrepreneur were recounting her experiences over time – rather than give everyone full airtime, because the topic is itself wearisome and this way we'll get to the point a lot quicker. In reality, the members of this chorus of interview subjects were at different stages with their ventures:

> The greatest barriers for us are financial. Capital is our number one obstacle. We need money to be able to hire people to work full-time, to pilot the model, and really get started.
>
> It's frustrating because we have to spend a lot of our time and resources on fundraising just because we need to get through this sort of early-stage phase. I spend most of my time raising money and I wish I'd spent it building my business.

As the organization grew, the demands of fundraising did not decrease:

> I'd say maybe 25–30% of my time is everything from taking meetings, to trying to identify donors, to cultivating some of our previous contacts, to focusing on stewarding our current donors. And, especially as we're growing, that's obviously a focus: to make sure we're continuing to grow our donor base.

Money is needed both for programs and administration – and is always in short supply:

> So there's this tension between all the money going into the projects, which is what we want, and yet some needs to stay so that we can develop kind of the infrastructure to support what we see for the future.

And, inevitably, the need for funds becomes greater, not less:

> The pure capital requirements were more than we had anticipated, so that was increasing our budget every year. The whole team had moved to India to be close to the end consumers, but the fundraising was all happening in the U.S. where the philanthropy market is much more developed, and the U.S. was also where we had our roots. What ended up happening was: I would shuttle back and forth between India and the U.S. and spend somewhere between 70 and 80% of my time fundraising. I think most executive directors spend that amount of time, and it was very difficult for

me to properly be running the business, which also required so much of my attention, and to be fundraising at the same.

(A quick aside for the benefit of *domestic* social entrepreneurs: sorry to have to tell you but, while you won't accrue equivalent frequent-flyer miles, fundraising will be only fractionally less onerous.)

> I hadn't considered the sheer amount of time the executive director in a year will have to spend on fundraising itself. And when you're trying to do something very novel that requires so much time on the ground – figuring out distribution, figuring out manufacturing, there are so many pieces going into it – it's not an effective use of time to be spending all of that time fundraising.

And, as the organization becomes even more mature, with notable acclaim for all the good it was doing, alas fundraising remained a perpetual chore:

> Even now [after decades], fundraising is still really hard – *really* hard. I mean, I spend most of my life fundraising.

AND YET IT REMAINS NO LESS ESSENTIAL.

36 Investors

To SPEAK TO INVESTORS, speak their language. Not simply by echoing their terminology, but by understanding the logic that guides their thinking. This revolves around making money, naturally, but how different are everyday investors from impact investors? Angels from later-stage?

Investor-speak

THOUGH THEY SIT ACROSS THE TABLE FROM YOU, investors are not your adversaries: they want you to succeed. Not simply to *try*, mind you, but to succeed – which is why they ask you the hard questions and expect well-thought-out answers. And, although their language is probably full of jargon, it's good to understand someone's jargon if you want a conversation to move forward. Here are some key financial ideas that funders will explore:

- *Burn rate*. Operational (or gross) burn rate is the amount of money you're spending each month; it can be converted to net burn rate by adding back your company's monthly revenues.
- *Cash flow*. Cash flow essentially means the cash moving into your business minus the cash moving out. Cash flow positive means monthly revenue exceeds monthly costs.
- *Runway*. How much time until you burn through all your money.
- *Break-even point*. That point in the future when your cumulative profit covers money received as an investment (you no longer "owe" anything).

To HOW MANY DECIMAL POINTS must you calculate answers to satisfy investors' curiosity? The answer may surprise you. One investor explains:

> The first thing I tell entrepreneurs when they show me their projections is, 'I pretty much guarantee you're wrong. I can tell you right now that you're wrong. It's not going to be like that, because you can't really make projections that early.'

That should reassure you; you don't need to be a mathematician. But there's more:

> But what social entrepreneurs would be good to do is show the market opportunity. 'Water sanitation: billion-dollar market opportunity. We're focused on this segment of the market, which is maybe a $750 million market opportunity, and here's how we're going to [enter it].' Then let the VC [venture capitalist] kind of figure it out.
>
> Have an idea of what you can make, and know the metrics for: this is what we're selling, here's how we're going to sell it, how much we're going to sell it for, here's our cost structure.
>
> But in terms of how many customers you're going to get, be careful not to limit yourself. You have to think big, but also think realistically. I think that if social entrepreneurs think bigger in terms of the financial side, they'll do really well because they're conservative thinkers by nature when it comes to the financial side.

One thing she expects ventures to be clear on is their cost of gaining a new customer.

> I think it's more important to understand how are you going to reach customers, and how much it costs to reach them. Because, if it costs $10 to reach a customer and you get $100 from that person, the VC is going to do the math and think, 'Every $10 in, I'm getting $100 back.' They'll make the investment and say, 'We can blow this up, as long as there's enough customers.' That is, the market's big enough to reach those goals.

Ross Baird, president of Village Capital, sums up the investor's perspective:

> I would learn about finance if you are an entrepreneur, because you have to be able to look at things through the lens that investors are going to look at them. Learn about debt versus equity versus revenue-sharing-based investing – all different ways that you can raise money.
>
> But one thing that I've seen – the concept of an exit – holds back more social enterprise investments than pretty much all the other factors combined, mainly because people who are raising investments don't have a good answer for how the investor will get their money back one day, and I think they need to. If you are selling your company for equity, make sure that that equity is worth something, and have an explanation for how that money might get paid back one day. That is really, really critical.

Ready? No.

PIVOT WORKS WOULD HAVE TO WORK ITS WAY up before becoming attractive to large, *financial* investors who have big wallets and who adopt aggressive targets for profiting from their investments. A rung beneath them on the investment food chain are *impact* investors, who generally invest smaller amounts but are more lenient in terms of when, and how much, they must be repaid.

When I spoke with Pivot Works' Ashley Murray, even impact investors weren't ready to accept Pivot Works' results:

> At this stage, impact investors are an easier target for us [than are traditional investors], and even they tell us we're still too early-stage. That's why we had to raise our money from angels [angel investors] [with significant help from the Unreasonable Institute].

UNREASONABLE BROUGHT IN ANGELS – individuals with soft hearts, clear heads, deep pockets, and primed to make small, very early-stage investments. Acknowledging that "the investment we got as a result of Unreasonable was incredible," Ashley was equally quick to acknowledge that she was the rare social entrepreneur who would ever meet a *social* venture angel – "they don't advertise themselves like impact [investment] companies do" – let alone have a group of them assembled and brought before her at a social venture accelerator. What, I ask her, can the more typical social entrepreneur do at a comparably early stage? Not surprisingly, she urges him or her to work through others:

> Build relationships and maintain relationships and really leverage people in your network who have larger networks. ... Find that person who says, 'You've got to talk to this person. This person will be really interested in what you're going to do.' The role of the CEO is so much about wrapping your organization with resources – that's relationships, that's employees, that's money. It's the whole web that surrounds the company. That's my job.

Still ...

IT IS A MISTAKE TO DISMISS venture capital out of hand. When April Allderdice realized that the carbon markets that she was selling into by producing cleaner energy for citizens living at the base-of-the-pyramid were measured in tens to hundreds of billions of dollars, she knew MicroEnergy Credits was playing high-stakes poker. When Ashley Murray realized the economics of shit (to be more delicate: that "fecal sludge" could be converted into saleable fuel), she recognized she was playing the same game. In cases like these, sources of sizeable funding are necessary to promote scale and expand your business. Funders with deep pockets become essential, and they are often looking to enrich themselves. It is worth recognizing that these sources may play a role later in your organization – not right now. In the interim, grants to get you going may be vital (as both April and Ashley found). But, as Ashley describes, the investor you simply chat up today may become a key funder tomorrow:

> We've done a really good job, mostly led by my business partner, of reaching out to investors. We've been cultivating relationships for about a year and a half, and I think it was a really good idea on his part to start approaching investors really early and being able to say, 'I'm not asking you for money. I just think you're going to be excited about us in a year or two years from now. Give me 30 minutes.'
>
> It makes it a really easy, no-stress conversation, and a lot of investors were excited enough that they said, 'Keep us posted.' They wanted subsequent meetings, and we have a long, long list of investors. But even when we were actively starting to raise funds, they'd say, 'You're early-stage. Come back to us after you've generated some revenue.'

When we spoke, MicroEnergy Credits had just exceeded its funding goals.

What's the what?

IF YOU'RE READING THIS, you've probably heard of venture capital. And there are decent odds that the idea of social venture capital, sometimes known as patient capital, has activated a neuron or two in your gray matter. This would place you far outside the mainstream of everyday knowledge. But let's step back to review.

More than a few of those I interviewed claimed there was more myth than matter to the idea of social venture capital. Not in the sense that they don't believe it exists, but more in the sense of Halley's Comet, which they know about but will never see, at least not again until 2061. And more than a few interviewees were frustrated by social VC's unrealized, mythical promise.

LESLEY SILVERTHORN of Angaza gives shape to the situation. First, of course, obtaining venture capital can be fiercely competitive, and becomes World Cup level when you throw the idea of "changing the world" into what you're offering investors:

> A lot of what we did in the beginning was just trying to craft our story. Why are we in Africa [selling solar products]? ... How are we different from our competitors? Crafting that story in a way that even people who don't understand necessarily the real market in Africa can immediately gravitate toward.
>
> This is a long process, too, with many iterations. As a for-profit enterprise, we're walking the fine line between our social mission − we're out there to alleviate poverty − but, on the other side, we are going to

make money. ('And here's why you, Mr. Traditional Investor, should pay attention.')

When investors thought they understood the story, they began to write a fairy-tale ending: outsized returns on their investment, garnered quickly. Saying that they helped change the world would be nice to crow about, too:

> It made sense to investors on a very high level [that we could be mission-oriented and also profit-minded]. The really hard part came down to investors saying, 'We get it, we understand: we're aligned with you in terms of how you can make money. But what's your exit? Where's your company going to be in five to ten years? Show me precedents of other companies exiting and making this very rich financial return.' Because this is a young space, we don't have precedents in terms of specific energy companies having traditional exits.

LESLEY ULTIMATELY DECIDED THAT ANGAZA should give up on telling a story that would appeal to traditional investors' sense of social mission but might require them to sacrifice some financial return and take more risk. Instead, Angaza would seek investors who more readily accepted how mission-oriented investments differed from traditional investments. At least that would be its tack in its early stages.

> I don't want to say we've given up, but basically we've stopped approaching the more traditional VCs and even the more traditional angel groups around here [i.e. Silicon Valley]. And now we're approaching more the angel groups who get what a social venture is and the more traditionally social investment firms. One of the things that we had to learn the hard way was that we wasted too much time talking to people who were never going to be convinced that you could have a for-profit social venture.

And this is where myth comes in:

> 'Impact investing' is becoming a term that's pretty common, but I think there's a lot more talk around impact investing than actual action. We're at a leading edge in terms of impact investing and we're an early-stage social venture.
>
> The problem is that early-stage capital, where the risk is much higher, is still very hard to find in the social venture space. I don't think we will have any problem once we raise a lot of debt capital to [provide enough working capital for] our pay-as-you-go [i.e. large-scale] solution. There's a lot more options for us out there. But at the early-stage capital, it's pretty few and far between.

Their solution? To cobble together

> a creative approach where we've raised a little money from a lot of sources: business plan competitions, some small accelerators, some [angels]. It's been frustrating because we had to spend a lot of our time and resources on fundraising just because we need to get through this early-stage phase.

Fortunately for Angaza, this amalgam proved a success:

> We're just seeing the light at the end of the tunnel now where we're about to deploy the pay-as-you-go units on a large scale. We've got a lot of distribution contracts in place, and we're about to hit a growth stage where we fit the mold of the larger social investment firms.

LESLEY WOULD LIKE OTHER SOCIAL VENTURES to have an easier go than she did:

> One of our personal goals is to really show that you can have a for-profit company with a social mission that will make money and will also be able to scale and make a lot of difference. A lot of our [motivation] is born out of our frustrations that there's no really strong example yet that we can point to.

No interest

WHEN ASHLEY MURRAY CULTIVATES RELATIONSHIPS with investors, she focuses neither on how her organization will provide urban sanitation (remarkably, it pays for itself) nor how it produces a renewable fuel source for heavy industry. Instead, she focuses on Pivot Works' economic returns: "We don't pitch blended value. We think we're going to be a very profitable company."

MARY LEMMER, who has sat at the investment table as a venture capitalist, echoes Ashley's sentiments, but from the perspective of an investor:

> The main thing that I want to get across to social entrepreneurs is that traditional investors almost get scared at the word 'social' when you put it in front of 'entrepreneur,' because, to them, it is the same as saying 'We're not going to make a lot of money: we don't care about money' – which isn't true all the time; it's just you have other goals as well.
>
> And so, when you approach an institutional investor, or a VC, or even a bank – really any outside funding except for grants – you really don't need to emphasize 'the social' as much. It is important, and I think it's important to include as you tell your story. But, at the end of the day, you're an entrepreneur. You're trying to solve a problem. Your problem is unique compared to other problems in that, if you solve it, it's going to change people's lives.

Mary uses Wello – the venture that produces and distributes rolling water drums – to illustrate her point:

> Cynthia is a great example of this. She is solving a huge problem – huge! A problem that is going to impact the lives of tons of people. But there's a business model behind that. And if the economics make sense – if the cost of what she's doing is less than the money she can bring in – it's a [viable] business. I think that that's the story that isn't being told about social entrepreneurs and their ventures.

37 Fundraising tips

Now that you've become acquainted with some of the inconvenient truths about fundraising and investors, here is a short chapter with some positive, useful advice about fundraising from those in the know.

Fundraising tip: Authenticity

The approach that Mark Hecker uses to ask for money is never to ask. He tries to learn and, without a hint of guile, often returns to his venture with a fuller wallet.

> If you go there with the intention of asking for money they will just rip you apart and tell you everything that's wrong with what you're doing. But the way to actually have a fundraising conversation, in my mind, is to say, 'You fund great organizations and you've really been successful in how you've been able to choose what's good. So what should we build in to what we do? How can we become the organization that you would want to support?'
>
> And, honestly, probably half the time I'll walk out of that meeting with money. There are all sorts of people that give advice on fundraising and they talk about going in with this specific ask and this is how you do it. I have never, in a face-to-face meeting with a grant maker, mentioned a dollar amount in my life.

Fundraising tip: Spare change

Well, not quarters or small bills. But foundations, businesses, and even government agencies, often have modest amounts of money on hand that they are able to disburse without complex approval processes. Depending on the organization, there may be a threshold of $10,000 to $50,000, which you want to stay below in requesting support.

When Charlie Cavell began his workforce development organization, he was an earnest teenager with a tantalizing idea who would outwork any two people and didn't need a lot of money to do it:

I was asking people for $10,000 to $25,000. Or from MEDC [Michigan Economic Development Corporation] I asked for $50,000, but that was after meeting with Kevin for three months, one week at a time. It helped [me succeed] that I wasn't asking for, say, half a million dollars.

I think it was that, tied with my willingness and passion and then also being naïve enough to go after it. [And] the confidence of feeling, 'Damn, if I'm going to do this, I might as well do it 100%, right?'

Too soon

ECONOMISTS, WHO LOVE LANGUAGE THAT IS UNNECESSARILY OBSCURE, explain that money is *fungible* – meaning that what you save to buy a car you could spend instead on a wild weekend in Paris. In contrast to wool socks, which are not intended to be worn as mittens or stretched so far that they can be worn as hats, there are no restrictions on how you use money. So, it would seem that having money now, and lots of it, would always be a good thing, because you could choose to spend it now or spend it later, and on whatever you choose. But it's not.

Ross Baird, whose Village Capital funds social entrepreneurs, has seen the problems they face when money comes in too fast:

When [social entrepreneurs] go out there and say, 'We're going to raise a million bucks and be very successful,' [they may not have done their homework]. They might go through their revenues compared to costs and realize they only need to raise maybe $300,000. So if you're out fundraising, getting the fundraising number right is important.

Still, why? Ross continues:

An example of financial flameout is a company that came real hot out of the gate, raised $500,000, spent it all down, and ran out of money. They went to do additional fundraising and everyone asked, 'What happened to the $500,000?' And they responded, 'We spent it too fast learning all these lessons, but now we've learned them. Now we're really ready to go.'

No longer the darlings of investors, or even in business, these entrepreneurs added: "If we had raised $150,000, we probably would still be around today because we were going to blow whatever we raised. But we learned with too much money, and look what happened."

IN A FUTILE, self-conscious EFFORT to appear hip, allow me to quote a social entrepreneur I interviewed, who opined, "Mo Money, Mo Problems." Noticing his reference had flown past this Crosby, Stills, Nash & Young era author, he kindly translated. First, this was a the title of a song by the late rapper The Notorious B.I.G. (who knew?) and, more to the point, when investors, donors, or others pump money into your social venture, they'll want you to spend it – not sit on it – so that you can demonstrate that you're putting that money to good use. But with "mo money" than a capacity for using it well, it's not going to end well: you may attempt what you're not experienced enough or well enough staffed to take on, or you may take on things that you can do but which don't create much impact. So, on top of whatever problems you had before, you now have "mo" of them – possibly many "mo."

38 Fundraising trajectories

THERE IS A MOMENTUM to attracting funds, but how do you begin from a standstill? Others can serve as examples, but never as templates. Here then are examples – from Zambia, the United States, and Mexico – addressing education, anti-trafficking, and technical assistance.

Trajectory: Zambia

LIKE A PAIR OF OLD JEANS, you can outgrow your funding strategy and need to replace it. You need money to start a venture, more to prove your worth, more still to grow, and you need money just to get money. Where does it come from?

The early funding trajectory of Impact Network, a U.S. nonprofit operating in Zambia (familiar from Chapters 4, 12, and 14), is a case in point. It set out to transform education in that country by using technology to create e-learning schools. It was launched with a combination of the co-founders' own money, small grants, and "funds from our close networks – friends and family and co-workers, things like that." At the time I spoke with co-founder Dan Sutera, it was running ten e-schools, "top to bottom." The founders hoped that these first efforts could demonstrate the effectiveness of e-learning schools, even leading to a new model for nationwide education. To get there, Impact Network would need to form a partnership with the Zambian government. And this would require new sources of funding, from larger, and well-respected, sources. Dan describes his funding strategy, which obeyed the law of circular funding – the need to have money to raise money:

> We're starting to move toward that next phase of mid-size and large funders. And since we're looking at a [future] government partnership, and also because my two co-founders are both really high up in the evaluation world, we just contracted with an American university at a highly discounted rate of $50,000. Typically, [evaluations like we want to do] are much, much more.
>
> But these are the kind of evaluations that you would want to get partnerships with USAID and DFID and the World Bank [all of which support

economic development]. That is the gateway to money and government partnership.

It's pretty tough to jump right into a government partnership, but with an evaluation like [we're doing] plus some backers on the international organizational level, that can motivate talks with government on a national scale.

Trajectory: United States

WHEN DEREK ELLERMAN FIRST BECAME INVOLVED with the issue of human trafficking, he lacked deep knowledge and anywhere near the funding that would be necessary to propel his nonprofit to a position of national leadership a few years later. Bit by bit, he bootstrapped his way, using funding to create new opportunities, and these opportunities to secure ever larger funding.

Polaris Project began as a nonprofit totally dependent on the contributions of friends, relatives, and associates of its co-founders:

The initial fundraising we did was simply sending letters to our circle of family and friends asking for donations. And also using alumni connections from Brown [their alma mater] to reach out and ask for donations. It was very much an individual donor-focused approach, and that was pretty much where we got our initial funding for about the first year-and-a-half.

Although such funding may appear pedestrian, it is anything but:

Frankly, those were some of the most impactful donations ever, because the entire future of whatever social impact we were going to have was based on those early donors. And it's really a great opportunity you are giving people to be able to invest that early [to support you].

Donors believed in Derek and his co-founder and put their faith in what they thought the two might accomplish to prevent human trafficking, even though they had no experience, let alone a record of accomplishment. The funding from these early donations provided a base from which to operate. With this base, Polaris was able to establish its track record. Polaris began to work alongside Washington, D.C., law enforcement, lending a softer touch to hard-nosed police raids. The issue of human trafficking was also gaining attention – at the local, state, and federal levels. This burgeoning interest, combined with the skills and reputation Polaris had begun to establish, led to its first large sum of money:

Based on the work we were doing on the ground and the work we were doing in collaboration with law enforcement, we got funding from the D.C. government in our second year. That was our first grant – for $75,000 – which at the time was an unbelievable amount of money.

As Polaris expanded the scope of its activities, its accomplishments and reputation grew, too. As they did, additional funding sources became available:

> By developing relationships with different congressional champions of the issue, we actually received a congressional earmark in our second year. We were just a startup, and no other organizations would have given us that level of startup capital. That was what helped get us started with grants and, pretty much, we came to rely upon government grants and foundation grants for most of our growth.

ONCE IT BECAME ESTABLISHED AS A NATIONAL LEADER, Polaris began to receive support from major individual donors and corporations, and to complement donations it received with revenue it earned from various services it performed. But Derek hastens to add: "But early on, really, it was government funding and foundation funding that was our primary strategy."

Potatoes, large

ALL VENTURES KNOW THAT having enough money is a priority, but the way many go about it can make it difficult. There is a cost to raising money, and it is often ignored.

Derek Ellerman explains the fundraising mistake that many social enterprises make, including his own:

> One of the common mistakes is engaging in inefficient fundraising. Because capacity is so limited early on, usually it's just one or two staff people, oftentimes it's just the social entrepreneur, him- or herself.
>
> I see people spending a lot of time doing events and other stuff that's going to bring in a medium amount of small donations, but often a tremendous amount of work goes into that. That's what they imagine when they think of fundraising, and so they just kind of do that. It very rarely makes sense for an organization to do that unless they actually have significant capacity in terms of fundraising staff and so on who can make that efficient.

YOU MIGHT THROW CHASING business plan competition money into the same category, as Leticia Jáuregui Casanueva, founder of CREA, a Mexican training and advisory firm supporting low-income women, explains:

> I would be very strategic in what competitions I choose to compete in. Because otherwise it ends up absorbing all of your time. And your full-time job ends up being writing the plans of the business plan competition or writing the applications for another award. You really have to look at all the options but choose the ones that work for the organization and for you.

DEREK ELLERMAN RETURNS TO what you should do at an early stage to make best use of your time to secure funding:

> What is usually the most efficient is focusing on building a base of medium to large individual donors and then focusing on proposal writing for either foundation or grant money. It's just many orders of magnitude more efficient. For four hours of writing a grant proposal you may get $75,000, compared to throwing an event and pulling in $2,000 with 30 hours of work. That's certainly a mistake we made. We had a couple of different initiatives that were just wrong-headed in terms of that fundraising efficiency.

Potatoes, small

THERE IS AN EXCEPTION to the rule of going after sums of money only if they reward your effort above minimum wage – and that is to do something that creates exposure and credibility that can be leveraged later. The clearest examples would be pitch competitions (sometimes in bars or restaurants) or business plan competitions (usually more sedate, with contestants wearing dress shoes and ties). By getting your name and ideas into the world, you create new opportunities, after all.

Detroit SOUP, as an example, hosts $5 dinners where diners get soup, salad, and bread and hear four four-minute presentations on a project to help the city of Detroit. Diners then vote for the project they feel would benefit the city the most, the winner going home with the purse. Charlie Cavell describes his experience:

> We got $1,200 from SOUP from the pitch competition. But that $1,200, though, we were able to leverage basically into another 20 [thousand] because of crowdfunding. That was the value. Because $1,200 – you can't do a lot with that. But 400 people that are there listening – that's something.

AT CERTAIN BUSINESS PLAN COMPETITIONS, including those run by Village Capital, the Mentor Capital Network, and the Unreasonable Institute, angel investors are invited to hear pitches. As you may recall, angel investors are wealthy people who provide small amounts of money at an early stage of a startup, mainly to keep it going until it has other financial options.

39 Funders' perspectives

THIS IS THE LAST OF THE FIVE promised chapters on fundraising and investors. Thank you for bearing with me on this arduous but crucial topic.

The lens that any given funder looks at you through will be its own – some evaluate using quick heuristics, some study your work deeply, others broker direct relationships between potential lenders and recipients.

Each follows his or her own set of rules, and some of these rules seem to say: "I appear to be – but don't act as – an impact investor."

Your rule: know your investor.

Funding: No work for you

SOME FUNDERS OPERATE SO DIFFERENTLY from each other that comparisons seem like antimony to zirconium. But dig under the surface, and you may discover possibilities as precious as rare earth elements.

THE PEERY FOUNDATION is a family foundation whose investments rest on a "belief in the uniqueness of philanthropic capital in being able to absorb ultimate risk," as Jessamyn Lau, its executive director (Chapter 6, "The siren call of social entrepreneurship"), explains to me. This is why the foundation supports early-stage social entrepreneurs through philanthropy and investing, and why it uses "philanthropic capital where the risk is greatest and ... makes sure that a good proportion of our fund is used at that early stage where other capital just doesn't have the flexibility to really get involved."

Peery is "very light on paper and heavy on trust," preferring that social entrepreneurs not jump through funders' hoops but aggressively attack societal problems. According to Jessamyn:

> [Founder Dick Peery] really thought it could make sense to know the entrepreneur really well and for [him or her] to be at a point where we trust them, we believe in their capabilities and their potential, and for them to be the right person to solve this problem – no matter what happens with the assumptions [underlying their approach]. And that no matter what life throws at them, they will be the one to iterate – push through the weeds to figure out what the solution is and make it work in real life.

And so we really don't invest in people in our portfolios unless we believe that they are the right people and that we can absolutely trust them with our name and with unrestricted funding.

But before you get too excited at the thought that this unrestricted, paper-work-free source of funding is exactly what you'd always hoped for, please understand a few more things. Peery does not solicit or accept proposals. It will seek you out (and is more likely to meet you at your office than its own). Its due diligence involves examining information that you're almost certainly producing anyway: information on your website, or documents you produce in the ordinary course of your work. It is investing in *you*, based on your life experience to date, not your promise:

> I want to see that they've spent a deep amount of time – not just six months to a year – researching, that they have spent time working in the industry within which they're trying to solve a problem, and that they understand all of the moving pieces and have seen it from multiple angles.

Peery assesses its funding recipients using a broad spectrum of criteria:

> Where do they come from, and what has prepared them for this? Do they have the right expertise? If there are gaps in their expertise, are they the right person to be able to draw people to them who will be able to fill those gaps? Are they able to approve the right kind of board members? Are they good at telling their story? Can they mobilize funding resources? [We try to understand] a whole plethora of things about that individual as we sit across a café table.
>
> [Too many] individuals have all the heart and the passion but don't have the life experience yet. They have the potential to be the right person, but they're not that right person just yet.

Jessamyn echoes a refrain explored at the beginning of this book:

> If you fully believe you are going to be a social innovator or a social entrepreneur, please take your time! Please be deliberate in your understanding … Fully understand from all angles the depth and the complexity of the [issues] that are reinforcing whatever problem … you want to solve.

Then, perhaps, Peery will seek you out.

Funding: Fair

RSF SOCIAL FINANCE SUPPORTS social investors, for-profit and nonprofit social enterprises, and local communities. Don Shaffer, RSF's past president and CEO, explains that RSF, itself a nonprofit organization, is "basically like a bank and foundation combined" by providing some grants but mostly loans "exclusively to social entrepreneurs and social enterprises that would not exist but for the deep positive social and environmental mission that is part of their founding impulse and their founding vision."

For its part, RSF's purpose statement is "to transform the way the world works with money," which it implements by giving equitable voice to its various stakeholders by deploying a variety of unique funding strategies.

A favorite of mine: lenders and loan recipients meet each other – first to better understand their conflicting desires on interest rates, and to then reconcile them in order to jointly establish rates that will govern loans for the next three months. Don explains:

> Every quarter, we bring together representatives of our borrowers and representatives of our investors and of the RSF staff to meet and discuss needs and intentions in a very transparent way. Then we seek counsel and input from our investors and our borrowers as to what rate of return the investors should get and, therefore, what rate of interest the borrowers should pay.
>
> We call this community-based pricing, or RSF Prime. It's an incredibly powerful thing because of how radical it is for the investors to actually see, and meet, and interact with the people where their deposits are going; and for the borrowers to actually see, and meet, and get to know the people whose money it is that they are using.

Rather than brokering these conversations to produce an agreed upon interest rate, RSF stands to the side:

> We try to be kind of Switzerland, really and truly. We try to provide a little bit of context as to where rates are generally, a little bit of the history of recent past where rates have been for us, and then we kind of open it up to the group. ... You can see how [our desire for] direct, transparent, personal values come to life in this example.

RSF aims to serve those who create opportunities within the communities where they are located, focusing particularly on enterprises with long-term commitments to food and agriculture systems, ecological stewardship, and education and the arts. Among those to whom it has provided loans is Guayaki, a yerba mate beverage company with a 50-*year* business plan that acts to fortify it against advances from larger beverage companies like PepsiCo that might want to acquire it.

A/B testing the virtual reality of monetizing

INVESTORS IN STARTUPS LIKE TO CONSIDER themselves tuned-in, hip, the smartest ones in the room. From an inves*tee*'s perspective, this can seem laughable.

According to one social entrepreneur (whose identity I'll protect so he can get future funding), investors fear *true* innovation, seeking comfort in the incremental:

> VCs [venture capitalists] constantly say they're looking for entrepreneurs who are very different, who think differently, who challenge the status quo, and things like that. But if you look at VC behavior, it's very scared. They have a very herd-like behavior in the sense that, once one person commits – puts the term sheet down to an entrepreneur and his or her venture – then all of a sudden the other ones suddenly get interested in it. But not before that. It's sad.

Another money seeker, who will also be kept in the witness protection program, more bluntly dismissed the abilities of venture funding to identify meaningful opportunities where financial opportunities and social change overlap:

> Every investor is bitter and remorseful they didn't get in on Facebook – Facebook or Twitter or Google, you name it. They're all looking for the next Facebook – the *next* next thing. Put together some conglomeration of buzzwords you've heard, and that's what they are seeking: gamifying mobile social; uberization of cloud-based analytics; the internet of mobile deeply learned things [I won't tell you which of these weren't in the actual interview transcript]. It will blow your mind. So if you're pitching an idea, you somehow need to align with one of these 'trends' that are on their radar.

The physics of funding

RELATIVE TO FUNDERS, YOU ARE SMALL, so the physics of attraction means that you will accelerate more quickly toward them than the other way around. Or, to put this in terms that don't conflate the laws of gravity and business: they have the money, you don't, so they set the rules. If you're not careful, this force can move you out of your orbit.

Peter Luckow, co-founder of Last Mile Health, felt this shift as the organization moved beyond its founding:

> Many of the donations and the grants that fueled our early work were from really compassionate individuals who believed in our work and believed in our leaders. They saw that there was value in providing care in a place like Liberia and were willing to just give, and give, and give.

As Last Mile Health (then named Tiyatien Health) received growth funding, its concept of care was wrenched toward results, however, as Peter explains:

> Some of our more recent funders, I think, would classify themselves as investing in social entrepreneurs. Those types of funders look for really

clearly defined models, strongly articulated theories of change, and are very demanding in terms of the metrics that drive the work. And we think all that is good; it has helped to push us to define what we're about.

And yet that emphasis clashed with the values forming the basis of the organization. According to Peter, social entrepreneurship in the United States, where his organization is registered, is "defined, first and foremost, by cost and scale: if an idea cannot be scaled, then there is no value in it." And that definition presented direct challenges to the services Tiyatien was providing:

> Our funders say we should not be giving any money to the women's center because that's mission drift; that's not what we're about. That what we're about is building a front-line [community-based] health worker model. And we need to invest 100% of our time and energy and focus into that.
>
> But, for us, the value in the work that we are doing comes from the people like Phillip, or Mary, or all these other patients, these *individuals*, these people who now we consider friends, who are living healthier lives. And [some in our organization] say, 'To hell with scale. [Our unqualified commitment to our patients] can't be replicated. And even if we invest an insane amount of money and resources and talent so that there's one individual who's now living a better life, that is of value.'

Peter rather grudgingly acknowledges that funders had an important point, even if Tiyatien's strategey would also be to draw them closer to its own perspective on care:

> We do generally believe that this model that we're building, in addition to providing that level of care that Mary needs, that Phillip needs, can be one that can scale across Liberia, across the country.
>
> We've learned that language of social entrepreneurship, we've learned that language of cost-effectiveness. We've learned how to advocate for our work in front of those funders in a way that doesn't compromise or take away from the whatever-it-takes approach that we know we need to bring to Liberia.

Social? No, risky.

TWO STORIES FROM AFRICA let us know where we stand with social investments. Chid Liberty was born in Liberia, the son of an ambassador to Germany, where he lived until his family relocated to the United States. He drifted through his early studies and might have continued to do so through his career had the right opportunities not come along – first planting him in the corporate world where, as an accountant and comptroller, he "had a good job, a very nice car, a good house in Sausalito but ... was pretty miserable", and then drawing him back to Liberia where he co-founded Liberty and Justice, a fair trade, employee-owned apparel manufacturer that provides jobs for Liberian women and support services for the communities where they live. Now approaching 1,000 employees, Liberty and Justice may not yet be able to pledge a better workplace for all, but it does aim to transform manufacturing into an ethical, non-exploitative activity that handsomely rewards those whose fingers and backs provide us with our T-shirts and handbags.

So, when investors would fly to Liberia to visit him at his factory, Chid was delighted. A quick glance at Wikipedia would show that Liberia was a low-income country and had emerged from a protracted civil war in 2003, and certainly these investors had done more research than that. They must be enlightened enough to see West Africa's future, rather than its problematic past. And then they would astound Chid, who relates:

> What surprises me sometimes is people come to Africa and say, 'Yeah, we're interested in investing in Liberty and Justice.' And we get to talking, we get into due diligence, and they'll say to me, 'But you know this is really risky because it's in Liberia.' [And I would think,] 'You flew here to meet me in Liberia. You would think that the risk was already part of the equation.'

Chid tried to reconcile investors' attraction to social enterprises with their intolerance for risk:

> People are very attracted to social entrepreneurship right now, so much so that they're willing to spend a lot of money flying all over the world and going to conferences and talking about how great of an idea it is. But when it comes to check-writing time, … you just start coming up with all of these reasons in your own head of why not to write the check. …
>
> I don't really see how people expect the miracles that we want to happen out of social entrepreneurship and impact investing if we're having this conversation about downside risk. If [they] want to operate as a commercial bank would, then we're really limited in the kinds of investments and the kind of ventures that we can get going in places like Africa, Asia, India. At some point, in order to create something like we are attempting to, you need to take some very, very serious risks.

Sanga Moses, it bears retelling, grew up dirt poor in Uganda, far from a diplomat's son. Yet, like Chid, he found his way first to the world of corporate finance and then to social enterprise. When his investors saw how his enterprise, Eco-Fuel Africa, might profitably convert agricultural waste into fuel, they were interested. But they, too, mainly saw risk – or actually "risk" (sneer quotes required), for what they objected to were the inefficiencies in production that give livelihood to women villagers, the very "inefficiencies" (they're needed again) on which Eco-Fuel was based. Their true motivations verged close to being 100% financial:

> [Creating social value] has not gone down with some investors, and it has delayed our growth – the fact that we are trying to create value for so many people. There are people who believe that we should be creating value for only the business and not anyone else. I tried to raise venture capital and some of the people who wanted to make the investment wanted us to drop that piece. So it's a piece that has cost me rapid growth and made it hard somehow to raise investment.
>
> I have found many investors who believe [if something] doesn't make money, it doesn't matter if it makes someone's life better. They all want to see that.

These investors would urge Sanga to build a central facility, make and sell everything himself, and avoid the associated costs of training and quality control from supporting a network of local, unsophisticated female producers:

> We would make twice as much money. It would be much more profitable and more attractive to venture capitalists. But I don't know, I don't know. That's something that I don't think I will ever do.
>
> If we had wanted to take on capital quickly and took on every investor that threw money at us, we would have raised a lot of money by now. But I didn't want to take money that would compromise my emotional values.

40 Seller, beware

WHO YOU SELL TO AND FOR HOW MUCH goes a long way toward defining your venture. But consider: the highest bidder may not be your ideal customer.

'GBENGA SESAN OFFERS COMPUTER TRAINING to poor Nigerian youth, charging them $3 to fill out a form to apply. The mandatory fee guarantees applications will come only from those serious about receiving the training. Those not selected get the fee refunded. After completing their training, students are connected to a paid internship or are supported by Paradigm Initiative, 'Gbenga's organization, if they choose to build their own business. For 12 months, they pay 10% of their earned income back to the project.

> "It's a way of telling them, 'We will train you to earn an income and we will get 10% of it. The only way we get our money is if you begin to earn money.' It's kind of a guarantee."

It is also how students pay for their training.

'Gbenga briefly offered his training to Nigerian nonprofits as well:

> And that became a problem. I started doing it out of passion to help them. And a couple of organizations actually asked us to train all their staff members across Nigeria, and said they'd pay for it. That was very attractive, but we had to say no, eventually, because it was diverting us from our deeper mission [of training youth].

IN ADDITION, some buyers may fool you:

Solar Sister, whose mission is "to eliminate energy poverty by empowering women with economic opportunity," supports a network of African entrepreneurs who sell products including solar lamps, solar panels, and solar phone chargers to poor, African households. For many of these end consumers, what they buy may be the most expensive thing they will own. When I asked Katherine Lucey, Solar Sister's founder and CEO, about providing consumer financing to help them pay over time, she explained that this was often unnecessary:

People do pay, and they pay in full, more than you often expect. It's conventional wisdom that people at the base-of-the-pyramid can't make those kinds of payments, and it's just not really true. I'll give you an example of one of our customers, who explained it this way. He is a coffee farmer, and so in January when he harvests coffee, he gets maybe $200 or $300 for that. He may not have any other income again until June, so he's got to live off that $200 or $300 for six months. So actually, for him to make a payment on a lamp right then in full is a better economic proposition than for him to try to hold onto that $200 or $300 and pay it out in $2 a week installments, because, as he said, 'A lamp is an investment. But cash in your pocket? Your brother will come visit you.'

Part 6

More than you: Impact

EVERY SOCIAL ENTREPRENEUR must consider impact, and for many this means achieving large scale. Most imagine serving populations far greater than they currently do. But please recognize that this is not the only route to achieving impact.

If impact is a concept, metrics are concrete. Keep score of everything that matters. Measure – as well as you can – even as you acknowledge the shortcomings of your measurement methods. Collect data to guide the day-to-day – and conduct fuller evaluations at regular intervals – to confirm your activities are producing the desired results.

41 Scale

IT'S NEVER TOO SOON to set your sights on scale. The enormity of certain problems demands it; economies of scale may require it. Recognize how others have paved the way, and build on what they have done. Understand how your incipient efforts today may result in broader market solutions tomorrow, even as many organizations share in the spoils. Think scale, but recognize that scale at all costs is not necessary to achieve impact.

Early-stage scaling?

THIS BOOK IS MAINLY AIMED at early-stage social entrepreneurs: those who are, those planning to be, and those wanting to understand what it's like. Why, then, discuss scaling – something that by definition means big (when you are small), obsesses over results (when you're still proving yourself), and is latter-stage (when you're still early)?

From my interviews, I heard several reasons to consider scale very early on:

> The problem you're tackling affects so many people (or perhaps our entire planet) that success will only come from efforts devoted to massive change.
>
> The very nature of your solution requires scale. You either go big or you don't succeed.
>
> What you do now sets you up for what you do later. You can climb to the top of tree with a ladder but not the top of the Empire State Building. Don't buy ladders: they'll later prove wasteful and ineffective.
>
> Thinking 'scale' creates an ambition that drives you, even when times are tough.
>
> A focus on scale helps you in making decisions about your product line or program offerings.
>
> Knowing your intended scale shapes your thinking about how and when you exit.

Destiny

HORACE GREELEY — newspaper editor, abolitionist, dismal politician — is famously (many say falsely) credited with saying, "Go West, young man" to encourage the United States' Manifest Destiny. A century-and-a-half later, he might well have said to social entrepreneurs, "Go big, young man" – although maybe not the "young" part. And not the "man" part.

As it turns out, not everyone agrees on the inevitability of scale, or its importance. Or even its definition.

Put a penny on a scale and see how much it weighs. Can you create a weight a hundred-thousand times as much? An easy way would be to get $1,000, all in pennies. Another way might be to take a roll of pennies, add some nickels, dimes, and quarters, and top that off with a few hammers and screwdrivers. Those represent the two ways to scale: do what you are already doing, just more so; or complement what you are already doing with a suite of products of services. The first way argues: more people in a village, more villages, more countries. The second: a broad array of more tailored services for those whom you are already serving. (I'm not sure the math quite works out with the coins and tools.)

Waste not

IN THREE QUITE DIFFERENT WAYS, my interviews led to conversations about waste. Ashley Murray tells me about converting fecal sludge (you remember what this is, right?) into fuel. Parag Gupta describes bringing dignity and fairer wages to human waste pickers. Paul Saginaw couldn't stand by when perfectly good, and uneaten, food was being thrown out by restaurants, food retailers, and food wholesalers. Coincidentally (or not), each of these conversations hit on the same point: their efforts would be futile if they didn't achieve scale. But not in identical ways.

FOR ASHLEY, THE ISSUE was economies of scale, just as you would learn about in business school. Her industrial process of creating energy from human waste depended on a significant financial outlay for equipment. Just to recoup the investment, she needed a large sales volume. The more sludge she converted into fuel, the more the equipment paid for itself.

On top of this, her primary customers were in heavy industry, including cement makers and power plants, and they were interested only in purchasing huge volumes of "Pivot fuel"– the hygienic, clean, energy-rich solid fuel she produced, which they could use in their industrial kilns and boilers.

Not least was the social motivation for creating her business in the first place: providing modern sanitation to those who never had it before. One-third of the world's population lacks adequate sanitation. In sub-Saharan Africa and Southern Asia the figure is two-thirds.[1] Thus, the magnitude of the situation is such that only large-scale efforts can address it.

PARAG, LIKE ASHLEY, WANTED TO MAKE a difference in the lives of people who live without the protections and human rights that we in the West can take for granted. Waste Ventures supports those whose income depends on work that most of us find unimaginable – picking through garbage heaps to salvage what is of value (see Chapter 5, "Originality is not necessity"). Worse, it is done with few, if any, safeguards for health. Worse still, the bulk of the revenue from the pickers' efforts goes to those who employ them, not the pickers themselves.

For Parag, these unconscionable practices needed replacing, and Waste Ventures was formed to provide improvements in health, better livelihood, and greater dignity for Indian waste pickers. His earlier work at the Schwab Foundation had convinced him of the need to focus on large-scale, global solutions, and in conducting due diligence for the foundation he saw waste-picker organizations everywhere he went in Eastern Europe and South Asia.

Parag needed to delicately navigate the shoals of scale. On the one hand, focusing on this issue of fundamental decency with small-bore solutions would be no match for the enormity of the problem. And Parag was acutely aware that his firm would need to be joined by others to make a meaningful difference. But, on the other hand, he was disturbing entrenched interests, in particular the financial interests of those who were currently appropriating most of the value from waste pickers' work. They would want no part in giving pickers more money for their efforts, or providing clothing or masks to reduce their hazards – such things would cost them money. So Parag began to consider how to grow bigger without attracting attention, hoping at some point to have developed the capabilities and attracted the allies necessary to take on those who would oppose him.

PAUL SAGINAW SELLS THE BEST sandwiches in Ann Arbor, Michigan (my hometown), and some food publications place Zingerman's, his deli, on the list of best delis anywhere. Yet, shortly after the deli's founding, Paul was concerned about those who would never be able to afford his sumptuous sandwiches and were instead worried about simply having enough to eat (see Chapter 8, "A taste for equity"). The nonprofit he established, Food Gatherers, saw opportunity in food waste – collecting what would otherwise go to waste from those selling and serving food and distributing it to dozens upon dozens (now 150) of nonprofit agencies that provide food support to the community.

Yet, important though it is to help those in need receive nourishing food, food insecurity is deeply entwined with issues of poverty, affordable housing, and other building blocks of a secure life. Accordingly, Food Gatherers is now involved in those issues as well, aiming to address the roots of food insecurity as well as its more obvious symptoms.

PARAG'S WASTE VENTURES VIEWED SCALE from the vantage point of getting others involved in similar efforts by creating networks and developing infrastructure – and establishing new norms for waste pickers in India and, later, elsewhere. Paul's vision also viewed scaling as building a coalition – not only to harvest and distribute uneaten food, but as a stark acknowledgment of the many faces of food poverty. For Ashley, scale was an economic, operational, and societal imperative.

Anticipate

IF YOU REMEMBER ANYTHING from chemistry class, maybe it's that a catalyst makes a chemical reaction take place or else makes it happen faster. When John Anner headed the East Meets West Foundation (see Chapter 21, "Smart and gray"), he viewed the foundation as a catalyst for high-impact solutions to difficult societal problems. Like a catalyst, East Meets West didn't want to become part of any permanent change itself. It hoped to leave behind lasting improvements owned by others. Instead of paying for heart surgeries for a few Vietnamese children, it would use the same money to increase Vietnam's capacity to perform those surgeries on its own. It adopted a similar approach in improving the country's literacy and education and, in fact, it applies it to all its areas of focus, including water, sanitation, and infrastructure, and in all locales it operates.

Being catalytic also means thinking about scale all the time, especially ahead of time. A simple application of this philosophy is in procuring systems. Rather than purchasing systems that barely cover what you do now, John recommends buying more than you need and growing into them. This positions you for growth without messy, techy details holding you back in the future.

YUSUF RANDERA-REES HAS NEVER met John, but in this aspect his approach to building the Awethu Project (see Chapter 10, "In-*credulous*: Talent doesn't have hues") is straight out of John's playbook. Awethu identifies and supports resource-poor (but not talent-poor) entrepreneurs and gives them the tools and resources to become lifelong, and world-class, entrepreneurs. In a country of more than 50 million people, Awethu aspires to change the destinies of tens of thousands of people and possibly even far more. And so, even as a startup, it resisted the temptation to create systems proportionate to its current scale and instead developed an approach on par with its ambition.

Yusuf explains how scale was foremost in his mind even as he began Awethu: "Systematizing is [key]. The whole time, and everything I've done, actually, has been thinking with scale in mind even though we weren't big. I tried not to do anything that I felt can't be replicated."

Awethu's training for early-stage entrepreneurs, its main focus, illustrates this point. Still early as a company, Awethu received funding from the South African government to prove that its ideas, "which we right now can prove that with a lot of goodwill and a lot of effort and a few people can make a few businesses work," could be just as effective in creating a thousand businesses.

> That has to be done completely systematically. So that is the way we've done the personal development [of aspiring entrepreneurs]: for example, where everything's done on cell phones and you can use the cheapest possible cell phone so it's not reliant on someone having a BlackBerry. And in the way we've structured our mentorship so that it's as hands-off as possible and is much more about providing guidance and having an entrepreneur execute than it is about working together [with them] to solve a

problem. We tried that at the start and it just creates [too great] a reliance on our portfolio managers [and thus will not scale].

From day one, even if you're starting in your garage, you're thinking, 'How does this thing get to scale?'

RETURNING TO JOHN ANNER, his advice about buying systems that you will need later ("interview the organization you want to be in two years and ask them what systems they use") is only one way he produced solutions at scale. As he points out, "being successful on a boutique level does not mean success at the next level": to be successful there requires you to gain control over a more complicated, likely more geographically spread-out, set of activities. East Meets West relied on these pillars: training, regular check-ins, and formal monitoring and evaluation.

Once East Meets West felt it had gotten a solution right in one location, it instituted intensive training and monitoring in its next locations to achieve uniformity and similar results. For instance, every hospital under its auspices would be called every single day, asked the very same questions, be visited and thoroughly reviewed once or twice a year, and be advised about the best use of all equipment delivered to them.

True success to John means having influence on a province or entire country. But you don't need to be operating at that scale at the moment to anticipate it in the future.

Build on top of

POOR PEOPLE IN DEVELOPING COUNTRIES don't have the luxury of building a home that accommodates their needs all at once. Instead, they often build by buying cement, wood, and other materials when they have enough money and adding on a room at a time.[2] Scaling can work like this – where growth comes from building onto something rather than erecting something complete, all at once, on a bare patch of earth.

Shivani Siroya had seen the need for financing established micro-entrepreneurs. Though typically running single-person businesses, their requirements for capital to expand their business could not be met with small microloans, and yet they were too small (and poorly understood) to get a larger bank loan from traditional banks. With this problem in mind, Shivani founded InVenture (now Tala). Tala uses mobile phone data to understand the creditworthiness of these micro-entrepreneurs (as well as non-businesspeople), offer them loans, and help them run their businesses more effectively.

SHIVANI HAD WORKED in West Africa and in India with the United Nations Population Fund. And West Africa seemed like the location to launch InVenture's early-stage data capture tool:

I initially wanted to go very small and so we started in West Africa because we felt like that's where a lot of the new innovations are coming out.

We really thought that it could be a place where people would be able to understand the model quickly.

They found, instead, that it was better to build on financial services that had already taken hold, and that meant locating elsewhere:

But what we realized is, actually, where the model works best is in more developed markets, where microfinance has been really established and we have borrowers who have taken out loans, sometimes for five to eight years. Because they're really hitting that [financial] ceiling, and this is really where our product fits the best.

Tala is now operating in Kenya (where its credit product was begun), Tanzania, the Philippines, Mexico, and India.

The market giveth and the market taketh away

YOU KNOW THOSE WOODEN SIGNPOSTS with any number of arrows all pointing in different directions? The ones you must read on the fly as you barrel toward a fork in a country road: "Southern Uplands," "Upper Southlands," "Brook's Ferns," "Fern Brook?" Markets can seem like that when you try to scale, pointing you in directions that can be confusing, hard to read, and even conflicting. Here's where they can lead you.

KATHERINE LUCEY, who founded Solar Sister to bring lighting to African villages and economic opportunity to female entrepreneurs (Chapter 2, "Mission, not profit, lights the way"; Chapter 17, "Chosen few"), envisions scale by building brick by brick, or perhaps solar cell by solar cell:

In order to have large-scale change … it has to be demand-pull. It can't be some kind of humanitarian push … That only goes so far. It's got to be 'I want better light and I will spend my money for it.'

We're investing in building a market, training entrepreneurial women who are at the base-of-the-pyramid, building our distribution channels that don't exist in rural Africa. It's not necessarily going to get an immediate return to us. If we build out the market for solar in rural Africa and increase awareness for it and increase distribution channels, we'll benefit from that, but so will a lot of other people.

LESLEY SILVERTHORN creates solar products that Solar Sister distributes (see Chapter 8, "Flexibility," Chapter 29, "Aspiration versus illumination" and "Analogs," Chapter 36, "What's the what?"). As described in these chapters, Angaza, Lesley's company, was a bit off-target with its first solar offering: "We realized we were only really hitting the top tier – those with more buying power – in the rural villages." To achieve its mission of providing light to the very poor, it would need to find a new way. Fortunately, the success Angaza had already achieved was enough to introduce its pay-as-you-go technology, as Lesley explains:

> We actually couldn't start building that until we had a [sufficient scale] of manufacturing of SoLite. We were selling it in six countries ... Our pay-as-you-go focus was kind of born out of what we learned from selling the SoLite initially.

ANGAZA IS CERTAINLY NOT the only company that moved "downmarket" to embrace less-well-off customers after first selling to the more affluent. Ross Baird, who makes impact investments through Village Capital, is generally wary of companies who can trade away societal impact for pure profit. But he likes the Indian mobile payment company Beam:

> They have 14 million customers. Their first 10 million customers were all middle-income. Probably 90% of their most recent 4 million customers are people living below the poverty line. They had to build up enough cash flow to build a team, to go into rural areas, etc.
>
> I don't mind that Beam didn't really go after poor customers from day one because we knew the management team and the mission. If Beam serves 800 million people in India and only 200 million are living below the poverty line – well, there's currently no mobile payment company that's serving more than 1 million. Beam serves more low-income customers today than any other mobile payment company in India, even though it took them a while to get there.

THE FOREGOING EXAMPLES REMIND US: you might need to build your market, by convincing people they want your product; react when your market rejects you, by changing what you sell; or revise your market, by targeting an entirely new group of customers. But, even when there is demand for what you produce among the people you target, market failure can rear its head. I return to the words of Kevin Starr of the Mulago Foundation:

> Market failure means people really want something and the market is failing. They can't get it at an affordable price. Or it isn't going to get distributed to them. Or it's going to cost too much when it does. Or basically all the various reasons why the market doesn't work for poor people. [And this] is generally a problem where a social enterprise can step in to overcome the challenges.

Martin Fisher's work at KickStart illustrates how to build a new market and then eliminate all obstacles so that it succeeds. With dogged determination, KickStart has been creating demand for pumps that no one knew they wanted; creating infrastructure to distribute, sell, and repair them; and setting up interlocking incentives so that everyone having anything to do with a pump – from making it to stocking it to selling it – makes money. Over a period of more than two decades, KickStart has succeeded in creating more than 200,000 jobs and lifting five times that many people out of poverty. The road has been anything but easy – far more difficult than selling something like cell phones, which the same people who might buy pumps jump at. But KickStart continues its important work of building economic systems for eliminating poverty for farmers and for the network of businesspeople KickStart works through to support them.

Kevin summarizes these efforts: "KickStart is one of the few places where you can 'ka-ching' – invest in an organization and a family can really vault out of poverty. It's kind of amazing."

Jenga

A SOCIAL ENTERPRISE ALMOST ALWAYS creates some kind of disruption – acting in ways that are contrary to current norms, removing a barrier, filling a gap, bringing a new perspective. But, as it settles and grows, it should take care, too, not to disturb parts of the ecosystem that are working. And, as part of a pathway to true success, it should also identify those parts of the ecosystem that complement its own efforts. Let me make this notion concrete.

Root Capital, which we met in Chapter 17, "Rooted in business," provides financial and technical support for small and growing businesses, such as food cooperatives, which themselves support some of the half-billion families that are scratching out an income of a few dollars a day as small farmers. Root Capital might provide a pre-harvest loan of between $50,000 and $2 million to a Latin American or African cooperative, which would use the money to make partial advance payments to small farmers for their crops and provide them the balance after the crop is grown and delivered. This provides smallholder farmers income before harvest, allowing them to purchase quality seeds and fertilizers when money is scarce and resulting in high-quality crops commanding attractive prices on world markets. Root Capital also helps connect the cooperatives with large buyers such as Starbucks and Whole Foods, who distribute food products around the world. After harvest, accounts are settled: farmers turn over the crops to the cooperative, which ships them to buyers; payments from these large buyers go toward repaying Root Capital for the loan it has provided to co-ops (with interest); and the balance of these payments is returned to the co-op and its farmer-members.

Root Capital is not content to stay small. In 2011, it disbursed $24 million in loans to 93 small and growing businesses. By 2014, those numbers had swelled to $178 million and 279 small and growing businesses. In 2015 Root Capital reported that its loans were indirectly supporting 550,000 small farmer-producers, collectively representing 2.5 million farmers and their families. Impressively, these smallholder farmers' products generated $1.2 billion in sales on world markets, $980 million of that going directly to the small famers.

As it proves the validity and profitability of its own approach to lending, Root Capital wants to invite others to join its efforts. Altogether, more than 99% of Root Capital's loans are repaid. Ironically, however, the cooperatives and other loan recipients still can't turn to banks or other institutions for affordable loans. Rather than harangue local banks for being so unobliging, Root Capital's goal is to demonstrate that it is profitable and safe to make loans that can provide the connective tissue linking smallholder farmers and word markets, helping lift them out of poverty. As Willy Foote, Root Capital's founder and CEO explains, "Our financial strategy is to scale but not to crowd out private capital that can help build on what we're doing and make it bigger."

Build, don't topple.

Small and right

As a professor who teaches the "other" kind of business, the "other" kind of business students often seek me out when they matriculate, asking for advice. I tell them that there is a swift current that can carry them toward Wall Street (although there are more terrifying destinations, such as pharmaceutical companies that jack up the prices of life-saving drugs from $13 a pill to nearer $750; or companies that knowingly save pennies but put our safety at risk).[3] Stay true to why you went to business school, I tell them.

When they graduate, many of them have been swept up by the current, taking them to mainstream (and certainly respectable) jobs rather than something specifically "social."

Likewise, there is a strong current among social enterprises to grow bigger, to scale. In most cases, this is laudable. Many of the problems we face are massive and longstanding. Confronting them requires might and size. But might size be the wrong solution ... *sometimes*? I believe so. I've heard some persuasive arguments.

The most compelling is that deep community engagement is vital to a venture's success and must unfold bit by bit and be unrushed. Only this type of foundation can provide the trust necessary to create opportunities for long-neglected, sometimes abused, and always mistrustful communities – perhaps most so when a venture is headed by people who look different, have a different native tongue, and are not themselves part of that community. Strategies to auto-replicate community engagement miss the mark, and they risk shallow commitments instead of true partnership. They can be insufficient for getting much done. At worst, they can further damage already fragile relationships between struggling communities and outsiders, walling them off from organizations that respectfully defer to communities' own skills, resources, and talents and then lend their own.

MARK HECKER, whose work with Reach Incorporated was described in Chapter 7, "You don't know your own venture," is intent on staying local:

> I'm a little different than a lot of the Echoing Green crew in that I'm a believer in community-based nonprofits, so I don't really have any intention of growing this specific organization outside D.C. In five years, I see us maybe getting into 15 or 20 different sites, hopefully with some background services for our kids, opportunities for alums of our programs, as well as some summer programming.

Mark's ambitions run against the grain, especially with funders who seek scale.

> The biggest challenge for us currently is funding. I think that, specifically, funders today are most interested in hearing about [ever-expanding] organizations. They want me to tell a story where we will be nationally serving 100,000 kids in three years. And, because I'm not interested in that process – and I feel very strongly that this push to scale quickly is weakening the actual efficiency of what can be promising programs – there are definitely people out there who are just not even interested in talking to me. That's the biggest challenge.

The story that Reach Incorporated is interested in telling is one of how the kids its serves are succeeding:

> Metrics will be a big focus of what we do this year – really trying to get down to not only academic growth but looking at issues of school engagement and being able to check in on those kids. The bottom quartile of students, which we focus on, are 20 times more likely than the average student to drop out of high school. We'll be looking to see if our kids actually finish school. There's a lot of information we're going to track, and we definitely intend to prove that we're being impactful. There's just this huge focus these days on numbers served and whether you're in a bunch of different cities or not.

A few years after this initial interview, Reach Incorporated reported this on its website:

> Our average tutor arrives in high school reading between the 4th and 6th grade level. This year, 75% of our 11th grade tutors are reading at or above grade level.
>
> In our first two tutor cohorts, over 90% of program participants have graduated on time.

A COMEDIAN, MIKE BIRBIGLIA, writing in the *New York Times* on his "Six tips for making it small in Hollywood. Or anywhere," offered this tip: be bold enough to make stuff that's small but great.[4] Like Birbiglia's comedy, Reach's efforts to educate are small, daring, and outstanding.

Think exit early. Stay small

JASON CAYA (see Chapter 9, "Ready? Really?") knew when the time was right to start his women's empowerment program in the Indian state of Rajasthan – he's the one who realized he was ready only when he could cancel his lease, break up with his girlfriend, and go live there – and he knew from the beginning that this was not going to be his life:

> We don't want to be running Ek Duniya [which means "One World" in Hindi] in five years. That would mean we failed. Maybe five years is a bit ambitious, but at some point if ownership isn't transferred and the women aren't taking it and running with this idea of collaboration then it would be better to put our efforts and resources toward an organization that is able to [get things done] like SEWA.

When we spoke, his nonprofit had authority that it wanted transferred to the poor Rajasthani women whom he was supporting. When that happens, he can walk away:

> Our goal is to make this successful and self-sustaining. We'll re-see ourselves playing a role of offering opportunities around resources and still trying to make connections for people that are willing to donate or people that want to do projects [but stepping back from decision-making]. For example, there was a fire department that likes to build schools. We connected with them and they wanted to come over and build a school. We had to tell them no, because we weren't ready for that. We'll be ready when we can take that opportunity to the women in the community and they can decide: do they want it? Where do they want it? Where does it make sense? They will take ownership of it. That's what we see our long-term role being.

Ek Duniya would stay small, but be governed by those it serves.

Exits

GETTING MORE INVESTORS TO ENTER social investing will require more social ventures to have exits. Lesley Silverthorn, whose for-profit company is helping light Africa, bemoans the lack of exits for startups, something that had limited the sources of capital available to her. Ross Baird, who funds social ventures, has seen some, but not enough, ventures with the exits required for a healthy social investing environment. Part of this is the conservative nature of investors.

The rest is the trouble many founders have when it comes to explaining their company's economics. According to Ross:

> An exit strategy seems like a very 'inside baseball' investor thing. But, simplified, it's telling investors how they would get their money back if they invested in you. I think that that is something that every entrepreneur needs to have a good answer for.

The ability to exit is getting a bit easier though, as latter-stage investors start to gobble up earlier investors in an emerging impact-investment food chain. As first-stage impact investors find second-stage investors to whom they can sell their shares, they become more comfortable making a financially risky, but socially impactful, investment – not just once, but many times over as they plow their money back into other early-stage social startups. Ross explains how this behavior applied to Village Capital, the fund that he directs:

> Our fund is a nonprofit [though his investors can themselves profit]. We return 80% of the returns beyond the principal, and we reinvest the remaining 20% into new programs. And what's probably going to happen is: if investors get a return from us, most of them will probably go in for another round.
>
> We had five exits from the investments that we've made, and all of the people [his investors] who have gotten liquidity [money back] have put it back in the pool [for us to reinvest]. And so, in the impact investing world, the later-stage investors know that if they buy our shares in a company, that that money is probably going to go into a new startup next year. So you're starting to see a lot of second- and third-round buyouts, too.

JUST AS INDIVIDUALS use their returns to enable Village Capital to fund new startups, social investment firms are rotating funds into early-stage ventures:

> I'm also seeing a lot of later-round impact investment funds … starting to give exits to some earlier investors, because they know [those earlier investors will put their money into another social venture]. Mainly, it's like ecosystem building. … That's way more common than when I started, actually.

EXITS ARE NOT EQUALLY likely across all types of social ventures. For instance, mobile companies that have sizeable enough base-of-the-pyramid markets to be lucrative are attracting latter-stage investors. Other areas that are quickly gaining customers, including some health clinics in emerging markets, can also be attractive takeover targets for companies who begin to see that their product or service can serve (and be profitable) with rich and poor customers alike. It remains a mistake, however, to count on your for-profit social enterprise producing an exit.

Notes

1 "Global WASH fast facts." Global Water, Sanitation & Hygiene (WASH), April 11, 2016. Retrieved 13 July, 2018 from: https://www.cdc.gov/healthywater/global/wash_statistics .html

2 CEMEX's "Patrimonio Hoy" initiative in Mexico was established to engage with this reality. See Segel, Arthur I., Chu, Michael, and Herrero, Gustavo, "Patrimonio Hoy." Harvard Business School Case 805-064, November 2004 (Revised July 2006). Prahalad, C.K., *The Fortune at the Bottom of the Pyramid: Eradicating Poverty Through Profits* (Upper Saddle River, NJ: Prentice Hall, 2006).

3 Pollack, Andrew, "Drug goes from $13.50 a tablet to $750, overnight." *New York Times*, September 20, 2015. Retrieved July 17, 2018 from: https://www.nytimes.com/2 015/09/21/business/a-huge-overnight-increase-in-a-drugs-price-raises-protests.html. Lawrence, Eric D., "GM settles deadly ignition switch cases for $120 million." *USA Today*, October 20, 2017. Retrieved July 17, 2018 from: https://eu.usatoday.com/s tory/money/cars/2017/10/20/gm-settles-deadly-ignition-switch-cases-120-million/7 77831001

4 Birbiglia, Mike, "Mike Birbiglia's 6 tips for making it in Hollywood. Or anywhere." *New York Times*, August 30, 2016. Retrieved July 17, 2018 from: https://www.nytimes.com/2 016/09/04/movies/mike-birbiglias-6-tips-for-making-it-small-in-hollywood-or-anyw here.html

42 Measure

MEASURE – the right things, the right way, with proper attribution of cause. What you can measure might be limited; and what you want to measure may be too difficult, even impossible. Still, measure. Acknowledge that creating impact in one area – say, better health – may require measuring something completely different – very possibly dollars. Measure as well as you can. But do not be seduced by bigger numbers into forsaking genuine impact – that's why you're doing the work in the first place.

If a tree falls in a forest ...

YOU PROBABLY KNOW THE REST: "... and no one is around to hear it, does it make a sound?" We might tweak this philosophical dictum to guide a discussion of impact: if a tree falls in a forest ...

- Should I measure its length or diameter?
- Was it cut down or blown over?
- Was it the right tree?
- Will a funder now buy me a bigger saw?

Who means why

THE ANSWER TO THE QUESTION *"why measure impact?"* is ... it depends on who is asking. The purest answer, the one addressing a concern of the heart, is to know if your efforts are making a difference. But the answer can be far more pragmatic. Funders want to know if their dollars are well spent. As a manager, you need to understand your progress toward goals. And so *who* you are measuring for determines why. And *why* you are measuring determines *what*.

Impact machines

COMPUTER PROGRAMS CAN BE THOUGHT OF as perfect machines, ones that take in inputs and give back outputs. They are perfect, at least when written without bugs, insofar as the answer you get is exactly the one you should. If a program calculates square roots, it will convert the number 144 to the number 12. If it calculates taxes, it will convert your income and other relevant financial data into the precise amount of tax you owe. Much as we might want them to be, social enterprises are not perfect input–output machines. Some definitions, with comments, are in order.

Social enterprises can be considered to have *inputs*: they get funding (from donors or investors), may receive technical assistance, have employees and volunteers join the organization, along with other resources they may "take in."

In turn, they produce *results*. A nutrition program may serve healthful lunches in schools; a training program may provide job-seeking assistance to those under- and unemployed; an environmental cleanup program may work to restore a habitat.

These results can be measured, but how? For the nutrition program, we could count the number of lunches served or, perhaps, the number of students receiving them. The job training program might track total student-contact hours. These are measured directly. These are *outputs* of the programs.

But are they the right things to measure? Serving healthful lunches is laudable, but the actual point is something larger: better health – but how and when is *that* measured? Or maybe the larger point is taken to be reducing hunger so that students pay better attention in school. But that is part of an even larger (and more distant) ambition, but what *that* is can be debated: better grades? Better graduation rates? Better employment prospects upon graduation? Results that are more distant from the inputs than outputs are, both in time and ambition, known as *outcomes*.

But attributing outcomes to program activities is difficult, as might well be imagined. Suppose graduation rates do rise. Was the food program responsible, even a little? How could we ever know its effects when other factors – let's say an improving economy overall, or the hiring of better teachers – were also in play?

AND, SO, WHEN AN ORGANIZATION SAYS it's "measuring impact," it may really be measuring inputs (grants received, volunteers recruited – which confuses causes and effects), outputs (easy to count – usually – but not very satisfying as an indication of accomplishment), outcomes (increasingly difficult to observe the further they occur from a program's activities), or, rarely, genuine *impact* (the effects of your organization over an extended period, when the effects of other causes are subtracted).

When someone claims, "We produce X units of impact for every grant dollar we receive," you can demur, knowing that social enterprises are not perfect impact machines.

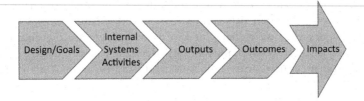

And now it gets messy

MOST FOUNDERS UNDERSTAND the input–output–outcome–impact measurement conundrum. Yet, faced with the need to demonstrate the benefits of what they do, they collect what information they can, often planning to be more rigorous later and hoping that the underlying logic of what they do will help fill in some gaps. It's something like inferring the history of humanity from the highly incomplete fossil record. If you push them to reveal it, every organization can tell you the logic behind what they do. They, their funders, and others who care are often justified in inferring from limited data a contribution to outcomes that are still some ways from materializing.

WHEN BOBBY SMITH TAUGHT FENCING to Detroit schoolchildren, he knew who he was dealing with. These were young people whose only meal before school might be a bag of sugar they bought from a gas station. Their direct experience of the world had a radius of blocks or miles, even if their digital radius underscored what they lacked but others had. Bobby's personal goal is "to be a national leader in urban social entrepreneur development." His approach? "To design critical systems that really engage and change the way we solve problems within urban areas." As for En Garde! Detroit, was it practical? Was it engaging? Was it changing the approach to solving urban problems? Check. Check. Check.

But all of what Bobby envisioned would never come at once, as he knew well. He kept track of what he could: the number of partnering schools ("I called exactly 58 schools before I got my first 'yes.' Now we're definitely working with more schools every day."); how many students were being exposed to different types of healthful activities; and the number of ways their cultural boundaries were expanding ("they have to learn a little bit of French"). These are early points on the chain leading from inputs, through programming, toward genuine impact. Bobby was fully aware that fuller analysis was necessary to support the logic underlying En Garde! Detroit: his program would induce changes in attitudes about healthful lifestyles and self-efficacy. These would lead to changes in behavior, resulting eventually in students growing into adults who escape lives of deprivation:

> I'm not building programs and speaking from the goodness of my heart when we come in – 'We're saving the children! We're teaching them something beautiful and great, and it's helping them with self-esteem and feeling good about themselves and other things you can't measure!' No. I'm literally coming in and saying, 'We'll do baseline BMI [body mass index] testing to see where the kids are [and how this changes]. I'd like access to a blind data sample of their attendance records last year, and [again] after we're here for a year to see if we're lowering [absenteeism] through preventable illness.' Because you could have Einstein teaching in your school, but if the kid isn't there to learn it doesn't matter.

While changes in BMI and even improved attendance are not the end goal, they help form a logical chain of events that leads toward genuinely profound outcomes. The logic of Bobby's work, along with the evocative stories that went with it, won it recognition by the governor and other state officials as an intervention meriting emulation and broad adoption.

Net improvement

IN RARE CIRCUMSTANCES, you can measure one thing to accurately infer another. Bednets are an example. It is well established that bednets prevent malaria when they are used properly. And in many locations the prevalence of malaria is well documented (let us suppose that it is one out of three people every year in a particular location). Then, for every three new nets you place in use there, there will be one less case of malaria. But, again, only if the net is used correctly, meaning that it covers all of one's body, including the head and appendages.

Calculating impact is thus easily deduced, and without counting people who show up at clinics or report their illnesses. (This would be problematic anyway, since both people who use and don't use bednets contract malaria and may appear at a clinic; and self-reports about diseases may not be reliable.) Simply: count the number of bednets you distribute (via sales or donations) and determine the number of people using them correctly. This might be done by creating a statistical sample of recipients and studying their behavior. Then take the number you find and divide by three: that is your impact, measured in cases of malaria avoided.

Change what you change

THE LOGIC OF HOW AN ORGANIZATION creates societal change, sometimes called its theory of change or its logic model, may actually change over time. Steve Mariotti, who gave us his thoughts on recruitment in Chapter 14, "Basics of hiring," originally introduced the topic of entrepreneurship to academically disinclined inner-city students to get them to get them to settle down, to gain some control over his class, and simply to be able to teach without getting locked out of his own classroom. But as Steve and his Network for Teaching Entrepreneurship (NFTE) grew, the logic became more encompassing. A classroom where students were captivated by entrepreneurship could launch them as entrepreneurs. But a more broadly encompassing logic suggested that learning entrepreneurship – engaging as it was – was really just *learning*: and that would prepare students for post-secondary education and then for a variety of different kinds of careers. When Steve and I spoke, the logic had shifted once more:

> The ultimate technology [we offer] is the tool of ownership, in my opinion. [Our course tools] are just a reflection of that process. We've won all

kinds of awards for our curriculum, we've had a distinct niche in teaching technology, and we have been the largest partner with Microsoft and have a major partnership with Google. But I never forget that, ultimately, [we offer] ideas of the technology of ownership.

By this point, what Steve thought needed to be measured had changed a great deal, too. When it was simply getting students' attention, absenteeism and visits to the principal's office might have been an appropriate measure. As recognition dawned that an entrepreneurship-based curriculum could help students launch businesses and, after that, could lead to enrollment in college or other career-training programs, those became a focus (and were measured with the help of various evaluators).[1] And, as Steve began to view entrepreneurship as a gateway to ownership – not just of possessions but of one's future – NFTE's focus shifted to influencing the field of education and tracking those changes:

> Our tag line, "Owning Your Future," has never been part of the standard [for evaluating educational success]. Then we co-wrote a paper for the World Economic Forum; it redefined the role of ownership and entrepreneurship in the educational systems around the world, and I thought it was a huge home run for our field.[2]
>
> So, having a[n impact] standard that includes the ultimate source of power [the ability to create and then own what your produce] would be something you'd want, rather than ... these multiple choice tests and things.

Through funders' eyes

FUNDERS HAVE AN INTEREST in impact, naturally, although each has his or her own way of thinking it through. Some perspectives to ponder:

Small foundation: The Mulago Foundation, with limited funds, delves deeply into your work and imposes a series of checklists to evaluate you. These include an attempt to anticipate whether you will create and deliver social value and to ascertain if you actually did so.

Progressive financial institution: Don Shaffer, president and CEO of RSF Social Finance, is looking to marry investees' good behavior with more favorable investment terms. Already, every incoming borrower has to complete the GIIRS (Global Impact Investing Rating System)[3] survey and is evaluated using RSF's proprietary methodology developed over three decades to deeply get to know potential investees. This is all done to identify, and encourage, exemplary societal behavior. As Don says:

> It has benefits from a financial risk management and diligence standpoint, but equally, if not more, it's coming from us trying to understand what their social-environmental impact is: where it's come from, where it is today, where it's going.

One of the Holy Grails for me is if we could have an enterprise come to us for a loan, go through the process, and get a loan from us; and then, from the day we sign the papers and wire the funds and start the relationship formally, we would also have a benchmark of where they are with their social-environmental impact at that moment. And, if they could show us steady increases in their social-environmental impact and performance over time, they could earn a lower and lower interest rate commensurate with that. That is something I believe our investors will support … and we should be able to achieve.

Investors' money compared to grants from a foundation: Ashley Murray, who has received money from both the Gates Foundation and private investors, explains their very different expectations:

It's not Monopoly money anymore. There's a huge difference between grant money and an investment. The Gates Foundation is almost as happy with a failure – you've tried to develop this technology and you've realized it just can't happen and you hit a wall – as they are with [discovering a solution].

Philanthropists: The Aspen Institute of Development Entrepreneurs (ANDE) commissioned a study of high-net-worth individuals' charitable giving.[4] As Randall Kempner, ANDE's executive director, explains:

One of the biggest insights is that most of these [individual or family foundation] impact investors don't actually look very deep into the metrics. [Thus,] you can totally over-invest in your metrics work, which is a hard thing to hear. The investors only want to see that you have some sort of impact assessment strategy, that you put it on the front page of your website, and that the metrics you have make sense.

But are they really comparing your impact methods to someone else's? Do they go in and deeply question you about your methodology for capturing numbers? Very few people do that.

It's a good insight to know that, as you're starting up, you need to have a story about what you're going to do that is easy and effective and understandable, and you need to get it out there. And, you should have a long-term strategy for impact assessment, because even if the investors don't really care, you as a social entrepreneur should.

THE LESSONS? Research the funders best suited to your needs. Appeal to what they hope to gain by funding you.

Notes

1 Nakkula, Michael, Lutyens, Miranda, Pineda, Dray, Claudia Amy, Gaytan, Frank, and Huguley Jay, *Initiating, Leading, and Feeling in Control of One's Fate: Findings from the 2002–*

2003 Study of NFTE in Six Boston Public High Schools. Harvard University Graduate School of Education, June 2004. Retrieved July 17, 2018 from: https://www.nfte.com/wp-content/uploads/2017/06/harvard-nfte_study_02-03_full_report_6-6-04.pdf

2 Full disclosure: the author was an advisor for this report.

3 GIIRS is the widely accepted standard for measuring and managing a fund's social and environmental impact.

4 Hope Consulting, *Money for Good: The US Market for Impact Investments and Charitable Gifts from Individual Donors and Investors* (May 2010). Retrieved July 17, 2018 from: https ://thegiin.org/assets/binary-data/RESOURCE/download_file/000/000/96-1.pdf

43 Poets versus Quants

IMPACT RESIDES in your gut and on spreadsheets: neither is always right. Your choice of what to measure, by what indicators, using what collection methods, determines the value you can extract from your measurements.

At times, what seems most obvious to measure may be less important than something else: understand your context and its underlying logic.

Measurement can be difficult, especially when sophisticated. You can learn to do it, but pros can be hired.

Softball

IN THE BUSINESS SCHOOL WHERE I TEACH, softball games were "Poets" against the "Quants." The Quants considered themselves far more muscular (at least in an analytical sense); the Poets felt too much math meant missing too much of the point. If you read the social enterprise literature, you'll see similar sides forming.[1] And so it shouldn't be too surprising to see both teams represented here.

RCT

JUST AS THERE ARE VARIOUS THINGS TO MEASURE – from outputs, to outcomes, to genuine impact – there is a variety of ways to measure them. The gold standard is considered the randomized control trial (RCT). Evaluations conducted in this fashion emulate medical research (which, we're learning to our dismay, more often produces false and irreproducible results than we blithely suspect[2]) by arbitrarily dividing people into two groups: one which receives an intervention and one which does not, and then comparing results (often without evaluators knowing who received the intervention).

RCTs have been used to assess social impact, with a fair number of studies taking place in microfinance.[3] A single study typically investigates a highly specific variable (such as whether microloan repayments that begin immediately compared to those with a few months' grace period lead to recipients investing more in their microbusinesses). Unfortunately, such "small" results aren't additive – meaning you can't run a number of small

RCTs and then combine their findings – while studies that investigate many different variables at once make the effect of any single variable uncertain. The results produced must also be understood as having a particular context (a particular region or village; a situation where microfinance was already well known or not; one where loan recipients borrowed individually or as a group) rather than applying more generally. RCTs use before–after testing, with somewhere between ten months and three years being the usual interval between measurements. They are best used to help prove that a specific intervention is effective and ready to scale. They are unable to provide periodic, actionable information that you need to run your organization.[4] Not incidentally, a single study can cost several hundreds of thousands of dollars to conduct.

Mostly for this last reason, of those I interviewed only Steve Mariotti's Network for Teaching Entrepreneurship (NFTE) conducted an RCT (with the help of Brandeis University), although most everyone else was certainly aware of them. Impact Network explored using an RCT to evaluate the effectiveness of the eSchool education it offers poor schoolchildren in Zambian villages, but David Seidenfeld, one of Impact Network's co-founders and a research scientist with a PhD in educational testing, decided it would be too unwieldy and too costly. Instead, Impact Network conducted an 18-month non-experimental study comparing eSchools at five sites with five nearby government schools and five nearby community schools. This approach – trading off rigor for a study that is easier to administer and less costly – is one that still yields defensible results, despite its lack of randomization, and is often advisable until an intervention needs to be more carefully studied before great sums of money are poured in to scale it.

In the case of Impact Networks, the results were encouraging. Impact Networks serves students from the Eastern Province of Zambia, where villagers live in huts without electricity or running water and where families are considerably poorer and less well educated than those sending children to government schools. Despite this disadvantage, with Impact Network's "learn by doing" approach – relying on tablet computers, interactive software, and intensive teacher training – students showed improvements on all specific skills measured by standardized tests of math and literacy, typically at a level at least as high as (and often higher than) government and community schools, but for only one-third of the cost. The fees families pay are just 2% of what families pay for their children to attend government or community schools. The motivation of both students and teachers improves, too.[5]

Impact as dollars

REMEMBER KEVIN STARR'S WORDS FROM CHAPTER 22, "YOUR TWO BUSINESSES": everything flows from impact. And let me remind you: although you strive for genuine impact, you may need to frame impact in the terms of others.

When Rebecca Onie was a fixture at Boston Medical Center (then Boston City Hospital) as an undergraduate, talking to patients and their families and their doctors, she began to recognize the enormous potential of coupling the social aspects of health care with the medical aspects, and for the hospital to consider them together. Yet, as Health Leads was contemplating how to document to Boston Medical Center the health benefits of providing coats, food assistance, help with utility bills, housing and the like, she was told it was the wrong thing to do:

> We had a trajectory-changing conversation with a group of physicians whom we asked to tell us what we should measure. It was almost an emotional conversation for them where they said, 'Please do not spend a penny proving to us that if our patients have access to healthy food that they will be healthier, because it's a no-brainer.' The truth is that point has been already well researched and well documented. But what they did say was, 'What we desperately need help doing is having the data available to us that allows us to go to the leadership of our institution and make the case for why this is something that should be paid for.'

Power in numbers

THERE IS A QUOTE OF UNKNOWN PROVENANCE WHICH GOES: "In God we trust. All others must bring data." Data can be presented to make progress look better than it really is or can measure what is easy (outputs) yet rather uninformative. Still, data well collected and analyzed can be convincing to funders and anyone else who is concerned about genuinely making a difference (you), as the following two examples illustrate.

AFTER REBECCA ONIE'S "TRAJECTORY-CHANGING CONVERSATION" with the physicians who pleaded that it was a waste of time to measure the well-established connection between improved health and providing patients with health-promoting resources like housing or quality food, her focus became one of demonstrating their economic value for health care institutions. The question was: what should be measured? Health Leads commissioned an outside firm to find out by interviewing around 40 chief executive officers, chief financial officers, and chief medical officers and asking this question: "If you were going to pay for Health Leads out of your operating budget [two years from now], what's the data you're going to need to see?"

These executives mentioned 14 metrics. As an example of how one of them was put to use, Health Leads was able to create a direct link from filling social prescriptions to bottom-line results, as Rebecca describes:

> We're in a clinic in a very low-income neighborhood in Boston, and we're able to show that, pre- and post-Health Leads, the social workers in that clinic had a 169% increase in capacity with respect to therapeutic billable clinic hours. All of a sudden we've become a revenue-generator for that clinical site.

KATHERINE LUCEY CAME TO SOLAR SISTER from the world of investment banking, where numbers are treated like – well, money. So it should be no surprise that she has carefully thought about how much impact her organization creates from the Solar Sister network of entrepreneurial women who sell solar products to African households who suffer from both economic and energy poverty. What came as a surprise – at least to me, and a very happy one at that – is quite how much economic impact each dollar invested in Solar Sister generates.

As Katherine explains it to me, here's what happens if you donate $20 to Solar Sister. First, it buys a $20 solar lamp and places it with a female entrepreneur who then sells it for the same amount to one of her customers. The entrepreneur keeps 10% (or $2) from the sale, giving the rest back to Solar Sister. Benefits accrue on the customers' side from each sale. Where a customer would previously have spent $100 annually to repeatedly fill old coke bottles or other containers with kerosene to burn as a source of light, that expense drops to zero, or close to it, for the outlay of $20 on a solar lamp – a net saving of $80.

Now Solar Sister has $18 left of your money. So your $20 initial investment can be put to work ten times just as I've described until it is exhausted. All told, then, the $20 you donate to Solar Sister generates $820 in financial benefits to entrepreneurs and customers combined. This is more than a forty-fold return on a $20 donation. And this does not count other benefits that are strikingly important in terms of social welfare and economics when you include these facts: women who buy these lamps now have more time in their day when they have light for other economic activities. Their children can go to school. And this $820 windfall from a single donation circulates through the economy many times over, with most of the money saved or earned being used to make other purchases including food, school supplies or fees, and sundries; and each time money changes hands it economically benefits another seller, who in turn generates additional economic activity with some of the money received from *that* transaction.

Katherine explains the importance Solar Sister places on understanding its impact and how it can confidently claim impact of more than forty-fold:

> We track for impact because it's a part of what we do. Because we are a sales organization, we're tracking every single dollar that comes in and is used to buy product, and per product we know exactly which entrepreneur it went to, in which region, how much she sold it for, how much she made, and how much money came back to us.

Underlying its impact assessments are some assumptions by organizations, such as the World Bank, who study how much kerosene a solar lamp replaces as well as Solar Sister's own projections about its sales activity. But Katherine is confident in the impact Solar Sister is achieving:

> As you look at that number [820] – that's a projection that's based on our expectation that they can sell ten lamps per month and roll it over. And,

in reality, we have some who do that, we have a lot who don't, and then we have some who bust through it and make much, much more. I could come back and give you an actual figure of what Solar Sister's impact is, but it's not going to be too different from that number because that is about the average.

But even these numbers do not communicate what Katherine knows in her heart. She relates the story of Florence, a tailor and a mother who used to leave her children at home at night because the only time she had a chance to do her sewing was after her kids were in bed. She walked to the next town to rent a room that had a light in order to do her work:

> When she bought a lamp, her expenses of course went way down. She didn't have to rent a room, she didn't have to pay for the electricity in the room. She didn't have to walk back and forth in the dark. She didn't have to leave her children at home alone. So much improved in her life that she started up this whole other business. Now she wakes up in the morning and, because she has the light, she makes chapatis – fried bread – and her children deliver that to people in the community and they buy it for workers who use it for lunch.
>
> And, because she's doing so well and is successful and she's the first lady in her village who has a light, the people in her community have come to her and asked her to run for town council because she's obviously so wise. So she's now a leader in the community.
>
> This all happened within six months. She's completely gone from this hard-working, but barely-making-ends-meet, kind of situation to really being a leader in her town and being so happy about it. Wow! That's what it's about!

Fitbit

FINDING OUT HOW LAZY you are now requires no effort at all – just slap on a Fitbit. You move (or don't), and it keeps track. Ongoing monitoring and evaluation of impact can work like that. If you can, build impact evaluation into your operations so that they're tracked as you go about your work (although I'm unaware of any wearables that might help you). First, it will be more efficient, and likely more reliable, to do so on an ongoing basis than to look back and reconstruct what you've done. Second, you get feedback that you can use to improve your operations right away.

FOR HEALTH LEADS TO DELIVER ON ITS PROMISE, Rebecca Onie knew she'd need data – and lots of it – so the organization is sure that it is delivering the right resources, to the right people, at the right place, at the right time. As Rebecca explains, Health Leads' "core metric" is whether a patient actually receives resources, not whether he or she gets information about it. "For example, do they have the right dollar amount on the EBT card for their food stamps?"

Health Leads relentlessly stays in touch with patients until they receive the resources they need:

> Part of our operating model is that we follow up with the patients until they get the resource. That's something that we do to both facilitate those connections but also, of course, to understand the outcome.

Health Leads tracks each of these interactions, plus its own interactions with potential resource providers:

> Every client encounter is documented in a database. That enables our on-the-ground program staff to go through the database and actually track how many points of contact the family has had: have we been in touch on a regular basis? And so we're not only able to do outcomes measurement with respect to our success in creating the resource-connection, but we're also able to look at some of the indicators around, for example, the quality of our follow-up.

Rebecca elaborates this last point to show how tracking and analyzing data can lead to improved performance:

> [We're] able to look at our data across clinical sites, across desks within clinical sites, and even across our volunteer advocate workforce on a volunteer-by-volunteer basis. So we can say, 'Given that food stamps is an entitlement program and in theory any eligible family should be able to receive it, why do only 30% of [a particular volunteer advocate's] food stamps cases come successfully to resolution versus 60%, say, for their peers?'

And, armed with such knowledge, Health Leads can make adjustments so that it continues to offer as much benefit to patients as possible.

Evaluation mistakes

KEVIN STARR CAN CUT THROUGH THE B.S. as well as anyone. Here are the highlights from his advice about capturing impact:[6]

1. Figure out what you're trying to accomplish. He advises using the eight-word mission statement.
2. Pick the best indicator (just one) to demonstrate success.
3. Get real numbers, and at the right times, that show a change.
4. Make the case for attribution.
5. Calculate bang for the buck.

When we speak about this, he points out how evaluation problems often occur:

> Where people go wrong the most is knowing exactly what they're setting out to do – this notion for us of an eight-word mission statement where

we really force people to say this is the thing that above all I am trying to accomplish. When I do workshops for budding social entrepreneurs, we end up spending more time on that than anything else, because if you don't get that right, the rest of the process doesn't really matter. And from that, then figuring out what's the right thing to measure. Those two steps are just huge ... If there's something I do that's useful [note to readers: everything he writes is worth reading], it's that.

I ask him what you should consider to make sure you get real numbers (tip #3). He explains that a skilled approach and doing your homework are vital in assessing impact:

> Ultimately, trained people have to do it, and the best organizations actually hire trained people within the organization to do this. The actual surveyors, if the survey is well enough constructed, don't need to be that sophisticated if it's sufficiently scripted.
>
> But typically what I see is that somebody takes M&E [measurement and evaluation] seriously and they bring qualified people in and they figure out what's actually been done in that sector [in terms of measurement]. For example, measuring income in small landholder farmers is just notoriously difficult, and you need to familiarize yourself with the literature and understand what pitfalls await you and who has circumvented them successfully, and what proxy measures are out there that would then validate them, etc. But you can't just invent systems. There really is a way of determining how others have asked the right thing in the right way.

Gut

MEASURING – yearly, quarterly, monthly, weekly, even daily – is essential for an organization whose success is not absolutely assured. And, as a business school professor, I can tell you that the success of your venture is *never* assured. So ... measure.

Yet, beyond the numbers lies the intuition that information is better seen and heard, even felt, than simply put into a spreadsheet. Craig DeRoy voices this sentiment. A careful, thoughtful speaker (after all, he's a lawyer), and former president of a New York Stock Exchange-listed company (which, incidentally, is utterly reliant on data), Craig advises not to overlook your gut when you manage and make decisions. As our interview is wrapping up, Craig has one thing he wants to stress:

> Fundamentally, the only way you actually break through in [developing] markets is to be a sponge and try and pick up as much as you can, apply your reasoning and logic as an entrepreneur ... It's finding those missing things that will make you successful or unsuccessful. I'm still hunting them after 40 years in the business community.

Both in the private sector when we were pursuing commercial business in a very sophisticated way as well as with MEDEEM [his land rights company in Ghana and Zambia], it is really important to take a step back all the time and just be able to say, 'What are we missing here? What could be better? Or how could we approach this differently? Or are we hitting the mark?' ... It's actually more important to know what's missing and what can be fixed. You need to know what's working well, but you really need to know what isn't.

I ask Craig if an appropriately designed set of measures or metrics could capture that:

It's more subtle. I think the world has moved to metrics as an easy way to communicate, but it's a mistake, in my view. It was a mistake we tried not to make at First American [where he was president]. Big companies depend on metrics because there's no other way to communicate in a succinct fashion ... But, fundamentally, it always boiled down to a less concrete analysis, a gut-level feeling: are those guys doing a good job? Do they understand that market? Do we understand that market? Have we addressed this challenge honestly? I know what the numbers say, but does it feel right? Does it seem like you're succeeding? That gut-level feeling is really important.

And this is where you put away your laptop, stop sending emails, and talk:

Engage beyond the numbers; get people's reactions. ... We gain a lot more when we sit with somebody ... Face-to-face is irreplaceable by any technology. You gain a lot more when you engage.

As a young entrepreneur, you really should be a sponge. You should be out trying to talk to as many people physically face-to-face as possible, by phone if that's not possible, and use written communication as the last alternative.

Help wanted

How do you go about conducting an impact evaluation? Each of these ways was used by someone I spoke to. The order in which I list them goes from what you can do on your own to what is best left to others. I also might have said: in order of increasing sophistication, or in likely order of increasing cost.

- If you know what you're doing, you can conduct an impact assessment yourself. Be aware that you may introduce bias (seeing what you want to), you may influence results (if, for instance, you're a white American working in Africa), this will take away from time you devote to your programming, and this is best left for early-stage and smaller studies.

- Engage the services of university students with the requisite methodological skills and a strong curiosity about your organization (or possibly about your location). These services will typically be free.

- Solicit expertise via social media or by reaching out into the world through your website, newsletter, etc. You'd be surprised at those you may hear from who are willing to help you. This support again may be free or at a deep discount.

- Engage the services of a partner, perhaps a supplier or distributor, who is familiar with what you do and whom you serve, and who shares your desire to measure impact.

- Hire an organization that specializes in impact assessments. The more you have at stake – going after a large grant or governmental contract to scale, for instance – the more sophisticated the regimen you may need to employ. (RCTs, at the most sophisticated end, require considerably more care than stakeholder interviews.) Long intervals from start to finish of an intervention, or great distances among research sites, are another reason for hiring an outside evaluator. Be prepared to pay, but social enterprises may get very favorable rates.

Real impact is not gamed

WE'VE JUST COVERED THE MECHANICS of impact evaluation, short of attribution of cause (which can be done through a compelling narrative, strongly grounded empirical associations between behavior and results, or sophisticated methodologies, especially RCTs). But none of this touches on ethics. That is what I want to mention now. I'm not talking about obeying institutional review board guidelines or anything of that sort. I'm talking about being faithful to what you truly set out to do, and keeping score the right way, even if the temptation is to be expedient and make compromises.

MARK HECKER, FOUNDER OF REACH INCORPORATED, rules out compromise. His organization employs a workforce of high-school students to tutor grade-school children. On his organization's website, he describes the consequences of strictly adhering to, and then measuring, a mission to serve highly underperforming students:[7]

> Throughout our history, we have chosen to serve the most challenging students, even when that commitment may make our program outcomes look less impressive.
>
> In the context of today's testing, all students are organized into four categories: below basic, basic, proficient, and advanced. Schools are judged on how many students they can move to proficient and advanced. For this reason, it makes sense for schools to spend limited resources on moving basic students to proficiency.
>
> At Reach, we are focused on the most challenging work. We intentionally recruit [as tutors] those students who are labeled as below basic,

even when we know it may take years to get to proficiency. This is just one way that we choose a standard higher than many others.

Neither is this the only way that Reach has resisted expediency. As Mark notes, these decisions have had consequences: "That is the standard to which we hold ourselves accountable. By doing so, we have lost funding opportunities, yet we remain committed to the most challenging participants, even when this comes at a significant cost."

Impact, business, impact

SANGA MOSES NEVER FORGOT why he launched Eco-Fuel Africa. Never far from his mind was the plight of girls missing school because they were carrying firewood and becoming women who lacked opportunities for meaningful livelihoods. Having learned about the possibility of converting agricultural waste into fuel, he got to work learning how to build simple technologies appropriate for the job in Ugandan villages. Having created the technologies, he devised his business model.

Originally, the model revolved around three parties. Farmers would collect agricultural waste such as coffee or sugar cane husks and burn it in simple, easily operated kilns made from modified oil drums to create char – a powdered, carbonized substance – which they would then sift through screens to make an even finer powder. Eco-Fuel Africa would purchase the refined char and compress it into bricks, which were then sold by women owning and operating small retail kiosks in villages. All parties profited: farmers, by processing and selling their waste; Eco-Fuel Africa, by making bricks and selling them to kiosks; and retailers operating the kiosks, by selling the bricks to consumers. The environment won, too, as no new trees were felled, kilns burned cleanly, and no dung or kerosene was burned by consumers. And end consumers got a product that was cleaner and more healthful than the fuels they were accustomed to using, cost less money than other purchased fuels, or saved them the time normally spent chopping and carrying wood – time that they could use for income-generating activities and attending school.

HOWEVER, WHEN SARAH ARRIVED ON SANGA'S DOORSTEP, he began to realize how inclusive his business could be. You will remember that he had given up a lucrative career and sold all his possessions to start his business (and, in the process, almost lost the woman whom he would later marry). When he finally launched Eco-Fuel Africa, he had just $500 to his name. He could have been excused for wanting to recoup his investments of time and money:

> A lady walked in my office, a lady called Sarah, and she was crying. At first, I didn't realize she was crying because it was raining and she was all wet, but she told me that she had kids and they hadn't had a decent meal for two days, two or three days. She told me, 'My husband left me for another woman. I have no job. I didn't go to school. I can't find a job. I can't feed

my family – help me.' I looked at this woman and I was very confused. That's actually how we started creating micro-franchises.

THE LORE OF MODERN-DAY MICROFINANCE often begins with the telling of Muhammad Yunus lending a total of $27 to 42 Bangladeshi villagers with little or no expectation that he would ever be repaid. But repaid he was, leading to what became the Grameen Bank, for which Yunus would receive a Nobel Peace Prize. Sanga, like Yunus, acted out of an impulse to help, not to profit, when he met Sarah.

> When Sarah came to my office, the last thing I thought was, 'Are we going to make money out of her operations?' The first thing I thought was, 'This is a woman who cannot feed her family. This is a woman who is worried that she could see her children starve to death. How can we help her?' …
>
> Sarah couldn't afford our technology, but she was really convinced that she could make a living using our technology because she knew the market was there, she knew the raw materials were there, and she knew this is a simple technology she could use in her village. It doesn't require electricity. She only needs to pump the jack, so she could use it. So we took a bet with Sarah and trained her and leased our technology to her, and, to our surprise, six months later she had paid off the technology, and she now employs three people in her village. She meets the energy needs of about 50 households in her village. So that's when we started considering changing our business model.

Today, independent micro-franchisees like Sarah add another dimension to Eco-Fuel Africa's business. They lease brick-making machines from Eco-Fuel Africa, receive training to ensure that there is no difference in quality between the bricks they make and those that Eco-Fuel Africa makes itself, and "make the final product in places where we either don't want to own our own production center or where we think that they can supplement what we make." Franchisees operate under a contract that requires them to sell all the bricks they produce to Eco-Fuel Africa. Though they are independent business people, they are very much part of the Eco-Fuel family. "They are like part of us," Sanga continues. "They operate on our brand. These are people who previously had no source of income."

REMEMBER: *EVERYTHING FLOWS FROM IMPACT.*

Happy ~~ending~~ progress

WHEN SANGA AND I FIRST SPOKE, a few years ago now, Sarah was serving the energy needs of 50 households. Altogether, Eco-Fuel was serving 3,500 households.

> Sarah was the person who has totally transformed the way we do things, but that was a bonus [compared to helping her].

It took about four months before we realized that it could really work. At first, we thought, 'Maybe we won't even recover our money. Maybe she will not take the opportunity seriously: she will just work when she wants. But at least we have tried.' ... Sarah proved that these people like her – that have no skills, women that have never been really given a fighting chance – if you just trust them and give them the resources they need to do something with their lives, they can be some of the best partners you will ever have. And they are very dependable. They don't want to disappoint you. That really changed the way we think.

THE UNREASONABLE INSTITUTE, which provided Sanga with expert guidance and connected him to funding, produced a video describing Sanga's accomplishments.[8] In it, Sanga explains:

Many people got opportunities. Many kids are going to school. Many young people with limited skills have got jobs. ... I feel good about the impact we have now. I feel that it's only the beginning. We still have to reach so many other people.

TODAY, ECO-FUEL AFRICA provides the energy needs for more than 100,000 households every day. It has 36 full-time employees and has a network of thousands of farmers and micro-franchisees. And it is a profitable business, with $1.2 million in revenue.

Notes

1 See for example Quinn Patton, Michael, "Week 4: The top ten developments in qualitative evaluation over the last decade – part 1." Better Evaluation: MQuinnP's blog, January 16, 2014. Retrieved September 9, 2018 from: https://www.betterevaluation.org/blog/top_ten_developments_in_qual_eval. Quinn Patton, Michael, "Week 5: The top ten developments in qualitative evaluation over the last decade – part 2." Better Evaluation: MQuinnP's blog, January 28, 2014. Retrieved September 9, 2018 from: https://www.betterevaluation.org/blog/top_ten_developments_in_qual_eval_part2. Mulgan, Geoff, "Measuring social value." *Stanford Social Innovation Review*, June 16, 2011: 38–43 (41). Retrieved September 9, 2018 from: http://stanford.ebookhost.net/ssir/digital/6/ebook/1/download.pdf

2 Ioannidis, John P. A., "Why most published research findings are false." *PLoS Medicine* 2(8) (August 30, 2005). Retrieved September 27, 2018 from: https://journals.plos.org/plosmedicine/article/file?id=10.1371/journal.pmed.0020124&type=printable

3 Jameel, Abdul Latif, *Where Credit Is Due*. Poverty Action Lab Policy Bulletin, February 2015. Retrieved July 17, 2018 from: https://www.povertyactionlab.org/sites/default/files/publications/where-credit-is-due.pdf

4 May, Maria A., "RCTs: Not all that glitters is gold. A look at the limitations of randomized control trials." *Stanford Social Innovation Review*, August 28, 2012. Retrieved July 17, 2018 from: https://ssir.org/articles/entry/rcts_not_all_that_glitters_is_gold

5 Impact Network, *The eSchool 360: An Evaluation of Impact Network's Education Program in Rural Zambia* (2014). Retrieved July 17, 2018 from: https://static1.squarespace.com/static/57f7ed65d482e9a19e46ca88/t/5807960ae6f2e13839d365c4/1476892170949/evaluation.pdf

6 His full account is available in Starr, Kevin, "How to Measure Impact." Mulago Foundation, September 15, 2014. Retrieved September 9, 2018 from: http://mulagofo undation.org/resources/how-we-think-about-impact

7 Hecker Mark, "Honesty and integrity in evaluation." Reach Incorporated, February 9, 2015. Retrieved July 17, 2018 from: http://www.reachincorporated.org/2015/02/hone sty-integrity-in-evaluation

8 The Unreasonable Institute, *The Unreasonable Ones: Moses Sanga* [video] (November 2015). Retrieved September 27, 2018 from: https://vimeo.com/146802104

Part 7

Beyond you

WE MAY REDOUBLE OUR EFFORTS, to produce more. We may excavate deep causes, then overhaul systems. We may work to instill new habits of mind, including the right (and skill) of everyone, everywhere to change the world around them for the better. We can all work to bring today's world one step closer to that world: a world of untrammeled human rights, unleashed opportunities; a world where our "our" world connects to "their" world.

FIRST, WE MUST DECIDE.

Part 7

Beyond you

44 This moment

EVEN BOULDERS TUMBLING into the ocean won't generate a tsunami. Tsunamis require the very different action of underground earthquakes or volcanoes.

So it is with societal impact, as we have been alluding to throughout:

No person can accomplish much without being part of a team or an organization. But organizations themselves have limitations, and for them to have the greatest impact they too must be part of something larger, something not yet present.

This is the issue that we turn to next.

Now, move

JERRY WHITE HAD TRAVELED a long way since 1984 when he stepped on a landmine left over from the 1967 Arab–Israeli War and lost his lower right leg. He had founded, with Ken Rutherford, the Landmine Survivors Network, which helped organize the International Campaign to Ban Landmines. The campaign resulted in the Mine Ban Treaty of 1997, signed by 122 nations and since then 39 more. Parties to the treaty must ban the production of new anti-personnel landmines and destroy existing stockpiles. In addition, they are obligated to clear existing minefields and provide assistance to landmine survivors.

For its work, the International Campaign to Ban Landmines shared the 1997 Nobel Prize, with Jerry being one of the Prize recipients. The Nobel Committee lauded:

> There are those among us who are unswerving in their faith that things can be done to make our world a better, safer, and more humane place, and who also, even when the tasks appear overwhelming, have the courage to tackle them. Such people deserve our admiration, and our gratitude. … You have not only dared to tackle your task, but also proved that the impossible is possible.[1]

By the time Jerry was celebrating the Nobel in Oslo, he had become a father, traveled the world, and resumed a physically active lifestyle including playing tennis and downhill skiing. Yet he still hadn't mastered the essence of a movement.

Volatile

AT A TALK I ATTENDED, Malcolm Gladwell explained that entrepreneurs operate from the premise that the world is volatile. That wasn't a comment so much about their reaction to terrorism, political extremism, or horrific atrocities as much as their recognition and understanding that the world of tomorrow is not the same as the world of today. Among other statistics, he pointed out that, in a single generation – and without it being predicted beforehand or understood afterwards – the murder rate in the United States dropped by one-half, as did the incidence of teen pregnancy; and, in just half a generation, the country's views changed from rejecting the rights of same-sex couples to marry to it becoming the law of the land and supported by a majority of U.S. citizens.

Accepting that the world today will not be the world tomorrow provides opportunity to help more people through restructured social initiatives. If the world today views medical care as the province of licensed doctors and nurses, the world tomorrow sees an expanded health care workforce populated by students and others filling prescriptions for food or shelter, and the world beyond that involving a lay medical workforce drawn from traditionally non-medical populations. Rebecca Onie explains about bringing better care to more patients:

> We need a diversity of workforces to be able to address our resource [i.e. medical staffing] needs ... Part of what Health Leads has demonstrated is that we can effectively deploy into our health care system a number of motivated and committed lay workforces that are well trained, have the right technology backbone, and are well supervised. And in fact we should be doing so.
>
> Historically, in our health care system, there's been an aversion to integrating non-clinicians, and that is an aversion that is not present in the developing world, obviously, because it's feasible. One of the beauties of the pressure that our health care system now feels is that we are now finally seeing a much more expansive approach to this notion of who is a health care provider. That I actually think is an amazing opportunity for us to restructure care in a way that is much more responsive and also more rational.

Subversives

EDGAR DEGAS, THE FRENCH IMPRESSIONIST PAINTER, is claimed to have said, "An artist must approach his work in the spirit of the criminal about to commit a crime." This was not a comment about stealing paint, of course, but about overthrowing convention. Like any great artist, a daring social entrepreneur must also be subversive. For her, the business model becomes a canvas for expressing the next idea.

YUSUF RANDERA-REES SAW PAST the worn clothes, dilapidated housing, and other outward derelictions in South African townships. He saw, instead, a source of talent, abundance, and the capacity for renewal. His beliefs formed the foundation for the Awethu Project, a firm that identifies ambitious individuals with a bent for entrepreneurship, and then supports them with capital, business skills, technical support, and mentorship.

> The only premise we had when we started was that there is world-class talent in poor communities and under-resourced communities, so let's figure out a way to find that talent.
>
> We considered all the usual ways of doing it like educational background, or whether you have a business, or your work experience, and we just felt that, for various reasons, inside Africa there's all sorts of measures of entrepreneurial potential – not that they don't matter – but they're not the be-all or an end-all in identifying an entrepreneur.
>
> For example, in South Africa I think every person with an income supports about nine people. So that's totally different than someone in, for example, Silicon Valley when you're considering whether you can take a risk. If you've got nine people to feed – and, literally, it's about feeding them – you probably don't take a risk; you just go get a job as a security guard instead of starting a business.
>
> So, we felt that it's not good enough to say, 'If you haven't started a business you aren't an entrepreneur.' In the end, we just said, 'Let's just get rid of all traditional prescreens, and let's create a process where people can compete and prove their entrepreneurial potential.'

THIS UNORTHODOX PERSPECTIVE has spawned a number of different opportunities. Training is provided for high-school students with an idea and talent for entrepreneurship; and those already running informal spaza shops learn how to keep financial records, register their business, manage their staff – all in support of becoming formal businesses that gain far greater opportunities for profit and growth.

Awethu's subversive perspective has captured the notice of the South African government, which fully funds a training program for 500 informal business owners or would-be entrepreneurs at a time, to the tune of 20 million rand (more than $1.25 million) per program. This is money well spent, with each informal or startup entrepreneur creating, on average, 2.2 new jobs (and there being 5 million of them in South Africa).

AWETHU ITSELF has a 300 million rand (about $20 million) fund to invest in entrepreneurs – from those graduating from its training programs to established black industrialists.

Note

1 Sejersted, Francis, "Award Ceremony Speech." NobelPrize.org, 1997. Retrieved July 17, 2018 from: http://www.nobelprize.org/nobel_prizes/peace/laureates/1997/presentation-speech.html

45 Beyond scale

As SOCIAL ENTREPRENEURS step back from the world they inhabit, they will see similar organizations, first-cousin problems, the spectacular universe – if not the full moral arc. They begin to see tomorrow. This unfolding will be particular, however. It will be through work in education (as a human right); or food systems (as a human right); or financial systems (as a human right). Those whose eyes are trained on the farthest galaxies see each of us as social entrepreneurs of a sort, each seeing and reacting, shaping a just world, bending the arc.

Passage to change

POWERFUL SHIFTS OCCUR as the locus of change moves from working through an organization, to a changing a social system, to forging a new way of thinking.[1] An organization that provides direct service through a product or service can affect only relatively few people until it finds a way to scale. Even then, delivering impact on a grander scale requires something more: overhauling a system. The Thirteenth Amendment abolishing slavery, the advent of labor unions, or the adoption of Medicare as law all suggest how this can occur. But anyone reading a newspaper (or following a newsfeed) knows that, despite these measures, racial discrimination, wealth and income inequality, and inadequate access to affordable health care still remain problems.

Because societal problems are so enduring and so pervasive, something even greater is required than changing systems. Just as we no longer think as we once did about feudalism, witches, voting rights, civil rights, and human rights (and let's face it: the fact that we are now always supposed to be online, connected, and communicating), we can shift our views about who and how change is created. Ashoka insists on "everyone a changemaker" – a world where parents, teachers, and neighbors all have the skills, perspectives, and desires to create change, not just social entrepreneurs, politicians, and others of high station.

This is "framework change." Its promise is a world where problems are defused before they escalate and where those that can't be are tended to by those skillful in forging solutions.

Think exit early. Grow large

ON A CONTINUUM OF EDUCATIONAL CHANGE, from better tools, to better schools, to a better system, Impact Network knew where it wanted to lie – changing the very nature of education in the southern African country of Zambia. By almost any measure, Zambian students are short-changed. In any particular school, there may be no textbooks, not even pencils and paper, and a teacher who, if she shows up at all, lacks the skills and resources necessary to teach. Nationwide, fewer than 10% of students meet acceptable educational standards.

Impact Network redresses these deficiencies through a combination of mid-tech and high-touch. The "tech" part is based on a Zambian company's project-based, customizable (eight local languages plus English) version of the national primary-school curriculum. Teachers are supported with more than 6,000 lesson plans, each one guiding them through the best use of interactive lessons covering literacy and mathematics. These multimedia lessons are loaded onto a low-power tablet computer hooked to a projector used for display. The "touch" part is probably more important. Locally hired teachers each receive weekly feedback from experienced teachers, professional development, technical support and, not incidentally, a paycheck providing a living wage. The school is integrated with the local community through its PTA's engagement with parents and by other activities that create outreach to the community. The school itself is supported in all other necessary ways: with school supplies, reliable power (in the form of solar) to support the e-learning hardware and provide lighting, and a safe, secure, respectable schoolhouse.

WHAT CAN A NEW YORK CITY-BASED ORGANIZATION truly expect to accomplish in Zambia, and how? Dan Sutera, Impact Network's co-founder, explains:

> We have a specific agenda, and we're solving a problem more than we're building an organization. We've bitten off one problem, and it's not a small problem, of quality in the schools and the lack of structure in community schools specifically. What we're doing is building these ten schools as a pilot, evaluating them to show that we're providing high-quality education at a lower cost, and then looking to partner with government or with other large organizations to take it to scale.
>
> Unlike a lot of other school-building organizations that want to scale up to 1,000 schools or whatnot, we have an exit strategy, I suppose you could say, and that's to take our model and hand it off to the relevant parties. At the end of the day, we're working in public education, and public education is just that – it's a government property.

Impact Network believed it had the right skills to succeed; more important was its approach, reflected in its name:

> [We initiated the project] because we felt like we were uniquely positioned [in part due to the co-founders' backgrounds in technology and

education and their roots in Zambia] and had a model. But our name is Impact Network and that really reflects our philosophy as well in terms of getting all partners on board. So whether it's the hardware that we're using or the curriculum or the training, we're really trying to put together a coalition, because, as I said, at the end of the day, we're trying to solve a problem, not to grow an organization.

We're trying to figure out who are all those fragmented partners out there that are doing the best work, bring it together, and then package it up and hand if off to the relevant party that can scale it, which is not everybody. It's like the BRACs of the world [BRAC is a huge, highly effective NGO in Bangladesh] and then the governments, in theory. Scaling is very different than innovating.

Volatile: Money and food

DON SHAFFER'S HIGHLY PROGRESSIVE, yet eminently practical, social investment firm RSF Social Finance envisions a future where people who bank know how their money is used. (Do you have any idea what kinds of loans are made using the money you have in the bank?) And these uses will be in the service of noble aims, like supporting local businesses, better food and agriculture, a healthier planet.

With major banks around the world racking up billion-dollar fines and pleading guilty to serious financial sins, everyday people are angry and looking for alternatives, as Don explains:

> Forget the Armageddon side. Just look at it from the positive. People that have bank deposits or the equivalent can actually know where their money is going and feel much better about it. And entrepreneurs can look at having a much more robust set of funds and financial institutions aligned with their values. That's why a lot of our borrowers come to us – because they say, 'I can't get my money from Wells Fargo [creators of fake bank accounts] or Citi [massive deception leading to the financial crisis] or BofA [misrepresenting to investors and the government the quality and risk of securities backed by toxic loans] anymore. I just can't do it.' That's a trend I see.

As RSF MAKES INVESTMENTS, it looks for shifts in the economy that it might help propel forward. One of these is local food:

> I think food alone as an industry is going to change dramatically in the next five to ten years. I think the big retailers should be scared to death. CSAs [community-supported agriculture] and farmers' markets are just the beginning. There's going to be a lot more ways to get your food directly from farmers – with a kind of a light distribution layer in between [farmers and consumers] that's going to cut out a lot [of middlemen]. It's going to

start in the usual places – the Bay Area and the Ann Arbors and the Ithacas and the Boulders. It's going to continue to get charged with being elitist and everything else, but, over time, the volume is going to be there and the prices will come down as you cut out a bunch of the middlemen who have been mopping up most of the margin. And the farmers will be able to get more, and the consumer will be able to pay less.

So we [are considering investment in] regional food processing and distribution. I mean, it has to be on the whiteboards at Walmart and Kroger and Safeway and everyone else. Whole Foods should be most scared because it's their target audience that's going to go away to these kind of CSAs-on-steroids.

That's where I see the financial markets going, and what I think the opportunity is for investors to [more consciously use their money].

Not just a loan

TALA WOULD APPEAR to provide a mobile app that helps individuals receive small loans. But appearances can be deceiving. The app is part of a financial revolution.

There are two completely separate financial worlds: the formal one where you and I transact, and the informal one which accounts for 2.5 billion people. People in the informal financial world have familiar financial needs – obtaining credit, saving safely, obtaining insurance, and more – but far fewer affordable and reliable options for meeting them. Hernando de Soto, the well-known Peruvian economist, points to a more fundamental difference: formal economic systems create information that identifies what you own, what you owe, who owes you, and transactions that you've made. True capital, de Soto recognized, is a kind of abstract representation – a point that is made extraordinarily clear when, in the informal economy, it doesn't exist. There, you can't list your house or business for sale, use it as collateral, or even prove what you own. The informal economy operates without a system of legally recognized public memory.[2]

The gap between the informal and formal economies is vast in terms of the amount of money swirling through each system, but is even wider still because, without legal public memory on your side, jumping from the informal economy to the formal economy is nearly impossible. Enter: Tala, which sees its mission as making available global credit to anyone with a mobile phone. It is moving them out of the financial shadows and providing them with a financial identity. Tala ingeniously determines credit scores for those in the informal economy who don't have pay stubs, formal receipts, bank accounts, or other trappings of a formal financial identity. By getting users' consent to analyze their cell phone usage history, Tala can make strong (and mathematically sound) guesses about one's creditworthiness. The likelihood of repaying a loan can be tied to whether you are consistent in whom you call, if you have a broad network, if you call at night when rates are higher, among, literally, 10,000 other data points.

Using money it has raised, Tala provides loans typically $10–500 in size (average size of $100), mostly to small businesses who use them to buy supplies, travel, or perhaps even expand their business. Tala has originated more than $650 million in loans, most with durations of 3–4 weeks, with business customers often returning for further loans every few months.

Shivani Siroya, Tala's founder and CEO (see Chapter 41, "Build on top of"), explains her firm's ambition to change the face of lending:

> We're unlocking credit in emerging markets. There are 3 billion people around the world who are underserved and there's a $2.1 trillion unmet need for credit, according to the World Bank. ... We're developing a whole new system and a new way of thinking about risk and identity.[3]

Tala has served more than 2.5 million customers, with lifetime repayments exceeding 90%, well in line with bank repayment rates. Nearly three-quarters of loan applications can be evaluated, with payments delivered, in under five minutes, using country-specific mobile money transfer systems (such as M-Pesa in Kenya and Tanzania), remittance centers, and, in some cases, bank accounts.

But beyond what Tala is doing by itself as an organization, it is creating a pathway from informal to formal finance. By issuing small loans to those with no formal credit history and proving their ability to repay, it is demonstrating the loan-worthiness of such small businesses, paving the way for them for the first time to get loans from traditional banks. By devising algorithms that accurately analyze economic and social behavior from cell phone usage, it is creating an awareness of new means to assess the creditworthiness of all borrowers. More broadly, Tala is redefining the very definitions of risk and trust and showing how those in the informal economy, where financial options are limited, can be brought into the formal economy, where they have access to financial products we may take for granted but, for them, can, literally, change their lives.

Mind of God

THE FIRST ACT OF THORNTON WILDER'S 1938 PLAY *Our Town* has a character describing a letter sent from a minister, the address on the envelope reading "Jane Crofut; The Crofut Farm; Grover's Corners; Sutton County; New Hampshire; United States of America; Continent of North America; Western Hemisphere; the Earth; the Solar System; the Universe; the Mind of God."

I'M REMINDED OF THAT as I think about a social venture's place in its own universe. At the smallest level, it's one person or several, working to get a few things done. Zooming out a bit, it's an organization, focused on tasks, trying to produce, trying to stay afloat. Next, it's one organization among others, working jointly to address a particular problem bedeviling society. Finally, in the "Mind of God," it's working to create a more perfect world.

Derek Ellerman helped me think about social enterprises this way – how people, activities, organizations, and even causes nest within each other to create movements. This was something he sensed when he co-founded Polaris Project and came to understand more fully as Polaris navigated these layered connections.

> A trap that people can fall into in the early stage is focusing a lot on their innovation. There's such a focus on innovation in the social entrepreneurship field as a whole. In a sense I think it can be very misleading. It creates a very micro-focus.

I believe that Derek could have chosen the word *intervention* rather than *innovation*. The idea would remain that what any organization does is still "micro," – whether it's novel or the adoption of an existing approach – and that there is always a broader focus to consider. He continues:

> What a successful, really transformative leader needs to focus on, from the very beginning, is operating at multiple frames. Yes, they need to be operating at the level of making [specific interventions or programs work]. Then, there's the frame of 'What do I need to do to have my organization be successful and sustainable and impactful?' That's usually where people stop. They feel that's their primary area where they really need to focus.

Yet, Derek explains, this misses the larger opportunity: "What's incredibly important and makes a huge difference is, from the very beginning, training yourself to also have a very strong emphasis in continuing in two other directions." The first is grounding yourself in personal development and spiritual leadership, as Derek expounded on earlier. The second is:

> To grow your organization … to have its values around a movement-orientation. Ultimately, it's very rare that a single organization is going to scale its impact to the degree needed for a particular issue. And, even in those few cases where there's really widespread scaling, more can always be done through building the overall ecosystem rather than just focusing on your impact as an organization.

A deliberate course toward movement

EVEN WHEN POLARIS was an early-stage nonprofit, it was looking ahead toward shaping a movement against human trafficking. It began by gaining experience and expertise in one aspect of human trafficking and then looked for related opportunities. These would broaden its qualifications and expand its programming but also do something much more: prepare it for broad-scale change. Derek observes:

> The conventional wisdom is often focused on a niche area: get really good at it, be the best in your field in it, and generally kick butt in that area. … In the social change world, if what you are trying to create is really transformative systemic change, it's very, very hard to be effective if you're

only doing advocacy. Or if you're only doing services. Or if you're only doing training. Or you create some small-bore innovation that's funky and new and you're just scaling that.

Really, what you [want] to change is the ecosystem around whatever issue you are dealing with. Strategically over time, you want to be positioning yourself to have leverage at multiple different points in a particular field.

Derek explains how Polaris developed the broad base that became the foundation for its national impact:

A lot of the reason we have been able to have the impact we have is that we do work on the ground and so we're exposed to the reality of the issue [of human trafficking] and we get the information – incredibly high-quality data. We really keep abreast of what's happening and what's changing in trafficking from year to year.

We engage at the state and federal policy level so we're shaping the legal structures of our field. We do training and technical assistance and so we're helping to build the movement all around us, and build the infrastructure.

Polaris added to its foundation bit by bit, each addition creating more expertise, greater opportunity, and more secure funding. And, with these advances, the further it could range to make more systemic changes to the field:

Working at all these different levels, there's an incredibly powerful synergetic effect that happens over time. It creates a deeper organizational-development logic that I call a *dynamic stability*. One: you're creating the opportunity for cross-fertilization. Two: you're also widening your base of support. For example, just at the level of funding, if you are only doing direct services, you are only going to have a certain basis of funding available for direct services. If you are only doing advocacy it's going to be the same thing. Whereas, when you diversify your programming, you are constantly creating new opportunities for different revenue bases. ...

In the long run, if you are able to do that effectively you have a much stronger basis for stability as an organization as you grow than just working in one narrow area alone. That is a general principle of development that is important to understand and have as a framework. That's something we did early on.

As Polaris expanded its own capability, it also recognized the importance of reaching out to other organizations that would be instrumental in combatting trafficking:

Our initial programming was to create a website which was aimed at filling a gap in the field at the time by having a lot of information available for free, and easily accessible, and so on. We even created a service where we were helping other small trafficking organizations build their own websites. It was very short-lived. But it was about wanting to grow the movement as a whole.

As Polaris came to realize, human trafficking was hiding in plain sight:

We came to understand that the mainstream field developed around foreign nationals who were being trafficked into the country. Even though the federal law in large part also covered domestic victims, pretty much it was ignored; that wasn't considered trafficking. If you were a 14-year-old African American girl who ran away from home and then a pimp sex-trafficked you on the street for your entire childhood, took all your money, and was incredibly physically and sexually abusive, for the most part that wasn't considered sex trafficking, early on.

Because we were working on the ground, we saw the reality of this, and to us it was just obvious that this is not only sex trafficking, it's one of the most violent forms of sex trafficking, one of the most prevalent forms in the United States.

To create significant change, Polaris would need to open others' eyes and enroll them in efforts to prevent trafficking:

Early on, we had a tremendous focus on broadening our field [and asking], 'Who are all the organizations that are working on this? You guys don't consider yourselves as a [anti-]trafficking organization but you are.'

There [were two] shifts that we were part of: making the mainstream field of existing human trafficking organizations expand their definitions to include domestic [victims]; and helping bring in to the field, so to speak, all these other organizations that were working on what was thought of as child prostitution issues, or commercial sexual exploitation of children issues, and helping them realize that what they were doing could also be called trafficking. They could be accessing all these resources and support in the trafficking field.

If we had been just focused on our own organization, I'm not sure we would have taken that same strategy. But because [we had] such a strong movement orientation, we put a lot of time and effort into helping build the movement to be broader and to bring more organizations in. It's counter-intuitive to some of the standard thinking that might be present that often looks at organizations as more competitive.

Beyond organization and cause

THERE IS A STILL MORE EXPANSIVE PERSPECTIVE TO TAKE on a social venture's passage from Grover's Corners, through North America, the Solar System, and toward the Mind of God. Derek explains:

Even the movement-orientation is a micro-orientation. Not in a negative sense, but the work we do in our field is [a microcosm of broader social change work]. The *macro* mission that all of us have, whether we explicitly realize it or not, is a much broader one. It's one that's shared by all the organizations pretty much, and all the different leaders who are doing this kind of work. It's the macro vision for a world that's more free. That's more prosperous, etc., etc.

He continues by urging the rising generation of leaders to embrace this broader conception of their work:

Where our identity is a particular issue that we're working on, we don't feel a responsibility, we don't feel skin in the game, for crossing into another silo. So if I'm working on hunger, then I'm a 'hunger person,' and I'm a 'hunger organization.' If I try to engage in broader work, even if strategically it's very relevant to hunger issues, my board of directors, for example, often blocks that and calls it mission drift.

We need to break out of that mind-set and be able to both have an explicit commitment to a macro mission and to a macro vision that enables aggregation of political power way beyond just our fields alone. And balance that focus [and connect it] with what will probably remain our primary focus: the micro mission and micro vision around just our field or our particular issue.

It's a really important strategic orientation. It's another one of those key shifts that needs to happen in the social sector in order to make it overall more effective compared to what exists now, which is just very highly fragmented.

THE RIGHT TO HEALTH CARE is a civil right, as Dr. Martin Luther King understood; civil rights, which are enacted by law, are but one part of the human rights to which we are entitled by virtue of our birth; even human rights are lodged within the rights of the planet to sustain itself, even if it voices its needs and discontents in terms far different from our own.

That is the perspective we need in *Our Town* – make that *Our World*. That is the way forward with our mission.

Pragmatics of care

IN MEDIEVAL TIMES, an ill traveler on a long journey might have received care from what was then called a hospice. Not until just after the Second World War did the term acquire its current use, when Dr. (Dame) Cicely Saunders created St. Christopher's Hospice outside of London to care for those at the end of their lives. Nearly a decade later, the practice of hospice care was transplanted to the United States and, over the next decades, legislation in that country was introduced and voted down, hospice care was more rigorously studied, the idea of palliative end-of-life care crept into mainstream consciousness, until finally, in 1983, Medicare established a Hospice Benefit to cover the costs for those in hospices.[4] Since then, the number of patients receiving hospice care has risen above 1 million per year (nearing one-half of all end-of-life patients), studies have shown that those in hospice with certain conditions live longer than those being treated to keep them alive, and the U.S. Postal Service has issued a stamp in recognition of hospice care.

Despite hospices providing dignity and comfort in death, what has likely been most consequential in the growth and increasing acceptance of hospice care is its cost-effectiveness, with studies showing that it saves money for Medicare.[5] Today hospice costs are almost entirely paid for by Medicare, with certain states providing similar benefits through Medicaid.[6]

And now, this

WE DON'T KNOW HOW THIS WILL TURN OUT, but it may be following the same trajectory as hospice care. I'm talking about what counts, and gets paid for, as regards medical care in the United States. When an official from the Office of Economic Development told Dr. Jack Geiger (see Chapter 4, "On whose shoulders?") in 1965 that he couldn't use the money they were providing him to pay for food for his poor, malnourished patients, and he sharply replied, "The last time I checked my medical textbook, the specific treatment for malnutrition was food," this was just an early salvo in a dispute over what qualifies as medical treatment.

When Rebecca Onie took up the same cause as Geiger (only 30 years later and unaware of that bit of history), she was joining a movement directed at addressing the social determinants of health – the eminently sensible idea that even fantastic doctors and hospitals can't compensate for lack of income, food, housing, and other factors that lie at the root of illness and mortality. As a college sophomore, that too was something she would learn about only later. But the doctors she doggedly followed to learn what kind of support she might provide by marshaling the energies of volunteer college students were all too aware of the problem, and pained that it was out of bounds. They didn't have the time or training, personally, to find coats, heating assistance, or housing for their patients whose health might depend on them. And if they took that task upon themselves, no one would support them – financially or with added personnel. They'd foot the bill without any help from the medical practice, clinic, or hospital to which they belonged, and, God knows, insurance companies were not going to reimburse them.

Nevertheless, a study followed. The World Health Organization's Commission on Social Determinants of Health issued an in-depth report on the matter,[7] which some critics of the status quo claim the United States tried to conveniently ignore. Relying on evidence rather than anecdote, the Commission decried the lack of action being taken around the world, despite accumulated evidence in favor of the importance of social determinants, and pointed toward remedies that could be immediately taken to improve daily living and the broader, underlying socioeconomic conditions of the poor.

WHEN I SPOKE WITH REBECCA, I wondered out loud how she hoped to convince potential philanthropic funders or health care providers themselves about the importance of combining traditional medical care with its social complement – and paying for both. She explains:

> By demonstrating that access to essential resources also is an economically valuable activity from the perspective of health care payers and providers. The question is less around which is more cost-effective, the antibiotics or the food, but more establishing that addressing resource needs has a positive impact on a set of existing metrics for which there are already financial rewards associated.
>
> If Health Leads is successful, where we will make the most significant contribution will be to drill down and say what the metrics are that we're able to influence that have pre-existing financial incentives associated with them, so that institutions that have long understood the importance of these resource needs now have the economic justification to deploy their resources [to meet] those needs.

She points out, quite rightly, that public health provides benefits for society as a whole. "But that's distinct from who's the customer that will pay for your services, right?"

FOLLOWING ITS FIRST REPORT, the World Health Organization addressed the economic issue that Rebecca placed at the center of the struggle. Among its recommendations were the need to improve public health by investing in education, social protection, and urban development and infrastructure.[8]

The United States appears to be stepping up, though cautiously. Rebecca wrote the following in 2016, explaining an announcement by the Centers for Medicare and Medicaid Services Innovation Center to support trials of Accountable Health Communities:[9]

> The view of what counts as health care in the U.S. is beginning to shift toward Dr. Geiger's, through both new care delivery and new payment models. The payment framework around the Accountable Health Community model … requires providers and payers to think about how a value-based alternative payment world enables screening for and effectively addressing [social determinants of health]. Furthermore, the Accountable Health Communities model can also be seen as an extension of the health care sector's commitment to patient-centered care and population health as a way to create greater value for the U.S. health care system. It is hard to imagine a truly 'patient-centered' health system that ignores the reality of patients who are hungry, experiencing violence at home, unable to get

to a medical appointment or go to the pharmacy, need behavioral health services, or are homeless.[10]

FOR ITS PART, Health Leads is determined to show the economic value of coupling the social determinants of health with conventional medicine, as Rebecca explains:

> We take pretty seriously as a mandate that our evaluation efforts [should focus] on how to establish the economic value associated with this activity. It's not about changing what people believe. It's about really being able to get them the data that justifies financially acting on that belief.
>
> The prevailing paradigm is that the health care system does not pay for the work of connecting patients to resources, and what that looks like in practice is two social workers for 24,000 pediatric patients. As a consequence, in addition to it obviously being bad for patients, there is no data. When you have two social workers for 24,000 patients, they're not doing follow-up, they're not able to collect data around patients presenting resource needs, the resolution of those needs, and then there's no ability to triangulate that information with claims data from the payers, productivity data from the clinic, health care utilization data from the electronic health record. And then, of course, as a consequence, there is no business case and nobody pays.
>
> So Health Leads' approach began with the idea that we would start by working to raise significant philanthropic dollars upfront. We would use those dollars to deliver our infrastructure at scale and then, in doing so, not just provide excellent direct service delivery across these clinical sites, but deliver the infrastructure in a way that enables us to collect this data over time and bring to bear [significant] analytical horsepower to really understand how that data establishes a case for why this is something that health care institutions should be paying for.

Health Leads also walks its talk by adopting a hybrid revenue model combining philanthropy and revenue from participating hospitals and clinics, both for its own sustainability and to help tip the system:

> We have a very well-defined aspiration to increase our earned revenue over time, but already over half of our clinic partners pay some or all of the cost of the program. That is certainly our long-term goal, not just for Health Leads' sustainability, ... but more fundamentally because our belief is that health care is what's paid for by the health care system. When you think about true systemic change, if we're not changing what's paid for, we're never going to really change the operating model.

DR. GEIGER'S (AND REBECCA'S) VIEW is not yet entirely the norm. But a host of government pilots now treat essential resource needs as a medical necessity.

Health care organizations increasingly recognize that expenditures of this sort can yield better patient outcomes and reduce overall costs. And private insurers are just beginning to acknowledge the positive economic payback and value of reimbursing for so-called "non-medical" services.

A movement is afoot.

Seeing

JERRY WHITE'S JOURNEY HAD TAKEN HIM from a makeshift, ocean-side "theater" as a child, where bed sheets served as theater curtains; to Israel as a college student, where he traveled to spend a study year abroad; to the Nobel stage in Oslo, as a laureate; and back to the Israeli Knesset (parliament) to work *against* landmines and *for* human security. He had been to hell, and back. He had won, lost, and then won again in his quest to eliminate the devastating, indiscriminate destruction of landmines.

As he transitioned through life, his idea of "seeing" changed. "Landmines bore me," Jerry tells me (even though they tore off his leg). "Fake legs bore me, even though I know I need one and want one. But most humanitarians, most investors, and most NGOs like to see things." This was Jerry's shorthand way of saying that many in favor of social change are enamored of innovative "things" (say, prostheses or perhaps bednets), stopping short of progress in the form of fundamentally overhauled systems. And, perhaps more, overhauled beliefs.

Wearing the scars of political battle alongside actual scars that were a legacy of the Arab–Israeli war of 1967, Jerry speaks of what he hopes to "see" now: "I'm looking for the problems of our day. I'm looking for collective breakthrough. I think that is where you'll see Bill Drayton [of Ashoka and other organizations looking to change entire systems]."

Liberation

SEVEN YEARS AFTER RECEIVING THE NOBEL PRIZE in Oslo, Jerry White returned to Israel, the land where he lost his leg and also regained his life. His mission, the Mine-Free Israel Campaign, it would seem, would be relatively easy. After all, he had already helped draft and negotiate the Mine Ban Treaty, signed by over 150 countries; he'd hung out with celebrities including Princess Diana; and that Nobel Prize wouldn't hurt his negotiating power either, would it? It would prove anything but easy. So much so that the campaign was put on pause for five years.

Yet Jerry would discover how transformation must occur. In an article on transformational leadership he subsequently wrote,[11] he describes the three attributes necessary to work at the level of creating systemic change. One: *understanding* – an ability to discern root causes and old patterns, leading to constructive, enduring alternatives; two: *knowledge* – the knowhow necessary to bring to bear the required parties and resources to bring about transformation. What Jerry came to realize that he lacked, however, was the third requisite: *wisdom*.

That point was driven home to him by an Israeli colonel who called him out: "את מי למה (lama-mi-ata)?" Translation: "Why: who are you?" Without exactly saying so, the colonel, whose support Jerry needed, was saying that Jerry's ego was crowding out his *wisdom*. Thus, Jerry's effort to impose "his" solution went nowhere. The colonel asked him if he was "ready to do this in a way that is not about you? Something more low-key that will take several years of quiet work and patience?"

Knowing *how* to mobilize a cause, even when you also have a strong under-standing of underlying patterns and causes, is insufficient. Wisdom is essential. "Wisdom, born of a deep reverence for life," Jerry explains, "unleashes our inherent resilience, potential and powers, and helps replace fragmentation with unity, shortsightedness with vision, and fear with courage."

The colonel had stimulated in Jerry his desire for personal liberation. Jerry's quest for Israel became its liberation from landmines – "a systemic shift in thinking and policy." True liberation would go far beyond only addressing landmines and military security and instead encompass human security through a model based on citizens' safety and overall well-being, all the while maintain-ing legitimate security interests.

Jerry discovered an unlikely ally, an 11-year-old Israeli boy who had also lost a leg to a landmine, and through grace and courage became the face of this new campaign. Together their efforts would ultimately result in the Mine-Free Israel Campaign being passed by a unanimous vote in the Knesset.

WISDOM IS YOU AT YOUR CORE, at your best, how you show up. It is time-less, it is collective. Leaders who move the world possess wisdom, and their organizations are animated by the collective wisdom of their members. As Jerry wrote, "Wisdom cuts across borders, boundaries, and social, religious and national identities. That's why it is a great unifier and liberator."

Cosmos

AS WE SPEAK, Jerry riffs on "the lifecycle of a social entrepreneur who is evolv-ing, as opposed to getting stuck," being careful to caution that "you can get stuck at any phase." It seems clear to me that those reaching the latter phases Jerry describes are steeped in wisdom:

Ego

"Most for-profit and NGO entrepreneurs begin from ego." He quips, "'I am Steve, and I just thought of something. A light bulb just went off.' At this stage, it's all about you. There's 'founderitis.'"

Orgo

You get affirmation and get going: "'That's such a great idea: malaria nets,'" someone compliments you. 'You have to create an organization.' So ego turns into *orgo*: "You form an organization, as a 501(c)3 or whatever, and people say, 'Wow, you've built an organization. You're a social entrepreneur.'"

Logo

"Then that becomes about the logo very often." Pride in organization (and proprietary protection) take hold. "People want to brand their logo." Your attention has shifted, from your idea to your organization – from *you* to *You, Inc.* "A social entrepreneur gets trapped by the logo and the idea you have to fundraise, you have to plan. It suddenly becomes management [versus serving the greater purpose]. It never should have become that."

In the best cases, these phases yield to more expansive phases, each an advance, and each with its own seductions and traps that can keep you from moving even further ahead.

Yes/no

"It's women helping women or survivors helping survivors. You start to work as more of a coalition and you might practice at first with your tribe – people with disabilities, or women, or girls, or whatever the issue is."

Global

You "scale [your efforts] through others' networks and campaigns." As an example, Jerry cites his own campaign, the International Campaign to Ban Landmines. It is interesting to note how attention is now far away from identifiable actors: specific individuals or any specific organization. It is anchored in purpose, in a cause, in a movement. And then, even beyond the global stage, there is something more encompassing ...

Eco or cosmo

The most successful ... social entrepreneurs are doing collective entrepreneurship, but not just their own. They've reached a phase I would call *eco* ... or *cosmo*.

You have to get to a point where your generosity in giving back is almost of a spiritual nature .... By the time you reach the *eco*-system, which has set up systems for collective entrepreneurship that benefit others, not just your orgo or your ego, [you see that the] key ingredient of the best global, leading social entrepreneurs is a spiritual discipline. These people know how to breathe, not just act.

You've got some people, starting with Bill Drayton: you look at him, and he's secular in every respect. But he's deeply infused with this idea that the world is going to be something; that not only can it be changed, but it will change. He appears to be a very selfless kind of guy. He's doing it for the world, or for the planet.

Notes

1 A clear introduction to this transition is provided in Kim, Marina, "Rethinking the Impact Spectrum." Ashoka, April 30, 2015. Retrieved July 17, 2018 from: http://ash okau.org/blog/rethinking-the-impact-spectrum

2 DeSoto, Hernando, *The Mystery of Capital: Why Capitalism Triumphs in the West and Fails Everywhere Else* (New York: Basic Books, 2000).

3 Adams, Susan, How Tala Mobile is using phone data to revolutionize microfinance." *Forbes*, August 29, 2016. Retrieved July 17, 2018 from: https://www.forbes.com/sites/forbestreptalks/2016/08/29/how-tala-mobile-is-using-phone-data-to-revolutionize-m icrofinance/#185bc66c2a9f

4 "History of hospice care. Hospice: a historical perspective." National Hospice and Palliative Care Organization, March 28, 2016. Retrieved September 27, 2018 from: https ://www.nhpco.org/history-hospice-care

5 Kelley, Amy S., Deb, Partha, Du, Qingling, Aldridge Carlson, Melissa D., and Morrison, R. Sean, "Hospice enrollment saves money for medicare and improves care quality across a number of different lengths-of-stay." *Health Affairs* 32(3) (March 2013). Retrieved September 9, 2018 from: https://www.healthaffairs.org/doi/full/10.1377/hlthaff.2012. 0851

6 https://www.medicare.gov

7 Commission on Social Determinants of Health (CSDH), *Closing the Gap in a Generation: Health Equity through Action on the Social Determinants of Health* (Final Report of the Commission on Social Determinants of Health, Geneva, 2008). Retrieved July 17, 2018 from: http://www.who.int/social_determinants/final_report/csdh_finalreport_2008.p df

8 World Health Organization, *The Economics of Social Determinants of Health and Health Inequalities: A Resource Book* (Geneva: WHO, 2013). Retrieved July 17, 2018 from: http: //apps.who.int/iris/bitstream/10665/84213/1/9789241548625_eng.pdf

9 Centers for Medicare and Medicaid Services, "Accountable Health Communities Model." May 3, 2016. Retrieved July 17, 2018 from: https://innovation.cms.gov/initiati ves/AHCM

10 Perla, Rocco, and Onie, Rebecca, "Accountable health communities and expanding our definition of health care." Health Affairs Blog, March 2, 2016. Retrieved July 17, 2018 from: http://healthaffairs.org/blog/2016/03/02/accountable-health-communities-and -expanding-our-definition-of-health-care

11 White, "Explosive Wisdom."

46 Our moment

OVER HISTORY, human rights have been trammeled by ugly and ignorant restraints. Still they always peek into view. Professionals and laypersons; women and men; young and old – whether through outrage or from a sense of calling, there will always be those who are first to see with clarity and react.

Just as any of us might do, when we decide.

It's all about us

THERE IS A SHORT CHAPTER in Paul Loeb's edited volume, *The Impossible Will Take a While*,[1] in which Paxus Calta-Star tells a story that shows the far-reaching effects our actions can have, which goes like this: In December 1996, a corrupt and unpopular Bulgarian government has developed plans to complete an as yet unfinished nuclear reactor. Bulgaria's existing reactor is extraordinarily dangerous, and there is no reason to believe that this one will be safer. In response, an 18-year-old student protests outside Bulgaria's parliament, joined by 20 friends. Media attention has the effect of swelling the group to 20,000 by spring. By April 1997 the government has collapsed and a new government is swept into power.

Bulgaria's economic crisis and other factors were at play, of course, in the government's collapse. Yet one student's efforts played a headline role. She was focused on preventing the reactor and took the most direct route to that outcome – ousting the government. She used one of the most powerful tools at her disposal: uniting people in common cause to generate a movement.

Yesterday. Tomorrow

IN THE 1940s, DRS. SIDNEY AND EMILY KARK introduced the first community health centers – in apartheid South Africa, of all places. These centers focused on both the health of individuals and of their communities: black townships and later white communities with alarming levels of malnutrition, typhoid, infant mortality, and other diseases of poverty. They offered immunizations, drugs, and other services typical of medical practice, with further attention to epidemiology to assess unmet needs, and home visits by nurses to increase health access. They also provided programs covering gardening, diet, and maintenance of latrines. Such concerns would later become known as "public determinants of health."

In 1957, Jack Geiger, an American physician, trained at two of these South African community health centers. Inspired by what he had seen an ocean away, Geiger brought the idea for community health back to the United States and is widely credited as the pioneer of community health centers in that country. The National Academy of Medicine bestowed upon him its highest honor in 1998 "for creating a model of the contemporary American community health center to serve the poor and disadvantaged, and for his contributions to the advancements of minority health."[2]

As we've seen in Chapter 4, "On whose shoulders?" and Chapter 45, "And now, this," none of this was known to Rebecca Onie when she entered college in the mid-1990s looking to find a way for herself and other students to do meaningful volunteer work. At first, as a project, students were enlisted to fill social prescriptions (for utilities, coats, food, childcare vouchers, support in enrolling in GED [General Educational Development] programs, among 50 identified resource needs which doctors could then begin to write). As we've seen, the project became the award-winning social enterprise Health Leads, which now works across the country with leading hospitals and clinics. For her efforts, Rebecca received a MacArthur Fellowship in 2009.

TODAY, THE RELATIONSHIP BETWEEN living conditions and health is unquestioned. More importantly, efforts initiated by the Karks and brought forward by Jack Geiger and Rebecca Onie are finding broader acceptance in practice. Efforts such as theirs led to the Declaration of Alma-Ata,[3] which called for "Health for All," defining health as "a state of complete physical, mental, and social well-being" and insisting it is a human right.[4] In the United States, programs such as Comprehensive Primary Care Plus, Accountable Health Communities, and 1115 Medicaid Waivers are enabling health systems across to country to address social needs as an essential part of care.

These ideas have crossed continents, spanned decades; they have won support across generations and from physicians and laypersons. These ideas have led to dignified care for members of the Zulu tribe, poor farmers on the Mississippi Delta, those living in urban poverty in Boston, and rural poverty in Appalachia. Because these ideas are, in one sense, timeless. They are just and right. It takes us all to keep them moving forward.

Decide

I MET SANDY WIGGINS FOR BREAKFAST in the restaurant of the Amway Grand Plaza Hotel in Grand Rapids, Michigan. We were both there to attend the BALLE (Business Alliance for Local Living Economies) conference. A leader in the green building movement, Sandy tells me about his professional trajectory: learning to be a carpenter, then a builder, then managing building projects. Each step opened new opportunities and shaped an ever-widening view of possibility.

IN THE PLEISTOCENE ERA of the ecological building movement, an architect friend introduced Sandy to a paper on building with the environment in mind. "We muddled our way through it, trying to figure what we were reading – reading the labels on paint cans and stuff like that, but not really understanding what to do about it." Eventually, Sandy found others in his hometown of Philadelphia who wanted to engage in this exploration, and they formed a local nonprofit that *would* understand, which could direct green building efforts, including their own. From that point on, Sandy became a major influencer. As we saw in Chapter 2, "Are you a social entrepreneur? (Take two)," he was the founding chair of the Green Building Certificate Institute, served as chair of the U.S. Green Building Council, and was on the executive committee for LEED (Leadership in Energy and Environmental Design), co-authoring LEED for Neighborhood Development. All the while, he was building homes and commercial buildings and helping develop communities that met the highest standards for environmental sustainability. And his philosophy continued to broaden. Although LEED gained widespread acceptance as a model for sustainable building, he began to find it lacking: "LEED becoming mainstream is good in some respects and not so good in others. It's a tool for moving the needle in the right direction, but even the highest-graded building is still just doing less bad."

As building issues verged into environmental issues, Sandy felt something more important was really at stake:

> Tired old architects, engineers, developers, manufacturers started to light up as they climbed this ladder of awareness and began to recognize that what they were doing in their day-to-day work lives had a direct connection to these profound global problems that they were beginning to understand, and it brought meaning and purpose to their life.
>
> The engine that was driving the sweeping change in the industry wasn't about the buildings. It was about the people and the personal transformations they were going through. It was about places, and the way that buildings affected the relationships of people in those places.

SANDY BEGAN TO CONTEMPLATE how enlightened banking could nourish people and their communities, supporting more socially and environmentally aware business activity. "We're trying to understand how we can change or redirect the flow of capital so that it's supporting rather than impeding progress." Again, this would require changing minds:

> What are the points of engagement where you can grab [someone] and help them move up that ladder of awareness? ... We had to reframe everything in the language they [Federal bank regulators] could accept [so we could offer favorable loan rates and terms to green businesses]. ... We were

successful in convincing the regulators because we sussed out the data to show that investing in green buildings is a better risk proposition from the bank's perspective. Operating costs are lower, there's increased asset value, and higher tenant retention rates, things like that. So, it's just a better business proposition.

He waxes philosophical:

You really need to change individual mind-sets. It's all about people and helping them connect the dots, so that they then see own their role in the world and begin to think, 'How can I create change with what I'm doing in my life?'

I HAD DRIVEN TWO HOURS from Ann Arbor to Grand Rapids to attend the BALLE conference without giving the environment a second thought. Sandy had flown in from Philadelphia. I ask him if he had purchased carbon credits to offset the carbon from his flight.

I do that routinely. It's a mind-set issue. Once you begin to understand, once you know something, if you don't act on it, you're culpable. The fundamental increment for change is the individual human decision. We make big decisions, but it's the thousands of little decisions we make every day that matter.

Notes

1 Loeb, Paul Rogat, ed., *The Impossible Will Take a Little While: A Citizen's Guide to Hope in a Time of Fear* (New York: Basic Books, 2004).
2 "Gustav O. Lienhard Award for Advancement of Health Care." National Academy of Medicine, 2017. Retrieved July 1, 2018 from: https://nam.edu/about-the-nam/gustav-o-lienhard-award
3 World Health Organization, *Declaration of Alma-Ata. International Conference on Primary Health Care, Alma-Ata, USSR, 6–12 September 1978.* Retrieved July 18, 2018 from: http://www.who.int/publications/almaata_declaration_en.pdf
4 "Social determinants of health." World Health Organization. Retrieved July 1, 2018 from: http://www.who.int/social_determinants/en

Appendix 1: Methodology

THE MOST FUN PART of this project was interviewing the set of amazing people you've met in this book (and many others who didn't make it into the final draft). The least fun, but arguably most important, part was then laboriously coding each interview so that I could piece the book together. Every passage in every interview became a brick, a piece of wood, a steel beam, or a sheet of glass. I created the blueprint of the book out of a knowledge of those elements. Many of those pieces were never used – now stacked in my writer's garage. From others, this book emerged.

This section presents a more formal description of the process. To begin with, I used a questionnaire template to prepare for all interviews. Before conducting each interview, I did as much research as I could to understand the interviewee and her organization, and modified the template to include issues I thought would prove particularly insightful. Such a customized template guided all interviews. The interviews followed a semi-structured approach[1] – with a good deal of "semi" – where I would push for further detail, clarifications, and examples, and had the freedom to explore all ideas that arose during our conversation. I conducted all the interviews myself, both in person and using voice-over-internet. Interviews typically lasted one to two hours. All interviews were recorded and then professionally transcribed. I followed up with many people for clarification or extension, either talking to them again or using email, using those responses as additional source materials.

There was nothing systematic in whom I chose to interview, but the majority were at the very early stages of their ventures. Some were teenagers, others grandparents. Some were just getting their footing, others were social entrepreneur rock stars (certainly in my estimation). By interviewing well over 100 people, and looking for distinctions – not just commonalities – among them, I felt that any lopsidedness from my sampling would be washed away.

Thus began the coding. At first, a research assistant and I read a dozen or so interviews apiece. Both of us looked for every important idea in the interviews we read, then captured that idea in a single sentence. We then printed these captions, cut them up, and put each on a separate Post-it note – creating for ourselves a big, qualitative, unorganized mess. Over the course of many hours, we placed each Post-it on a huge whiteboard, trying to identify thematic clusters. Clusters were merged, split apart, and reformed entirely, as necessary. At the end of this process, we had a hierarchically organized set of topics spanning the contents of the interviews we had analyzed. Before the coding of the complete corpus of interviews began, an experienced practitioner-researcher reviewed this classification and found it corresponded to her perception of the topics describing social entrepreneurship. This became the initial coding scheme.

Next, all interview transcripts were coded. This involved carefully reading the transcripts and applying the topics in the coding scheme as "tags" to pinpoint, and later identify, the specific content contained within the thousands of pages of transcripts. These tags were applied to sentences, paragraphs, or larger blocks of text as appropriate. Each of these text *excerpts* could be coded with one or more tags. An excerpt coded by one tag might overlap with an excerpt coded by another. Within a single transcript it would not be uncommon for 50–100 excerpts to be identified and tagged, with the total number of (non-unique) tags applied in that transcript being two to three times that many.

Transcripts were coded using NVivo, a software package used for qualitative research and analysis which allows "hierarchical coding": the ability for topics to be arranged in parent–child relationships (in the sense that *hiring* can be considered a child of the topic *team*, and *compensation* a child of *hiring*). This feature was especially useful later when, for example, an excerpt tagged *compensation* would be returned when searching for the tag *team*. All transcripts were coded by at least two people: trained research assistants and me. Multiple coding helped ensure that every important idea was detected and tagged. "Over-coding" or erroneous coding was not harmful, since tags were not used to produce careful numeric counts for quantitative analysis. Periodic coding reviews were held to allow coders to see and discuss each other's coding, potentially allowing them to adapt their own approach.

The research approach followed what can be called a general inductive approach for qualitative data.[2] This approach has been used to explore the intersection of social entrepreneurship and information and communication technology.[3] A characteristic of this approach is that the coding scheme can be revised as more documents (transcripts) are read. This is because the scheme does not reflect pre-established questions or hypotheses that the research is exploring; rather, it is an emergent structure representing what the underlying texts reveal.

In the early stages of coding, a few topics were added at the "leaf" (no child) level of the hierarchy to accommodate topics not yet encountered. After nearly 50 of the over 100 transcripts had been coded, a more serious overhaul of the entire coding scheme took place to produce a more balanced coding-tree structure. This revised coding scheme was used to re-code every already-coded transcript and was applied to all remaining transcripts. The coding scheme suggested an overall architecture for the research that would follow, but it was never intended to capture the full complexity of the interviews. For instance, one of tags with no children was *volunteers*. Yet this tag was applied in discussing: the benefits of having volunteers, the challenges of using them well, how to attract them, and a number of other issues.

This fuller picture of the interviews emerged from interrogating the Nvivo database. NVivo software supports full-text search (searching for exact text, stemmed text, and word relationships such as "benefits" NEAR "staff") plus searches for tagged text. Using these methods, I explored topics in great detail. For instance, a search for *skills*, one of the refinements of the more general topic of *preparing yourself*, returned 560 "hits," which, when printed out, amounted to 128 single-spaced pages.

On top of this, I also retrieved 393 annotations, amounting to an additional 29 single-spaced pages of text. Annotations were brief captions (typically a phrase or a sentence or two) I created when examining already-coded excerpts, which allowed me to impose some judgment and interpretation on what was already tagged. Annotations might consist of reminders of something particularly noteworthy, subtleties I noted, or cross-references among different interviewees' ideas about a certain topic. In effect, my annotations acted informally to extend the coding scheme. Returning to the example of *volunteers*, I might have added any one of these annotations to a particular excerpt of text: *volunteer-benefits*, *volunteer-challenges*, or *volunteer-attraction*. I also added sentences, even short paragraphs. These extensions (themselves searchable) served as early thoughts about the different aspects of volunteering that I might write about later.

The next step in the process was entirely manual (by which I mean sitting at my desk, thinking). I read through the 560 excerpts and 393 annotations on *volunteers*, all 157 pages, often returning to the relevant point in the associated interview transcript from which one of these was drawn in order to study it in context. And I thought. And thought some more. And then started to write. What I've reported are the words of my interviewees, with only the slightest revisions to improve clarity.

The effort I exerted in examining a single topic was vanishingly small if measured in foot-pounds – that mainly deriving from constant trips to the refrigerator or the coffee pot "to think something through." In terms of the mental energy I exerted, however, it sometimes seemed this task would be never-ending. Yet necessary. Even as I repeated this process for all 71 topical codes in the entire coding scheme.

THE RESULT IS the book now before you.

Notes

1 Harrell, M. C., and Bradley, M. A., *Data Collection Methods: Semi-structured Interview and Focus Groups* (Santa Monica: RAND National Defense Research Institute, 2009). Retrieved July 18, 2018 from: https://www.rand.org/pubs/technical_reports/TR718.html

2 Thomas, David R., "A general inductive approach for analyzing qualitative evaluation data." *American Journal of Evaluation*, 27(2) (2006). Retrieved September 20, 2018 from: http://journals.sagepub.com/doi/10.1177/1098214005283748

3 Fraizer, L., and Madjidi, F., "ICT and social entrepreneurship: Implications of change making for the future ICT workforce." *Research in IT* 8(2) (2011). Retrieved September 27, 2018 from: https://www.researchgate.net/publication/254003293_ICT_and_social _entrepreneurship_implications_of_change_making_for_the_future_ICT_workforce

Appendix 2: The entrepreneurs and the organizations

1. The entrepreneurs

Andre Albuquerque
Terra Nova
Chapter 2, "Are you a social entrepreneur? (Take two)"
Chapter 30, "Running your *business* business"

April Allderdice
MicroEnergy Credits
Chapter 4, "Complexity from simpler parts"
Chapter 10, "Too cool for school?"
Chapter 13, "Pluripotency"
Chapter 14, "The people the people you know know"
Chapter 17, "Learners and rockers"
Chapter 23, "TAM SAM SOM matter"
Chapter 26, "Every link matters"
Chapter 27, "Fresh eyes"
Chapter 36, "Still ..."

John Anner
East Meets West
Chapter 3, "Faux immersion"
Chapter 21, "Smart and gray"
Chapter 31, "Ninja management"
Chapter 34, "Waves roll in, waves roll out"
Chapter 35, "The challenge of fundraising"
Chapter 35, "Hot truth"
Chapter 41, "Anticipate"

Ross Baird
Village Capital
Chapter 5, "Is it necessary – *Really* necessary?"
Chapter 7, "You don't know your own venture"

Chapter 11, "If the bus comes"
Chapter 13 (intro)
Chapter 18, "Inward and outward"
Chapter 19, "Who's your mentor?"
Chapter 29, "Minimum viable product"
Chapter 36, "Investor-speak"
Chapter 37, "Too soon"
Chapter 41, "The market giveth and the market taketh away"
Chapter 41, "Exits"

Lisa Ballantine

FilterPure
Chapter 3, "Experienced with meaning"
Chapter 9, "Acting from values"
Chapter 11, "There's no "team" in 'I'"
Chapter 16, "Your team in the cloud"
Chapter 24, "Why you?"
Chapter 29, "Pure"

Malvika Bhatia

DIIME
Chapter 10, "Now, just a product"

David Bornstein

author and journalist
Chapter 2, "Are you a social entrepreneur?"

Deborah Burand

lawyer; formerly University of Michigan, now NYU Law
Chapter 33, "Legal turn"
Chapter 33, "U-turn"

Bena Burda

Clean Clothes Inc.
Chapter 2, "Are you a social entrepreneur? (Take two)"
Chapter 19, "Others' shoes"

Martin Burt

Fundación Paraguaya
Chapter 7, "Stress and risk"
Chapter 7, "Misunderstood"
Chapter 21, "Smart and gray"

Edward Cardoza

Still Harbor, Partners in Health
Chapter 4, "The doctor and the priest"
Chapter 6, "The siren call of social entrepreneurship"

Chapter 8, "Nonproductive persistence"
Chapter 9, "When your venture gives you lemons"
Chapter 9, "Critical 'whys'"
Chapter 13, "Organization structure: Benefit or crutch?"
Chapter 18, "Inward and outward"
Chapter 27, "Take the money and ..."

Adam Carver

Impact Everyday
Chapter 10, "Too cool for school?"
Chapter 12, "Critical feedback"

Charlie Cavell

Pay It Forward
Chapter 3, "Real life"
Chapter 9, "Ready? Really?"
Chapter 9, "Charmed 'whys'"
Chapter 10, "Ask"
Chapter 10, "Too cool for school?"
Chapter 10, "Credibility"
Chapter 10, "*In*-credible personalities"
Chapter 19, "Who's your mentor?"
Chapter 19, "Moments, lifetimes"
Chapter 23, "Your *business* business"
Chapter 31, "What you didn't sign up for"
Chapter 37, "Fundraising tip: Spare change"
Chapter 38, "Potatoes, small"

Jason Caya

Ek Duniya
Chapter 9, "Ready? Really?"
Chapter 41, "Think exit early. Stay small."

Jane Chen

Embrace
Chapter 7, "Awards notwithstanding"
Chapter 12, "You or 'yous' in control"
Chapter 13, "Embracing new roles"
Chapter 21, "Formation"
Chapter 27, "Jazz"
Chapter 29, "As a scientist"

Katherine Fulton

Monitor Institute
Chapter 5, "Markets don't define necessity"
Chapter 6, "Joining the chorus"

Chapter 10, "New mistakes"
Chapter 11, "It's not about you"
Chapter 12, "Start together"

Ophelia Dahl

Partners in Health
Chapter 4, "The doctor and the priest"

Ami Dar

Idealist.org
Chapter 3, "Off the track"

Craig DeRoy

Medeem
Chapter 14, "Away from home"
Chapter 17, "Adaptive hiring"
Chapter 28, "Small businesses, still complex"
Chapter 43, "Gut"

Patrick Donohue

Chapter 3, "Real life"

Raquel Donoso

Latino Community Foundation
Chapter 35, "Hot truth"

Bill Drayton

Ashoka
Chapter 18, "Emote different"

Derek Ellerman

Polaris
Chapter 7, "Work intensity"
Chapter 7, "Burning your social enterprise"
Chapter 7, "Myths and shells"
Chapter 9, "Breathe out"
Chapter 16, "Volunteer structure"
Chapter 16, "Select and train"
Chapter 18, "Inward and outward"
Chapter 19, "Others' shoes"
Chapter 31, "What you didn't sign up for"
Chapter 31, "Managing: Pro tips"
Chapter 38, "Trajectory: United States"
Chapter 38, "Potatoes, large"
Chapter 45, "Mind of God"
Chapter 45, "A deliberate course toward movement"

Carol Erickson

Carol A. Erickson Associates
Chapter 21, "Your board: Get interested"
Chapter 21, "Boards 101"
Chapter 21, "Formation"
Chapter 21, "Don't shake on it"
Chapter 21, "Yes, you raise money"
Chapter 21, "Smart and gray"

Paul Farmer

Partners in Health
Chapter 4, "The doctor and the priest"
Chapter 16, "Local talent is not voluntary talent"

Martin Fisher

KickStart
Chapter 1, "Lessons left on the ground"
Chapter 2, "Business can't do it alone"
Chapter 2, "Which market?"
Chapter 6, "Joining the chorus"
Chapter 8, "Act for yourself; act for others"
Chapter 8, "Persistence"
Chapter 9, "Always stepping on the gas"
Chapter 29, "That's a *what?*"
Chapter 29, "Aspiration versus illumination"
Chapter 30, "Rows and ducks"
Chapter 31, "What you didn't sign up for"
Chapter 34, "Afloat"

Theresa Fisher

DIIME
Chapter 10, "Now, just a product"
Chapter 34, "Afloat"

Ian Fisk

Mentor Capital Network
Chapter 10, "Data"
Chapter 14, "Mindful hiring"

Willy Foote

Root Capital
Chapter 41, "Jenga"

Katherine (Kat) Chon

Polaris
Chapter 7, "Burning your social enterprise"

Chapter 7, "Myths and shells"
Chapter 16, "Volunteer structure"

Dory Gannes

Olevolos Project
Chapter 3, "Faux immersion"
Chapter 21, "Your board: Get interested"

Saul Garlick

Think Impact
Chapter 18, "Like them. Trust them. Be yourself."
Chapter 33, "U-turn"

Parag Gupta

Waste Ventures
Chapter 5, "Originality is not necessity"
Chapter 6 (intro)
Chapter 6, "Joining the chorus"
Chapter 13, "Organization structure: Benefit or crutch?"
Chapter 41, "Waste not"

Jacob Harold

GuideStar USA
Chapter 19, "Facets of support"

John Hatch

FINCA
Chapter 21, "Smart and gray"

Mark Hecker

Reach Incorporated
Chapter 6, "Necessary and unwelcome"
Chapter 7, "You don't know your own venture"
Chapter 8, "Reframe"
Chapter 20, "Free lunch?"
Chapter 37, "Fundraising tip: Authenticity"
Chapter 41, "Small and right"
Chapter 43, "Real impact is not gamed"

Cheryl Heller

The Measured Lab
Chapter 2, "From the sweet spot toward profit"

Nikki Henderson

also known as: Nikki Silvestri (married name)
Green For All, People's Grocery

Chapter 19, "Facets of support"
Chapter 19, "Menteeship"
Chapter 21, "You are not perfect"
Chapter 31, "Ninja management"

Gillian Henker

DIIME
Chapter 10, "Now, just a product"

Grace Hsia

Warmilu
Chapter 7, "Work intensity"
Chapter 7, "Misunderstood"
Chapter 10, "Climb with others"
Chapter 13, "Warm relationships"
Chapter 27, "Jazz"

Leticia Jáuregui Casanueva

CREA
Chapter 38, "Potatoes, large"

Van Jones

Green For All (now at Dream Corps)
Chapter 19, "Menteeship"

Wanjiru Kamau-Rutenberg

African Women in Agricultural Research and Development
Chapter 19, "Facets of support"

Zachary D. Kaufman

American Friends of the Kigali Public Library
Chapter 3, "Immerse yourself"
Chapter 3, "Knowing versus understanding"
Chapter 3, "Unflinching"
Chapter 18, "Organizational software"

Randall Kempner

Aspen Network of Development Entrepreneurs
Chapter 10, "Too cool for school?"
Chapter 42, "Through funders' eyes"

Marina Kim

AshokaU
Chapter 3, "Immerse yourself"
Chapter 4, "Sludge"
Chapter 4, "Strong "number 2s""

Chapter 12, "Start together"
Chapter 19, "Facets of support"

Jim Koch

Global Social Benefit Incubator
Chapter 6 (intro)
Chapter 10, "Language of enterprise"
Chapter 19, "Who's your mentor?"

Cynthia Koenig

Wello
Chapter 30, "Design"
Chapter 30, "Get moving"
Chapter 31, "Stranger in a strange land"
Chapter 32, "Taken seriously"

Jessamyn Lau

also known as: Jessamyn Shams-Lau (married name)
Peery Foundation
Chapter 6, "The siren call of social entrepreneurship"
Chapter 19, "Who's your mentor?"
Chapter 39, "Funding: No work for you"

Mary Lemmer

TerraPerks
Chapter 12, "Building partnership"
Chapter 18, "Like them. Trust them. Be yourself."
Chapter 18, "Think different"
Chapter 36, "No interest"

Jonathan Lewis

MicroCredit Enterprises
Chapter 33, "U-turn"

Chid Liberty

Liberty and Justice
Chapter 39, "Social? No, risky."

Katherine Lucey

Solar Sister
Chapter 2, "Mission, not profit, lights the way"
Chapter 10, "Learn"
Chapter 17, "Chosen few"
Chapter 25, "*E pluribus* business model"
Chapter 41, "The market giveth and the market taketh away"
Chapter 43, "Power in numbers"

Peter Luckow

Tiyatien Health (aka Last Mile Health)
Chapter 8, "Act for yourself; act for others"
Chapter 10, "Soft skills"
Chapter 16, "Local talent is not voluntary talent"
Chapter 18, "Like them. Trust them. Be yourself."
Chapter 20, "Relationships"
Chapter 20, "Help with your taxes, and maybe a hug"
Chapter 39, "The physics of funding"

Steve Mariotti

Network for Teaching Entrepreneurship
Chapter 14, "Basics of hiring"
Chapter 42, "Change what you change"

Nick Moon

KickStart
Chapter 1, "Lessons left on the ground"

Sanga Moses

Eco-Fuel Africa
Chapter 1, "Sanga's birthday"
Chapter 2, "Are you a social entrepreneur? (Take two)"
Chapter 3, "Immerse yourself"
Chapter 3, "Life comes at you hard"
Chapter 4, "Impulse to act"
Chapter 4, "Developing an idea"
Chapter 8, "Your goodness or mine?"
Chapter 9, "Ready? Really?"
Chapter 9, "Charmed 'whys'"
Chapter 10, "Becoming technical"
Chapter 12, "You or 'yous' in control"
Chapter 14, "Vision attracts talent"
Chapter 19, "Wise moments"
Chapter 24, "Why you?"
Chapter 39, "Social? No, risky."
Chapter 43, "Impact, business, impact"
Chapter 43, "Happy progress"

Chris Mueller

Chapter 4, "Strong 'number 2s'"

Ashley Murray

also known as: Ashley Muspratt (married name)
Pivot Works
Chapter 3, "Invite the world in"

Chapter 4, "Sludge"
Chapter 6, "The siren call of social entrepreneurship"
Chapter 19, "Others' shoes"
Chapter 19, "Who's your mentor?"
Chapter 20, "Network of support"
Chapter 25, "Poop and carbon"
Chapter 31, "What you didn't sign up for"
Chapter 36, "Ready? No."
Chapter 36, "No interest"
Chapter 41, "Waste not"
Chapter 42, "Through funders' eyes"

Rebecca Onie

Health Leads
Chapter 4, "On whose shoulders?"
Chapter 6 (intro)
Chapter 10, "Seizing opportunity"
Chapter 16, "Select and train"
Chapter 18, "Inward and outward"
Chapter 19, "Others' shoes"
Chapter 30, "Mimic"
Chapter 43, "Impact as dollars"
Chapter 43, "Power in numbers"
Chapter 43, "Fitbit"
Chapter 44, "Volatile"
Chapter 45, "And now, this"
Chapter 46, "Yesterday. Tomorrow."

Raj Panjabi

Tiyatien Health (aka Last Mile Health)
Chapter 8, "Act for yourself; act for others"

Yusuf Ranera Rees

Awethu
Chapter 10, "In-*credulous*: Talent doesn't have hues"
Chapter 27, "Competition ain't a model"
Chapter 41, "Anticipate"
Chapter 44, "Subversives"

Melissa Richer

Ayllu Initiative
Chapter 30, "Running your business business"

Paul Saginaw

Food Gatherers and Zingerman's
Chapter 8, "A taste for equity"
Chapter 41, "Waste not"

Rupert Scofield

FINCA
Chapter 21, "Smart and gray"

David Seidenfeld

Impact Network
Chapter 4, "Intention for impact"
Chapter 43, "RCT"

'Gbenga Sesan

Paradigm Initiative
Chapter 2, "Are you a social entrepreneur? (Take two)"
Chapter 15, "Compensation: Experience"
Chapter 21, "Your board: Get interested"
Chapter 40 (intro)

Don Shaffer

RSF Social Finance
Chapter 39, "Funding: Fair"
Chapter 42, "Through funders' eyes"
Chapter 45, "Volatile: Money and food"

Yuwei Shi

Chapter 19, "Moments, lifetimes"
Chapter 29, "As a scientist"

Noor Siddiqui

WorkShare
Chapter 2, "A new wave"

Lesley Silverthorn

also known as: Lesley Marincola (married name)
Angaza
Chapter 8, "Flexibility"
Chapter 29, "Aspiration versus illumination"
Chapter 29, "Analogs"
Chapter 35, "Strings attached"
Chapter 36, "What's the what?"
Chapter 41, "The market giveth and the market taketh away"
Chapter 41, "Exits"

Shivani Siroya

InVenture (aka Tala)
Chapter 41, "Build on top of"
Chapter 45, "Not just a loan"

Bobby Smith

En Garde! Detroit
Chapter 10, "Prepare thyself!"
Chapter 34, "Afloat"
Chapter 42, "And now it gets messy"

Whitney Smith

Girls for a Change
Chapter 30, "Rows and ducks"

Maria Springer

LivelyHoods
Chapter 19, "Facets of support"
Chapter 31, "What you didn't sign up for"

Derek Stafford

Unión MicroFinanza
Chapter 7, "Work intensity"
Chapter 7, "Burning your social enterprise"
Chapter 33, "Legal turn"

Kevin Starr

Mulago Foundation
Chapter 4, "The doctor and the priest"
Chapter 5, "Is it necessary – *really* necessary?"
Chapter 5, "Markets don't define necessity"
Chapter 8, "Persistence"
Chapter 14, "Bad language, bad hires"
Chapter 22, "Your two businesses"
Chapter 22, "Mission statement"
Chapter 27, "Jazz"
Chapter 29, "Aspiration versus illumination"
Chapter 29, "Analogs"
Chapter 41, "The market giveth and the market taketh away"
Chapter 43, "Evaluation mistakes"

Dan Sutera

Impact Network
Chapter 4, "Intention for impact"
Chapter 6 (intro)
Chapter 9, "Pushing forward"
Chapter 12, "Invest together"
Chapter 14, "Talent is everywhere"
Chapter 38, "Trajectory: Zambia"
Chapter 45, "Think exit early. Grow large."

Alan Webber

Fast Company
Chapter 6, "Joining the chorus"
Chapter 11, "It's not about you"

Jerry White

Landmine Survivors Network (now at giStrat)
Chapter 3, "Survivor"
Chapter 4, "Recover, integrate, act"
Chapter 9, "Wisdom"
Chapter 18, "Emote different"
Chapter 44, "Now, move"
Chapter 45, "Seeing"
Chapter 45, "Liberation"
Chapter 45, "Cosmos"

Sandy Wiggins

Consilience LLC
Chapter 2, "Are you a social entrepreneur? (Take two)"
Chapter 15, "Compensation: Values"
Chapter 46, "Decide"

Barry Zuckerman

Health Leads
Chapter 10, "Seizing opportunity"

2. The organizations

American Friends of the Kigali Public Library

Chapter 18, "Organizational software"

Angaza

https://www.angaza.com
Chapter 8, "Flexibility"
Chapter 29, "Aspiration versus illumination"
Chapter 35, "Strings attached"
Chapter 36, "What's the what?"
Chapter 41, "The market giveth and the market taketh away"

Ashoka, AshokaU

https://www.ashoka.org, http://ashokau.org
Chapter 2, "Are you a social entrepreneur? (Take two)"
Chapter 3, "Immerse yourself"
Chapter 10, "Soft skills"
Chapter 12, "Start together"
Chapter 18, "Emote different"

Aspen Network of Development Entrepreneurs (ANDE)

https://www.andeglobal.org
Chapter 10, "Too cool for school?"
Chapter 14, "P.S."
Chapter 17, "Rooted in business"
Chapter 42, "Through funders' eyes"

Awethu Project

http://www.awethuproject.co.za
Chapter 10, "In-*credulous*: Talent doesn't have hues"
Chapter 27, "Competition ain't a model"
Chapter 41, "Anticipate"
Chapter 44, "Subversives"

Ayllu Initiative

Chapter 30, "Running your business business"

Clean Clothes Inc.

also known as: Maggie's Organics
https://maggiesorganics.com
Chapter 2, "Are you a social entrepreneur? (Take two)"

Consilience LLC

http://www.consilience.net/
Chapter 2, "Are you a social entrepreneur? (Take two)"

Detroit SOUP

https://detroitsoup.com
Chapter 38, "Potatoes, small"

DIIME (Design Innovations for Infants and Mother Everywhere)

also known as: Sisu Global Health
https://sisuglobal.health
Chapter 10, "Now, just a product"
Chapter 10, "Climb with others"
Chapter 23, "Your *business* business"
Chapter 33, "Legal turn"

East Meets West

also known as: Thrive Networks
http://thrivenetworks.org
Chapter 21, "Smart and gray"
Chapter 41, "Anticipate"

Echoing Green

https://www.echoinggreen.org
Chapter 6, "Necessary and unwelcome"

Eco-Fuel Africa

http://ecofuelafrica.com[1]
Chapter 9, "Ready? Really?"
Chapter 14, "Vision attracts talent"
Chapter 24, "Why you?"
Chapter 39, "Social? No, risky."
Chapter 43, "Impact, business, impact"
Chapter 43, "Happy progress"

Ek Duniya

Chapter 41, "Think exit early. Stay small."

Embrace

now known as Embrace Innovations
https://www.embraceinnovations.com
Chapter 7, "Awards notwithstanding"
Chapter 12, "You or 'yous' in control"
Chapter 13, "Embracing new roles"
Chapter 21, "Formation"
Chapter 27, "Jazz"
Chapter 33, "U-turn"

En Garde! Detroit

Chapter 10, "Prepare thyself!"
Chapter 34, "Afloat"
Chapter 42, "And now it gets messy"

FilterPure

https://www.facebook.com/filterpurefilters
Chapter 9, "Acting from values"
Chapter 16, "Your team in the cloud"
Chapter 29, "Pure"

FINCA

https://www.finca.org
Chapter 21, "Smart and gray"

Food Gatherers

http://www.foodgatherers.org
Chapter 8, "A taste for equity"

Fundación Paraguaya

http://www.fundacionparaguaya.org.py
Chapter 7, "Stress and risk"
Chapter 7, "Misunderstood"
Chapter 21, "Smart and gray"

Global Social Benefit Incubator (GSBI)

https://www.scu-social-entrepreneurship.org/gsbi
Chapter 10, "Language of enterprise"
Chapter 14, "P.S."

Grameen Shakti

http://www.gshakti.org
Chapter 23, "TAM SAM SOM mat … ter"

Green For All

https://www.greenforall.org
Chapter 19, "Menteeship"

Guayaki

https://guayaki.com
Chapter 39, "Funding: Fair"

Guidestar

https://www.guidestar.org
Chapter 21, "Don't shake on it"

Health Leads

https://healthleadsusa.org
Chapter 4, "On whose shoulders?"
Chapter 16, "Select and train"
Chapter 18, "Inward and outward"
Chapter 30, "Mimic"
Chapter 43, "Impact as dollars"
Chapter 43, "Power in numbers"
Chapter 43, "Fitbit"
Chapter 44, "Volatile"
Chapter 45, "And now, this"

Idealist.org

https://www.idealist.org
Chapter 3, "Off the track"

Impact Enterprises

http://www.impactenterprises.org
Chapter 12, "Invest together"
Chapter 14, "Talent is everywhere"

Impact Network

http://www.impactnetwork.org
Chapter 4, "Intention for impact"
Chapter 12, "Invest together"

Chapter 14, "Talent is everywhere"
Chapter 38, "Trajectory: Zambia"
Chapter 43, "RCT"
Chapter 45, "Think exit early. Grow large."

KickStart International

formerly known as: ApproTec
http://kickstart.org
Chapter 1, "Lessons left on the ground"
Chapter 2, "Which market?"
Chapter 6, "Joining the chorus"
Chapter 8, "Persistence"
Chapter 9, "Always stepping on the gas"
Chapter 24, "Why you?"
Chapter 26, "Chained value"
Chapter 29, "That's a *what?*"
Chapter 30, "Rows and ducks"
Chapter 41, "The market giveth and the market taketh away"

Landmine Survivors Network

http://landminesurvivors.org
Chapter 4, "Recover, integrate, act"

Last Mile Health

formerly known as: Tiyatien Health
http://lastmilehealth.org
Chapter 8, "Act for yourself; act for others"
Chapter 10, "Soft skills"
Chapter 16, "Local talent is not voluntary talent"
Chapter 20, "Relationships"
Chapter 20, "Help with your taxes, and maybe a hug"
Chapter 24, "Why you?"
Chapter 31, "What you didn't sign up for"
Chapter 31, "Managing: Pro tips"
Chapter 39, "The physics of funding"

Liberty and Justice

Chapter 39, "Social? No, risky."

LivelyHoods

https://www.livelyhoods.org
Chapter 19, "Facets of support"

Living Goods

https://livinggoods.org
Chapter 14, "Bad language, bad hires"

Medeem

http://medeem.com
Chapter 14, "Away from home"
Chapter 17, "Adaptive hiring"
Chapter 28, "Small businesses, still complex"

Mentor Capital Network

formerly known as: William James Foundation
http://mentorcapitalnet.org
Chapter 10, "Data"
Chapter 14, "Mindful hiring"

MicroCredit Enterprises (MCE)

now known as: MCE Social Capital
http://www.mcesocap.org/
Chapter 33, "U-turn"

MicroEnergy Credits

http://www.microenergycredits.com
Chapter 4, "Complexity from simpler parts"
Chapter 13, "Pluripotency"
Chapter 14, "The people the people you know know"
Chapter 17, "Learners and rockers"
Chapter 23, "TAM SAM SOM matter"
Chapter 25, "Poop and carbon"
Chapter 26, "Every link matters"
Chapter 27, "Fresh eyes"
Chapter 36, "Still ..."

Monitor Institute

http://monitorinstitute.com
Chapter 5, "Markets don't define necessity"
Chapter 6, "Joining the chorus"

Mulago Foundation

http://mulagofoundation.org
Chapter 4, "The doctor and the priest"
Chapter 14, "Bad language, bad hires"

Network for Teaching Entrepreneurship (NFTE)

https://www.nfte.com
Chapter 14, "Basics of hiring"
Chapter 42, "Change what you change"

Olevolos Project

http://www.theolevolosproject.org
Chapter 3, "Faux immersion"

Paradigm Initiative

https://pinigeria.org
Chapter 2, "Are you a social entrepreneur? (Take two)"
Chapter 15, "Compensation: Experience"
Chapter 21, "Your board: Get interested"
Chapter 40 (intro)

Partners in Health

https://www.pih.org
Chapter 4, "The doctor and the priest"
Chapter 16, "Local talent is not voluntary talent"

Pay It Forward

Chapter 3, "Real life"
Chapter 9, "Ready? Really?"
Chapter 9, "Charmed 'whys'"
Chapter 10, "Ask"
Chapter 10, "Credibility"

Peery Foundation

http://www.peeryfoundation.org
Chapter 6, "The siren call of social entrepreneurship"
Chapter 39, "Funding: No work for you"

Pivot Works

formerly known as: Waste Enterprisers
Chapter 4, "Sludge"
Chapter 6, "The siren call of social entrepreneurship"
Chapter 25, "Poop and carbon"
Chapter 36, "Ready? No."
Chapter 36, "No interest"

PlayPump

http://www.playpumps.co.za
Chapter 5, "Markets don't define necessity"

Polaris

also known as: Polaris Project
https://polarisproject.org
Chapter 7, "Burning your social enterprise"
Chapter 9, "Breathe out"
Chapter 16, "Volunteer structure"
Chapter 16, "Select and train"
Chapter 18, "Inward and outward"
Chapter 38, "Trajectory: United States"
Chapter 45, "A deliberate course toward movement"

Practice Network

Chapter 20, "Help with your taxes, and maybe a hug"
Chapter 31, "Managing: Pro tips"

Reach Incorporated

http://www.reachincorporated.org
Chapter 20, "Free lunch?"
Chapter 41, "Small and right"
Chapter 43, "Real impact is not gamed"

Root Capital

https://rootcapital.org
Chapter 17, "Rooted in business"
Chapter 41, "Jenga"

RSF Social Finance

https://rsfsocialfinance.org
Chapter 39, "Funding: Fair"
Chapter 42, "Through funders' eyes"
Chapter 45, "Volatile: Money and food"

Schwab Foundation

http://www.schwabfound.org
Chapter 5, "Originality is not necessity"

Solar Light for Africa

http://solarlightforafrica.org
Chapter 10, "Learn"

Solar Sister

https://www.solarsister.org
Chapter 2, "Mission, not profit, lights the way"
Chapter 10, "Learn"
Chapter 17, "Chosen few"

Chapter 25, "*E pluribus* business model"
Chapter 40 (intro)
Chapter 43, "Power in numbers"

Still Harbor

http://stillharbor.org
Chapter 6, "The siren call of social entrepreneurship"
Chapter 8, "Nonproductive persistence"
Chapter 9, "When your venture gives you lemons"
Chapter 9, "Critical 'whys'"
Chapter 13, "Organization structure: Benefit or crutch?"
Chapter 18, "Inward and outward"
Chapter 27, "Take the money and ..."

Tala

formerly known as: InVenture
https://tala.co
Chapter 41, "Build on top of"
Chapter 45, "Not just a loan"

Taproot

https://taprootfoundation.org
Chapter 31, "Managing: Pro tips"

Teach a Man to Fish

https://www.teachamantofish.org.uk
Chapter 21, "Smart and gray"

Teach for America

https://www.teachforamerica.org
Chapter 6, "Necessary and unwelcome"

Terra Nova

http://grupoterranova.com.br
Chapter 30, "Running your business business"

TerraPerks

Chapter 18, "Like them. Trust them. Be yourself."

ThinkImpact

https://www.thinkimpact.com
Chapter 18, "Like them. Trust them. Be yourself."
Chapter 33, "U-turn"

Unión MicroFinanza

now known as: Aldea Development
http://www.unionmicrofinanza.org
Chapter 33, "Legal turn"

Village Capital

also known as: VilCap
https://vilcap.com
Chapter 5, "Is it necessary – *really* necessary?"
Chapter 7, "You don't know your own venture"
Chapter 11, "If the bus comes"
Chapter 13 (intro)
Chapter 18, "Inward and outward"
Chapter 41, "Exits"

Warmilu

http://warmilu.com
Chapter 7, "Misunderstood"
Chapter 10, "Climb with others"
Chapter 13, "Warm relationships"
Chapter 27, "Jazz"

Waste Ventures

https://wasteventures.com
Chapter 5, "Originality is not necessity"
Chapter 6, "Joining the chorus"
Chapter 13, "Organization structure: Benefit or crutch?"
Chapter 41, "Waste not"

Wello

http://wellowater.org
Chapter 25, "Accounting 101"
Chapter 30, "Design"
Chapter 30, "Get moving"
Chapter 30, "Becoming sophisticated"
Chapter 32, "Taken seriously"
Chapter 36, "No interest"

WorkShare

Chapter 1, "A new wave"

Note

1 At the time of writing, Sanga's URL had been hijacked.

For more information about the topics covered in this book as well as related ideas, please visit profmichaelgordon.com.

Index

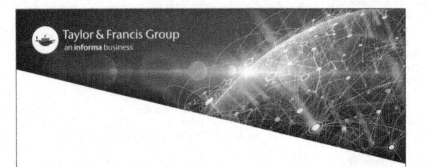